Because ,
Seriously
America,
Seriously!

Joshua Grant

I

Cover designed by AUTHOR: Joshua Grant

ISBN: 978-1-7366594-0-3
Independently Published & Printed in:
The United States of America - 2020

This book is dedicated to my Father, whose the reason why I am the man I am today, but whose also taught me so much I can only wish I've made him proud. This book is also dedicated to my loving mother. You were the beautiful angel with a smile that brightened every ones day.

Table Of Contents

Introduction:
We now live in a very Cynical World!

Chapter 1:
The word `seriously`, is the best adverb we can use to explain all this nonsense.

Chapter 2:
The hatred is pushed by the ignorant, followed by the ill-minded!

Chapter 3:
Taking God out of everything, won't fix your problems!

Chapter 4:
What's ours is ours, you don't get it, simply because you want it.

Chapter 5:
More likely to happen or likelier to happen, That's your argument?

Chapter 6:
Chaos & Confusion, always causes, Disruption & Delusion!

Acknowledgments:

References & Research:

Introduction & Lead:
We now live in a very Cynical World!

I am no Einstein, nor would I ever claim to be Einstein, but there are a few things I am pretty sure of, like how white American colonists did not start the enslavement of minorities. In addition, I am pretty sure police officers and white people are not the ones killing minorities, at least not more than minorities are killing themselves. Maybe the one main thing that I am pretty sure of is the fact that, all white Americans living today, do not owe minorities anything, especially for something that mostly everyone's ancestors profited and participated in, hundreds of years ago.

"History is not there for you to like or dislike. It is there for you to learn from it. In addition, if it offends you, even better. Because then you are less likely to repeat it. It is not yours to erase. It belongs to all of us."

What many people fail to realize is, everyone makes mistakes, it is a given, but that does not mean you make those people pay for those bad choices for the rest of their lives, unless they are career criminals of course. Sometimes good people make bad choices constantly, it does not mean they are bad people, just means they are human. I for one am nobody who is perfect, but I have seen enough to know what is best for my family and me and that is what every American should be sure of. Before we continue, let us also just get something straight, calling me a racist before you even get to know me, only makes you the racist one.

Instead of jumping the gun and assuming I am a bad person, just listen to what I have to say, then you can go back to hating me. Here is a little back-story about me, I am a 40 year old and have been in the customer service world for over 2 decades, from warehouse management to store management. I recently had a heart attack, where it was discovered that I had a rare heart condition and should have already been dead. One of my heart valves was not working right, my mitral valve had an inch gap in the valve, and this inch gap was letting blood into pockets, where oxygen was supposed to go.

Due to the rare condition, the valve itself was not repairable and therefore needed to be replaced, although the only thing they could replace my heart valve with, was a mechanical heart valve. Thanks to amazing doctors, numerous amazing nurses and a 6-hour heart surgery,

1

I was once again able to breathe. My life is now a little different with my mechanical ticker, which honestly sounds just like a ticking clock when you are sitting in silence. Also no, for those that may ask, there was no light, I did not see a light at the end of the tunnel, although these doctors did stop my heart, there was no dramatic sequence where I met the Lord above.

That would have been awesome though. I was simply put out after a simple ten count, which I think I got to five before I was out. I woke up groggy 6 hours later in the hospital recovery room, and was said to be shaking everyone's hands. Unfortunately, my heartbeat was not where it was supposed to be, so I had to stay a few extra weeks in the hospital. Sad thing was my window view was of a huge cemetery that was located right next to the hospital. During my time in recovery, I sat there in my hospital room contemplating about life and my own life experiences, something I never really did before.

Which is also something you usually do not do until your life comes to a halt and stops you in your tracks? One thing I am certain of is the experience of sitting in my hospital room waiting for the day I could go home, is an experience I never wish to go through again and something I wish on no one. One thing that did stick out during my recovery time is the fact that, I got to watch as the world around me fell apart. I watched every day as the country I loved, fell further into chaos, all brought on by our very own people. As I sat their getting better, day by day, I watched as our very own American State Senators took turns in slowly ripping apart America from the inside out.

These State politicians were causing as much chaos and destruction as they could, we seen this by watching hundreds of people rioting and destroying everything in sight, as these politicians just stood by and watched them do it. One sad thing about the whole situation is that, these democratic politicians were often seen on television pushing these people to riot and burn everything to the ground, especially Maxine Waters and Kamala Harris. The reason they wanted it done was shocking though, it was not because they wanted equality, it was not because they wanted justice, no, it was all because of their own hatred for President Trump.

These State Senators hate President Trump and everything he stands for, which honestly makes no sense because President Donald Trump stands for America and putting the American people first. Something

2

Democrats have not done in years, let alone decades, although they constantly preach that they are, the evidence always proves them wrong. It was amazing to watch the greatest nation in the world being destroyed by un-American State Senators from the inside out.

It was amazing to watch because these State Senators took no form of responsibility of what was occurring; instead, they turned around and blamed it all on one man, President Trump. In reality, it takes organized people to create the chaos and destruction these state officials have created today. This was not just a one off; this was an orchestrated attack on America and our American rights and freedoms. It's crazy when you think about it, people used to question the truth or they questioned things before they made their decision, which unfortunately does not happen today.

Today, we live in a very cynical world, people assume everything or assume they know everything and they have no problem telling you what they think you are doing wrong. With this way of thinking, these people tend to only be concerned with their own interests, they do what benefits themselves, they are not interested in any point of view, but their own. This thought process often comes into play in every conversation people now have because certain people assume they know everything. This motivates these self-described know-it-alls and they act on these selfish assumptions by destroying others, simply because they think they know better.

Assumptions kill everything, but people do not bother to learn the truth about the incident, until after all the damage and destruction is already done. Even after these people learn the truth, they still justify their selfish actions. It's crazy how people no longer wait for the truth or facts to come out, instead they act on their assumptions. Seriously, these people rather just make assumptions then learning the truth or facts of the situation. Besides being very cynical and assumptive people, these people also have a simple distrust of other people's motives. These days, people tend to believe that other's only look out for their own self-interests or what benefits themselves.

This is often why people are very cynical towards others; it is also because people believe other's do things for a reason, instead of doing it just to do it. It is a very contradictive theory though. This is because they themselves base their actions and assumptions on opinions and statements made by others, rather than the actual truth. People often believe what they want to believe, they listen to what they want to listen to, and they usually do what they want to do. It is just like the paranormal field, certain people believe there are ghost, while other's need to see it to believe it.

However, for those people that do not believe in ghosts and have never seen a ghost, will always claim that ghost do not exist. Not because there might be ghost's out there, but because they have not seen an actual ghost and just because others say there is ghost, does not make it true. It is a back and forth game now; you have half the people in the world following the word of others, while you have the other half following the truth and facts. Trump's deplorables. Accountability is one of the major things that comes from a thought process like this because people are no longer held accountable for their actions.

Since people are no longer held accountable, they do not worry about facing repercussions for the damage or chaos they cause. I can say this because State Senators have literally put in place bail reforms, so that anyone held accountable for the destruction they caused, would be instantly released of any wrongdoing. We watched this chaos taken place in America, we watched as these so-called peaceful protests turned very violent. These protesters started off very peaceful, but quickly turned into violent and destructive rioters when anyone who had a difference of opinion or point of view, shared it.

This was often how these so-called peaceful protests started, people based their actions on their opinions or assumptions of the situation, rather than waiting for the truth and they acted on these opinions and assumptions, whether they were truthful or not. After people witnessed something they didn't like or agree with, they started protesting, but soon that protesting turned into rioting and causing as much damage as they possibly could. This honestly makes no sense because you are trying to stop the violence toward your people, by committing more violence against others, not much sense there. Once one person sees something as a problem, they start to convince other people that there is a problem and once the word spreads, you now have thousands of people feeling the same way, thinking they all have the same problem.

It is not hard to be a follower, since most people tend to be followers, but it is hard to be a leader, which America seems to be lacking right now. We currently have a great American President, but President Trump is too busy being threatened by impeachment, all for simply doing his job. It is the democratic way though, they blame their problems on other people and they blame the situation they are in on other people, rather than facing the music themselves. This insane and crazy thought process has been adopted by millions of Americans, especially minorities.

Millions of minorities have been tricked into believing that they are still being enslaved in America, not because they are being kept on farms or enslaved to a room, but because democrats have convinced these minorities into thinking that they are still being oppressed and treated like slaves. Democrats, along with rich blm leaders, have somehow convinced minorities that they are being oppressed by President Trump's systemically racist government, yet, they're the ones seen causing all the division. Democratic State Senators are also the ones responsible for allowing all this chaos and violence to take place.

Not only is this a major problem, but it causes major confusion between Americans because now we have minority professors and teachers trying to teach children that slavery was the reason for America's growth. These are the very same professors that are now claiming that slavery was the reason for the Revolutionary War, which we all know is far from the truth. In addition, this to me is crazy, because we all know that Americans wanted to become free and independent from the British Parliament, so they started a new revolution for their own independence.

It had nothing to do with slavery and everything to do with Independence, but this is the ignorance being pushed onto our kids these days. Honestly, look it up, slavery was not even an issue at the time or a reason the war was started, Americans did not even know about slavery. American colonists wanted to be free from the grip of the Great Britain Parliament, who controlled most of the established American colonies. This is the same ill-minded ideology coming from people that want to teach elementary kids about civil rights and civil rights movements. Because really, why do children need to learn about their ABC's, before they learn about their civil rights, something they clearly will not understand.

It has become a very sad day in America, the people that we chose to represent us as Americans, the people we elected to represent us, our very own American State Senators, have turned their backs on America and the American people. Americans watched as these democratic State

Senators sat idly by while hundreds of people continued to destroy dozens of communities, loot and destroy grocery stores and cause billions of damage to American cities. Their actions were questionable at best because we watched as these democratic Mayors and Governors allowed people to protest against President Trump, by the hundreds, but they did not allow Americans to have funerals, attend their churches, celebrate their Independence or even have weddings.

It was all because democrat's claimed these family gatherings were too much, they don't want people gathering in big crowds, but they praise and push for protesters to get out and protest by the hundreds, side by side, against President Trump. Ah, the Irony, you have to love it. Seriously though, how does that actually work? Protesting by the hundreds against the President of the United States is okay, but family gatherings is not, seriously? This is the democratic logic that I fail to understand, how it is safe for hundreds of people to stand side by side, some without masks, so they can protest President Trump, but it is not okay for people to have a funeral to celebrate a person's life or bury one of their own.

Funny how a State Senator dies and they have a funeral, not only that, democrats, including Obama, used this dead State Senators funeral to bash the current President. That is the character we are being led with right now; democrats feel it is okay to bash the President at a dead State Senators funeral. The logic is really just overwhelming, they claim it is not okay for people to have a funeral to celebrate their family members' life or can't even go to church to worship God, but it is okay for them to have funerals and use hundreds of people to protest President Trump.

I am sure by now, there are many Americans, like myself, who are confused about the logic that these democratic mayors and governors' use or the fallacious arguments they make, which is aimed to make their lies and deceptions seem better than they actually are. It honestly makes no sense at all, we have un-American State Senators, Mayors and Governors, letting people destroy our American cities, simply because they hate President Trump and will do anything to make him seem like the one responsible for the damage they have caused.

This is why democrats, led by Nancy Pelosi, have helped push these violent protests, also the reason why democrats joined the hateful blm movement. It was all designed to damage President Trump's character.

Democrats and the Democratic Party were constantly exposed for pushing this violence, this is the reason they tried to bring forth a fake impeachment, the violent protest were not working. The information they were using to accuse the President was based on assumptive opinions, false allegations and false accusations and it was proven. Any other American would be jailed for what these democrats have done, said and claimed.

From Nancy Pelosi tearing up actual government documents in front of the world, to all democrats using false allegations against President Trump, any normal American doing this would be arrested for treason and thrown in jail for life. Somehow, though, democrats are getting away with it and it seems as if they honestly could care less whether the American people agree with them or not. Do not believe me; think about this for a second, democrats spent millions of American tax dollars, close to over 50 million dollars, on a false impeachment that lasted 2 and half years, basically to get rid of President Trump. The allegations? Proven, in court, to be false allegations.

This wasn't during the impeachment, this was proven in the very first week of the impeachment, but still, democrats, knowing the information was false, knowing they had no base to their impeachment, continued to spend the next two and half years to try and impeach President Trump. The kicker, Hillary Clinton and Barack Obama, were found guilty and convicted of what democrats were trying to accuse President Trump of doing. Do not forget what happened in Benghazi and who was in charge and in the White House at the time this tragic event occurred.

The democrat impeachment honestly made no sense, democrats spent millions of dollars on lawyers and investigators to try to find dirt on President Trump, but they all found nothing. President Trump honestly did nothing wrong, yet, democrats still tried to impeach him, simply because they hated him. In reality, they hated President Trump because President Trump focused on the American people, not other countries or what money he could steal from the American people.

What should be worrisome to all Americans is the fact that, every single allegation and accusation brought forth against President Trump by democrats, were deemed to be false before the impeachment even started. The facts did not matter though, knowing they had no real evidence, knowing their accusations were false, democrats, led by Nancy Pelosi, still continued to try to impeach President Trump. Not only did they choose to impeach President Trump on false allegations, they spent millions of taxpayer's dollars over 2 and half years, knowing all along that they had no real evidence and they were basically not going to win the impeachment.

This is their democratic logic though, they do not actually care about the American people, all they care about is the power they hold and how they can get more. We know that democrats only look out for themselves; we know this because during President Trumps four years in office, they did nothing for the American people. Instead, democrats constantly focused on getting rid of President Trump, simply because Trump was taking money out of their pockets and giving back to the American people.

This is the cynical world we live in today; millions of people follow these democratic State Senators who only look out for their self-interests and their rich buddies. This to me make no sense and often leaves me confused, because these people are being told lie after lie, but they continue to follow and listen to these people. I mean, how many times have we heard Nancy Pelosi say thank you to George Floyd, a criminal, who did nothing for his community, but rob it. Floyd was a career criminal and yea, he should have not been held down, but he also should have not been on fentanyl and Meth, passing counterfeit bills in another State.

However, when someone like President Trump disrupts the democratic process, democrats attack them and try to destroy their character any which way they can. When democrats cannot destroy your character with their fallacious arguments and false allegations, they spread false information about you, so anything you say or claim, is always to be questioned by others. This cynical theory is what is pushing most of these hateful and violent movements occurring today, people have the opinion that all white people are racist and only do things to better their own self-interests.

This is all because democrats have forced this assumptive opinion upon the American people, they spent the last four years trying to trick millions of people into thinking, and believing these assumptive opinions are right. In reality, these politicians and their followers, only do things that better their own self-interests. They could honestly care less about what the American people want or need, they do what benefits their pockets and power. It is all sort of puzzling and interesting because we are witnessing democrats, liberals and even rich Americans; work with convicted criminals, convicted felons and hate groups to push their assumptive opinionated theories.

Democrats have convinced these criminals that they will take care of them and erase all of their past troubles, but only if they vote their way, the democrat way. Democrats are only interested in what will benefit them in the end, they do not care what is best for America, they do not care what is best for the American people, and they only care about what is best for them. This is crazy because, these are the very same people that were hired to represent the American people, not criminals or convicted felons. This is also what makes the 2020 election so scary, President Trump should win by a landslide, but democrats are doing everything in their power to give them the edge over Trump, this includes making plans to steal the election with their mail-in ballot schemes.

Democrats know the only way they can win the 2020 election is to steal the election from Trump. This is why democrats have invested so much money into mail-in balloting, illegal immigrants and convicted felons. They need these extra votes counted, votes that normally would be counted as invalid, they are going to count as valid, all so they can give Joe Biden the edge over President Trump. We know there will be plenty of corruption, especially seeing that convicted felons, the people who lost the right to vote, have democrats fighting to give them that right back, but only if they vote democrat.

What makes you question their motives is when you see that democrats are pushing for mail-in ballots, instead of people going to vote in person. This is because with mail-in ballots, they can easily push the numbers they are going to need to pass President Trump. It is not hard for democrats to easily add thousands of extra absentee ballots and claim they are valid, when in reality, they are far from valid. In all reality, they are merely pushing their cynical views on to the American people, trying to destroy the character of our current President, so they can put in someone in that they can control.

It is unfortunate for us Americans that this person just so happens to be Sleepy Joe Biden, a person who is not even aware of what he is saying. We've seen the evidence, we've watched as Americans who disagree or have a difference of opinions then these democrats do, being silenced on social media, but also having their character dragged through the mud, this includes our President. This is what has become so scary to watch, Trump supporters, are being labeled traitors to America, yet, it is democrats and their followers that are the ones betraying America and the American people.

Democrats could not impeach President Trump, so they thought causing chaos and destruction would help them in their mission to get rid of him. It is their assumptive opinion that the more chaos and destruction they push, the more they can blame it on President Trump. This falls in line with people assuming other people only do things that benefit themselves. Everything President Trump did, democrats said and often claimed Trump did it for another reason, other than just wanting to help out the American people. It is funny because President Trump is the only one that seems to care about the American people, what the American people want, and our American interests.

Seriously, how can a President who puts the American people and America first be bad for our country? This is the ultimate question that needs to be answered because President Trump has stated repeatedly, that he puts America first and always will. Democrats have said this is a bad thing, literally! They have continued to go on television and claim the president Trump is bad for the American people because he puts the American people first. Democrats, the people that were hired to represent the American people are complaining that the President is racist for putting the American people first.

Think about that Irony for a second. And seriously, we need to question this, why would our very own American State Senators, the ones hired to represent us, not be okay with our President putting America first? I mean, that is the job they were hired to do, these State Senators were hired to represent the American people, and they were hired to look out for our best interests. This leaves me seriously wondering why democrats are trying to get rid of a President who continues to put America and the American people first.

It is very puzzling when you think about it, during his first three years in office; President Trump has had to deal with more adversity coming from our very own American State Senators, than the world leaders who hate us. What we also talk about a little more and what makes no sense to me, is the fact that, these State Senators have been in our government for decades, not just years, but decades, yet, they are blaming the problems on a President that's only been in office for three and half years. One thing we will discuss is, the blame game, this is the specialty of democrats and blm, they cause all the chaos, they infuse all the violence, they push all the riots and protests, only to turn around and blame it all on President Trump and white people.

Most of these democratic State Senators tend to be walking, talking contradictions, they say one thing, only to retract that statement and say something very different. Most of them just claim they never said it in the first place, although they were on tape or in an interview caught making the statement. Although bad themselves, their statements are not really what we should all be worried about, what we should all be worried about is the fact that, our American State Senators are allowing America to be torn apart, bit by bit.

Like I said before, we've already seen evidence of this taking place, these State Senators have been working with protesters, creating new legislature, so these protesters can be bailed out, instantly after they've been arrested for rioting or destroying property. Think about that for a second though. Democratic city mayors and governors, who are supposed to represent their American citizens, but also look out for public safety, are bailing out the rioters, destroying their cities. The people who are out in American cities causing chaos and destroying property are being bailed out and as if that was not bad enough, its American taxed money that they are using to bail these rioters out with.

It's insane when you think about it because these rioters are destroying dozens of homes, destroying dozens of businesses, destroying dozens of communities, doesn't matter though, they know if they get caught and jailed, they will easily be bailed out. It makes no sense and often leaves you confused because people have turned our American streets into war zones. Our American cities are under siege, rioters and looters continue to destroy everything in sight, while these democratic mayors and governors sit back and do nothing at all to stop this destruction. Each one of these City officials denied help from President Trump simply because; they were doing all of this to blame it on President Trump.

We know this because we witnessed it every day on our news stations, democratic city mayors and governors were on television blaming all the chaos and destruction on President Trump, although it was their job, not his. If you are not familiar with the law of the land, it is the City Mayors and Governors job to be the ultimate protectors of their citizens living in their States, not the President. The President can only help if he is asked to. The kicker though, while these city mayors and governors sat there and did nothing to stop the destruction and denied Trumps help, they turned around and asked the government for funds to help them rebuild their cities.

Democratic State Senators always play the blame game though; they go on television so they can blame all the crime and violence occurring in these cities on President Trump. It's amazing to watch these State politicians sit there and blame all the crime and violence on President Trump, especially when these State Senators, Mayors and Governors, are the ones who are in charge of public safety and the first line of defense for the American people. That is one thing that people fail to realize, the President can only interrupt in city affairs if he is asked to, the President does not have the power or authority to send people in to fix the chaos occurring in these American cities, he has to be asked to intervene.

Democrats will not tell you that though, they always skip over that little fact, while they blame President Trump for the crime and violence occurring in their cities. Honestly though, if you knew about this little fact, their blame game would never work, so you will never hear this coming from them. If they did admit that it is their entire fault, which it really is, they would never be able to blame Trump for causing all the chaos, violence, and destruction. The sad thing is, democrats know this, and they know they cannot really blame the President for their own wrong doings, but they do it anyway.

They do it because they know that whatever they say or claim, their followers will believe, and their followers will believe their word over the actual truth. This is partly why America has become so cynical, State politicians have convinced people that President Trump only does things to benefit his racist white supremacists friends. It is their assumptive opinion that President Trump is a racist President, who only does things for himself and his friends, but since this is their opinion, this is what they push onto anyone who will listen.

Since this opinion is now shared by millions, the millions of people that support President Trump are labeled as supporters of his racist white supremacist administration. Often being referred to as

12

deplorables. The logic behind it makes no sense at all and I fail to understand why these people call Trump a racist, but also a white supremacist, when he has done nothing but denounce white supremacist organizations. The truth is simple, Trump does what he does because it benefits the American people, it does not make him a racist because he chose to put the American people first.

You also cannot call Trump a white supremacist, especially when you have no evidence to back up the claim; your hateful opinion is not evidence. Hateful and assumptive opinions seem to be the one thing that has taken over, people's opinions are controlling their actions, they are no longer bothering with the truth. The crazy thing about all of this is what these assumptive people say and believe, is what they consider to be the truth, whether it is right or wrong. It has gotten much worse in America though, democrats have slowly divided and separated the country with their hateful assumptive opinions of the President. I honestly think this was the narrative d agenda all along.

What also seems to be very interesting is the fact that, to these assumptive people, their opinion is the only opinion that seems to matter. These people do not debate or converse with others, if you do not believe their opinion or what they believe to be true, then you are the one who is wrong. This is honestly why everyone became so cynical of President Trumps administration, democrats used their power to spread as much nonsense as they could. Since their opinion is the one being listened to, also followed, the hatred for the President grew, leaving millions of people thinking the same thing about President Trump.

The one thing I fail to understand is how they convinced millions of people to hate President Trump, although Trump has done amazing things for the country. Since democrats claim that he is an un-American white racist President, people start to judge him and join in on the claim. People with a brain or even common sense, know that this is far from the truth; people know President Trump is far from a white supremacist, but democrats have to make this statement because it's all part of smearing his name and destroying his character.

This is the dirty game these politicians play, President Trump tries to focus on bettering America, democrats do not, instead of helping Trump better the lives of the American people, democrats rather focus on getting rid of Trump. This is why they analyze President Trumps every move, everything President Trump does is torn apart and scrutinized, not because it is a bad idea, but because democrats want to discredit anything he does for the country or the American people. This scrutiny leads to major division in America, these State Senators scrutinize what Trump does, but the American people see what he is doing and support him for it, which in turn labels them as racist Trump supporters.

We have all seen what Trump supporters have been called, which is sad because supporting the President of the United States should not label you as a racist, but this is the logic that democrats push onto others. Seriously though, does that make any sense? What's pretty obvious about this is that, this hateful opinion is mainly coming from democrats, people like the Clintons, the Bushes and the Obama's, politicians who have been in our government for years and are more corrupt then any mob member living today.

It honestly leaves me confused, these politicians are calling people who support the United States President, deplorables, but they are only calling us deplorables because we will not take their democratic side or follow their idiotic ideology. It is honestly sad to watch, these cynical State Senators could really care less about the American people and more about their motives and agendas. Everyone has watched and witnessed as our country slowly went from being one of the greatest nations in the world, to being a country divided and separated, where it is now black versus white.

This is what has taken place in America, once again assumptive opinions of the few, now command the many. As you may have noticed, everything with a white label, anything colored white or related to white, is now being deemed racist, this includes us white people. I am not too sure where or when the switch happened, but the America that once was, is not the America that we live in today. Today, we are dealing with millions of idiots who thinks everything should be handed to them, whether they have worked for it or not. This is all thanks to State officials and blm leaders, who claim that minorities deserve everything handed over to them simply because of what their ancestors went through.

Oh and because white people are all racist and only got what they got because the color of their skin, so minorities deserve the same. Since everything white is now racist and white people supposedly only

14

got their stuff because their white, minorities think this gives them the right to cause chaos and destroy communities, along with businesses and residences. It makes you question the sanity of these people because; they claim that the way to end all the violence against their people is to cause more violence against other people. These are the very same people that have no problem with destroying American cities and disrupting other people's lives, especially if it betters theirs.

Seriously though, before you continue to read on and we discuss in further detail about what is happening to America right now, just ask yourself. If the people in charge do not mind seeing America being burnt to the ground, do you seriously think they care about providing a better future for you or your family?

-- Chapter 1 --
The word `seriously`, is the best adverb that
we could use to explain all this nonsense!

Honestly, the word `seriously`, is the best adverb that we can use to describe all the nonsense going on because although it's a word used to modify verbs, adjectives and even other adverbs, the manner in which people act, think and speak these days, makes the word `seriously`, seems more like a blank statement, rather than a word modifier. It has become obvious that it is more of a blank statement more now than ever before. This is because people no longer take the time to bother with the manner of the incident, the cause of the incident and the circumstances that led to the incident.

Instead, people destroy cities and communities, but also start riots, before they even know the degree or manner of the situation. This is why the word `seriously`, has become more of a rhetorical blank statement, especially after you see everything going on in America. All you are really left doing is questioning and asking, seriously? It is heartbreaking to see what is occurring in America right now, hundreds of Americans and non-Americans are following the logic and theories of the weak and have taken part in the destruction of our very own American culture. America is no longer the America we all grew to love and cherish; these simple ill-minded democrats have turned America and its American cities into a political chess game, where Americans are continually used as the pawns.

Even using the word `seriously` in front of or after any question, still leaves you puzzled and failing to understand the logic that these people use. You are often left with a blank statement on your face. Today, you are often left wondering what will happen next; this is because we have a country that seems to be on the brink of another Civil War. This is all based on racial tension and the division that is being pushed by our very own State Reps. You are left asking yourself, are American State politicians really allowing this to happen to our American communities and American cities right now?

Did Nancy Pelosi, our very own Speaker of the House, seriously just claim that she "Doesn't care much for American monuments and statues because they represent white supremacist men"? I mean, seriously, Nancy Pelosi is the Speaker of the House; she is the third person in charge of our nation and takes over if anything was to happen to the President and the Vice President. She is supposed to represent our American values, which includes our symbols of American freedom, but she claims she could care less. That is the scary thing about Nancy Pelosi; she becomes President if anything happens to the President or Vice President. It is especially scary when our very own Speaker of the House, is stating that she could care less about our American national monuments and statues.

Besides the fact that Nancy Pelosi is by far probably the worse Speaker of the House we have ever had or seen she constantly claims that she loves the American people and represents the American people, yet, she does nothing for the American people. Then again, can we seriously rely on someone who has let their entire represented city go to hell? Nancy Pelosi's very own city is in total dismay, but she spends more time focusing on President Trump, then she does focusing on her own city. Another sad thing about her failing city is the fact that, her city plays a huge part in California's homeless problem.

The homeless have literally taken over California's city streets, but it is honestly because they have nowhere else to go. For those of you not aware of the situation in California right now, California's city streets are littered with homeless people, numerous homeless men, women and children, have literally taken over entire city blocks. Due to the huge homeless problem that California is now faced with, the Mayor of California actually created an entire separate police force to try to control the homeless problem that has taken over most parts of California.

So, do we honestly think a woman, who cannot even control her own city, would be successful as the Speaker of the House, I honestly do not think so. Pelosi has spent more time going after President Trump, then she has in helping President Trump or helping the homeless. Nancy Pelosi has also focused more on destroying Trump's character, then she has on bettering the lives of the American people. What is sad is the fact that she is part of the powerful elite, the ones who want to keep Americans divided and their pockets filled, but they cannot do that with President Trump in Office.

Think about their democratic logic for a second though, these democratic mayor's and governor's have went as far to ban family gatherings, this includes the Fourth of July, Thanksgiving and even Christmas. They put in these restrictions because they believe family

17

gatherings are too dangerous. What democrats think is not dangerous is hundreds of people gathering together to protest in the streets about how bad of a President, Trump is. It is an insane way of thinking because these democrats are completely okay with hundreds of people gathering in the streets, standing together, protesting against President Donald Trump, but are not okay with families gathering together.

Unfortunately, it does not stop with our American State politicians, nope, millions of Americans have started to follow these weak-minded individuals we call our American State Senators. Prime example of all this ignorance is when you see that these millions of Americans protested to ban a cartoon characters' guns because you know, fake cartoon guns are very dangerous. The reasons, along with the logic they use to make these blank statements is mind-boggling to say the least. The fact that cartoon characters are being called racist or offensive, really only shows you how big of a problem we have in America.

The problems that we should be addressing are not being addressed; instead, we have people claiming everything is racist and offensive to them and needs to be changed. This to me makes no sense at all, it's just as astonishing as the people who are under the assumption that they can do whatever they want, simply because the color of their skin. Question after question, runs through your mind, all thanks to the simple-minded logic that these democratic American State politicians have instilled into these people's minds. It is always still a constant question of, seriously, come on, seriously?

I think this expression has become rhetorical itself, every question, every thought that is provoked tends to go unanswered and the answer you do receive is never the right one. Like, is Barack Obama really talking crap about President Trump, when President Trump did more in 3.5 years, than Barack Obama did in 8 years, seriously? Barack Obama's morals tend to get worse and we seen this immoral display when Obama literally used a fallen American State Reps. funeral to bash President Trump. Speaking at the American State Reps. funeral, Barack Obama thought that instead of giving a eulogy about his fallen friend, it was a good time to tell Americans just how bad of a U.S. President, President Trump was and continues to be.

I am afraid his wife is much worse, Michelle Obama, literally went on record to claim that President Donald Trump puts her into a state of deep depression, although they have no daily interaction. It is funny

18

how someone who she has no interference or contact with at all can somehow put her into a state of deep depression. It is honestly exhausting to watch her talk; this is because all she talks about is how white people hate her and how Donald Trump is a bad man and bad President. When Michael or Michelle, is not talking about the subjects above, she is often spreading lie after lie or pushing more hate speech.

The sad reality of it all is, these two individuals, the Obama's, use their huge influence to spread hate and division, rather than unity and peace. What is crazy about that is, the Obama's are more cynical then most Americans, they will often lie straight to your face and tell you they are doing things for the American people, yet, their actions speak louder than their words. This is not just me saying this either, their actions often contradict what they claim or say and this tends to repeat itself constantly. One thing we know about the Obama's is that they are always complaining about a wealth gap, according to them, there is a wealth gap between black and white people that needs to be changed, although they are multi-millionaires.

This to me is somewhat funny because they are constantly on television, especially Michelle Obama, complaining that they are not making as much money as white people, yet, they are richer than most white Americans and even most minorities living today. I think one thing Americans need to remember when it comes to these two non-American individuals is the fact that, the Obama's were not rich until Americans made them rich, this can also be said for people like, Ophra, and Lebron James.

This is often why what Michelle Obama claims and says means nothing, these people are quick to blame white people on their so-called money problems, yet, combined they have more money than most Americans living today or will even make in a lifetime. It is sad because the same people they are degrading and belittling, white men and women are the very same people that helped turn them into millionaires and billionaires. It honestly makes no sense to see people that have plenty of money sit there and complain about so-called wealth gaps, while most Americans, white and black, are forced to live paycheck to paycheck.

We do have a wealth gap problem in America, but it is more of an, American middle class wealth gap problem, rather than a millionaire making more millions wealth gap problem, like these people tend to

19

complain about. I also find it funny how rich people always complain about making more money and it's always their mission to get more for their so-called people, yet, the people that are really struggling to feed their families and survive, never seem to receive any of the money.

Watching millionaires complain about making more money, while other people struggle to live paycheck to paycheck, is not right and this is something we should be taking a stance against. We should do this because people should not have to work to live, especially while we sit and watch as multi-millionaires complain about a so-called white and black wealth gap. The only man to put a stop to this was President Trump; he focused on giving the American people a better life and the option of making a decent living, instead of having to work to live.

Democrats hated this though; they cannot stand the fact that President Trump took the money from their pockets and gave it back to the American people, the people they stole it from in the first place. There was never really a wealth gap problem; there was the money democrats were making off the American people while Trump was not in office, compared to the money they are making now, since President Trump took office. One thing democrats do not like is people messing with their not hard-earned money and now that President Trump is putting more money back into the pockets of the American people, democrats deem to stop him any way they can.

This is often why we see democrats scrutinize and criticize everything President Trump does; it is because they are looking for a way to get rid of him, so they watch his every move, ready to pounce when they think he has done something wrong. It gets more interesting when they can't pin anything on President Trump because then these sneaky State Senators bring forth false allegations and accusations, trying to get something to stick. It seriously keeps you puzzled, but it gets worse when something does not stick, because then they create violent movements and back violent protests, so they can push their false narrative of hate. It is all very interesting because you see these same people talking about equality and having equal rights as everyone else, yet, these people do not extend that same option to all others.

Instead of allowing others to enjoy the same equality, they try to cancel their entire existence and try to erase their entire culture. It is never equal though, these people do not care about equality, they only care about what betters their lives. We have already seen this racism and discrimination take place by watching white Americans being punished for simply being white, the nationality they were born as. Southerners are being punished for displaying or supporting their Confederate Southern flag, while minorities proudly fly the Black Panthers flag. Seriously, how are you asking for equal rights, when you are not giving the same option to your fellow American?

Seriously, if we had equal rights for all Americans, shouldn't celebrating your Southern heritage be just as important as celebrating your minority heritage? Why is it racist for white people to celebrate their Southern heritage, but it's not racist for minorities to fly a flag that only represent black power and supports their own heritage? It honestly makes no sense when you think about it or even say it out loud, but this is what we are experiencing in today's America, everything white is racist and if it's not black or doesn't benefit minorities, it's also racist and unacceptable.

You know, when I think about some of this stuff, I honestly feel that I am in one big dream because this cannot be America, this cannot be the country we all grew to love. How can everything white literally be considered racist, seriously how? Everything really can't be, but this is the America we live in, these people are following the logic of democrats and un-Americans, who have pushed the theory that somehow everything white is racist and should be stopped or erased, this includes the entire white culture. It is one of the most ridiculous things I have ever heard because how can you try to get rid of us just because we are white, that is offensive and racist itself, but according to democrats and minorities, it is not racist.

It is amazing to watch minorities or other people go online and make statements about white people, accusing white people of things that other people are guilty of doing, but they do not care, they do it anyway because they will always hate the white race. Their attitude and opinion will never change towards white people; they will always hate the white race and blame white people for their problems. This is why these people have taken to destroying public American national monuments and statues, they want to erase or destroy everything they deem white or offensive.

The democrats have backed this ridiculous theory, but helped push it even further, when most of them were seen on television pushing for the movement. We watched as Nancy Pelosi and her democratic cronies, let hundreds of people destroy public American national monuments and statues, all because their opinion was that these monuments and statues represent nothing but white supremacy. It is like seriously, did State Senators literally just sit by and let these people do this, I mean, seriously.

It is all just a ploy by the Democratic Party; they spread their assumptive opinion that everything is about white supremacy and all minorities are being oppressed by a white systemically racist government. Yet, they are the ones that have been in the government for decades and have done nothing but increase the divide between Americans. It does not make any sense because you are often left asking yourself, have minorities become so weak minded to where they believe they are still suffering from slavery? It is sad to see millions of people think this way when they have never experienced slavery in their lifetime, while there are currently dozens of women and children being abducted and sold into slavery every single day.

This huge issue does not concern these people though, they want everything to be about them, so these people claim they are being enslaved, because by claiming this, they can play the blame game and act as the victim. It is the ideology and opinion that is being drilled into their heads by democrats and blm leaders, this opinion and ideology basically lays the blame solely on white people, police officers and President Trump. Supposedly everything bad or terrible that happens to minorities, now somehow falls on the shoulders of white people, police officers and the President. All of this just makes you shake your head because you see minorities out there in the streets with signs claiming that all police need to, "just stop killing us".

Yet, minorities are the ones responsible for all the crime and violence that wrecks their urban communities, not to mention all the death occurring in these same urban communities. We will take a look at more statistics later, but just keep in mind that, minorities are responsible for more of their own people's death, than any other race and this is by the thousands. So holding up a sign and screaming about how other people need to, "just stop killing us", is somewhat contradictive to what is occurring in real life.

Seriously though, you have to ask yourself, how can minorities claim other races or police officers, are killing off their people when, over the last 50 years there have been close to over 22,500,000 minority babies aborted and thousands of minorities are shot and killed by minorities each year? These are very alarming statistics, these are the issues that are a problem for minorities, not police officers, not white people, these alarming and tragic statistics seem to be more of a problem then police brutality or this made up white violence.

Seriously, it's alarming because not only are there more minority babies being aborted each year, but each year most young minorities are left with fatherless homes, drug and gang infested communities and are subject to violence on a daily basis. This is not, because of police officers, this is not, because of white people, this is because other minorities take it upon themselves to sell drugs and join gangs, rather than go to school and follow those that work to better their life. So your honestly left wondering, are minorities really the victims here? I honestly just think they are using this so-called systemic racism, along with victimization to become superior to white people and the white race because that is what the white race is to them, superior.

This is not just the opinion all these people tend to have either, this is the ideology that these people follow and act on, they no longer worry about the facts because they believe their opinion, is the only one that is true. It is amazing to watch as these people no longer worry about the truth, because now, the truth is what they make it and the facts are what they say they are. This is why their hateful opinion will never be changed, these people will always think everything is racist and offensive to them, they will always complain about it, unless it is the racist and offensive things coming from their own race.

That's one thing that has me questioning everything going on right now, how is it that everything of one culture seems to be deemed racist, but the other culture, although very racist itself, is not deemed racist? I fail to understand how this would honestly work, but it does, because we have seen it taking place as we speak. The entire white culture is now being deemed racist or offensive by other people, while the minority culture is not. Nor are they supposedly discriminating against white people for claiming that everything related to the color white is racist and offensive.

This hateful opinion has started movements and protests that have ended in the white culture being destroyed and white people being attacked. These are obviously acts of racism and discrimination, but according to minorities and democrats, it is not and they are allowed to do it. The thing that all Americans should be afraid of is, these minorities have been taught this ideology; they have been fed this opinion by the same people that target our children because they claim, it is the democratic way. This is the same logic that is used by teacher's and professors, who believe that capitalizing the b in black is a step towards racial equality.

Because capitalizing a letter is so much more important than getting a good education and working to better your life. Then again, due to this idiotic ideology, this is often where the blame game comes into play and victimization starts to take over their lives. Education is a prime example because these people constantly blame white people and our government on their bad education, yet, these are the same people that attend all minority schools, but some chose not to even go to school, then protests about having a bad and unfair education.

This is where the complication of fair and equal rights for all comes into play because minorities separate themselves from others, divide themselves from all other cultures, only to turn around and complain that, they are the ones forced into separation. Seriously, we know the facts, minorities have their own personal television channels, their own personal support groups, their own personal television shows, but also their own personal schools and colleges. Doesn't stop there though, minorities also have their own personal radio stations, their own minority civil rights groups, their own personal minority political caucus and even their own personal NRA.

So seriously, are all white people really the ones responsible for keeping minorities oppressed, separated and divided? White people, are not the ones who push for the division in our country, minorities, along with democrats, blm and liberals, are the ones that are guilty of the separation and divide. What I say or think really does not matter though, because all these people play the blame game and use the victimization card. This is because they've all been deceived by democrats and blm into thinking that nothing is ever their fault and all white people owe them something for the struggles they occur and the pains of the past.

It is somewhat puzzling to me because minorities are the only people in America that can keep themselves separated from other races, but still complain about being separated and being discriminated against. I say it is puzzling because these people follow the lead of idiots like, Charlemagne the dummy and Puff daddy or Puff or Puffy or P. Diddy or Diddy or whatever he goes by these days. These two influential individuals spread lies, along with false information and use their influence to push hate, instead of unity. I mean, Charlemagne is no God and he should not even be allowed to have the moniker because this guy is a straight idiot and I know why most rappers and people who meet him want to punch him in the face.

The sad thing is, Charlemagne, thinks he is actually someone of influence, but in reality Charlemagne, is just someone that most people make fun of because everyone needs a good laugh. I bring up these two individuals because along with many others, they push more false information and false allegations than anyone else. Think about it, these two idiots went on national television, to claim that they will not vote for President Trump because President Trump does nothing for them or the minority community.

I guess they do not watch the news much because President Trump just signed a new bill to invest over $100 billion dollars into fixing urban communities and neighborhoods. Not only that, President Trump signed another bill that helps minorities receive a better education by funding all black schools, colleges and universities. President Trump, also just passed a new musician's bill that helps musicians and songwriters keep the rights to their own songs and their own music, not allowing producers to steal it from underneath them.

This is so these musicians and songwriters cannot lose their songs and music to producers and production companies; I guess that does not help out P. Diddy because he is a so-called Producer, even though I cannot tell you the last hit song he produced. President Trump, has helped out the minority community more than anyone thought he would, yet, these two idiots and many others like them, claim that President Trump does nothing for the minority community, although the evidence proves otherwise. It's not just coming from these two either and that's the puzzling thing about what they claim, this idiotic opinion coming from these two individuals, is being spread to millions of others all around the world.

The opinion of a few, has transcended into the opinion of many and it's not for the better either, if you don't agree with these people or if you don't agree with their opinion, you are the one whose wrong, you're the one following the lies. Seriously, the ill-minded logic that comes from these people tends to make you shake your head and question everything they do, but also everything they say. Minorities' blm and democrats, use this ideology and logic to push their fallacious arguments about a worldwide police brutality pandemic, where police officers all around the world are supposedly beating and killing minorities every time they step out their front door.

It is a fallacious argument because there are more minorities being killed in America by their own people, then there are minorities being shot and killed by police officers. In 2019, police officers were involved in killing about 14 minorities for resisting arrest, this does not compare to the over 7,400 minorities, who were killed by their own the same year. These are facts, these are actual proven data statistics, data reviews taken every year by the F.B.I., so they can maintain their information, but facts nonetheless, yet, people choose to ignore these facts and claim something very different.

What I honestly would like to know is how you can seriously be so blind to the truth, where you blame the thousands of your people dying on other people and other races, knowing your people are the guilty ones? It is puzzling to me because minorities are dead set on claiming that there is a police brutality pandemic, but the facts are there, more minorities have been shot and killed in the past decade by minorities, then there were by police officers. If you do not believe me, I understand, the truth hurts, but facts are facts and no matter what you think or say, the facts speak for themselves.

If you do think I am lying though, here's a little fact for you, in the past 5 years, police have shot and killed over 1000 people, most of these victims were white, not minority, like people claim. Over 1000 people have been slain by police, while an estimated 10,000 minorities, have been shot and killed by other minorities and I am being generous when I say estimated at around 10,000. Think about it, we just discussed that in 2019 alone, over 7,400 minorities were shot and killed by their own kind, this is a very alarming statistic that goes ignored by minorities and democrats.

This occurred in only one year; just imagine if you added up all the previous years, the actual number would probably blow your mind. You can honestly look at the statistics from last year to see that police officers were responsible for over 200 shootings that resulted in minorities either being shot or killed, while thousands of minorities were killed by their own kind, over 7,400 to be exact. So seriously, who is really killing their own kind here, who is really responsible for the thousands of death occurring in minority communities because ; I know it is not the ones who are being blamed for it? The sad thing is, these people use the blame game so they don't have to deal with the real problem at hand, for these people, it's easier just to blame it on others, rather than facing the truth.

This is why we often see real problems swept under the rug, since no one wants to deal with the real situation at hand; they rather just brush it off or try to erase it from existence entirely. This goes for all races and people of all color. I say this because yea, minorities are responsible for the thousands of death of other minorities, but if we look at the same statistics, the same thing can almost be said about white Americans. It may shock you that while there were over 7,400 minorities killed by their own kind, there were over 7,000 white Americans killed by their own kind. So it seems every race in America, seems to be their own worst enemy.

Statistics and facts like these are often buried and forgotten though; these truthful facts are more than often swept under the rug because these statistics and facts do not fit the narrative or agenda that these minorities and democrats are trying to push. We know the narrative, which is to paint all white people as the enemy and blame everything on white people. The agenda is to continue their push for dominance, but when statistics prove, what you are claiming is false, it is harder to trick people into believing what you want them to believe.

This is why it took black lives matters leaders almost 7 years to become relevant and form a movement because their movement was built on the hatred of the white man and their agenda was to get rid of everything white. Pushing that hateful narrative and having that hateful agenda was never a good thing, until now of course. Seriously, though, these democrats and blm idiots really demanded that white people needed to give up everything they have worked hard for their entire lives, simply because these democrats and blm Marxist leaders claim they should; they want dominance, not racial equality.

It's honestly mind-boggling to see some of the demands that these blm Marxist leader's are giving to white Americans, but it's also mind-boggling to see that these people went as far as to create an entire list of demands for white people to abide by and literally expected white people to follow these demands. That is the thing that gets me about these blm leaders, these people actually made a list for white people, a full list of demands, simply because these people claim that all white people owe them something. This is something that keeps me puzzled because these blm leaders actually consider themselves fully trained Marxists and they continuously go on record complaining about the entire white race, demanding that somehow all white people owe them something.

It honestly makes no sense to me because white people do not owe minorities anything; white people are not responsible for the millions of bad decisions that have been made by millions of minorities. This is what these blm idiots claim though; these people claim that white people are responsible for the millions of bad life choices that minorities have made, year after year, generation after generation. Michelle Obama is a key player in the blame game because she pushes her false ideology about unfair educations and wealth gaps, while her and her husband makes millions off the American people.

Contrary to what they claim, the Obama's do not care about the American people, remember, if you voted for President Donald Trump, according to Michelle Obama and her useless husband, "you are the problem". It was also Michelle Obama who went on record to blame Trump supporters for spreading the chaos and lies. She was the one that made the statement, "Let's remember that tens of millions of people voted for the status quo, even when it meant supporting lies, hate, chaos and division. We've got a lot of work to do to reach out to these folks in the years ahead and connect with them on what unites us".

What I want to know first though is, who does she mean by, "unites us", she does not unite anyone but her own kind, plus why is she even speaking in the first place, she has no seat in the government, so why is she talking? Second, it's funny how she refers to people following lies, hate, chaos and division, yet, it's exactly what her and her husband, along with all other democrats, have pushed for the past four years. If I am not mistaken, it was mostly democratic cities that were experiencing the up-rise in crime and violence thanks to these so-called peaceful protests.

It was also democratic mayors and governors, who were supporting and bailing out these protesters and rioters, after they were caught burning down communities and businesses. These same democratic mayors and governors were developing new bail reforms for rioters and protesters, so as soon as the protesters were arrested, instead of being held accountable for their actions, they were instantly released. Still, according to Michelle or Michael as some like to call her, the people who supported President Trump and the people who support our American traditions, are the ones that have followed the lies, pushed the hate, caused the chaos and push for the division.

It would honestly be nice if she would just go away, I mean honestly, she has no political office, she has no seat in the government, so why are we even listening to someone who's husband was one of the worst U.S. President's we've ever had? I always like to stick to facts, which is something the Obama's never tend to do, but it is always funny how people like them discriminate against others, only to turn around and claim that they are the ones dealing with the discrimination. You cannot forget that, according to her, her husband and just about every democrat, blm member and liberal, President Trump supporters, are all white racist Nazi clan's members, who represent white supremacy, all 75 million of us Trump supporters.

It's funny to think about because them making a statement and racist remarks towards the President like this, is not considered racist, yet, if the President or any white person says anything back to these idiots or tries to stand up for themselves, were the racist ones. This is the philosophy that many of these people tend to live by, they constantly blame other people for their faults, but they also berate and degrade others, while they cry wolf when it is returned.

For me, listening to these people, especially Michelle and Barack Obama, is like having to deal with that echoing and horrifying sound that comes when someone is scratching a chalkboard. It is also about facts and the main fact, the main "done son", is the fact that, white colonist, did not start the slave trade, nor did white colonist's start the enslavement of minorities, N. African Moors did. You can say no, you can try to deny it, you can scream to the high heavens, but the truth shall set you free because it is the truth and if you bothered to open your history book, you would see exactly what I am talking about.

People don't bother with their history any more though, they listen to what others say or claim, but also what others believe, rather than reading about their own history. Seriously though, why do minorities choose to ignore the truth and won't take into account that their own ancestors, North African Moors, sold them to white man, but also to the British Parliament. That is the truth; N. African Moors created and started the slave trade and the enslavement of their own people, not white American colonist.

Seriously though, North African and Arabian Moors, created several slave trades before the new Americas were even discovered, this was because for these African and Arabian Moors, their own people were their highest rated trade commodity. So you are left asking, why are minorities claiming that white people owe them something, when history proves that their own ancestors are the ones responsible for selling them to the so-called evil white man? It's all puzzling to me because history shows the facts and while there were many slave owner's, white and black, slaves in the Americas were treated ten times better than they were as slaves in Africa and the Middle East.

There were many slaves in the New Americas that became close to the family member's that enslaved them, thanks to this close admiration, these slaves were given better jobs, better lives and even better living arrangements. It was a huge difference because many of these indentured servants eventually received their freedom by the same people that they served, this did not occur in North Africa or even the Middle East. No one ever wants to discuss actual history, they want to make up their own history and only discuss what they think happened, rather then what actually did happen.

This is where this crazy process and idea of canceling cultures comes into play; people are literally trying to cancel an entire culture, the white culture. This is all simply because they claim the entire white culture is racist and offensive and does not represent the American people, it represent's white supremacy. Think about that logic for a second though because people are trying to cancel an entire culture, all because they claim it is a racist culture and does not represent them, yet, it's our entire American culture. It is like the stupid people have taken over in America, our four fathers built this country for the American people and they did what they did to improve the lives of the American people.

Our four fathers did not bother to worry about how good of a trade commodity you were, like North African Moors and Middle Eastern Moors did. Fact is, slave owners, including the first recorded slave owner in America, an Angolan man named Anthony Johnson, a prominent minority figure during the 16th century, owned more white slaves then minority slaves. This is another part of history and fact that people like, Ophra, Lebron James, Diddy, Whoopi Goldberg and other minorities tend to forget because the facts do not help them push their agenda and narrative of minorities being the only ones who suffered from slavery.

The fact of the matter is, minorities, were not the only slaves in America, nor were they the first slaves in America and white colonist did not start slavery, N. Africans Moors did. These are proven facts, so if you are going to blame someone for your bad life choices, quit trying to use the past as an excuse and take a look in the mirror. Either way you look at it, the world has gone haywire, being white is now a crime and what used to be normal, is not anymore, the new normal is whatever reality these simple-minded idiots make up in their head.

Some of what these people claim and most of these people's opinions of what they believe, are just so overwhelming and unbelievable that they leave you shaking your head because seriously America, seriously! Unfortunately, the reality of what is occurring today is far worse then what we could have imagined and as a nation, it is going to take a while to recover. The decisions these people in charge are making do not benefit the American people in any way and are hurting our traditional American values. For instance, did we seriously just see a federal court judge appeal a child pedophiles case, all because this pedophile appealed that pedophilia should not be a crime and should be considered a sexual orientation, seriously?

Pedophilia is an inexcusable crime, but also an inexcusable act on a child, but according to this federal court judge and child molester, pedophilia should not be considered a crime, it should be considered as an accepted sexual orientation. The fact that this actually happened in real life and the fact that the case was actually appealed should be worrisome to everyone walking God's green earth. This is just one case, think about if there were more cases, like this one we would soon see child molesters walking the streets without worrying about suffering any consequences.

Granted most of these child molesters would wind up dead and the parents of the children would wind up in jail because that is how our government and judicial court system works. Seriously, though, this

31

judge should lose his judgeship because there should have been no appeal granted in the first place and the fact that a federal court judge approved this appeal is what is wrong with our country today. These judges are approving and appealing cases that should not be approved or appealed, these people are guilty of heinous acts, but these federal judges could care less and they are letting them out or agreeing to appeal their cases.

We have seen this same thing happen with the Boston Marathon Bomber, where the killer's case was appealed and he now has more rights in prison, then most people have out in the real world. It doesn't just stop with these federal judges either, these State and city officials should also be fired, especially in San Francisco, where city officials stopped federal ICE agents from arresting convicted illegal immigrant felons, in front of their own courthouse. Seriously, these San Francisco city officials stopped federal ICE agents from basically arresting illegal convicted felons and you want to know why they stopped these agents from doing their jobs.

It was because these city officials claimed it was a, "violation of these illegal immigrants' rights". You get that, it was a violation of their rights, arresting people who are over here illegally, but who are also convicted felons, is a violation of their rights. The logic honestly makes no sense at all, but all you are really left wondering is, when did people over here in America illegally, get rights? We should all be worried about this because these San Francisco city officials are more worried about illegal immigrants and convicted felons being arrested and deported, than dealing with the homeless problem that has taken over their cities.

Unfortunately, this tends to be a trend that seems to be occurring in America, people deal with problems they should not be dealing with and the real problems get pushed aside, like the homeless veterans, who fought and died for this country, they get pushed aside for illegal immigrants. Another crazy and stupid trend sweeping America right now is the trend of everything being deemed racist, especially anything and everything white.

Prime example of this is trend is that we now have thousands of people claiming that food labels are racist, due to this racism, food companies need to change their food label designs. Label designs they have had for generations. Seriously, if you honestly feel that food labels are racist, you are part of the problem we have in America because you seriously have some deep issues to work on. These are not just regular food labels that are being labeled racist either; these are popular food labels that have been around for generations that were dedicated to certain people for their loyalty to their companies. Food labels such as: Aunt Jemima Syrup, Uncle Ben's Rice, Mrs. Butterworth, Eskimo Pie, Cream of Wheat and Land O' Lakes butter.

The sad thing about some of these food labels being referred to as racist is the fact that, some of these food labels are based on famous minorities, who were put on the label for their appreciation and dedication. So basically, you are discriminating against this minority, simply because they are on a food label that you deem racist. I am not really going to stress with you guys too much on this subject because seriously, like I said before, if you think something as simple as a food label is racist, you have some serious issues to work on.

Another sad thing is that, this does not just stop with food labels, even cosmetic companies are now being criticized and labeled racist for promoting colorism. It is weird because minority females have their own stores, but also their own makeup and hair brands, yet, they still claim cosmetic companies promote colorism. Sometimes I think these people are just making words up to try and sound smarter than they actually are and this might be one of them, but now, companies are being blamed for promoting colorism, which is honestly just another excuse that they can use to claim they are the victim.

The ideology they use is the same ideology that is followed by these mindless people that believe they are to be handed everything, simply because of their race. These people use their race as the excuse to as why they do not have to work for anything, while all others do. Excuses seem to be all these people come up with these days and now thanks to our democratic government and a 98.6% curable disease, something as simple as work has become outdated. I think what is crazy about all of this is, all of this is being pushed by American State Senators and American city officials, basically, the people who are in charge of our country.

These senators have pushed the opinion that hard work is something that should not be appreciated all because hard work is supposedly a "white characteristic"; therefore, it should not be something people focus on. One thing that makes all of this funny is, not only is this coming from minority senators, this is even coming from white State Senators and politicians. White State Senators are complaining about white privilege and how all white people and even minorities have "whiteness attributes".

It is crazy because these are the exact same State Senators that were seen pushing protesters to riot and destroy communities for racial equality; destroy national monuments and statues for racial equality and even burn down dozens of minority owned businesses, all for racial equality. I would honestly like to know how doing any of these things, would be the correct way of fighting or advocating for racial equality. To a normal thinking person like myself, it is not, it is not even the right way of going about doing something for a cause, but according to our current State Senators and blm, it is exactly the right way.

Once again, their democratic logic comes into play, because you honestly hope that these people cannot be that dumb, then they go ahead and prove you wrong, when you see them on television doing it all over again. State Senator Jerry Nadler even went on record to claim that these protests were peaceful; there was no destruction or violence occurring at these so-called peaceful protests. While State Senators like Maxine Waters and Kamala Harris went on record to add flames to the already lit fires. These two State Senators alone pushed for the violence, they were both seen in interviews telling protesters to riot and loot because that's the only way people are going to give into their demands.

It is funny how these Senators pushed for this violence, but then retracted their statements when they were asked about what they said, although they made the statements on live television. Unfortunately, we have seen this insane ideology being pushed every day by our State Senators, American State politicians have helped start this entire trend of trying to cancel our American culture because these senators, have followed the blm movement, claiming America is racist and built on white supremacy. It is honestly puzzling to see because these are actual American State Senators helping push this movement, the same people that Americans elected to represent us, are pushing to cancel our entire American culture.

It is overwhelming to think that the State Senators that are supposed to be representing the American people and looking out for our best interests, are trying to get rid of our culture, all based on their opinion of the past. As we know `opinions` is a very interesting topic because people seem to think their opinions should be followed by others, this is the democratic way, to these people, if you don't believe their opinion, you basically don't matter. I think what everyone seems to forget is that our four fathers wanted to be free men and they fought to earn that right, but they also fought so their people could also enjoy the right of being free, that is why they created a united nation.

America was not built on slavery, nor was it founded by slavery, slavery was alive long before the American colonists even discovered slavery, so people need to stop blaming white people for the actions perpetrated and started by their very own people. This is something we have to look at because these opinions have started national worldwide movements. People are rioting, looting and protesting, all because their opinion is that, everything is racist and offensive to them, especially if it is white.

I seriously fail to understand their logic behind this theory because with this theory, since everything is now racist or is claimed to be racist, teachers now claim that math, yes, regular math, is racist. Because math is supposedly based on white supremacy, this makes it racist. Their reasoning is even more idiotic, since $2 + 2 = 4$, is an equation based on simple addition, it's based on "Western Math", since the equation and the answer is based on "Western Math"; it's racist and based on white supremacy. I'm seriously lost for words on this one, but the sad thing about this statement being made, is the fact that, this statement is actually coming from teachers and professors at legitimate schools and universities, all over America.

Most of what these people claim makes no sense at all or is actually based on real evidence, facts, history or even truth. You do not even have to take my word for it, you can simply look at the facts and statistics that these millions of people so easily ignore. Every single American living today grew up learning basic `Western math`, which was addition, subtraction, division and multiplication. This was the traditional way of doing math, but now, all of sudden thanks to others opinions, math is racist and needs to be changed, it is like, seriously?

Not everything is racist and you cannot just call something racist, just because it is your opinion that it is racist, people are allowed to have their own opinions, but they are not allowed to tell other people what their opinion should be or what they should believe. That is what

35

is occurring in America right now, people are forcing their opinions and beliefs onto others and if someone has a difference of opinion then these people do, if they do not conform to their beliefs, they instantly write them off as the liars. To these people, the ones who think like this, others are no longer allowed to have their own opinion because they no longer want you thinking on your own.

These people want you to have the same opinion they do and they will constantly try to convince you that their opinion is the right one, no matter how wrong it is. If you do not agree with these people, if you do have a different opinion then they do and do try to think on your own, they claim you are the one that has the problem and you are basically the racist one. The reality is, we are all American, were not only white, were not only black, were not only Hispanic, we are American and once people start realizing that fact, we can start coming together, because we should all remember that it's, "We the People".

It is honestly the government and the people in charge that every American should be worried about because these are the most corrupt people in the world, but they have the power to pass legislature that restricts Americans even more. The fact that our government can do whatever they want, should scare everyone in America, freedom is not so free if the people in charge start to slowly take it all away from us. Seriously, these State Senators do as they please, that is why the United States government spent close to $5.9 trillion dollars of taxpayer's money on wars in the Middle East and Asia since 2001, wars that were fought on false allegations, false claims and oil.

If you think that is bad, we can always discuss the over $30 million dollars of taxpayers' money that the government spent on a false impeachment trial, where they accused our U.S. President of doing something he did not even do. The very same U.S. President that just so happened to be responsible for ending the wars in the Middle East and for the first time in decades, get countries to sign a Middle Eastern peace deal. Of course, all these democrats ignore the fact that Hillary Clinton did actually collude with the Russians, but not only that, Hillary Clinton was also the one convicted of spying on President Trump's Presidential campaign.

Just like her hundreds of emails, the facts and truth came out, but quickly disappeared into thin air because these democrats continued to blame Trump for everything she was convicted of. What these people do or what they tend to focus on, just makes no sense to me, it honestly makes as much sense as giving an Emmy Award to the New York Governor for his excellent leadership during the global pandemic. It is like, forget the U.S. President, who saved the lives of millions of people by enforcing a travel ban, but who also invested time and money into making sure the American people were protected from this virus.

We are going to give the Emmy award to a governor that, shut down his entire State, putting his State on lockdown, which in turn, caused millions of people to lose their jobs, lives and worry about their future. I mean, seriously, you are giving an award for leadership to the exact same State Governor, who just passed a bill that gives illegal immigrants the right to obtain a State drivers license. He gave illegal immigrants the ability to drive, although they are over here in America, illegally. The sad thing is that, it takes most Americans several forms of identification to simply renew our Driver's license, but illegal immigrants can now get a license with no identification at all.

When I think about this, the only question I am left with again is, when did illegal immigrants get rights? In the State of New York, we are double screwed because not only do we have a messed up State Governor, we now have a new un-American State Representative, who could care less about the American people and more about illegal immigrants. She is another special State Senator, who was hired to represent the American people, yet, she spends more time bashing our current U.S. President, complaining about border immigration and fighting for illegal immigrants to have rights.

We witnessed recently where State Rep. AOC and her crony, State Rep. Ilhan Omar, tried to pass a bill that would protect illegal immigrants and illegal foreigners from being deported after they commit a crime in America. Not to mention both of these American State Reps., think that if an illegal immigrant or foreigner commits a crime; their lawyer should be paid for by the American people. These State Senators should not have even been elected to be representatives of the American people. Neither one represents the American people, they both fight more for illegal immigrants and illegal foreigners, than they do for the people they were hired to represent.

Again, this is not just me claiming this either, you can easily look up the recent new Green Deal or basically any other bill that both of these State Reps. have supported, you will see exactly what I am talking about. American State Reps. like these two and many others like them, believe in the same philosophies, therefore they use the American people as pawns, especially the American people who supported and voted for President Trump.

This is something that we have been exposed to daily, numerous idiotic news anchors, State politicians and fake news journalists; go on record to claim that, President Trump supporters are brainwashed Americans that believe the lies and the chaos that Trump has supposedly pushed. If you simply bothered to look at the facts, we see that President Trump was not the one lying to the American people; President Trump was not the one responsible for the chaos occurring in American cities, democratic Mayors and Governors were.

State Senators helped inflame this chaos by their hateful interviews, where they pushed the hatred and pushed for the destruction. People tend to skip over this little fact, but without the approval from these democratic Mayors and Governors, the President of the United States, no matter who they are, has to receive the approval of the city, before they can provide any help to the city. These democratic politicians let their cities be destroyed and instead of stopping the chaos, instead of stopping the destruction of their city, they go on television to blame President Trump for all the chaos and violence.

It is funny because all of these democratic mayors and governors knew that it was not really President Trump's fault, they knew this because they never gave him the authority to come in to their city to help. It honestly made no sense when these mayors were going on to television, complaining and blaming the chaos and rise of violence on President Trump, although they themselves chose to do absolutely nothing to stop the chaos and destruction from occurring. It's interesting to me because numerous democratic mayors and governors, just sat idly by, while millions of American citizens, were forced to deal with their cities being destroyed and having to watch as dozens of people destroyed their communities and businesses.

What also puzzles me about what these mayors and governors chose to do is, they chose to ignore the fact that, these movements were based on racial dominance, rather than peace and equality. The evidence is clear, so you do not have to go too far to see what I am referring to because most of these protests were started by self-proclaimed Marxists. These people are basically on a mission to change our American traditions and cancel and entire culture. It is all very puzzling to me because these are the same people that protest about how they deserve extra rights, yet, they burn everything down and destroy community after community, then claim it is your entire fault.

The scary thing about what these people are trying to do is, they are trying to change and even erase our entire American culture. These people are focused on trying to get rid of the traditional way of life because it does not fit their ideology or idea of their new America. For the first time in United States history, we have State Senators, blm and their followers trying to cancel an entire culture, but not only cancel it; they want to remake history, so it better fits their narrative of history. We have seen this taking place already; teachers were caught trying to teach children that the Revolutionary War was fought over slavery, not over Americans wanting to be free and independent from the British Parliament.

This ill-minded ideology was being taught to our children, until President Trump put a stop to it, but still, what this really does is, shows you that people are stuck in their ways, they will always use the past as an excuse to blame other people. No matter what you try to do or no matter what white Americans try to do, to people that think this way, white people, will always be the enemy; they will always be the ones that were responsible for enslaving their people, although their ancestors are the ones who started the process of enslavement.

This is why you will always see minorities constantly showing support for the Black Panther's, a known white hate group. This is also the ideology that these people are trying to teach, they constantly use race as an excuse. Instead of teaching about our real American history, they rewrite American history, so it is more based on their opinions of slavery building America. Needless to say, these people are now under the assumption that children attending Elementary school, should be learning about their civil rights and civil rights movements, instead of learning about their ABC's or even how to count.

It honestly makes no sense because, children should be learning about their abc's, but also learning how to add and subtract, not learning about civil rights and civil rights movements, something they clearly don't even understand at their age. If that was not already bad enough, these politicians and their followers are, acting like slavery built this nation into the great nation it is today. Which is just straight nonsense thinking because they are claiming that all major inventions, advancements and progressions that made us who we are, were led by slavery. Did they somehow forget that slavery ended hundreds of years ago and we have advanced way beyond the years of slavery?

After slavery ended in the 1800's, there were hundreds of inventions and advancements that were not built by slavery and making this claim discredits any minority inventor or anything they did for their country. To even make a claim like this to me is crazy because if you are making that bold of a claim, you should have evidence to back it up, but we have all read about our American history, we all know that slavery was something that occurred to every single race, not just minorities. In the very beginning of the new Americas, when the concept of slavery was first introduced to American colonists, most slaves were white, not black.

Slavery also did not become dominant in the new Americas until North African and Arabian Moors set in place, slave trade routes, which then allowed these Moors to sell their people at a higher rate. To claim that slavery built this great nation is just ridiculous and if you are claiming or even thinking that, you should be revoked as a teacher because you should not be teaching anyone, let alone children. It is insane when you think about it because like I said before, slavery ended hundreds of years ago and every race was enslaved at one time or another.

Still, minorities deny this claim and instead, claim they were the only ones who experienced slavery, which is why they claim slavery, built this great nation into what it is today. This to me is overwhelming thinking, these people are spitting in the face of every phase of advancement and progression that influenced America, but also every single American, white and black, that fought and died to protect the very freedoms we have today. Progression and advancement creates nations, peoples influence and inventions creates nations, yea, slavery was wrong and bad, but also may have had a huge impact on the American people, but it did not build the nation we see today.

You can say slavery divided the country more than it did in creating the country because you have to remember, there was an actual four-year war over slavery, which divided our country in half and forced even family members to choose a side. This is not what built this country; slavery was another part of this country's history, a bad time during our history, but history nonetheless. Slavery did not build this great country into what it is today, nor was it even the cause of the Revolutionary War, people need to stop lying and face the truth.

Unfortunately, this kind of thinking is not good for no one, this hateful opinion, is good for anyone, but State Senators and other influential people continue to try to push this way of thinking onto anyone who will listen, starting with our children. It is getting worse though because these very same people, along with blm leaders, are convincing minorities that they are still somehow facing slavery today, like somehow minorities are still stuck living as slaves. We all know this is something that's not occurring and we know that most minorities living today have never experienced slavery, but democrats want minorities to think they are still be treated as slaves, so this is the narrative they help push.

Slavery is not something minorities are experiencing today, contrary to what democrats and blm want you to believe, you are not a slave, you live free, you do as you please and you make your own life choices, you are no slave. The truth is, minorities do not even know what it feels like to be a slave, some may have experienced segregation, but none have experienced slavery and no, you cannot just claim that you have experienced slavery, when you have never actually experienced it. Claiming that you have experienced something through the past and your bloodline means that you have never actually experienced it and you are using the past as an excuse to try to better your future because you are too lazy to work for it.

In addition, you cannot live off the past and no one else is responsible for your bad life choices, contrary to what idiots like Michelle Obama says, you are the one responsible for your actions. If you do not bother to work for something or get an education, you cannot blame anyone but yourself because it is your fault that you have no education and no money. No one else is responsible for the bad life choices that you have made during your life, especially white people, if you chose not to go to school to receive an education that is on you; no one else is responsible for you choosing not to attend school or just skip school all together.

This is what seems to be holding Americans back because people of influence are teaching minorities that it's not their fault that they mad bad life choices, it's other peoples fault and when that's constantly drilled into your head, you slowly start to believe it. What I find very interesting about all of this is the fact that, these influential people are actually try to blame having a bad education or no education at all on white people, it honestly makes no sense because for decades, minorities have had their own black only schools and colleges.

These schools only accept minorities, no other race, so you cannot complain about having a bad education, when it is your choice to receive that bad education. Then you have the latter, which has occurred for years, where black teens attending regular public schools tend to be very bad and destructive students. They could care less about an education because they care more about being popular, so they act out in class or try to skip class all together to make them seem cooler. Any way you look at it, the only people responsible for their bad education, is minorities themselves, no one else is responsible for their bad educations and now it's worse.

Now these State Senators and influential people claim that school is too hard, so they have to dumb it down for minorities, so this means getting rid of advancement classes. It honestly leaves me confused as to how all of a sudden, students that always messed around in school, but also never listened to the teachers or skipped school entirely, are the ones we are giving in to. It's confusing because these are often the teens that chose to skip school to sell drugs or chose to just sell drugs in school, but these are the ones being declared the victims of being forced to have a bad education.

This is why I fail to understand how people like the Obama's, can go on television and complain about minorities having bad educations, when we've witnessed time and time again that minority students are violent, destructive students, who often chose to act up in school. This may not account for all minority students, but it does account for a vast majority of them and we have witnessed this in public schools every year, but now, white people are to blame for their bad educations, seriously? None of the logic these people use makes any sense, these people are always blaming someone else for the problems they have, when they themselves, are the ones who are guilty of putting themselves in that situation.

This is just something they do though, they use the blame game to blame their problems on other people, this is often because this is what they were taught and raised to do. The only thing this way of thinking tends to do is, push the separation and divide of white and black Americans even further then it already is. I honestly think that is one of the main things that keeps everyone so puzzled because minorities are the only people that continuously keep themselves separated in groups and divided from others; yet, they are the main ones that are always seen complaining about this separation and division from other races.

Today, minorities are trying to separate themselves even further from everyone because they have chosen to play the African national anthem in front of our own American national anthem at sports events, which makes no sense at all because we are in America, not Africa. Since minorities want it to be all about them, they chose to play an African national anthem to represent them, claiming that is now their official anthem, not the American national anthem. Minorities chose to do this, they pushed to do this, no one else told them to do this, they made the decision to do this.

Minorities chose to have the African anthem played first for them, furthermore showing that, all they are doing is trying to separate themselves even further from white Americans. They won't tell you this though, instead, they will claim it's all for racial equality, but you know it's no longer about equality, when they start to demand that white people give up their very own homes and even their jobs. People also need to learn more about their own heritage, rather than learning about it from a website.

People need to take the time to learn their identities and where they actually come from because people claim they identify as one thing, when it is obvious they are not. Seriously, if you are from Africa, were born in Africa, your parents were born in Africa, your grandparents were born in Africa, you are African, if you are from America, were born in America, your parents were born in America and your grandparents were born in America, you are American, plain and simple. The African national anthem does not represent you because you are not African, not even African-American, although you may claim that it is your heritage, it is not, definitely if your family doesn't even originate from Africa.

You are represented by the American flag and the American national anthem, these are our American symbols of freedom, symbols that have been fought and killed over, these symbols represent Americans and your American freedoms, not racism and especially not white supremacy. It was not only white Americans, who fought and died in wars for this country, it was Americans from all different backgrounds. Following the opinions or ideologies of crybaby sports players like Lebron James, is not only disrespecting America, but it is disrespecting the thousands of Americans that fought and died, so you could be free.

We will get to crybaby Lebron James later, but it is amazing that this guy is even seen as an influential person, because he makes some of the most outrageous statements ever made. It started with the NFL though; they let minorities have their own little anthem before every game, which was the African national anthem, while they knelt to the American national anthem, although we are not in Africa. Basically, since blm and their followers demanded it, the NFL gave in and played it for them, which in turn lost the NFL hundreds upon hundreds of fans, who now see the NFL as traitors to their own country.

Seriously, when you witnessed this, all you were stuck asking yourself was, why is the NFL playing the African national anthem in front of our very own American National Anthem, especially when we are in America, not Africa? I know it's not time for the Olympics, so why would we being playing some other nations anthem in our own country, seriously, what sense does that make? It makes no sense to normal thinking people, but according to blm, leftists, minorities, democrats and liberals, this makes plenty of sense and is a good way to show a stance on so-called systemic racism.

It all backfired for the NFL though, due to their decision of playing the African anthem first, Americans stepped up and protested against the NFL, which led to the NFL having the lowest television ratings it has ever seen. The same can be said for the NBA after all their protesting, but the NBA tried to be a little smarter with it because they claimed their coaches and players went on strike, when in reality, the NBA's ratings dropped so low, they needed another out, other than the one they had.

When a late night television show has better ratings then you, you might have a problem and this happened to both the NBA and NFL Both of these sports leagues, along with others, experienced their ratings dropped drastically once they all started disrespecting the American Flag and the American national anthem. It was nice to see Americans actually come together for a cause and a purpose and

44

showed their support for our American symbols. It's amazing to see how American's can come together on some things, but not come together on the things that we should be coming together on, like unity, equality and peace for all Americans.

I say this because I am still a little confused as to why Americans were mad at the NFL and the NBA for disrespecting the American flag and American national anthem, but were not mad at the people that were burning the American flag and kneeling to the American national anthem. It often leaves you confused because these people were also burning down public monuments and statues, destroying dozens of communities and tearing apart American cities. Like many American State Representatives, people all around America tend to focus on what they think is important, rather then what is actually important.

Since it is their opinion that it is what is important, that is the issue they focus on, while they leave the rest of their issues on the back burner. Prime example of all of this is the destruction and defacing of our American national monuments and statues, millions of people have the opinion that these monuments and statues are racist and only represent white supremacy; therefore they need to be destroyed or taken down. It is their opinion, not everyone's opinion, just their opinion, but since it is now the opinion followed by millions, people acted on this opinion and we watched as numerous public national monuments and statues were defaced or destroyed.

The thing we should probably be worried about is the fact that, American State Senators, including our very own Speaker of the House, sat idly by and watched as these public national monuments and statues were destroyed or defaced. Even city officials took part in the action by secretly having numerous public monuments and statues removed from their cities, without other people even knowing about the removal or even getting to say anything to stop the removal. These are the very same State Senators, mayors and governors that watched as rioters, looters and protesters took over their city streets, basically destroying everything they could, including dozens of police precincts, federal buildings and businesses.

It is like, seriously, why are American State Senators, mayors and governors, allowing people to destroy American cities, destroy public national monuments and statues and burn American federal buildings and businesses to the ground? Seriously though, why is this being allowed to occur, why is this not being stopped? It is an honest question because the only thing this chaos and destruction seems to be doing is, causing more damage to already hurting communities, with some communities not being able to recuperate from the damage and destruction.

You tend to question if any of these people have a brain because these people honestly believe that if they destroy and deface national monuments and statues, if you burn down and loot minority owned businesses, but also destroy their communities, you are on the right track to fighting for equality. Let's be real though, it's no longer about racial equality, it's no longer about the betterment of minorities, these people want racial dominance and will do everything in their power to get it. The fight for racial equality was stopped after these people decided to verbally and physically attack white Americans that showed support for the American flag or the U.S. President.

This is where all the confusion starts to set in because if you are an American who supports the United States President and his American values, you are somehow the racist one, who is supporting a white supremacist President. I honestly fail to understand the logic behind this opinion because due to this shared opinion, Americans who show support for the American flag, the American national anthem and even the United States President, are being verbally assaulted and physically attacked.

I am serious, Americans, mostly white Americans, are being physically sucker punched while they are doing nothing other than walking or shopping for groceries, sucker punched for simply being white. If you seriously do not think something is wrong with this picture, you may be part of the problem; seriously, this is not something that should be seen as an okay thing to do. Unfortunately, with everything that is going on in America right now, the word `seriously` has become more of a rhetorical question, rather than a modifier because you're also no longer left wondering who, what, when, where or even how did it all occur, it's all so mind-boggling you're only left asking, seriously?

It is unfortunate that yes would be the answer and I am serious, influential people are using ill logic to push their fallacies onto others, mistaken beliefs that are often backed by opinion, rather than truth. You question them, you question their agenda, you question why they will not accept another's opinion, but these people will never have an answer for you, but they will however, always have the opinion they do and they will spread this opinion to whoever will listen. Their kind of like the people that always want more then what they are given, like the old saying, "you gave them an inch, but they took a mile".

What it really comes down to is deception, from a fabricated police brutality pandemic, to the fake enslavement of an entire race, to the canceling of cultures; these people aim to destroy America. The deception of the American people has already started taking place, like we discussed before, the democratic party believes that, American national monuments and statues, symbols of freedom that have been dedicated to our heroes, are racist and only represent white supremacist men. Since these American national monuments and statues represent white supremacy and are somehow racist, they are to be taken down and destroyed.

It does not matter that these monuments and statues were made to honor the men who paved a way for Americans. If it was not for President Donald Trump we would probably still be seeing monuments and statues of people like Abraham Lincoln, Thomas Edison, Thomas Jefferson and even Christopher Columbus, being defaced, torn down or destroyed. What I fail to understand is, when did everything white become racist, when did our four father's, the people who fought to free the American people, all of a sudden become racist white men, who only pushed white supremacy?

This is something that I would like an answer to because people with a brain, especially history buffs, know that this is far from the truth. Just because America was formed, found and built by white men, does not mean everything they did was based on white supremacy. Seriously, if you think this is true, you obviously know nothing about your own history, but you also know nothing about the wars between America and hate groups like the KKK. White Americans, including the President, have never supported white supremacy, nor have we ever supported known hate groups, but according to minorities, democrats and liberals, all white Americans owe minorities because everything white people do and have done somehow represents white supremacy.

This really all started when democratic politicians and blm Marxists leaders, pushed the idea that all white people have white privilege, which they claim gives white people an instant advantage over everyone else, simply because the color of their skin is white. The confusion starts to set in when you see that minorities, led by these blm Marxists leaders, are protesting that they deserve everything handed to them, not because they worked for it like most Americans did, but because the color of their skin entitles them to it.

It is a bit confusing because these people claim white people have an advantage, because they are white, but then turn around and claim they deserve an advantage, because they are black. It honestly leaves you confused because these people claim that one race is given an advantage and this advantage is the reason why they have what they have. It is not because of their hard work, but because their skin color is white. The assumptive opinion that has taken over is the opinion that, because of this advantage that white people have, minorities deserve everything handed to them.

Like I said, it is no longer about racial equality, they want racial dominance, so they will do everything they can to spread their false opinions and lies. One of these false lies is that, minorities suffer from the pain and agony of what their ancestors went through, so this entitles them to everything. You have to seriously ask yourself, if you've honestly never worked that much in your life and you've done nothing to deserve anything, how could you be demanding that everything be handed over to you, simply because of what happened in the past, seriously though, how?

Due to this opinion of theirs and since they claim that white people supposedly have everything through white privilege; minorities think they deserve everything just to be handed to them. What tends to make no sense about all of this is the fact that, white people are now being blamed for something we have never participated in, but also something that happened hundreds of years ago, before any of us were even born. Even Ophra, a television host billionaire, someone whose made money on people's emotions, but who was also made rich by white people, especially white women, decided to use her influence and speak up about this `white privilege`.

According to Ophra, "Every white person has a leg up, no matter what, if you are white you have an advantage", yet, myself, my family members, also most my friends are white and we have received no extra advantage for being white. We have no leg up to get anything we want, if we want something we have to go that old route of working hard to get it, something Oprha knows nothing about because she has more of a leg up then anyone. It is also funny to hear people like Ophra, talk about other people having privilege and advantages, when no one in the world has the privilege that she gets to enjoy.

I find it contradicting when it is coming from a lady who was made rich by white people because it was not all minorities attending her shows and watching her television shows, it was white people and white executives, who were watching, attending and producing her shows, which in turn made her filthy rich. It is also puzzling why a woman, who is a known billionaire, who is also probably one of the richest women in America, chooses to degrade white people, the very people that made her into who she is today. Instead of using her influence for good, she creates an entire show for white people, especially white couples, so they can come on and talk about their supposed white guilt.

Seriously, I wish I was joking, but Oprha, created an actual full-length television show on her channel, that had several white people coming on the show to talk about how they felt guilty for being white. It seems to me that she rather focus on making money off people's emotions, rather than focusing on interviewing the people themselves. It is crazy because how does Ophra choose to repay the millions of white people that helped make her rich and turned her into a television star; she embarrasses them on national television by bringing them on her television show to talk about how they feel guilty or should feel guilty for simply being white.

That is right though, a billionaire, made rich by white people, but who also has more privilege then most white Americans living today, created a full show to have white people talk about how they should feel guilty for simply being white. The white privilege thing really gets me because according to Ophra, Lebron James, Puff diddy and other rich minorities, all white people have special privileges, all because of our skin color. Yet, all these people listed above and their friends, enjoy more privilege then most white Americans living today, even most minorities living in America today.

You see the same ignorant logic being used by others when they are being interviewed on live television because these people have the opinion that white people can't even experience racism, supposedly every other race experiences racism, except white people of course. I am white, I have experienced plenty of racism, my friends are white, they have experienced plenty of racism, but to claim that white people do not experience racism, just shows you how ignorant you are. Doesn't matter if you are a millionaire or just a common citizen, to think that white people do not experience racism, is just ridiculous, white people probably experience it more, we just do not complain about it as much as certain people do.

The scary thing about all of this is, this statement is what gives these people the opinion that they can say anything they want to white people, do anything they want to white people and white people are just supposed to sit there and take it. It has become ridiculous because if a white person does any of this or says anything remotely racist to a minority, the white person is the one charged with either a hate crime or racial discrimination towards others. Yet, if any minority makes offensive or racist remarks or commits racism or discriminates towards any white person, it's okay and to be accepted.

What is makes all this puzzling to me is, Ophra and Lebron James are billionaires, not millionaires, but billionaires, who rarely deal with racism, because it is more like criticism, yet, they both claim that white people are racist towards them, although half of their fan base tend to be white. I fail to understand how two billionaires, along with many other influential millionaires, can be complaining about racism and white people supposedly owing them something, when they themselves personally became billionaires and millionaires, all thanks to the help of white people.

Most white Americans don't even live the way these rich people have the privilege of living because most white Americans and even minorities are working a 9 to 5 job, 5 days a week, so they can receive a lousy paycheck. This is why it makes no sense to see these millionaires and billionaires, crying and complaining about a systemically racist government and all minorities being oppressed. Especially when all these people live in gated off multi-million dollar homes, with their personal maids and personal chefs that do everything for them.

You seriously do not think any white person would change their lives for these millionaires' lives, white people struggle just like everyone else. I say it does not make any sense because according to these rich a**holes, white people, are all-racist and have an advantage or leg up, because our skin color is white, therefore we have an advantage. Most white people, including myself, also most middle class minorities, are stuck working dead end jobs for a living and the thought of being a millionaire, usually comes in the form of a dream. Most honest hard working Americans just want to be able to live comfortable lives, not having to worry about not making enough money or living paycheck to paycheck.

Nothing is just handed to us simply because we are white, unless we work for it, which cannot be said for rich people, who really enjoy all the privilege. That's the one thing that seems to be lost in translation, because think about it, if it wasn't for millions of white people all around the world or millions of white Americans supporting people throughout the years and decades, these minorities would have never become millionaires and billionaires. This is not me being racist either; it is just me stating facts because during the 70's, 80's, 90's and even the early 2000's, a third of the population in the United States of America was white.

It is not a lie, its reality; white Americans have always made up the majority of the population in the United States of America. Therefore, it is true when I say that, millions of white Americans have made everyone around them rich, while they themselves are left living paycheck to paycheck. It's funny how most white people, including myself, indentify as middle-class Americans, the people who tend to live paycheck to paycheck and get the s**t end of the deal.

It is honestly a lie to say the least or even think that all white people are racist and represent white supremacy because we are not and simply do not. Although we may hate some things about your culture, it does not give you the right to say our American culture is racist and needs to be canceled. Let's be honest here, there is no systemically racist government, if there was, there would have been no minority President, there would be no minority anything, let alone millionaires and billionaires, there would only be white Presidents, millionaires and billionaires.

Fact is that, the United States of America has the most millionaires and billionaires in the whole world; this includes minority millionaires and billionaires. Yet, America still has millions of people living in poverty, millions of people living homeless and millions of people struggling to work to provide a life for their families. What is interesting about this fact is that, hard-working Americans are not the people complaining about systemic racism, they are not the people protesting about a wealth gap. The people that are complaining about a so-called systemically racist government are the ones that have been made rich off that systemically racist government.

It is amazing to watch these rich millionaires sit there and complain about being held back by the government, being oppressed by the government, knowing they have more money in the bank, then most Americans have made in a lifetime. As the saying goes, the rich get richer, while the poor get poorer. What is puzzling about someone as influential as Lebron James is, you would expect him to unite the people, not go on national television and claim that minorities are being hunted down like dogs, but also shot and killed by police every time they step out of their front door.

Seriously, if you did not see it, Lebron James went on national television to tell people all over America that, police officers are hunting down minorities like dogs and killing them. The worse part about all of this is when Lebron went on to claim that, this happens every time minorities step outside their front door, this is also supposedly why minorities are dying at an alarming rate. Like we discussed before though, this statement and many others like it, has no base to them, they have no actual facts that prove what they are saying or claiming.

Honestly though, 14 minorities being killed by police officers after they resisted arrest, does not compare to the over 7,400 minorities that were shot and killed by their own people. Fourteen minorities, compared to over 7,400 minorities, seriously, you tell me who is really responsible for the alarming rate of death occurring in minority communities? Do not listen to what Lebron or people like him claim, listen to reason, listen to the truth, review the facts before you make your judgment, do not believe someone, simply because they believe it, do the research before you just assume.

People need to start thinking for themselves and go ahead, it is okay, you can think for yourself, I promise it's okay, you are an American and contrary to what these people claim, you have a right to think freely on your own. It is honestly crazy to think of because according to Lebron James, this is not happening to everyone, this is only occurring to minorities currently living in America, minorities are supposedly the only ones being targeted and killed by police officers. We know this statement is not even close to being true and the fact that, a basketball player with a huge influence and one that has a national platform like he does, would say something like this about the same people he uses as his security, honestly speaks volume to his character.

We have already seen things coming from him that make you question his character because Lebron James and his fundraising team thought it would be a good idea to pay the fines of convicted felons in Florida, so these convicted felons would be able to vote. Forget the fact that, the millions they spent probably could have helped out numerous urban communities redevelop, forget the fact that, the millions could have helped in providing a better education system for urban communities because Lebron James thinks it's smarter to invest in criminals, rather than communities.

Think about this logic for a second though, you are paying to give convicted felons the right to vote, something they lost when they committed a crime. Yet, you do nothing about the innocent minorities being killed in urban communities on a daily basis, but kneel to the national anthem and blame all the death on police officers. Let me also clear this up before we continue, I fully support the lives of all minorities, I support the lives of all people, I do not support the blm Marxist movement.

These people are not protesting and rioting for minorities, they are not protesting for racial equality, they are protesting for racial dominance and destroying anyone who gets in their way. Now, I know you might be thinking, well if you do not support the black lives matter movement, you do not support minority lives. Which is not true, blm does not support black lives, nor do they even focus on the betterment of minorities, they focus on taking over as a race and canceling an entire culture to do so. Seriously, look at these peoples actions, look at what these people are doing to urban communities, look at the money these blm people make off the death of their people.

They are not in the communities doing good, feeding the people, finding jobs for the people, educating the people, nope, they are in communities burning down businesses and looting grocery stores, claiming its reparations for the past. Seriously, how does this better the lives of minorities, how does destroying and burning down minority owned businesses, fight for the betterment of black lives? It really doesn't, but don't tell that to these blm Marxists leaders because they see this movement as a way of fighting for dominance, they destroy communities, burn down businesses, loot stores and kill each other, claiming it's all for the betterment of minorities. Seriously, ask yourself, if the blm movement was really about the betterment of black lives, why is it that minorities are still being slaughtered daily, by their own race, even at these black lives matters protests?

There is no betterment for black lives, there is no justice or equality for minorities coming from these blm leaders because if there were, you would not see innocent minorities, especially innocent minority children, still being shot and killed on a daily basis. It honestly makes no sense when you think about it, even when you look at all the facts, statistics and data analysis, you see that minorities are usually the ones responsible for the alarming rate of crime and violence occurring in urban communities. The facts do not matter to blm leaders though; these blm rioters and protesters still continuously blame white people and police officers for all their problems.

What you have to realize and what it always come down to is, white people, are not the ones in urban communities promoting the crime and violence. White people are also not the ones out in urban communities robbing and killing people, some might be, but in urban communities, it is mostly minorities, who are responsible for the violence. I think that's one thing that keeps everyone puzzled, not just myself because seriously, how can you blame the robbing, the shooting and even the killing occurring in your communities on people that don't even live in your communities?

It is a very serious question because that is what people like Lebron James, blm leaders and their followers are claiming, if it is not the police killing them off, its white people supposedly keeping them oppressed in their own communities. What's scary about all of this is that, these people are claiming, none of the violence is minorities fault, it's not their fault that their own people are constantly being slaughtered daily in their own urban communities, the blame somehow falls on police officers and white people.

I honestly think these people have seriously lost their minds, but this is the blame game they play, they blame everything on other people because they cannot face the facts. Seriously, it is not police officers killing thousands of minorities year after year, it is not white people killing thousands of minorities year after year, its minorities, who rob, shoot and kill each other by the thousands, year after year. It is overwhelming to me because we have seen this constant trend of crime and violence occur in urban communities and it has occurred for generations, not just years, but for generations.

Still, the blame always seem to fall on someone else shoulder's, never on the shoulders of the ones who are actually responsible. Minorities plague their communities with drugs, gangs and constant violence, which in turn, destroys their entire community; these are often urban communities that have been plagued by violence for so long because that is all they know. What really makes no sense and makes you start to question everything these people do is when, minorities started walking into suburban neighborhoods, yelling and screaming at white people, demanding them to give up their homes.

Seriously, Americans watched on the news as dozens of minorities went into several suburban neighborhoods and communities and literally started yelling and screaming at these white people, who were doing nothing wrong, claiming that these white people need to give up their homes because they belong to minorities. I seriously thought I was seeing things, but nope, clear as day; they were walking into these communities, making demands to white people, who were doing nothing to them. Seriously though, what honestly makes you think that you are entitled to go into a community or a neighborhood and start disrupting their lives, simply because you are mad that their community is better than your community?

I mean, honestly, what would make you think this is okay to do? Safety and security even came into play because these minorities blame white people for having too much safety and security in their communities, since their urban communities tend to be filled with crime, violence and barred up windows. I'd honestly still like to know what gives people the right to go into suburban communities, which contrary to what others tell them, does have minorities living in them, to make demands, simply because it's their opinion that, these suburbanites have a better life and too much safety and security?

I mean, seriously, does this make any sense at all, what in your brain would tell you that it is okay to disrupt other people's lives, all because your life completely sucks? Especially when you are the one that is responsible for making the decisions that has led up to where you are in life? This does not even float in the vicinity of common sense, but we are seeing blm, their followers and young minorities, do it all the time now. They act out like this because these people are merely following the idiotic logic and opinions of these blm Marxist and their followers, but also, State Senators and civil leaders.

I honestly fail to understand how millions of people could blatantly just ignore the facts or the truth, but also turn around and claim that these facts are not true. Somehow these people all think, minorities are not the ones responsible for more than half the crime, violence and death in America, although the evidence proves otherwise. This is why a lot of minority's mindsets or opinions will never change, they ignore the facts and instead, listen to these blm leaders, who have convinced them that they can blame their problems on everyone else, rather than face the music themselves.

Think about this for a second though because it is true, minorities make up about 14% of the U.S. population, yet, minorities are responsible for more than half the crime and violence that occurs in America. Maybe this is often why we see so many minorities in jail or prison, they account for half the crime in America. It is not because they are supposedly being targeted by the police daily, but because they are responsible for more than half the crime that occurs in the United States of America. People tend to ignore little facts like these, especially minorities; they tend to stick to what they believe to be true.

It's interesting to me how minorities will ignore the black on black homicides occurring daily in their communities, but will riot and burn down urban communities, when police officers kill one of their own. This is why it really makes absolutely no sense when you see these American sports celebrities, radio hosts, TV hosts, democrats, professors, teachers and actors, giving in to these blm criminals. They are all acting like these people deserve some kind of prize for ruining people's lives, burning down minority owned businesses and destroying dozens of urban communities. These are the same idiots that think #hash tagging something is a good way to fight or advocate for racial equality because going out into the streets and protesting the right way, is too much work for these people.

No offense to these self-proclaimed smart people, but burning down American businesses, destroying dozens of communities, looting grocery stores and hash tagging something, is not by any means, a step

56

towards fighting for racial equality. Besides, think about the way they advocated for equality, they started by destroying their own communities and followed that up with burning down minority owned businesses. They caused all this chaos and destruction for equality, but while all this chaos and destruction was occurring for racial equality, minorities were still being shot and killed, including children, all by other minorities.

You need to honestly ask yourself, how are these actions a good way to advocate for racial equality or justice, seriously, how is this a good way to advocate or fight for anything? The only thing these people deserve is probably a jail sentence; they should not be rewarded for causing chaos, pushing violence and destroying their communities. Yet, they are, these State politicians, millionaires and billionaires, reward them and bail them out for doing just that, causing chaos, violence and destruction.

Seriously, it's like congratulations, you just destroyed dozens of minority owned businesses, you just destroyed dozens of urban communities and thanks to your so-called peaceful protests, it's going to take years, also cost millions, to rebuild what you chose to destroy in seconds; great job. The alarming part is that innocent minorities, young and old, were actually losing their lives during these so-called peaceful protests, dozens were gunned down for no reason at all. When asked about these innocent killings of minorities, blm leaders and protestors just shrugged their shoulders and acted like it wasn't their problem, as they continued to riot for criminals.

Unfortunately, you will not see these innocent deaths talked about on the news or online media outlets because it does not fit the narrative of the democratic media, it does not fit the narrative of white people and police officers killing minorities. It is all really just a game of chaos and deception, cause as much chaos as possible, then deceive people into thinking they are the solution, not the problem. We've seen this exact scenario play out in the media over the past four years, once President Trump was elected as American President in 2016, he spent the last four years, fighting the same State Senators that were supposed to be helping him better the lives of the American people.

Instead of helping the U.S. President, these State Senators came after him with a false impeachment, using their fake news media to push all their false allegations, but when that didn't work, these

Senators stirred up chaos and destruction in the American streets. With the help of destructive riots and protests, they inflamed the violence occurring in American cities, pushing rioters and protesters to destroy anything in sight. This was because these State Senators tried to blame it all on President Trump, so the more chaos and people caused, the more these Senators could blame President Trump for causing it.

The sad thing is we seen State Senators like Nancy Pelosi, Kamala Harris, Jerry Nadler and Maxine Waters, all pushing people to cause as much chaos and destruction they can, but they were even pushing people to interrupt President Trump supporters lives as much as they can. We all know this is chaos was far from President Trump's fault, after a U.S. President is elected, no matter what your feelings are for the person, since they are the U.S. President, it's your job to help them, that's what you were hired to do. I mean, seriously, that is your job as an American State Representative, you are there to represent the American people and you're there to help the United States President better the lives of the American people.

Our crooked State Senators, led by Nancy Pelosi, did not do that though, instead, they chose to go after President Trump for the next four years. Coming after President Trump with false allegation after false allegation, which should have got them all arrested. That's what so puzzling to me, anyone accusing the U.S. President of what these democrats and liberals accused him of for the last four years, would be in jail, maybe even prison right now, so why are these State Senators not in jail, especially Nancy Pelosi because she tore up official government documents live on national television?

Hillary Clinton was accused and convicted of colluding and working with the Russians, she was also convicted of spying on President Trumps Presidential campaign, nothing happens to her. Former President Obama sold over 25% of our Uranium to Ukraine, but also funded ISIS, yet, no one seemed to care or do anything about it. These State Senators falsely accuse President Trump of colluding with the Ukrainian government, the same one Obama sold Uranium to and everyone starts a lynching mob, trying to get rid of him, but President Trump was guilty of nothing at all.

It is narrative and their agenda, this is what they focus on pushing, this is the narrative that democrats need to push upon the American people. The more they can lie to and deceive Americans into thinking

President Trump is the problem, the easier it is for them to get rid of him in November. Think about that for a second though, if these State Senators were willing to lie, cheat and deceive the American people to get rid of a sitting U.S. President, imagine what they did during this Presidential election.

I find it hard to believe that a person with very few people at his Presidential campaign rallies, would beat someone with half the country at his Presidential campaign rallies, there is possibly no way that Joe Biden would honestly and fairly win the 2020 Presidential election, like he did. These State politicians, blm leaders, with the help of corrupted news outlets pushed a false narrative of hate, which was based on fallacious arguments and false allegations, but they push these statements anyways. This was the only way they could pass their agenda and get the people to believe what they believed.

The interesting part is, if you look into who owns most of our news and media broadcast stations, but who also controls most of our news and media outlets, you will often see that they are owned and operated mainly by leftists, liberals and democrats, who hate America. These news and media outlets report what they want, this is why news has often become known as fake news, the facts and the truth are often ignored and the truth is stretched into what they want you to believe it is. These people own the news and media outlets, so they print what they want and no one can say or do anything about it because they own what you see and read.

It is partly our fault though, a lot of American's have become followers that easily follow the lead of other people, people who do not really have our best interest because all they really care about is pushing their agenda and spreading their false narrative of hate. Americans have become too familiar with politicians and their hidden agendas, this is mostly thanks to Speaker of the House, Nancy Pelosi and her crony democrats, who love to play the blame game because "It's all President Trumps fault," tends to be the only thing you hear from these people.

Our American traditions and civil liberties are slowly being stripped away, leftists, liberals and democrats, have created a country of chaos, innocent Americans are being targeted, police are being assaulted, white people are being labeled racist white supremacist and innocent white children, are being beat up simply for being white, this is our new America. Our American culture as a whole is slowly being torn apart and destroyed, what's worse is that, these American State politicians are letting it all happen and doing nothing to stop it.

These officials and politicians, are letting these people tear down and destroy our way of life all because the new opinion coming from them and minorities is that, white people offend everyone and the color of their skin makes them racist. Not all minorities are like this and feel this way though, but the ones that do, could care less about the white race as a whole, their mission is to cancel our entire culture and they will do anything to advance the destruction of America. We all know how Nancy Pelosi, our very own American Speaker of the House feels about our American national monuments and statues. She has been seen on numerous television interviews, time after time, stating how much she could care less about these American symbols of freedom.

According to Nancy Pelosi, all these American statues represent white supremacy, which is crazy because this is the statement and opinion coming from our very own Speaker of The House, the one who would become the next U.S. President, if anything happened to the current President and Vice President. Thanks to Pelosi and other democrats, this opinion, is now shared by millions, who claim our four fathers were nothing but racist white supremacists, who did nothing for minorities and everything for white supremacy. With all this going on, plus more incidents of ignorance occurring daily, there seems to be many seriously moments, these moments are leaving everyone confused, questioning, just what the hell is happening to our country?

Seriously, how are American State Representatives allowing these incidents to continue in America? Why is the U.S. President the only one that gives a damn about stopping the chaos and violence? Its question after question because President Trump is the one being blamed for the increase of violence, knowing all along that President Trump, needs their States approval to come in and fix the chaos they started. Honestly, with the way these people think and the logic that they use, you can tell they are not very smart and this is not me just making this up.

We see this occurring daily in America, news channels cover these stories and these State Senators are constantly berating the President, instead of taking care of the chaos that has overtaken their city. State mayors and Governors, especially the mayors from Chicago, Atlanta and Baltimore, were constantly on television blaming Trump for the violence and for not coming to their aid. What they failed to tell everyone is that President Trump needed the States authority, which they did not give him, instead, they sat back and let the people destroy their cities, while they went on news interviews, claiming how all the chaos and violence was and is due in part to President Trump's campaign of lies and hate.

What doesn't take long to realize is that, people assume things very quickly, the world is filled with assuming people, these assumptions often come in the form of fallacious arguments that are being used to deceive the people into believing their opinion is better than it actually is. Although their opinion may be wrong, since yours does not align with theirs, your opinion tends to be false, therefore you are not to be listened too or even talked too. This is what is happening in America and to our U.S. President because people are under the assumption that America is now a white supremacist country.

America, is somehow a racist nation and President Trump, is the racist President, who turned America into a white supremacist nation. What these hateful people fail to tell you is that, the people they are calling white supremacist are the people that are supporters of the U.S. President, the American flag and the national anthem. It is sad because the people that hate President Trump to their core will not talk to you if you support President Trump. Instead, these people will judge you and call you a traitor, just like they called the 75 million American President Trump supporters, deplorables, but also claimed that we are the ones responsible for pushing the lies, the hate and the chaos.

Imagine that though, the people that are in charge of the first defense of American public safety, State Mayors and Governors hate the current U.S. President so much that, they literally ignore the chaos and destruction occurring in their very own American States and cities. The unbelievable part comes into play when you see that these exact same State Mayors and Governors, created brand new bail reforms for rioters and protesters, so once protestors, looters and rioters were arrested for public destruction, they were bailed right out of jail.

Eventually, after these State Mayors and Governors could no longer maintain order, they finally allowed President Trump to intervene, but by the time the President was able to step in, numerous American cities were already dealing with massive destruction. Most American cities

61

are still dealing with massive city destruction. I think what tends to bother me about influential people like the Obama's and other political people like them, is the fact that, they claim that President Trump and his supporters are the ones that started all the chaos. Not only that, they also claimed that Trump supporters were the ones who caused all the division, yet, these people were constantly on television, pushing for more division than anyone else.

This is really the overwhelming thing about the Democratic Party, these politicians go on national television to talk about the separation and division President Trump is causing, yet, they are the ones pushing all the chaos and division. This is not just my opinion either, we have seen this repeatedly play out all over the news, democrats are constantly on television, berating and belittling President Trump, while their cities fall into disarray. Seriously, if most of the chaos and destruction is starting and occurring in democratic ran cities, who is really responsible?

I mean, I know the answer, probably more than half of America knows the answer, but according to democrats and liberals, who control these American cities, it is not their fault the violence has increased ten-fold, it's President Trumps fault. I honestly do not think I cared this much until I kept seeing this occur in America and kept seeing democrats and liberals telling us just how un-American we were for supporting President Trump. Literally, even today, American State Representatives are calling Trump supporters American traitors, still claiming that we should all be concerned about our future because we supported President Trump and his white supremacist administration.

I would honestly love to just walk up to these morons and slap some sense into them, but I honestly do not think it would work. Everyday these people seem to make more outrageous statements, which tends to be more idiotic then the statement they already made. It is funny how these exact same people have freedom of speech, but others do not, if other people say what these people say or make the bold statements that these people make, they are fined, fired and labeled racist.

If I am not mistaken the U.S. Constitution was made to protect our American rights, to protect our American freedom to speak as we please and the U.S. Constitution stop's people from trying to infringe on those rights. Two people that have seemed to forget this constitutional law, well, there is a lot of them, but the two main idiots are our very own Speaker of the House Nancy Pelosi and New York State Rep. AOC. These two useless American State Representatives, believe that the U.S. Constitution is something that can be changed and edited, but also something that does not apply to them.

Seriously, legislature after legislature, whatever helps them pass their agenda and push their narrative, they will try to pass and we have seen this already with the new bills that have been put forth by Nancy Pelosi, State Rep. AOC and their democratic cronies. Assumptions and false allegations play major roles when it comes to liberals and democrats because they assume all Americans will believe the deceptions they push, they assume that all Americans will fall in line with their new normal.

No one is allowed to have their own voice, no one is allowed to have their own opinion about something, you are expected to think their way and if you do not, you are the one who is un-American; you are the one believing and following the lies and the chaos, not them. That is one thing that we need to change, everyone assumes, people assume they know what is best for everyone. They assume their opinions matter more, but you know what they say about people who assume everything, it only makes an a** out of yourself. It happened this very morning, I woke up this morning to an online news article that was just another "Seriously" moment because people make crazy assumptions that they shouldn't and it's just getting embarrassing.

Thanks to these cynical and hypocritical assuming people, Garth brooks, a well-known and decorated country artist, was blasted at one of his recent concerts simply because people made crazy assumptions about the football jersey he was wearing. At a recent concert Garth Brooks, wore his favorite football player's jersey, Barry Sander's, he did this because Barry Sanders was one of his favorite players, but Garth Brooks was also performing in Detroit, home of the Detroit Lions. However, according to these assumptive people and their idiotic and outrageous assumptions, Garth Brooks wore the Barry Sander's jersey because he was a Bernie Sander's fan, not a Barry Sander's fan.

People instantly made the assumption that he was showing support and endorsing Berry Sander's, but in reality he was not, unfortunately, this didn't stop people from going online to blast Garth Brooks for wearing the jersey. Seriously, have we've become so low of a people where we are blasting someone for wearing something all because you assume you know why they are wearing it, rather than asking them why their wearing it, seriously? In addition, are people really assuming that Garth Brooks is a Bernie Sanders fan simply because he wore a Barry Sanders jersey to his recent concert in Detroit? It honestly makes no sense, Garth Brooks, even told the entire crowd before his show that he was wearing the jersey to show support for Detroit and his favorite football player.

Brooks wanted to show respect to Barry Sanders and the city of Detroit, so he wore the jersey to show his respect, but then got blasted for wearing it because people assumed they knew, instead of actually knowing. Hundreds of people assumed that he was wearing the jersey because he was a Bernie Sanders fan and since they assumed he was a Bernie Sanders fan, they did not hesitate to go online and blast him for wearing the jersey. Like most assumptive people, they never bothered to listen to what Garth Brooks said at the beginning of his concert, but since these people are used to assuming everything, they base their actions on their assumptions, not the truth.

We've all dealt with people like this, we've all dealt with people that can't seem to mind their own business and are famous for assuming they not only know everything, but they also have the answer for everything, but in reality, all their assumptions are based on fallacies. The real question is, what gives people the right to assume anything about anyone other than themselves, who are you to judge other people, definitely when the pretense you are judging these people off of is based on your opinion, rather than the truth?

People cannot seem to control their own lives, but feel it is their right to tell other people how to live, not only how to live, but what they are doing wrong in their lives. The government is trying to outlaw our guns, our civil rights and even our freedoms and liberties, but what they should be outlawing is these online trolls, who make it their mission to go online and tear other people down. We can use the case of Garth Brooks as an example because the fact that people assumed Garth Brooks was a Bernie Sander's fan simply because he were a Barry Sander's jersey, is really what's wrong with America.

One thing that has been stricken due to people assuming everything is privacy, people used to enjoy their privacy, everyone used to enjoy their own space, their own privacy, without having other people disrupting their lives, not anymore. Since most people assume they know everything, people tend to stick their noses where they do not belong and people who were once enjoying their privacy, are now forced to deal with daily interruptions all because of others assumptions. I think all of this can fall back on people not having discipline in their lives because a lot of these people were never subject to any form of discipline, they were usually handed everything they asked or cried for when they were younger.

Discipline, is the one thing that seems to be missing in America, due to no form of discipline, accountability has become a thing of the past, no one is being held accountable for their actions. It's sad because this opinion is shared by many and the people responsible for causing the chaos and destruction, the people that started the riots and looting, don't care about the consequences of their actions because they know they will not be held accountable. Character, manner's, discipline, morals, ethics, all these traits that we were once taught to us as kids have long been forgotten, these simple behavioral skills seem to be a bit confusing to understand for this newer generation of youth.

Learning these behavioral traits from home and disciplining your children, is not the same anymore, the confirmation is seen every day through the actions of today's youth. These young adults disrupt other people's lives daily because they are under the assumption that other people somehow owe them something, especially if that person is white. There is no accountability for their actions, so they disrupt others people's lives with no repercussions because they know they will not be disciplined or be held accountable for their terrible actions.

Since these people believe and think this assumptive way, their opinion will never change, they tend to act like their undisciplined, but all they are doing is showing that they have no morals, no manners and no ethics, what so ever. Seriously, these kids and teens these days will rob and steal from you quicker than anyone, children and teens, are now carrying guns and even shooting people without any hesitation. Some of these are kids are no more than 8 or 9 years old, but they have been taught that the only way to get by in life is to rob and steal from people because hard work is something reserved for white people.

Seriously, why wouldn't you want your kids to have a better future or grow up in a crime free community, why would not you want your children to live and grow up in a safe violent free community? I ask this question time and time again because minorities focus more on rioting and protesting for criminals, then they do for the innocent minorities that are being killed daily in urban communities all over America. Honestly, why wouldn't you want this to stop, why would you focus your energy on destroying your community and looting your community grocery stores, instead of focusing on the crime affecting your community?

If you were honestly so concerned about minorities being shot and killed at an alarming rate, you would be fighting to get rid of the drugs and gangs in your communities, not the police officers that are trying to keep your streets safe for you and your children in those same communities. This mindset and opinion has already been set though, these people believe white people and police are the enemy and they are dead set on getting rid of both of them, this is the reason why we now have numerous American cities dealing with massive increases of crime and violence.

This also brings us full circle back to assumptions; these are the same youths that assume everything, instead of finding out what really happened. Example of this was when police officers were responsible for shooting another minority, after the incident was reported, every minority in that town assumed the minority was innocent, therefore they took it upon themselves to destroy their communities by rioting. They assumed this criminal did nothing wrong and was killed simply because he was black, thanks to their assumptions of him being innocent, they instantly started city wide riots, before they even knew the facts of the case.

It later came out that the so-called unarmed black man was a criminal, who fired at the police officers and got shot in the process, but the damage was already done; the community was already destroyed because the destruction had already occurred. We all know assumptions are dangerous, but when they are coming from people that are undisciplined and uneducated, they tend to make you question what their goal really is because all they do is destroy things to get what they want. Everything going on today is just part of the confusion, it started off as police brutality towards minorities, then it went to police officers hunting down and killing minorities.

Then, after those claims failed, they started to claim white police officers were killing off minorities, but in the end, they finished it off with white people were killing off minorities, but it seems that these people can never quite make up their mind. None of it honestly makes any sense, you protest for racial equality, but at all these so-called peaceful protests, there tends to be violent confrontations that usually ends up with someone being injured, shot or killed.

It is crazy because when someone has a certain mindset and they think and act a certain way, it is hard to change their mindset, it is hard to change their hateful opinion of others. This is the mindset and opinion that democrats and blm leaders have instilled into millions of their followers and now State Senators are trying to pass another fallacious bill of legislature that will help push their destructive narrative of hate. This new legislature, the Breathe Act, is basically a legislature bill to give illegal's freedom, but will also shutdown or completely abolish the police and also get rid of life sentences for people incarcerated.

I mean, first off, there should be no life sentence anyway, if you kill someone, intentionally or not, you should not be allowed to live until you die, even if it is in a 10 x 10 cell, you took the life of another, you do not deserve to live, period. According to blm leader, Panda Cullors, she thinks sleepy Joe, should pass the far-left legislation that would lead to the abolition of police and prisons because she wants to destroy the American culture. She is just a hate group leader but her opinion is being pushed by democrats, who think the bill would be a good idea, but this only speaks for their character.

This crazy new bill of legislature that these Marxists and socialists are trying to pass would get rid of prison life sentences, as well as, the Drug Enforcement Agency, Immigration Enforcement, U.S. Customs Enforcement, Border Protection Patrol and even Immigration Detention Centers. The funny thing about this bill of legislature and the BREATH Act, is the fact that, they are trying to repeal the same exact bill that Joe Biden enforced back in 1994, with the Violent Crime Control and Law Enforcement Act. It is funny because these people claim that this bill would eliminate surveillance tactics that are used to disproportionately, one word that these people love to use, but this bill would help stop the disproportional targeting of minorities, brown people and Muslims.

This profiling will just suddenly all stop because it would prohibit predictive policing policies, but also limit racial recognition technology profiling and more. This isn't where the ignorance stops neither, no, these State Senators also go on to claim that they want to, "eliminate the use of electronic monitoring, including ankle monitors, Smartphone applications and any other tools used to track some ones location". Seriously, I do not even know where to start when it comes to all these fallacious arguments that they are making to pass this bill because none of these statements have any base to them and all of them would damage America.

It honestly gets worse though; these Senators go on with an even more shocking statement, one that honestly just leaves you shaking your head. The legislation that these idiots are trying to pass, calls for the removal of all police officers, school officers and armed security guards from schools. As if that was not enough, they are calling for all the metal detectors and cameras to be banned from schools, it is basically like giving these students free range to do whatever they want, including bringing guns to school.

Therefore, with this new bill, we go from a nation having security at schools to stop people from going in and shooting up the school, to basically just allowing people to do whatever they want because these blm leaders and State Senators want police enforcement gone. It makes no sense at all, if there were no policing in the world, crime would increase ten-fold and it already has in cities that have already defunded the police, but not according to these geniuses, according to these blm leaders and State Senators, crime would supposedly all just fade away.

It is overwhelming to think that these people honestly believe that, if there were no more police officers, armed guards or security guards at schools, the daily violence and school shootings would just suddenly stop and just go away. They honestly thought that the crime and the violence occurring in American cities would suddenly just stop and all go away thanks to their awesome idea of police being defunded and racist cops fired, but it did not, instead it increased ten-fold. What it all comes down to is the fact that, these blm leaders and State Senators want criminals to be free because they see them as supporters, not convicted criminals.

This is why they also want these criminals to be able to roam our streets freely, does not matter that these criminals were in jail for committing crimes, these State Senators see them as voters, not convicted felons. Not only do these people think that criminals should be free and able to roam our streets, they also think that illegal immigrants should be able to do the exact same thing. Especially seeing that the bill they are passing, the Breathe Act is also calling for the abolition of Immigration. These State Senators are pushing illegal immigrants to easily be able to come into our country and enjoy our American freedoms, without having to worry about becoming a legal citizen.

The statements that these State Senators make honestly have no base to them, it is like seriously, how could you honestly want to abolish police, abolish immigration completely and let lifetime criminals out of prison and on to the streets? The puzzling thing about all of this is the fact that, there is already a constant dose of violence occurring daily in urban neighborhoods and instead of stopping this violence, these idiots want to abolish police and law enforcement organizations, the only people left trying to stop all the crime and violence.

These so-called democrats and minority civil leaders are not fighting to stop the violence occurring to minorities, they are not in urban communities trying to get these people to stop killing each other. Instead they are on television claiming that police organizations should be abolished and police officers should be fired, basically so they can let crime run rampant. What kind of logic is that though, you want to abolish the police because you claim police officers are too violent and are killing people, yet, with less police officers, cities have been proven to become more violent?

Due to this increase in crime, minority kids are now subject to crime and violence on a daily basis, these innocent minorities are subject to daily gun shootouts and daily robberies, wondering if their next. Seriously, why would you want your kids to live like this, also, why would you blame all this violence on the police officers that are simply trying to help? This ideology easily sinks into the minds of children because these teens grow up seeing what is occurring and instantly blame it on the police because that is who they see their parents and other minorities blame it on.

Kids often follow people they look up too, parents being some of them, so if they see their parents hating on someone because of their skin color, what do you think the kids are going to do? Same thing as if these kids were not taught to understand the concept of hard work and instead taught that crying or complaining gets it for you. This to teens is influential, due to this influence, these teens start to assume that they should be handed anything they want, whether they worked for it or not, since that is the opinion of many, that is the opinion they go with. The old way of getting things, which was to work for it, is out the window, working for something is in the past, today, these kids are taught that they can use the color of their skin to get ahead in life.

Think about what this teaches kids, think about the harm this does to a kid who is forced to think this way, I do not think people realize the damage they are doing to kids these days. Unfortunately, this ideology was passed down to these children and teens by these blm leaders and democrats, who started this ideology and opinion because they want to push for racial dominance and their idea of a new America. It is seriously hard to figure out why these people would want these kids and teens to believe in the theory of self-entitlement and victimization.

It is also hard to understand why these people would want minorities to think they can get things all thanks to their skin color, rather than working hard for it. This opinion and theory takes away all desire to work for a better life, since these people are being told they are all victims of oppression, they tend to ignore work and go straight to protesting. Minority teens now feel as if they are the victims of systemic racism and victims of oppression because that is what they have been taught or raised to think. The problem comes when these teens start taking their frustrations out on the wrong people, which is white people, including white kids and teens.

It seriously makes you wonder how we could have gone so wrong as a country, all this because real victims, real people suffering, get pushed aside by the people who act like victims, but are far from it.

-- Chapter 2 --
The hatred is pushed by the ignorant,
followed by the ill-minded!

It honestly comes full circle because the same people that are claiming that they deserve everything because the color of their skin, are hating on and destroying the lives of others simply because, the color of their skin. Since this ideology and opinion is often shared by many in the minority community, this is what these parents teach their kids, they teach them about hate because that is all they know, but also all they see coming from other people. We already know that America has too many followers and not enough leaders; millions of people easily follow the lead of people who only see a benefit in helping themselves.

That's the crazy thing about what is going on in America, kids, teens and young adults, are seen committing some of the most violent assaults on other children not because these children or teens have done something to them, but because they're the wrong skin color. One of the things we will talk a lot about is "racism" because racism definitely comes into play in every conversation people have. Minorities constantly bring it up to use it as an excuse, while white people, constantly choose to focus on other things, rather than actually dealing with racism.

White people, even get punished for not wanting to deal with it, if we bother not to say anything about racism, not because we could care less about racism, but because we do not think people should give racism as much power as they do, we are automatically considered the racist ones. This is another important factor that you should take a second to think about, people give "words", more power than they should, people let words hurt them, physically and mentally, but they are just words, basic letters strung together. Americans, tend to focus on what they shouldn't, we as Americans, tend to let things like words affect us when we shouldn't, seeing that they are merely just words, used to try and hurt us.

If we do not give them any mind or attention, they are of no use, simply because they are merely words. Since people do let words hurt them more than they should, they also tend to follow the lead of people they definitely should not, listening to the words they say, believing everything they believe. These are the very same people that riot and protest for criminals, but while they riot and destroy their communities for criminals and felons, innocent people, including innocent minorities, are being killed in the process. Prime example is these protesters protesting and rioting for this well-known and documented lifetime criminal, George Floyd.

Yes I said it, because million of people started a completely racist movement for this lifetime criminal. George Floyd was a criminal, convicted of assault and armed robbery, he was no hero, it was proven that Floyd had a long criminal record. George Floyd was convicted of robbing and assaulting a pregnant woman and was just released from prison, where he was serving a sentence for armed robbery. Not only was he just released from prison, but he was on two heavy narcotic drugs and tried using counterfeit money to buy something at a convenience store, which would obviously send him back to prison, so he resisted arrest.

Seriously though, this guy is a hero to your people, this guy? I highly doubt that this guy is a hero; think about this, during another armed robbery, these useless pos robbed a pregnant woman by holding a gun to her stomach, then pistol-whipped the pregnant woman after he was done robbing her. So seriously, how is this useless pos a hero to you and your people, how do you justify starting riots and burning minority businesses and communities down in his name? It's puzzling when you think about it because Nancy Pelosi, our very own Speaker of the House, held a ceremony for this criminal's family, she held a folded American flag service ceremony, a ceremony and tradition that is only reserved for our fallen heroes, she held for this criminal.

Nancy Pelosi and her democratic cronies, literally held this ceremony and others for a convicted criminal, a life-time felon, but also a person who was definitely no hero to anyone, neither did he ever do anything for his country, he was a criminal, nothing more. It is funny how this does not just stop with this useless pos criminal, if any minority, especially minority criminals, are shot and killed by a police officer, no matter how bad of a criminal record they may have had, hundreds of minorities will instantly riot in their name.

We've seen this occur time after time and it's crazy because these people don't bother to learn about why these criminals were shot and killed, they don't bother to learn the facts about the case, they instantly assume these minority criminals were innocent, so that makes them just another innocent minority gunned down by police officers. In reality, it's just another minority, who resisted arrest, fought with the police and suffered the consequences of their actions, but when you are claiming something like, "hands up, don't shoot", you have to make sure that these criminals had their hands up, which we all know, was not the case in any of these police incidents.

Seriously, every single police encounter that ended with a minority being killed was the direct result of the minorities actions, the path these minorities chose to take and none of these minorities had their hands up. These are undeniable facts, it's a proven fact that, during all of these police encounters, none of these minorities had their hands up during the entire process, not a few of them, not some of them, none of them had their hands up. Every single one of these minorities chose to disobey direct orders from police officers, then when they were being detained, they started to resist arrest and then started fighting with the officers; they never had their hands up, not even once.

It honestly makes no sense that millions of people would even be advocating for criminals, but they constantly do, they ignore the truth of the situation and base their destructive actions on their assumptions and opinions of what happened, rather than knowing what actually did happen. It's insane how these people do not even bother to find out what these criminals were doing at the time of the detainment, nor why these minorities decided to not listen to the officers and resist arrest.

These people see another minority being shot and killed by police officers and since the victim was black, this entitles them the right to instantly go out, riot, loot and burn everything down in their name. Seriously, most of the criminals that were shot and killed by police either, resisted arrest, fought with the police, tried to steal their weapons, were seen as a public threat, had a weapon or was going for a weapon, that's why they were shot and killed. These criminals are not heroes, these criminals are not martyrs, these criminals are not role models, these people are convicted felons, who all had long extensive criminal records and who all did jail time.

All the minorities that were shot and killed, were well-known convicted criminals or felons, so can we please stop treating these criminals like they were heroes because they simply were far from it. You know what also makes no sense at all is, people are having a protest and rioting for a known convicted criminal, but not protesting and rioting for the 8 year-old minority girl, who was violently gunned down by armed minority men, during this protest. Seriously, this is something that should be answered because how can people justify burning communities and businesses down, for criminals who were killed by police officers, but ignore the killing of an 8-year-old girl?

It is very puzzling to me because minorities literally say nothing when it comes to innocent minority children being slaughtered by the dozens, but will scream to the high-heavens when another minority criminal is killed by cops. What is sad is, minorities do have major problems in urban communities, minorities do have a major problem with keeping their children focused on getting an education, minorities do have a problem with drugs and gangs in their communities, but when you blame the problem on other races, instead of facing the music yourself, nothing tends to change.

It's like yea, I completely agree with you, police officers shouldn't be killing people, they shouldn't be assaulting people, but at the same time, when you are resisting arrest and threatening their lives, your rights kind of go out the window. Police officers are taught to make sure themselves and their fellow officers go home at night, besides, people act like being a police officer is an easy job, name another job that requires you to go help and save people that despise you? These city officials want to abolish the police and use social service workers to deal with domestic disputes, but we've seen the outcome of what happens at some of these domestic disputes, it's not pretty.

Again though, we have the democratic logic train coming through because these people are on live television, telling the American people that they want to get rid of police officers and replace them with social workers. I guess they don't care much about the lives of social workers because domestic disputes can turn into violent confrontations, that can only be settled by force, so I ask you, what are these social workers going to do when someone has a gun? This is the mindset of these democrats and liberals though; they have backed these racist blm leaders, so they can push their false ideologies of their way of providing safety and security.

Police precincts defunded, law enforcement agencies disbanded, immigration and border patrols stopped, illegal immigration camps dismantled, all white police officers fired, all white teachers swapped with minority teachers. Welcome to the new America people because this is the logic and ideology that is now running our nation. Plus, let's all be real here, police are not the only ones responsible in George Floyd's death, the guy didn't die from the police having his knee on his neck, although a bad maneuver, George Floyd died from heart failure.

He was on a combination of meth and fentanyl, which if you did not know, are both major heart stoppers. The democratic narrative these people tend to push always changes though, it first started with minorities seeking justice for the death of this criminal, then it grew into minorities blaming all white police officers because the cop who planted his knee into criminal George Floyd's neck was white. This is the narrative they need to follow, they have rules to follow, they have priorities to meet and follow, so if it does not fit their narrative, they change it so it better fits their narrative.

That is why these people make no mention of the other three police officers involved in the incident because it does not fit their narrative, since they were not white, they were blamed, but the focus was solely put on the white police officer, not them. Like many, these blm leaders and democrats were focused on using the race card, claiming that since the police officer was white, the fault falls onto the laps of white people, therefore white officers are the racists' ones killing off minorities. Once again, this to me seems to be centered on racial dominance because these people are doing things that will make them superior to other people, they want to get rid of everything that represents an entire culture.

They are trying to get rid of people simply because the color of their skin, does not matter what their profession is or what they have done, their white, therefore they must be fired or eliminated. Unfortunately, you cannot really say it is not about racial dominance because look at what is occurring during these riots and protests, if you do, you would see that there has already been 14-recorded homicides during these protests. The sad thing is, all these murders were perpetrated by minorities, not white Americans, not the police, minorities were responsible for these senseless murders.

It is interesting that this number just so happens to be the exact same number of minorities that were killed by police officers in 2019, while over 7,400 were shot and killed by their very own people. Look at the case of innocent David Dorn, Mr. Dorn was a retired minority police chief, who served as Police Chief for over 38 years, during the blm protest, David, was brutally gunned down by a young minority, who wanted to rob the pawnshop he was guarding. The young minority walked up to David Dorn and shot him in the head, then left him lying there in a pool of his own blood for more than ten minutes, until Mr. Dorn unfortunately passed.

Think about that for a second because this is one of the main points that people tend to skip over, a minority teen decided it was okay to end the life of a retired minority police chief simply because the retired police chief tried to stop him from robbing a pawnshop. Seriously, if you do not think there is a problem here, you are the problem, this teen chose to be judge and executioner, not because his life was at risk, but because he wanted to break into the pawnshop and loot it. Since retired Police Chief David Dorn would not let him break into the pawnshop and rob it, the young minority blatantly shot David Dorn in the head, so he could rob the pawnshop. This isn't alarming to you?

Seriously, instances like these have taken place during most of these so-called peaceful protests, yet, these blm leaders, claim that these protests are for racial justice for minorities, although minorities are killing innocent people in the process. Where is David Dorn's protest or rally for justice, this poor guy was innocently murdered for protecting his friends' property and not letting people loot his friend's pawnshop, why are you not concerned about the way he was viciously gunned down, he was a minority?

How are you honestly more concerned about what just happened to a criminal, rather then what just happened to an innocent man? It doesn't stop there though, the incidents just seem to get worse, David Dorn, was just one of the many lives that were innocently taken by other minorities, yet, these people's lives tend to be the ones that these protesters ignore. Let us take it one-step further, where is the justice for the 22-year-old minority mother who had to watch as her 20-month-old baby drew her last breath after being shot? This mother was driving trying to survive as her baby was fatally shot and killed by drive by shooter's, after a group pulled up and started shooting at them?

This scenario tends to play out many times in urban areas and communities, you can often watch videos on YouTube of young minority kids sitting in cars listening to music, while someone comes up from behind and shoots and kills them. There is actual video evidence of this occurring in urban communities, all thanks to the new thing called face book live. Since everything can now be streamed live these days, it's not too hard to look up any recent shooting that were caught on camera, which tends to mostly occur in urban communities and innocent minorities, just minding their own business.

This plague of crime and violence plays out in the entire community, yet, nothing is ever done to stop the violence; nothing is ever done to stop the killings from occurring because these people are too busy blaming their problems and bad communities on white people or the police. Rioting, looting and protesting, is something that really makes no sense, especially when it's been proven that everyday there are more minorities being killed in cities like Baltimore, Chicago and Atlanta alone, than any other city in America. What tends to be overwhelming about blm and their followers is they never deal with the fact that, urban communities have seen nothing but crime and violence for decades, not just years, decades.

Minorities living in urban communities have been exposed to a daily dose of crime, followed by gun violence and gang shootings for forever, this has never changed, this has never been dealt with. The only thing that has changed is the fact that now, it is supposedly not their fault, its white peoples fault, its police officers faults, but white people are also responsible for the crappy communities they live in. Seriously, you have to ask yourself, does blaming other people make any sense at all? White people, do not live in urban communities, if they do it's a very few, but one thing is for certain white people do not control the lives of the minorities living in urban communities.

White people do not promote black supremacy and white hate in urban communities, white people are also not the ones robbing, shooting and stealing from people in these communities, minorities are. There are even proven facts and statistics to back this up, statistics that are recorded yearly, show just what I am referring to, so you can see just how bad these communities are. That is why their logic seems to do nothing but leave me puzzled because how can you riot and protest for something that you are fully responsible for? Instead of uniting your people, your solution is to just skip all your problems and blame it entirely on white people, but how does that work exactly?

Seriously, how does that work because even if white people did come into your community and try to better your community, they would soon be accused of committing gentrification, which is something that is hated and frowned upon by blm. This to me is the puzzling part because like I stated before, white people are not in these urban communities telling these minorities how to live, white people are not the ones pushing the violence, drugs and gangs into these urban communities, so seriously, how can white people be responsible?

All of it honestly makes no sense, people are no longer being judged upon their actions, no one is being held accountable for what they do and your character no longer defines you. People do not care about what you may have overcome or any tragedy that you may have fought through because now it is all based on skin color and the color of your skin now defines you as a person. You are now judged by the color of your skin, you are labeled by the color of your skin, you are defined by the color of your skin and if you are white, you are automatically guilty because the color of your skin.

It all comes down to race now, unfortunately in today's America, your race plays a role in everything you do these days, people instantly judge you by your race and color of your skin, rather than by your actions and character. Minorities are really the only ones responsible for the crime occurring in urban communities, but now that people use race as an excuse, minorities have been convinced by black lives matters leaders and democrats that they can blame their problems on other people. There is a real bad education problem in these urban communities, there is a real huge wealth problem in these urban communities, there is an alarming rate of crime and violence in these communities, but that's on minorities, no one else.

Blaming an entire race of white people for the problems you have in your own communities, is not going to be the solution. The crime and violence in these communities will stop when minorities themselves, stop robbing and killing each other, but also when minorities decide to get rid of the drugs and gangs infesting their communities, not a moment sooner. This is what I wish I could drill into these people's heads, it is not white people, who are causing the troubles they encounter, minorities, are the leaders of their own demise and minorities, are responsible for their own bad decisions.

Think about this for a second; think about if these very same minorities put as much time as they put into organizing these so-called peaceful protests, into organizing ways to fix their communities. We would probably see a difference occurring in these communities, but you do not often see that. Instead, these people spend their time burning everything down and looting grocery stores, which leaves you questioning, if your fighting for a better life for you and your people, does destroying your own community and the community businesses in it, also looting and destroying grocery stores, make any sense at all?

It doesn't stop with just the destruction of their own communities, minorities, are killing each other daily, not police officers, not white people, but minorities are the ones out robbing and killing their own people on a daily basis, not the people actually being blamed for it. Their actions are often driven by pure hatred and minorities tend to do as they please, you can look at the case of Laroy Battle and the three minority teens, who Laroy chose to gun down simply because they were interested in how tall Laroy was. Three minority teens were at a mom and pop store, where they were standing behind Laroy Battle and thought he was awfully tall, so they asked him how tall he was.

At first, Laroy ignored the teens and continued to check out, then slowly walk outside. After being ignored the teens checked out and went about their day, leaving the store and starting to walk home. Laroy Battle, not saying anything, followed the three teens and while walking behind them, without warning, drew his gun and shot all three of them in the back, instantly killing two of them and seriously injuring the third. Again, this minority chose to be judge and executioner, just like the minority that killed David Dorn and the sad thing is, Laroy shot these minority teens all because they were interested in his height.

This was not a homicide committed by a white teen, these brutal killings did not occur in a white community, they occurred in an urban community, where minorities think they have the right to become judge and executioner, if anyone offends them. There is a constant plague of violence that occurs daily in urban communities, not in white communities, but white people are the ones claimed to be responsible for the crime and violence that occurs in urban communities, seriously, how does that work? The sad reality we are faced with is, trying to provide justice to the right people, without people fighting for justice for the wrong people.

People should be protesting for real justice, but you cannot burn down your own community and you cannot destroy minority owned businesses, then turn around and claim that you are protesting for racial justice and equality. Once again, the logic that comes from these people, tends to never be understandable, they destroy their own neighborhood, although they rob and kill their own people. They also destroy minority owned businesses, while they claim it is all for justice and equality. You are often left puzzled because if your own people are responsible for causing all the death and violence that seems to be occurring in your community, how can you blame someone else?

We have talked about this a lot because this is the problem, this is why there is so much chaos and destruction in America, minorities are killing each other at a very alarming rate, but, the blame is not falling on the minorities causing the violence. Nope, blm leaders and minorities are going on record to blame white people and police officers as the ones being responsible for the drastic rise of crime occurring in urban communities. This is the real problem though, if you are protesting for minority justice, you cannot claim that white American's and police officers are killing off your people at an alarming rate, when the evidence proves otherwise.

It has literally been reported and verified statistical facts that, minorities commit more than half the crime reported in America, although they only make up 14% of the population. This could be the reason why minorities tend to fill our jails and prisons faster than anyone else because they are responsible for most of the crime and violence occurring in America. However, you have to remember that, our State politicians, democrats and blm leaders, want prison reform and police reform, which would allow criminals to roam freely amongst the American people.

It is crazy because it is all based on the hatred of an entire race, the white race, people are so offended by the successes of white people that they are literally blaming the entire white race and culture for their problems. This hatred is often deep and their actions often reflect this hatred, we've seen this hatred take place daily on television with people berating and belittling white people all because the color of their skin. This way of thinking unfortunately starts at home and comes from the sins and behaviors that are passed down by minority's parents because people who are filled with hate, only teach hate and no matter how hard you try, you will never change that hatred.

You do not have to go too far to see white Americans being harassed and berated by minorities, but it makes no sense because these are the same minorities that turn around and claim that they themselves, are the ones experiencing the racism and discrimination. This is interesting to me because we have clearly seen minorities committing racist acts towards other people and we witness as minorities constantly continue to discriminate against all others. I say it is interesting because minorities are the ones who swear up and down, they are not responsible for discriminating against others because they are the ones being discriminated against.

We've seen this play out with kids and teens, which shows you exactly what's wrong with this country, time and time again, we have watched news videos about white kids and teens being bullied or beat up, simply because they are white. This deep hatred started at home, these minority kids were taught to hate white kids simply because the color of their skin, which is sad because all this really shows you is that no matter what white people do, to some minorities, they will always be seen as the enemy. It's really hard to watch because people are no longer judged by what their character, now, people are being judge on the color of their skin and they are not only being judged, but they are being executed and beaten.

Then of course, you have the people that say, well, little white children are abusing minority children too, it is not just one way, but it is. Honestly, prove it, I am sure the cases that I have seen on television that I used to reference in this book, were minority children and teens picking and beating on white kids, not the other way around. This thought process is also what is plaguing America, people think they have the right to discriminate against others, not because these people have personally done something wrong to them, but because their ancestors kept them as slaves.

It just makes you shake your head because people will try and justify what these minority kids are doing to white kids, they will try and justify their hateful actions towards these white kids. We have seen an example of this hatred play through in the case of the two little minority girls, who picked on a little white girl, who was only trying to play with these minority girls and even went as far as to offer her toys.

Instead of playing with the little white girl, the two minority girls were antagonized to be mean to the little white girl, so they in turn decided to start calling her names simply because she was white. Now, this was not the parent's antagonizing these two little girls to be mean to this little white girl, no, it was the minority girls' older brother, who was encouraging his minority sisters to be mean to the innocent little white girl. Once his parents found out about the incident, they did offer an apology, but that's the point, for the brother to force his little sisters to act hateful towards this little white girl, just shows you the hatred he has seen and was raised with.

These minority children and teens are raised to hate white people and this hate has no boundaries because the brother, an older minority teen, was literally taking his race issues out on a little white girl. This should not be occurring in America, it is not white people who are at fault for your bad life decisions, it is not white people's fault that every ones ancestors did some horrible things to people hundreds of years ago in the past. It is puzzling to me because why would you want to live in the past, slavery ended hundreds of years ago, if you are not a slave today, why would you want to act like you are being treated like one?

Like I stated before, white colonists did not start slavery, contrary to what you were all taught to believe, slavery was started hundreds of years ago by North African and Arabian Moors, years before white colonialists and settlers even decided to try to form their own nation. North African and Arabic Middle Eastern Moors, sold their people all over the world, to anyone that would pay, this is where the slave trade and the enslavement of people, originated. Think about that for a second because your ancestor's that you somehow claim were found, kidnapped and abducted, were actually sold by your own people.

North African Moor's sold and traded their very own tribes men, women and even children, for money, food and blankets, to just about everyone. Seriously, it is not too hard to look up your American history, the real history and not the history these teachers are trying to make up. If you do take a look at your American history, you will see that North African leaders, also known as, North African Moors, along with Arabic Middle Eastern leaders, were the ones who started slavery. These Old World leaders, were responsible for creating slave trades, they were responsible for enslaving thousands of their own people, not white colonists.

Plus, I fail to comprehend what these people are claiming because their blaming the entire white race because our ancestors participated in slavery, yet, their own ancestors were the ones who started the slave trade, but also continued to profit in slavery, after the Americas and Great Britain abolished it. You can also see this by examining what is currently going on in parts of Asia and the Middle East, but also most of the world. You will see that most Europeans, Middle Easterners, Africans, Nigerians and other nations, are still involved in some form of enslavement today.

Unfortunately, we do have a real problem with slavery, women and children all around the world, are being abducted and enslaved daily, these women and children are being forced into sex trafficking or child enslavement, but, these real issues get sidelined because minorities claim that they are still being treated as slaves. It is insane to think of because minorities are actually protesting that they are still being enslaved and oppressed just like their ancestors were, while others are losing their lives and are being abducted and enslaved.

In reality, white American colonists are the ones who stopped the savagery of slavery, you can easily ask yourself, who was the one responsible for abolishing slavery, a white U.S. President named, Abraham Lincoln. We all know this is true, we all know President Abraham Lincoln was an honorable man that thought all people were created equal and even wrote, the Emancipation Proclamation and the Gettysburg Address to try to unite everyone. Still, the truth does not matter because according to this new democratic logic, President Abraham Lincoln, did absolutely nothing for minorities and actually promoted slavery, instead of fighting to end it.

I honestly wish I was making this up, but we have seen this ideology and this opinion play out in America, statues of former President Abraham Lincoln, are being defaced and destroyed all because hundreds of people honestly believe he did nothing for them. It is honestly sad to see because these people actually believe that President Lincoln did nothing for their people, but only because that is what these democrats and blm leaders want them to believe. Think about that amount of power for a second because we have seen the outcome of this thought process, but think about the power this instills into our government and these people have behind this hateful movement.

State Senators, along with these blm leaders, claimed that statues of President Abraham Lincoln, along with statues of President George Washington, Christopher Columbus and other founding fathers, represent white supremacy, not minorities. People not only believed them, but people destroyed American public national monuments and

83

statues because of them. After these people planted this belief and opinion into the minds of the people, you soon started to see numerous public national monuments and statues, being defaced and destroyed. All because people honestly believed that these monuments and statues represented white supremacy. It was crazy to watch because even the police officers trying to protect these public monuments and statues, were being belted with rocks.

The officers fought hard to stand their ground, as they tried to stop hundreds of people trying to destroy and deface these monuments and statues. It was all because democrats, along with these blm Marxists leaders, claimed these white men supremacist never did anything for the minority people, but also did nothing but promote the enslavement of minorities. This is the part that leaves me lost and asking, seriously? Because I am not too sure how these people could make this statement or claim about former U.S. President Abraham Lincoln, the United States President, who lost his life because he thought everyone should be free.

I think what should scare everyone is the fact that, millions of people in America, easily followed the opinion of a few and started destroying public American national monuments and statues. Somehow these people in charge and their followers, were able to convince others that these monuments and statues were racist, an opinion that was solely based upon the hatred for white people. These people with power push their narrative of hate onto others, which usually tend to be the people that they know will easily follow every word they say and believe what they deem to be true.

This is why we have seen so much chaos and destruction occurring in the last year, more then we have seen in decades, the chaos needed to be started, because democrats needed something to help them push their narrative of hate. It is also because it was an election year and democrats and liberals, had to do anything they could to make sure they regained control from President Donald Trump. Democrats know if they did not, it would be another four years until they got another chance, but if you honestly do not think these politicians would not steal an election to seize power, you got another thing coming.

Seriously, shouldn't we be scared and worried about this, I mean, if democrats and liberals, are willing to steal an entire election, do you really think Americans are going to be able to stop them? You think I am lying, think about this for a second, these State Senators claim that Sleepy Joe Biden, supposedly got more American votes then Barack Obama did, during both his election and re-election. Take his running mate Kamala Harris for instance, she was a State Senator who ran in the 2016 Presidential election, against Joe Biden, she also called him a racist bigot, who pushed racist legislature.

Former California State Senator Kamala Harris, was forced to withdraw from the 2016 Presidential election because she had the lowest vote count between the nominated candidates, but now she is somehow the most popular women in America and a representative for minorities. Besides Barack Obama, Kamala Harris, is another one that cannot seem to make up their minds about their identities. Kamala, used to identify as an Indian-American, but now she claims to be an African-American simply because this fits more into the democratic narrative.

We all know that Barack Obama has yet to provide an actual birth certificate, Obama claims to be American, yet, he has citizenship in two other nations. This is a no-no, but it is also what hinders other people from becoming U.S. President, just not Obama. These two are among the many politicians that are pushing the belief that all of our American national monuments and statues represent white supremacy, but also that all of our U.S. Constitutional laws are racist and our entire way of life, needs to be changed.

Think about that democratic logic for a second because according to this newer generation of minorities, led by senators, politicians, teachers, counselors and professors, Abraham Lincoln, the U.S. President, who abolished slavery and created the Emancipation Proclamation, did nothing for the minority community or minorities themselves. They also claim that President Lincoln promoted the enslavement of people and promoted white supremacy, which is far from the truth and they should be jailed for making that claim. Seriously, minority teachers and professors at schools, colleges and universities, are still claiming that these American symbols that have stood for hundreds of years, are racist and should be destroyed.

Think I am joking, take a look at Wisconsin University Minority Student Union President, whose name is not worth the mention, but this idiot claims that the Abraham Lincoln Statue on Bascom Hill needs to be taken down and removed. This is all because this idiotic professor went on record to claim, "For President Lincoln to be at the top of Bascom Hill as a powerful placement on our campus, it's a single-handed symbol of white supremacy". It is crazy that a real professor, an actual professor, would make this kind of statement because President Abraham Lincoln's statue, a statue of the former U.S. President, who abolished slavery, is not, a symbol of white supremacy, not even close.

It is a symbol of our great nation, a symbol of freedom and this professor should be fired for making this statement. It is like, forget the fact that, President Abraham Lincoln, fought to free the enslaved, forget the fact that, President Lincoln, was the one who started the abolishment of slavery, while N. African leaders continued to profit from it because these people obviously have. It is mind-boggling when you think about it, but, this is why minorities are now claiming that President Abraham Lincoln's statues are racist and should be taken down because these politicians have convinced them that these monuments and statues represent nothing but white supremacy.

These politicians, teachers and professors, are straight morons and you really wish you could smack some sense into them for pushing this bad ideology onto others. To honestly believe and even claim on national television that President Lincoln promoted the enslavement of minorities and was a symbol of white supremacy, just shows you how ignorant you really are. You should not be a teacher, nor should you be a professor, you are simply an idiot and the fact that you have a job as a teacher or professor, just shows how messed up we are in America.

I think the sad thing about all of this was that this professor actually went on record to make this ridiculous claim, a claim that obviously is so far from the truth, it makes you look stupid for making it. It also shows you just how far these influential people are willing to go, they will make bold claims and literally try to rewrite American history, just so they can trick you into believing what they believe. It's kind of crazy when you think about it because these people, mainly blm leaders, minorities and democrats, will easily change the past to better fit their narrative, whether it's the truth or not.

It does not matter which founding four fathers it is because think about it, according to these morons, the former United States President, the one that has probably done the most for women and minorities, needs to have his statues removed. This is simply because they are trying to make the claim that former U.S. President Abraham Lincoln statues represent white supremacy, it is like seriously?. It is funny because these are the same moronic school authorities that think a 70-ton rock should be replaced because it supposedly represents a racist past. Does not matter that this 70-ton rock named, Chamberlain Rock, was dedicated to the former Wisconsin University President, Thomas Crowder Chamberlain, its racist.

It honestly makes no sense because these people will go on national television and talk about these American symbols being representatives of racism, yet, they are symbols and statues that were dedicated to people who cleared the path for everyone else. The same Wisconsin University idiot of a union president claimed that, with this rock being displayed, "You clearly see what the rock was called and you can't deny its history. Additionally you cannot deny the way it makes people feel. If you are going to move the things that are disrespectful to us because other students love it, put something up that us minority and brown students can celebrate."

I mean, seriously, where do I even start, the first thing you notice is that it's always the same racist statement being made by minorities, something is supposedly racist, so it needs to come down, but it's always a double standard because it doesn't go both ways. Minorities fight to take down every racist symbol they deem hateful, but it's always about taking down our American national monuments and replacing them with statues of their own. Now, I know some of you are thinking, you guys have statues dedicated to white Americans, while minorities do not have any, but you do, each national monument and statue standing today, is dedicated to a person that influenced the nation you live in today.

These great Americans did not do what they did because they thought it would better the white race only, contrary to what these idiots want you to believe, everything they did was not always about the color of your skin, our four fathers did what they did because they knew it would benefit the American people. Our Four Fathers and the Presidents that came after them, wanted to advance their country so they focused on progression and advancement, they did not focus on enslaving people because they hated minorities.

When you tear down monuments and statues of our founding four fathers like, George Washington, Christopher Columbus and Abraham Lincoln, you are no longer American and there is no way you are going to be receiving equality, you should honestly be banned from the country. The sad thing is, democrats and liberals, did nothing about this destruction occurring, they denied the very existence of it, the destruction was only stopped after President Trump passed a bill of legislature that made it a federal crime to deface, destroy or tear down any national monument or statue.

The excuses these people often used for defacing or tearing down these statues were just ridiculous to say the least and the fact that others liked the statues and they didn't, but it still needed to come down, just shows you that these people could care less about equality and more about racial domination. No offense but, if you are offended simply by a rock, by a huge 70-ton rock, that was placed their as a dedication to the former University President, you seriously have deep disturbing issues and need to seek some serious help for. The Chamberlain Rock, is something that all students get to celebrate, contrary to what these idiots believe.

Because the statue represents the entire school, every single student and teacher, seeing that the University President represents the entire school. This is another thing that makes absolutely no sense, these statues and monuments were dedicated to the people that changed the lives of others for the better, still, they are being deemed racist. The unbelievable thing is, no matter what anyone says, if it's different then their opinion, it doesn't matter, these minorities will still ignore you and go on to claim these American statues and monuments are racist. They represent white supremacy, so therefore they should all be taken down and destroyed, not put into museums either, just destroyed.

In reality, these people are just tired of seeing white people do better than they are and this isn't because of this so-called white privilege, it's because other white people and even other minorities, actually give a damn about their history, their future and work hard to make sure they actually have one. Real Americans don't complain like most of these minorities and democrats are doing, real Americans, don't use race as an excuse like most people are doing right now, real Americans go out and work for what they have and need because they know the only way they will get it, is to work for it.

There is no special card that we can flash that gives us white people everything for free, rich people like, Ophra and the Obama's can though, but they will swear up and down they don't, white people do.

Think I am joking, I am not, Barack Obama is king at doing this because he has recently been blaming white people left and right, this includes President Trump, who he accuses of being a white supremacist President. I mean, this guy should just go away, but of course, since he loves the lime light and thinks he has an opinion that matters more than most, we are stuck dealing with his ugly Indonesian mug on our television channels and shows.

This moron, who I call a fake American because seriously, when you hand Congress a fake birth certificate, you don't prove that you are American, all this does is speak volume about your character. Now, according to Barack Obama, the President who stole the U.S. Presidency, "You've seen created, in Republican politics, this sense that white males are victims. Which obviously doesn't gibe with both history and data economics." There was more to the statement that was coming from Obama, but it just got so ridiculous you just ended up shaking your head and wondering where the country is headed.

I mean, is Barack not watching the same news everyone else is watching or is he just making up news, so he can be in the spotlight? In reality, everything Barack Obama stated was just a ploy to help him sell his new book and make more money off the American people, like he has done since his Presidency. Now, Obama claims its Republicans pushing the chaos and violence, but they are also the ones that have instilled the thought of white people being the victims, especially white males. I seriously think that Barack Obama hates the fact that he himself, is half-white. Honestly, we have all seen it,

Obama and other democrats were the ones responsible for pushing the chaos and the division, they were the ones convincing minorities that they were the victims and the ones being oppressed. Since the truth often does not fit or jibe with their democratic narrative, Barack Obama and other democrats use fallacious arguments to try to convince people that they are the solution, not the problem. Its influential minorities like Lebron James, the Obama's and civil leaders that play the victim card, but who are also the ones pushing millions of people to feel this way.

Still, the truth does not matter because according to Barack Obama, it is Republicans and white people, who are supposedly claiming to be the victims, not minorities. It is obviously not the numerous minorities we constantly see on television interviews complaining about being victims of a systemically racist government, it is supposedly

89

Republicans and white males. I mean, seriously, if this guy had a brain, he would be dangerous and if these people actually cared about the American people, the Obama's would not be causing as much division as they do between white people and minorities.

I think Barack Obama honestly has a Martin Luther King Jr. complex, but what Obama fails to realize is that, Martin Luther King Jr., was a better leader, better person and all around better advocate for his people, then Barack Hussein Obama will ever be. Barack Obama's character will always be in question, he is the only U.S. President to provide a fake birth certificate to U.S. Congress. He is not a very respectable guy because you have to remember during his Presidency, Obama sold about 20% of our Uranium to the Ukrainian Government. Obama also helped ISIS gain military weapons, helped China makes billions of dollars off the American people and was also said to have helped Hillary spy on President Trump's presidential campaign.

I do not think anyone is really surprised about Obama being involved in spying on a campaign because Barack Obama along with Joe Biden, spied on millions of Americans during his entire 8 year run as the U.S. President. We know Obama was spying on Americans because Edward Snowden, a true American hero, was instantly labeled an American traitor by Barack Obama, when he exposed the truth to us. This was after Snowden exposed the truth to the American people about how Barack Obama and his administration was secretly spying on Americans, invading on our privacy.

It's crazy because what does Barack Obama do when him and his administration gets exposed for spying on millions of people, he doesn't offer an apology, he doesn't apologize for spying on millions of Americans, nope, Obama, instantly labels Edward Snowden an American traitor. Unlike Barack Obama, Martin Luther King never created the separation and division that Obama and these democrats are pushing today. In addition, Martin Luther King Jr. never once told his people to tear down American national monuments and statues during his crusade for racial equality.

Martin Luther King Jr., never would have pushed his people to burn down or destroy urban communities, Martin Luther King Jr., would also never have pushed his people to burn down minority owned businesses, as a way of advocating for racial equality. It's sad because I wish I was making all this stuff up, but we've watched day after day as it was taking place in America, hundreds of people were destroying and defacing statues of Thomas Edison, Christopher Columbus, Thomas Jefferson, George Washington and even Abraham Lincoln.

All because these idiots claim that all of our founding fathers were racist white supremacist, who only promoted white supremacy and fought for the enslavement of all minorities. These American men are the people responsible for founding the nation we all love, these American men cleared the path for Americans today, still, none of this matters because according to these un-American morons, our American founding four father's were all just slave owners, who didn't care about the freedoms or the lives of anyone who supposedly wasn't white. If this statement being made by Obama and other minorities were even slightly true, there would have honestly been no Civil War.

Remember the Civil War, which occurred for four years from 1861-1865, was fought because the North, led by President Abraham Lincoln, wanted all people to be free, but the South, still wanted to enslave people. This included minorities living in the South, contrary to what these people claim, there were minority slave owners and plantation owners, that fought for the South because they did not want slavery to end. People ignore these facts though, they ignore the truth about all races being enslaved and minorities owning slaves because this is not what fits their narrative of a white racist culture.

What makes all of this democratic logic so puzzling is the fact that, these people are claiming that President Abraham Lincoln was the one who promoted the enslavement of people, although he was the U.S. President who started an entire war to end slavery. He was also the President that passed an amendment to abolish the enslavement of his people and was killed for doing so. Still, these people claim that President Lincoln fought for the enslavement of minorities and wanted to continue to this enslavement, not end it. That is one thing that gets lost in translation too, obscured by this minority hatred for white people and the white culture.

President Abraham Lincoln, considered all living Americans, his people, including minorities, President Lincolns mission was to make sure all people were free of the savagery of enslavement. It is funny how people can easily ignore their own history simply because others have the opinion that it is racist and offensive to them, but in reality, they are making this claim because it does not fit their democratic agenda or their narrative of slavery. History proves that America and Great Britain, are the nations that started in the movement to abolished slavery, while N. Africa and the Middle East, ignored the abolishment of slavery and continued to profit in selling their people.

If you bothered to read Abraham Lincoln's speech, you will learn that Lincoln was an advocate of everyone enjoying their American freedoms, not just white people. President Lincoln, wanted his entire nation to be a free nation. No offense, but like I said before, President Abraham Lincoln died for your right to be free. President Lincoln, was killed by a Southerner for starting a war and passing an amendment all because Lincoln believed all men and women were created equal, while others did not, this included minorities.

In addition, like we discussed before, people fail to realize that during the Civil War, there were minority property owners and slave owners that fought for the Confederacy, they fought for the right to keep their people as slaves, minorities did. These prominent minority property owners did not want slavery to end, they were making too much money off it, since they did not want slavery to end, they sent their own people to fight in the war along with other Confederates. Of course, these prominent minorities of our past are ignored and this part of history is hidden because it does not fit the narrative of all white people being racist, but also being the only people who profited from slavery.

American history will soon become a thing of the past, it is often because these kids choose not to bother with school or bother with learning about their own history, but it does not help when people are trying to distort that history. It's come down to these people choosing to believe what they hear and see and if what they believe doesn't match up to what they've heard, they write it off as false information or false allegations, mostly what they call today as fake news. This is also because people base their reality and their history on false deceptions, fallacies that have been displayed in front of them all nice and neat, laid all out in fallacious arguments, so the information is better than it actually is.

It is a delusional mix of truth and reality, but this is where their narrative comes into play because these people, along with others, are not to question or even ask whether the information they are pushing is right or wrong, even if the evidence proves their theory is all wrong.

This is honestly what helps these leftists and democrats push their agenda, people see it, instantly believe it, then spread the information to whoever will listen to it, without verifying whether the information is true or not. The same democratic logic and hateful opinions that pushes these theories, are constantly being drilled into the minds of children all over America.

Kids no longer get to be kids, they are being forced to grow up faster, so they can make decisions about things they cannot even comprehend or understand. It's often because in today's new America, these parents follow ridiculous parenting trends and listen to people, who know nothing about parenting, but still feel they have a right to tell other people how to raise their own kids. This is why I often say the nonsense all starts from home because home is not what it used to be. Not only are these kids confused about the new world they were born in to, but some are also forced to grow up confused as to who they are as a person or as an individual.

This of course is because parents have chosen to no longer parent their kids or use common sense, instead, they have started to follow this trend of not declaring your child's sexual orientation. It's sad because due to this ridiculous trend, you have little girls being raised as little boys and little boys being dressed up like little girls simply because their parents think it's a cool trend to follow, like I said, follower's, not leader's. I am always reminded by my mother's famous words, "Just because someone jumped off a bridge, would you do it to", think about it, you are forcing your children to grow up as someone they may not identify as because someone else thinks it is a good idea.

You are the parent of that child, you are the one that has to make the life decisions for these children until they get older, forcing these kids to live as something they don't identify as, shows you how bad you failed as a parent. Think about it this way, back in the day, men who dressed up as woman were known as transvestites, drag queens and cross-dressers, this was not seen as something that was okay or even normal, nor was it something that was accepted. Now, in our messed up society, these people force their sexual orientations down every ones throats, telling us we need to accept it.

They parade around and intermingle with normal people, trying to tell everyone that they are just as normal as we are, but we know these people are far from normal. What we think does not matter though, since these people now have State Senators fighting for them, they are allowed to do as they please and if we say anything about it were the ones labeled homophobic. Since these people cannot make up their own mind to figure out who they identify as, children are forced to watch these embarrassing people on television.

All thanks to Obama and others, who told the American people that we should be more accepting of this nonsense and pushed Americans into having to be okay with this sinful act. It is wrong, we know it is wrong, we have been taught that it is wrong, we know we do not accept it, but it is not the same as it was back then. Now, if you show any discrimination towards these people or offend these people in any way, you are charged for committing a hate crime. It is like no, we do not accept that you are a man whose trying to identify as a woman, it was wrong back then and it is still wrong today. It will always be wrong, no man should be dressed up as a woman, unless it is for Halloween, then maybe you might have an acceptable excuse.

Just because you do not like our opinion about your gay tendencies or you do not like the fact that we do not accept your sexual preference, does not give you the right to belittle straight Americans. Men are not women and vice versa, but we indentify as one or the other, not both, you should not be dressing up as the other gender, it's wrong and the fact that Americans are seeing this as okay, also the fact that Obama pushed for this, just shows you how messed up in the head these people really are. Their democratic logic and thinking is questionable, their arguments are questionable, their statements are questionable, everything about these people is questionable, including who they are as a person.

Normal parents already have a hard enough time trying to discipline their own kids, without having people butt into their business, now parents have to show them that being gay is okay and if you don't accept these people, you are somehow racist and committing a hate crime. What gets me is that straight American's, white, minority, Asian, Hispanic, whatever, straight Americans, are being laughed at and belittled because we believe in the concept of Adam and Eve, not Adam and Steve.

The problem might be that you cannot discuss anything with these people, you cannot discuss the fact that they look like idiots when you see men dressed up half-naked in women's clothes. These people often

94

think since they should be accepted, they have the right to parade around like mindless and tasteless idiots, which they do not, but if you do not give them this right, they claim you are racist. The famous word these people tend to use is homophobic, they use this word to describe anyone who doesn't accept gay people, in reality, most normal people don't mind gay people, but when we are forced to deal with it more then we want to, we get tired of it very quick.

Were not homophobic because it is our opinion that your orientation is wrong, it is our opinion, just like it is your opinion that normal people are homophobic for not wanting to be gay. The reasoning behind calling someone homophobic is also kind of puzzling to me, you are calling straight normal people homophobic simply because we do not choose to be with the same sex, but we also prefer the traditional standards of man and woman. In addition to that, we also do not believe in the sexual orientation you choose, but that does not make us homophobic, that makes us normal and you cannot say we are homophobic just because we do not accept your abnormalities.

In addition, you can forget about your so-called freedom of speech because if you say anything offensive or discriminatory to these people, you are supposedly a white racist devil, who should be castrated. It is their new self-entitlement status that these people seem to think they have, gay people, tend to think they can say anything to you, offensive or discriminatory, does not matter, they supposedly have the right to, but if you say anything remotely offensive back to them, its discrimination and you are racist for committing a hate crime.

I tend not to understand where we went so wrong in this country, but the fact that, Americans can easily become targets for our American beliefs and traditions, is the most overwhelming thing of all. It comes down to the question of, seriously, how do you justify discriminating against someone else or labeling them racist because they don't accept you? Seriously, this is what I would like to know because we have seen this occurring lately on television, these people have been literally forcing their opinions on to others and labeling them racist when they do not accept it.

It makes you question what these people are trying to prove because these people think they should be accepted and are mad that we do not accept them, so they react by going after people and trying to destroy their character. That's like the people who always have the great debate of whether Star Trek is better than Star Wars, just totally stopped debating and forced one side to accept the other, whether they liked it or not. You are forcing people into believing in something that they do not and if they do not believe it, you are ousting them as if they were outcasts, whose opinion is filled with lies and deceptions.

The worse part about all of this is, due to this mass confusion of delusion, you have little boy's being dressed up like little girls and being called princesses because their parents think it's an appropriate thing to do. Unfortunately, it tends to be puzzling because thanks to this illogical thinking, parents have started to follow these ridiculous trends of not identifying or claiming their babies' gender. Although they know whether they are having a baby boy or a baby girl, they follow the trend of not claiming the gender of their child because other people think messing up a kids head is a cool thing to do.

Please, just stop already with these ridiculous trends and parenting trends, they are not cool, they are not smart and the only thing they prove is that, you cannot think on your own because you follow the lead of other people. Honestly, it is not okay to dress your son up as a little girl, this is not normal, but what puzzles me about this is that, some of these parents actually force their little boys to grow up like little girls, although they don't identify as one. These parents raise their sons as little girls, then turn around and wonder why their sons tend to grow up to be soft and sensitive, but what do you honestly expect, you are parading your son around in dresses calling him a princess, this would turn any kid into a sissy.

We have witnessed this craziness take place right here in America, when an American mother, took her own husband to court, so she could turn her son into a girl. The sad thing is that, it does not just stop with this trend, numerous trends have been created by people, which only seem to get worse. Especially seeing that another trend for parents is to claim that there are other genders (other than the only two you can be born as), to claim when their children are born. Uh no, no there is not. You either have a baby boy or baby girl, there are only two genders, just two, so please stop claiming that there is more than two genders to claim when your baby is born because there is not.

This honestly makes no sense at all because seriously, how on earth would you possibly think this is true? In addition, the only thing you are really doing is confusing your own children as they grow up in this already messed up confusing world. Your baby doesn't come out born looking like an alien, demon or monster; they come out as a lovely baby boy or baby girl, so please stop confusing these little children, I promise it will benefit them in the long run. You would often see something different back in the day because you would often see gender reveal parties for people to guess what the gender was.

This was often usually the only party the man would attend, but still you only have two options to what you were having, a baby boy or a baby girl. Now, you have these men attending baby showers and I'm just sitting back like what the hell, that's not a man's party, men don't attend baby showers, they are usually for the mother, when did men start attending these parties? It is often because these men are also following new trends, but just because people want you to follow these stupid trends, does not mean you necessarily should follow them.

Especially trends like not claiming the orientation of your children, this should be stopped because your children should not have to suffer for your ignorance and stupidity. Let's be honest here, parents are seriously messing these children up, they are forcing them to grow up not knowing exactly who they should identify as, which forces these kids to live one way, when they have no clue to what that way is. Not only are these children trying to find their own way in this weird and confusing messed up world, you now have little boys being raised as little girls and the worse part of it all is that, their parents are the ones pushing this behavior.

Little boys should be gamers, they should be playing outside or playing with cars or GI Joes, they should not being playing with little dolls, nor should they be dressed up and raised like little girls. It is not right what you are doing to your children, they should not have to suffer for your ignorance, so please stop messing these kids up and let them be kids. This is what is destroying the minds of children today, their parents are teaching them based on the false pretense of what they believe or follow what other people start as a trend, rather than being an actual parent.

Don't get me wrong, there are parent's out there that have enough smarts and common sense to raise their children right, but the trends most of these other parents follow seem to be getting worse and we as American's need to stop this ridiculous way of thinking. The sad thing is that, these trends do not stop, they just keep coming and only get worse and worse. People have created a trend for just about everything you can possibly think of, all you tend to see is millions of people all around the world acting like complete idiots online because other people have convinced them that, it's a cool thing to do. Like I said before and say once again, followers, not leader's.

Learning about manners, morals and discipline, was something that was taught at home, you learned these behavioral traits when you were growing up. Not today's generation though, they do not understand the concept of morals, discipline or even something as simple as manners. From not having a single ounce of discipline, but also no proper manners, to not being educated enough on what's right from wrong, to basically having no morals at all; it seems to me that these parents have literally failed these kids, although these kids can be said to share some of the blame. If you have been out in the world lately or have seen what has been going on in American cities, you will notice that the people who are out causing all this chaos, are the children that grew up with no discipline and no manners.

Their way of acting out and solving their problems is to cause as much destruction as possible and they do not know any other way because they were never taught another way of how to deal with their problems. These kids grew up never being told no, never being taught morals, never being raised with any discipline or manners and because they were raised this way, they now assume they can do as they please, without any accountability. These youth's mindsets and opinions could be considered their own worst enemy because these newer generational youths do not want to work, they rather riot and protest that they deserve everything, rather than going to work to better their lives.

Imagine if we acted like these kids do today, not only would we probably be grounded for life, we would have had our backside paddled, but that's okay because that's real discipline, we acted out, got whooped and learned to never do it again. That's what is missing today, these children and teens are not afraid of anything, they do not know the fear a belt or paddle instills into a child, they don't know the fear of hearing, "wait till your father get's home," they are not punished for anything, so they don't know the concept of accountability.

It is crazy when you think about it because this is where we went wrong as a country, discipline these days is somehow considered a sin, if parents try to enforce discipline on their own children, whether it is in the form of a spanking or yelling, parent's are often criticized and berated by other people. In America, we are no longer a nation of privacy, people are no longer allowed to live their lives or raise their own kids because everyone seems to butt into other people's business or lives, whether they know them or not, especially when it comes to people online.

This is what seems to be holding American's back from disciplining their children because people, especially people who do not even know you, assume they know more than you do, even when it comes to raising your own children. Let's also get this straight for all you assumptive, pre-judging people, there is a huge and major difference, when it comes to parents physically beating and abusing their children, compared to parents who spank, yell or discipline their children for acting out and being bad. American's who can't seem to mind their own business, tend to forget this little fact, they tend to assume the opposite and the only ones left to suffer are the parents.

Like I stated before, there is a huge difference between spanking your kids to discipline them for acting out and being bad, compared to abusing and physically beating your kids because you're a very bad parent, but also a very bad human being. Back in the day, parents, family members, neighbor's, teachers, basically any form of authority, was allowed to put you in your place if you acted out, there was no harm in it because afterwards we acted right, we learned our lesson.

That doesn't occur with today's newer generation of America, in today's America, you yell at your kid, you go to jail, you spank your kid to discipline them, you got to jail. Not only do you go to jail, but you have the fortunate opportunity of DSS paying you weekly visits to make sure your children aren't being abused. All this new trouble thanks to your nosey neighbor who assumed you were abusing your children, not because they saw actual evidence of physical and mental abuse, but simply because they heard you yelling at them. Again assumptions are at the helm of all this trouble because people can't seem to mind their own business and stay out of people's lives.

Instead, they interrupt other people's lives under the assumption that they know better than them or because they assume they know what's going on. The huge question I am always left wondering is, how are parents supposed to discipline their children on what's right and what's wrong, when everyone thinks something as simple as yelling at your kid is child abuse? Seriously, it should be considered abuse when these children talk back to their parents, it should be considered abuse when these teens curse at their own parents, it also should be considered abuse when these kids force their parents into buying them whatever they want, whenever they want.

No one sees it this way though, the parents are the ones berated, while the children are made out to be the heroes, yet, the children are the ones that should have been watched. With no discipline and the ability to do whatever they wanted, these children grew up into the young youths you see out destroying communities and businesses today, the alarming fact about this is that, their doing it because they know they will not be held responsible or accountable for their actions. This tends to bring up one of the problems we already talked about before, we've talked about everyone blaming their own problems on other people, claiming it's never their own fault, this is the same ideology they use.

This ideology is the reason why we now have a whole new generation of teenagers and young adults, who think they are entitled to anything and everything they want and contrary to what any of us believe, they don't have to lift one finger for it. The ideology and opinion was pushed onto these people by blm leaders and State Senators, who continued to push this opinion onto minorities and anyone else they could. They want these teens to believe that they are being oppressed. What's worse is, since their ancestors were slaves, they somehow experience this pain today and because of this painful memory, they're convinced they deserve everything for free, whether they have worked for it or not.

Unfortunately, these are the very same people that claim all white people should suffer simply because the color of our skin is white and our ancestors took part in slavery, the very trade that their ancestors introduced to the New Americas. Don't try to negotiate or debate with these people or even try to communicate with them about what they think because they don't care what you say. These people could care less what your opinion is, according to these self-entitled people, their opinions are the only ones that matter.

Remember earlier what I said about forgetting your so-called Freedom of Speech, well that fits the narrative here, you don't have Freedom of Speech, they do, you don't. These young adults came from

100

the generation of sensitivity, unaccountability and seclusion, thanks to this seclusion, these teenagers grew up claiming they are to be handed everything, for doing absolutely nothing and they'll destroy your things if you don't give in. We've seen the outcome of where it all starts with these undisciplined children because we've all been in grocery stores and seen kids screaming and crying their eyes out because their mom told them no, but they refused to accept that answer.

The confusing part is, if the mom disciplines her kids in front of anyone, she is the one looked upon, questioned and harassed. Why is that though, does that honestly make any sense, seriously, she's trying to do the right thing, she's trying to discipline her children, why is she seen as the bad person? She is the parent trying to discipline her own children, she is the mother of those children, why is she the one that is seen as a bad mother for trying to discipline her kids? This is one thing that makes absolutely no sense to me, but still people all over the world do it daily, people stress about issues that are not important, while the real important issues, often are swept to the side or ignored.

Like the fact that, people butt into other people's business when they assume a child is being abused or in danger, yet, they do nothing about the 1.2 billion children all over the world, dying from hunger and starvation. Let's face it though, real child abuse is one thing that's ignored more than anything because Americans chose to focus on non-important issues, but when it comes to issues like, real child abuse and women and children actually being kidnapped and abducted, they turn a blind eye. We know this because the number one problem in the world is women and children being kidnapped, abused and sold into sex-trafficking, but this problem is swept to the side, while Americans deal with the dangers of plastic bags.

The same can be said when we talk about real physical child abuse, look at all the cases of innocent children who were killed by their own parent's because of extreme mental and physical child abuse. The government, the social worker's, the lawyer's, the child's lawyers, all did absolutely nothing to help these endangered kids, they all knew these children were being abused by their parents, yet, they did nothing to stop it.

All these officials left the children in the care of their parents and unfortunately all these children suffered the same fate, they were all eventually killed by their parents, thanks to the constant mental and

101

physical torture and abuse. This is real child abuse, this is real physical torture and abuse, not someone spanking their kids for acting like little brats or someone yelling at their kids to try to stop them from acting out. It doesn't make much sense, especially when you look at the case of innocent 8-year-old Gilbert Fernandez, a little kid that was mentally and physically abused, but also tortured by his father and stepmother.

Social worker's knew, teacher's knew, judges knew, lawyer's knew, hell everyone knew, yet, the only one that tried to do something about it was his real mother, but her calls for help went unheard. The calls for help, didn't help, her cries were drowned out as these people did nothing and of course after years of neglect, torture and physical abuse, the father and stepmother took the life of Gilbert Fernandez. The sad reality is, this is only one of hundreds of cases of real child abuse and neglect occurring all across the United States. Yet, no one seems to butt into these people's business or interfere into their lives to help save these children, only the innocent ones.

It's sad because the only way these parents are caught or turned in, is if the kids themselves escape or they are caught in the act. We saw an example of this occur just last year in 2019, where a couple was found guilty of starving, malnourishing and enslaving their own children for years, 13 children to be exact. The couple's eldest daughter, a 17 year old, was able to escape and eventually find a police officer to report her parents, thanks to her courage, her brothers and sisters were all saved. Think about that for a second though because this was a year ago and the eldest daughter was 17, so for 16 or so years, these parents tortured, malnourished and physically abused, their children, while everyone around them did nothing to stop it.

It honestly can be a little puzzling to think about because people interfere in other people's lives, people who seem to be doing nothing wrong, but raising their kids, when they should be interested in the thirteen children down the street, who are being physically abused and tortured. Instead you have people in reality and online trying to tell you how to raise your kids, discipline your kids and will report you for anything they think is abuse simply because they assume they know better then you.

I remember when we were growing up our parents always told us, "Don't butt into other people's business because their business doesn't concern you", basically saying stay out of business that you have no involvement in. People need to start thinking this way again, eventually people are going to realize that they don't know everything and they have no right to butt into other people's lives. People are allowed to have a difference of opinions, this is why we have debates and discussions, people talk about things so they can see both sides.

They don't just assume their opinion is better and not bother to listen to the other side. Contrary to what people tell you, you're allowed to have your own opinion, a difference of opinion is also allowed, you can't judge a person based on the reason of you not liking the opinion they have. This only means there is a difference of opinions, which you should be okay with because our very own history is based on debates and discussions, that's also why there's a Presidential Debate with a discussion of what's best for our country.

You can also look at the current Presidential election because there's actual proof that Joe Biden cheated, yet, there are millions of people whose opinion is that he didn't, although there is clear evidence that he did. There is no debating with these people though, there is no discussing the election with these people, they ignore the evidence that proves Biden cheated and they tell us to just accept the outcome because it was a fair and honest election. These people ignore the facts and incite riots and violence because their opinion is that Joe Biden miraculously won the election and since it's their opinion, we should all just accept it.

What all these people fail to realize is, you can't win a U.S. President Election based on fraud, if there is one slight hint or even one case that proves election fraud, you cannot become U.S. President, you automatically forfeit to your opponent. The fact that the Senate and the Supreme Court blatantly ignored the actual video evidence, proves that the election was clearly stolen. Think about the cases of other forms of fraud though, there were hundreds of Americans, who reported and claimed that they went to vote for President Trump, but somehow their vote was already mailed in on an absentee ballot for Joe Biden.

Actual Americans showed up to the voting centers to vote, but were told that there vote was already cast in an absentee ballot for Biden, so they were turned away, but I am left sitting here thinking, who shows up to vote, if they already sent in an absentee ballot? I mean, an absentee ballot is for the people that don't want to show up to vote, so honestly, why would these people show up to vote, if they supposedly already voted, seems to me like someone's lying here and it isn't the voters who are trying to cast their vote for Trump? These claims often left most people stunned, wondering how that could possibly happen, but the fact that, all these people were turned away so they couldn't actually vote for the person they wanted to, is another thing that proves voter fraud.

Seriously, how does that happen though, if someone is walking in to actually vote, showing up in person to actually vote, you think they would honestly forget that they sent in an absentee ballot because I seriously doubt it? This was clearly voter election fraud, peoples votes are being cast for Joe Biden, when in reality, these voters showed up as votes for Trump. Instead of being able to cast their vote for President Trump, people in charge told these voters that they couldn't vote again because they already sent in an absentee ballot voting for Joe Biden, that's clearly voter fraud.

You filled out absentee ballots on other peoples behalf, then told these same people that they couldn't vote, when they personally showed up to vote. I want you to think about that for a second though because people that request and send in an absentee ballot are doing so for a reason, they don't want to show up to vote or they don't want to wait in line to vote, it's why they call it an absentee ballot, you are absent from the voting machine. So seriously, you have to honestly ask yourself, why would Americans show up to vote, if they supposedly already sent in an absentee ballot?

Alternatively, you can ask yourself, how is it that all Americans who came to vote for President Trump, supposedly already had their votes casted in absentee ballots for Sleepy Joe Biden? Nope, that's not suspicious at all. It honestly makes no sense that a person would show up to cast their vote if they knew they already sent in their vote with an absentee ballot, no sense at all, but this is what democrats want us to believe. Honestly, you really have to question everything these people say because these democrats claimed this wasn't happening. All these democrats claimed there was no election fraud and the people that were coming in to complain about their vote being casted for the wrong person, are just mad President Trump lost.

Seriously, the Americans that came in to vote for Donald Trump, were all told they already sent in an absentee ballot for Joe Biden, so they couldn't revote, if they complained about this, they were called liars and turned away. While turned away most of them were told that their vote didn't matter anyway because if you were voting for Trump, you were voting for someone who lost. It's like these people were somehow predicting the 2020 election and knew the outcome, before it even ended, how is that?

These are the statements being made by these democrats, these democratic observers and counters could care less about whether you know they committed voter fraud or not. They could care less that you know they committed fraud to steal a Presidency, but they have the press, therefore they can mold and twist any information they see fit. This is why you often seen the voter fraud cases being brought up by President Trump and his administration, being easily dismissed because democrats made sure that they had their people in play. These lawyers made sure that any case of voter fraud was quickly dismissed by their judges.

Democrats also used the media and the press to their advantage, they used journalists and their news networks to push their theory of President Trump lying about the voter fraud, with this help they were able to convince others to look the other way, while they stole the election. That's another thing that has become a joke in this country, journalist and journalism because besides Tucker Carlson, Sean Hannity Laura Ingrahm and a few others, our news networks have become one big joke and the dignity of a journalist or news anchor is not what it used to be.

Journalist and news anchors used to have integrity, they used to have character, they used to base their journalism and news on truth and facts, you've seen the war movies about journalist, who seek to find the truth, that does work anymore, the truth is now what they say it is, even if it contradicts the facts. The journalist and news anchors of today's generation have lost the art of journalism. I honestly think they are not even to sure what their own job title is anymore because their job is to investigate the truth, these people don't bother to do that though, they investigate the lies and accuse the victim.

Our current American media and press does this to a tee, they berate and belittle the President with false accusation after false accusation, while they ignore Joe Biden and his son's corruption in China. Seriously, Joe Biden had connections to companies overseas and bribed them into getting what he wanted, while his son worked for criminals, who ran prostitution rings and worked with Russians to interfere in U.S. politics, so you tell me who the criminal is here? However bad this looks for the Biden's, this isn't journalistic news, this isn't headlining news, nope, these journalists and news anchors rather ask President Trump, why he is so racist and why Trump supposedly supports white supremacy, rather than, why Joe Biden tends to be so involved in Chinese corruption.

It was amazing to watch as numerous news anchors blatantly made up fake news and pushed false allegations and false accusations about the President, but said nothing about Biden or Biden's son. For some reason it didn't matter what Joe Biden was convicted of, Joe Biden could do no wrong and President Donald Trump could do no right. This opinion is often coming from everyone who hates Trump, not just State Senators and politicians, but also influential television host and actors, push their opinions of hate onto everyone, denying any voter fraud that may have taken place.

People like crazy Whoopi Goldberg should eat their words and when you tell Americans we need to, "shut up and just accept it," you should make sure your savior of a President won on merit and principal, not fraud. She is one of the many pushers of hate that are on television shows that think their opinion matters more than everyone else opinion, but every time she opens her mouth, you are left wondering whether she is sane or not. Everything she says is questionable, along with many others that have shared the same opinion, it's insane how all these people can sit there and claim that there was no cheating during the 2020 election.

Although there was plenty of evidence brought forth, including video evidence of suspicious voter activity. What you can't do is, just ignore another person's opinion simply because it doesn't match up to your opinion, nor can you force your opinion onto someone else just because you think their opinion is wrong and they should just accept your opinion. No one person has the right to tell other people what their opinion should be or that you should just accept other people's opinions, without questioning whether it's truthful or not.

People have no right to tear others down or make offensive comments towards others because they have different opinions then they do, but these democrat supporters do it to a tee. This to me is just insane to think of because American actor's, television host's, radio hosts, Senators, mayors, governors, State leader's, civil leaders and millions of their followers, are literally calling for the millions of President Trump supporters to be hated and treated badly because they supported President Trump and his so-called white supremacist lies.

It's crazy because these people make the most outrageous and racist statements towards President Trump and his supporters, but also claim that his followers should lose everything they've worked hard for. This is all for simply being an American support, but also a President Trump supporter, a supporter of the President of the United States. This is because it's their opinion that trump is a bad person, it's not the truth, it's just their opinion, but they push and force their hateful opinion onto others and those that don't accept their opinion, are considered racist traitors and deplorable Trump Supporters.

Think of that for a second because this should scare millions of people, these un-American people, including State Senators, are so dead set in their hateful ways and hateful opinions that, they will do anything and say anything they can to get the people to side with them. This includes calling millions of Trump Supporters white supremacists because they didn't take their democratic side. It's gotten worse now that we have social media platforms because these social media platforms have become social hot spots for people that want to push their hateful opinion onto others or anyone who will listen.

Not only do these become platforms for millions of people to spread their hate, they also become platforms for millions of people to easily tear you down if they think you offended them. People from all over the world, not just America, will go online and literally tear others down, especially if they feel that these people offended them, no one talks things through anymore, instead they go online and belittle you in front of millions of people. It's a dangerous game of cat and mouse because innocent people are castrated online by hundreds, if not millions of people, but it's crazy because it's usually done by people who don't actually know who or why they are bashing these people, but they easily follow others who are doing it.

Democrat's and their supporters are the same way, except these people don't even think you are allowed to have your own opinion, this is because they believe their opinion is right and yours is wrong, especially if you are a Trump supporter. Democrats, leftists and liberals, use this ideology to their advantage, they use the media and

107

push online news articles to deceive you into believing what they believe, if you don't believe me, just look at the 2020 election and how the whole thing played out. Anything that supported President Trump, from tweets to face book posts were banned and erased, news anchors berated President Trump about his false accusations of voter fraud, while sleepy Joe Biden and democrats used the media and these social platforms to extinguish any accusation of voter fraud.

This to me is crazy because Donald Trump is the President of the United States, who are you to ban him, who are you to stop him from posting anything because you honestly don't have that right? You are nobody to him, President Trump should be given the respect he deserves, he is the President of the United States, you might not like him, but that does not give you the right to stop him from speaking on your social media platforms. This is probably the first time in United States history, where a President has had to deal with more backlashes and discrimination, then any other former President of the United States, while all he is doing is looking out for the American people.

Democrats have constantly pushed this narrative of hate and since democrats tend to own the news and airwaves, they make sure they push more for Joe Biden, while they try to destroy President Trump's character, every chance they get. We've all seen their idiot of a former President, Barack Obama, talking about how bad President Trump is, but in reality, Indonesian Obama, was far worse as U.S. President, then President Trump ever will be.

It's mind-boggling how this guy is still even talking or showing his face because Barack Obama and his wife, stabbed America in the back every chance they could and now these two idiots are trying to divide us further, claiming President Trump supporters are the ones following the lies, chaos and deceptions, but we've also supposedly all lost our minds. In reality, we are Americans, supporting the American President, we are not following the lies, we are not following the chaos, we are not deceivers, democrats are. They've proven it every day by opening their mouths on national television, berating the American President for putting the American people first.

Now, before we continue, let me clarify one thing, I am not a republican, especially not a democrat, nor a liberal, nor a whatever, I am an American and I care for America and the American people and I don't need to pick a side for that because the only side is the American side. It should only be one side anyway, the American side, but democrats and liberals have pushed so much division between Americans, it will take years before we can undo the horrible separation and division that the Obama's and all other democrats have caused. It still keeps me puzzled as to how all these democrats, leftists and liberals, started the chaos, but also pushed for the division and destruction of American cities.

They also pushed for the destruction of American public national monuments and statues, only to turn around and blame it all on President Trump and his administration. Seriously, these State Senators and city council members blamed everything on President Trump, from the major increase of crime, to the violence overtaken their city streets. It honestly made no sense to me because like I've stated before, these democratic State Senators, Mayors and Governors, were clearly the ones at fault for the violence that increased ten-fold in their cities.

I say this because according to our American Constitutional law, State Senators, Mayors and Governors, control each State that they govern, they are the first line of defense for American citizens, the U.S. President is not. Therefore, it honestly leaves me confused as to why these politicians would do nothing about the crime and violence that has seemed to steadily increase in each of their cities. It's very confusing to me because these State politicians did nothing about the violence occurring in their cities, nothing about the destruction, but they did each make sure they went on national television, so they could blame all the violence and destruction on President Trump.

Crime and violence tore through American streets ten-fold after these State and city officials chose to either defund their police departments or disband them completely. This idea further divided the country because American citizens didn't think it was a good idea to get rid of the police or defund the police, while these State politicians did and went ahead with doing it anyway. The problem is that these so-called Americans State Reps and city officials, want everyone separated and divided.

They thrive on keeping everyone separated and divided into little groups because this helps them easier control others opinions and deceive these people into believing what they want them to believe. This is why democrats have latched on to the blm movement and helped push it even further. Blm leaders want themselves divided from white Americans and they push for the white culture being erased, the police being defunded, immigration being canceled and prisoners being released. It's the same agenda that democrats and leftists have, they want to push this narrative of their new America, where police and immigration don't exist and that's why they've helped blm leaders push their agenda of racial dominance, further adding to the division in this country.

Think about the United States in the 80's, 90's and early 2000's, we were known as the most dominant country in the world and we were number #1 in everything and people had freedom to say what they wanted and do what they wanted. Our children had a future, homes were filled with love, Americans didn't worry much about racism, we cared about each other and making our country successful. Fast forward to today and the last 16 years or so because democrats have slowly taken away our privacy and American freedoms and given them to illegal immigrants and foreigners, who get to enjoy our spoils.

Think about this for a second, Joe Biden claims that the moment he becomes U.S. President, Sleepy Joe, is going to push a bill through, which would give over 11 million people living in the U.S., illegally, the ability to instantly become U.S. citizens. So sleepy Joe Biden, is going to give 11 million immigrants living here in America illegally, instant American citizenship, which leaves me wondering, uh, how is this even possible, illegal immigrants are just what their title says, illegal? Any illegal alien or immigrant should instantly be deported, they are illegal, but somehow we have over 11 million illegal immigrants living freely in America, seriously?

It's puzzling to me because let's say these illegal immigrants all worked American jobs, so out of the close to 11 million illegal's working, even if we say close to 9 million illegal immigrants working, that's 9 million American jobs, that are being stolen by people over in our country illegally and the government knows it and approves of it. Illegal means illegal, you have no American rights, you have no American freedoms, the only right you have, is the right to a flight back to wherever the hell you came from because you are over here in America illegally.

We as Americans should kind of expect this though, our very own State Representatives, have let illegal immigrants roam freely in our country for years. They also constantly fight d advocate to give these illegal's more rights than American's, especially these four idiotic American State Representatives, who call themselves the brood. Americans are always being pushed aside for other people, but the funny thing about all of it is, these American State Reps., swear up and down they are fighting for the American people, they claim they are fighting for our American rights, but their actions proves otherwise.

This is because we often see them on television fighting to give our rights to illegal immigrants and foreigners. Democrats want our borders gone because they see all these illegal immigrants and foreigners as voters and supporters and if these democrats get their way, immigration and forms of law enforcement, would soon be a thing of the past. Unfortunately, most of these bills and legislatures that these State Senators are trying to pass would change many things, but immigration and law enforcement would change drastically.

We've already seen the outcome of police departments being defunded and reformed because certain American cities have already defunded entire police departments, but this defunding only resulted in a huge increase of crime and violence. It was a power and control move, they wanted to be the first in defunding the police because they thought it was a great step towards progress, but the only thing it did was allow criminals to have free reign on the streets. It's always about power and control though, to them, power is everything because the more power they have, the more they can stay in control.

Now that they stole an entire Presidency and forced Americans to believe it was an honest and fair election, they have all the power and control they need to do whatever they want. This includes passing bad legislature that only hurts America more, but since they don't honestly care about America, these State Senators pass their legislature through to Congress and the Senate, claiming it's what's best for the American people. This is what we should all be really worried about because these democratic State politicians don't know what the American people want. They often tend to claim they do, they even claim everything they do is for the American people, but their actions always prove otherwise.

It's honestly far worse then we all think it is because these State Senators have the power to deceive and manipulate people into believing what they believe, also into thinking how they think and with this power and control, they can very quickly destroy any ones

111

character. It's amazing to me how these State Senators and influencers were able to use this power to convince millions of people that President Trump was a racist white supremacist, running a racist white supremacist government, that's keeping minorities oppressed. It's far from the truth and we know that President Trump is far from a racist, but it is amazing to watch because the person they are backing, Joe Biden, has been on record several times making some of the most racist statements ever.

Mostly what we've talked about in this chapter, we've watched play out all on the news during this past year, we watched as these State Senators used the media and the press to falsely accuse the President of anything they could, while most of these accusations were fake and found to be untrue. The thing that's alarming about these allegations was the fact that, most of these allegations were identified as being false right from the very beginning, so technically these State Senators had no base to what they were accusing the President.

Still, it didn't matter, since democrats owned the media and controlled the press, they used them to push their opinion of hate, so they could spread this opinion to millions of people. Unfortunately, the opinion that they were constantly pushing onto others was solely based on their own hatred for President Trump. Due to this hatred, the only thing democrats focused on was getting rid of President Trump. It all came down to them wanting President Trump gone, since they wanted President Trump out of the Oval Office, they aimed to do whatever they could.

It's sad because these State Senators and others, didn't care who they hurt in the process with their opinion, they used the media to smear President Trumps name and the press to destroy his character. This opinion of theirs was dangerous because these politicians constantly pushed the theory that President Trump was a racist white President, who only cared about white people and did nothing for the minority community, so he needed to be replaced. That has always been the answer for these State Senators though, these Senators never really gave President Trump a chance from the beginning.

Once elected to be the President of the United States, democrats went after President Trump, calling Trumps Presidency a hoax, claiming that Trump stole the election and instantly needed to be replaced. It's interesting how this was the opinion from the very beginning, we watched as Nancy Pelosi, Hillary Clinton, Barack Obama and other democrats instantly tried to discredit President Trumps win and claim that he stole the 2016 election. Since discrediting him didn't work, they instantly tried to impeach President Trump with false allegations, which like we discussed, were often unverified accusations and allegations and we all know that most, if not all of these allegations, were proven to be false.

Everything these State Senators have pushed so far has been questionable at best and could be easily considered wrong. Most of their arguments have been led by false allegations brought forth by unverified information. They used this information to push their lies and deceptions. Thanks to these democrats constantly pushing these fallacious arguments, constantly pushing their hateful opinion, people started to hate President Trump and blame him for everything bad. It made no sense watching these people hate on the President because he was not the one stirring up the chaos, he was not the one stirring up the violence, but they still blamed him for it.

For the first time in America, we had a U.S. President, who was voted in by the American People, chosen by the American people, elected by the American people, still, democrats convinced these people to hate President Trump all because they claimed he was a racist U.S. President. Not only do these people constantly think and feel this way, but they often act on this opinion, they constantly berate and belittle President Trump for being racist and no good. The only thing President Trump is really guilty of is, trying to provide a better life for the American people, but also trying to better America..

Democrats, liberals and their supporters, were not trying to do that, instead, they were pushing lies and mistaken beliefs because they wanted President Trump gone and they were going to do everything in their power to make that happen. President Trump has honestly had to deal with more adversity in his first four years as President, then any other U.S. President before him and you have to ask yourself, why is that? It honestly makes no sense to me because President Trump has passed bill after bill, which all focused on helping the American people, including minorities.

So seriously, why are these State politicians claiming that President Trump's done nothing for minorities or the American people? I feel this question should honestly be answered by Nancy Pelosi because she was

113

hired to help President Trump better the lives of the American people, but instead, she chose to berate and belittle the President simply because she couldn't stand him as a person. This right here shows you the way these democrats think, this is their thought process, they base their actions off their hatred for one man and this hatred runs deep.

It's crazy when you think about it because these State politicians are willing to destroy the country they were hired to represent, along with destroying the lives of the American people they were hired to protect. From false Impeachment trials to an uncontrollable pandemic, to Russians interfering with the election, Nancy Pelosi, democrats and liberals, have tried just about everything they could to get rid of President Trump and they were eventually able to. Seriously, why does that not scare you, why does that not worry you about our future?

Joe Biden, Nancy Pelosi, State Rep. AOC, Kamala Harris and others, all do the same thing, day after day, they berate and belittle President Trump with false allegations and false accusations simply because they hate the man himself. It doesn't just stop with Trump, these so-called American representatives also berate the millions of Americans that support President Trump. These people aimed to destroy the character of Trump and his supporters and they lied to the people so they could deceive them into thinking President Trump needs to be replaced with Joe Biden.

Seriously though, why would you follow the lead of people who will lie to you and deceive you into getting what they want? Growing up we were told never to trust people like them, so what's changed? Why are millions of people following the lead of American State politicians, who want to stay in power and will do anything and say anything they can to remain in power? I ask this because these people never do anything good for the American people, like we've discussed before, these State Senators have been in our government for generations, yet, they've done nothing but cause chaos and spend millions on trying to get rid of American rights.

The proof is in the making because these democratic politicians spent millions of taxpayers' dollars on false impeachment's, which were all based on false allegations, led by false investigations. They spent millions just to try to get rid of President Trump, but every single time they brought a case against the President, the case was easily shut down because the case had no merit. That's what puzzles me the most,

President Trump, was voted in by the American People, yet, democrats and liberals, are so hell bent on getting him out of office that they have literally tried everything they could to get rid of him, this includes trying to impeach Trump on false allegations, not once, but twice.

I talk about this a lot because it's crazy to think that these American State politicians, led by Nancy Pelosi, have spent more than 30 million dollars of American tax-money on just one impeachment, simply to try and get rid of the U.S. President, a President that was elected by the American people. Real issues like poverty, hunger, starvation, the homeless, child abuse and people being abducted and enslaved are out there, but these real issues are ignored because these issues don't fit their narrative, which is to use chaos to help push for their new America.

The thing that worries me the most is the fact that, these are the same democrats that pushed for a more divided America, they've separated Americans into Trump supporters and democrat followers, claiming you need to take a side. In reality, it's their side they want you on and the one they want you to choose, if you chose the other side, then you are the enemy, you are the one following the lies and deceptions being spread by a racist President. This is what these people often do though, you can see most of these people on television using their influence to push their narrative of hate.

If they are not pushing their narrative of hate, their following their agenda of trying to tell just about everyone else what to believe and what to think. It get's bad when you don't take their side or listen to their opinion, like we've talked about many times in the book, these people often discriminate against you for choosing another side or having another opinion then they do. This world is filled with assuming people, they assume they know what's best for everyone else, they assume they also have the right to tell you what to believe in and they will go to tremendous lengths to make sure you do. This also goes back to people needing to stop accusing parents of abusing their children, but also telling these parents that spanking their kids is wrong.

They are really only trying to discipline their kids, trying to teach them right from wrong, which kids these days seem to be lacking. It's sad because the Gilbert Fernandez case is just one of the hundreds of major child abuse cases taking place in America, these parent's are physically and mentally abusing their children, but these are not the parents that are watched, the innocent parents, the ones trying to do right by their kids, are. It tends to make no sense because regular parents trying to discipline their children by spanking them are now seen as criminals committing child abuse, while the parents who are responsible for torturing and killing their own kids, are getting away with murder.

Obviously something doesn't sound right here and I would honestly think that something needs to be done about what is occurring today because this unfortunate circumstance now forces parents to become somewhat powerless when it comes to disciplining their own children. I also honestly think this is how a lot of people feel right now, millions of people feel powerless because democrats and others have taking to destroying their names and characters simply because they chose to support President Trump.

It was a constant onslaught of name calling and berating, but these democratic State Senators even went as far to claim people supporting President Trump needed to be fired from their jobs. This was their democratic opinion though, these democrats hated President Trump, but also everything he stood for and they punished anyone who supported him. This is the life Americans have become accustomed to, we see this take place every single day, these State Senators are constantly online or in other peoples ears, pushing their assumptive theories and hateful opinions.

When these people are not trying to force their opinion on you, they are trying to tell you how to live your life or what you seem to be doing wrong in your life. I think one thing that seems to be lost in all this confusion is the fact that, there is no longer a wrong or right, it's their way, the way they think it is and their way of doing things, whether their way is right or wrong. Although the way these people think and the way these people act is often wrong, it doesn't seem to matter, they are still able to convince millions of people to think and act the way they do.

We've seen this occurring from the young adults out in American cities destroying everything in sight because democrats, along with blm leaders, have convinced these young adults that they could do no wrong. Even though most of these young adults know it's probably wrong to be destroying a community or burning down a business, this thought doesn't cross their minds. They've been convinced by State

Senators and blm leaders that, they can cause as much damage as they want and it's not wrong because nothing they can do is wrong. Most of us were taught right from wrong at a very young age, while growing up, we learned what was the right thing to do and what was the wrong thing to do, this learned moment is no longer there when it comes to this newer generation of young adults.

These youths no longer care about right or wrong, they no longer care about the damage they create, they no longer care about the lives they destroy, they have an agenda and that agenda is pushed by hate. Even their parents seem to have no more control, as if they had any control at all, but since there is no control or guidance, these youths listen to no one and do as they please, which tends to be following people that are only looking out for their very own interests. The sad thing is that these youths have taken to destroying communities and destroying people's homes, all because of the hatred that has been instilled into their minds and the opinions that were constantly forced down their throats.

Eventually after being fed so much hate, they started to act out by causing destruction, but honestly, if you have the opinion that you can do no wrong, you tend to think that anything you do will instantly be forgiven because no one is being held accountable for their actions. we can look at something as simple as the act of acting out to get your way because acting out was a classic kid move, but this simple kid move, has been adopted by these young adults and as we've seen, they act out in a very different way.

These young adults don't simply just act out like the youths of the past, this newer generation of youth's causes as much destruction as they possibly can, until they get their way. They act out on purpose because this is something that these young adults have done time and time again, they know if they act out and destroy everything in sight, people will eventually give in to them, since that has always been the trend in the past.

This behavior often started from home with the parents who gave these young adults everything they wanted when they were kids, but also as kids they were never told no, they were never grounded, they were never put in time out, so the only form of discipline they had, was no form of discipline at all. These kids grew up with no discipline or control and are now out there destroying communities and disrupting other people's lives all because they are the under the assumption that they can do no wrong and no one can convince them otherwise. The thing that doesn't help anyone is the fact that, these teens and young adults were taught to think and act this way, if it wasn't their parents teaching them this behavior, they were learning it from other people, who were pushing their hateful opinions online or on television.

What tends to be confusing about why these teens and youths do what they do, is the reasons they give you for doing what they do. Since they grew up undisciplined, they often skipped school, also didn't bother with something like getting a job, but this is partly the reason they are destroying things, unequal education and unequal employment. These young adults make the claim that for decades they've been provided with bad educations and dead end jobs mostly because the color of their skin, but in reality, it's their attitude and it's their character that's got them where they are today.

The claim they make is not reality or even the truth, but it's the opinion that is now shared by many because they've been tricked into thinking that a systemically racist government is oppressing them. Some of this oppression comes in the form of keeping these young adults from gaining access to a better education and a better place of employment. This is far from reality because these young adults have just as much opportunity to get a job as anyone else does, but the only thing holding them back is that most jobs require experience, which most of them have none.

We've discussed this previously how people all around America have the same opportunity as everyone else, the only difference is whether you chose to do something with that opportunity or just squander it. This is life though, opportunities come and go, chances are sometimes missed, but it's up to you what you do with them when they do come. What people cannot do is, blame their lost opportunities and missed chances on other people simply because, they claim these people are the ones responsible. The blame falls on no one but themselves, these people are the ones who are responsible for not worrying about their education.

They are also the ones that chose not to work, which often led to the bad life choices that got them where they are at, no one else chose this path for them. I think what's so overwhelming about the whole situation and much of what we've talked about is, none of what we've discussed really matter's anymore, simply because the truth hardly matters anymore. We know this because we've watched all year as these young adults continued to riot, loot and destroy dozens of communities, all under the assumption that everything is racist and designed to hold them back.

This is the reason why they've received a bad education, this is the reason why they've been held back from getting better jobs, not because they chose to take that path, but because the government is racist and holding them back. The truth is that, their parents failed them, the truth is that, they also failed themselves, the truth is that, they chose the wrong path and now suffer the consequences of those decisions. Since their truth is what they make it, the real truth seems to disappear. This is why we've talked about what we've talked about because I honestly fail to understand how these people could honestly act and think this way or how our American State Senators could back this hateful opinion and push for a more divided country.

Doesn't matter that these people themselves chose not to go to school or often quit school when they were growing up, it doesn't matter that they often chose not to get a job or quit the job after taking it. It really doesn't matter what they've done wrong in their lives because others have convinced them that, they are not to blame for the mistakes they have made, other people are. It's all very dangerous thinking because we now live in a world where opinions are leading the actions of many and people act on what they think or believe, rather than acting on the truth.

It's a very opinionated world and these opinions are pushed by deep hatreds that simply bring out the worst in people and the only ones left dealing with the outcome of these racist opinions, are the innocent people that are caught in the wrong place at the wrong time. This is the racist opinion that has been separating America, blm leaders, led by certain State Senators, have pushed their opinion about Trumps government being racist, but also supposedly is the one solely responsible for holding back minorities for decades, although he's only been in Office and our government for no more than four years.

Thanks to President Trump and his administration supposedly being racist, these people have pushed the opinion that minorities not only deserve reparations for what their ancestors went through, but they also should be handed anything they want, simply because the color of their

119

skin. This is the opinion that has taken over and been pushed into the minds of minorities and young adults, seriously, instead of working for something, it's now their opinion that they don't have to work for it because the color of their skin allows them to receive it for free.

Since these people now think that everything should just be handed to them, whether they deserve it or not, they are under the assumption that they no longer have to work for anything because if you don't give in to their requests, they'll just start destroying things until you do. Unfortunately my opinion on the situation and many like mine, are one of the many opinions that is drowned out because I am white, so I am part of the problem. This is mainly since the government is supposedly ran by a racist white President, all white people are said to be the problem. It's really confusing when you think about it because on one side you have Senators telling these young adults that they've been oppressed by a racist government, so they can do as they please.

Then on the other side, you have people pushing the theory that they deserve everything without having to work for it simply because they're entitled to it. This is what comes with being uneducated and undisciplined, these young adults have no real idea what it takes to succeed in the real world because everything has been handed to them in one way or another and if it wasn't handed to them, they acted out in destructive ways until it was handed over to them. These undisciplined youths would have never lasted in the 80's and 90's, not with the discipline or accountability we grew up with.

Unfortunately, discipline has become a thing of the past, parents these days that do try to discipline their kids, only end up getting in trouble for it because people assume it's wrong to spank or yell at your children. It's the assumptive people like these people, who should be the ones held responsible for all this opinionated nonsense because these are the people that assume everything, including assuming that they have the right to tell you how to live and raise your own kids. They push their assumptive opinions on to anyone who will listen, this includes the young adults who they've convinced into thinking that, the only way they can get anything in life is to take it from the people that already worked hard to get it.

Like I said before though, these assumptive people out here lying and deceiving these young adults should be the ones held responsible. These people are the ones who have implanted their assumptive opinions into these young adults' minds, sending them on a destructive path. Thanks to thoughts and assumptions like these, all we are left with is unruly, undisciplined youths, who terrorize the streets, terrorize American citizens and destroy American communities all because they were told they could.

This is the assumptive world we now live in, people assume they know better then you or assume they have the right to tell others what they should think and believe. Although this is a very wrong way of thinking, they do it anyway and other people listen to them and act on their beliefs. It all really just leaves you wondering if this is seriously what's going on right now? People assuming everything, people instantly judging you by the color of your skin, people destroying everything in sight, people telling others how to live, it all just leaves you wondering, just what the hell is happening to our country?

The logic these people use makes no sense, the ideology these people follow makes no sense, everything about the way these people think and act makes no sense, yet, millions of people still follow these fallacious ideologies. With all the know-it-alls and nosey people we have today in America, for parents and people trying to do the right thing, it tends to become, you're damned if you do, but your also damned if you don't. You are damned by people who don't even know you, for disciplining your children so your kids behave and don't act out, but you're also damned by these same people if you don't discipline your kids for acting out.

Therefore, like I said before, you are damned if you do and damned if you don't. Another interesting little fact is that, did you know that moms are not at home as much as they used to be, moms are out working instead of being at home, which then forces the dad to become the stay at home parent. Except in minority communities because these kids' fathers tend not to be there, their specialty tends to be hit it and quit it and before you jump down my throat, just make sure you know that I make this statement because like we learned before, minority women have the highest recorded abortion rate.

These are facts, which are backed by data and statistics, these statistics are recorded yearly, but what's crazy is, every year these statistics show the same results, minority women have the highest rate of abortions in America. This newer generation of dads also don't have the patients for kids, this is why some of these kids are turning out to be self-entitled brats. It's because dad's can only deal with so much before they get annoyed, while mom's on the other hand, can deal with so much more. Haven't you ever heard the saying, "home is where the heart is" it's usually because home is wherever your mom is, but nowadays this very statement no longer holds true.

When you think about it, moms are at the center of our world, these are the women that we all look up to, the women that we all worship and the women that we would do anything for, but the moms of today, tend not to understand the concept of being a mom. The moms of today's generation, are too busy listening and learning how to be moms from other women or people, who are telling them how to live their lives or raise their kids. To me it is crazy because these are the very same women that are claiming that women are not respected enough, so to get the respect they deserve, all women should go out and work, instead of being at home moms.

Seriously, other women were blaming stay at home moms, for being the ones that are not empowering women, calling these moms traitors to women because they focused on being moms, instead of out their working. Moms should be allowed to stay at home with their children and not have to worry about work or proving themselves to other people, but what was once considered normal family values, is not considered the same family values today. The same ideology that has been used to destroy the American family, the feminists women use because according to them, if a woman is at home taking care of her kids, they are somehow doing an injustice to other women.

Therefore, a mom just being a mom is no longer allowed, these feminist women push their beliefs onto other women and force them to think the same way they do, which is that all women somehow need to be out working, instead of at home taking care of their family. It's all very interesting because these feminist women follow blm's ideology when it comes to having a normal family structure, according to these people; the family structure is toxic, no longer unacceptable and should be stopped.

This to me is just insane when you think about it because the family structure is not toxic, nor should it be considered toxic, but since most minorities have no family structure, they want to cancel the entire concept of family values. Seriously though, how can you claim that, since you do not have a normal family structure in your life or

122

community, the family structure should be labeled, `toxic`, but also be canceled entirely? Hateful opinions like these are what destroys our American values, but these are the hateful opinions that are being pushed by millions of people and like I stated in the title of this chapter, the hatred is pushed by the ignorant and followed by the ill-minded.

-- Chapter 3 --
Taking God out of everything
won't fix your problems!

I tend to blame all of this useless nonsense on the fact the we took God out of just about everything, thanks to the opinions of these atheists, non-believers and foreigners because these are the people who think they have a right to change our American history and beliefs to better suit them. We all come from different backgrounds, so we all need to chill out because Americans should not have to change our beliefs in God simply because you don't believe in him, you rather believe in some kind of Prophet. We now have numerous religion's that you can now claim and our God, is being replaced by these false Prophet's and crazy religious leaders, who personally believe they are their own Prophet's of God.

Unfortunately, these people are not Prophet's of God and most of them are only really in it for the money, yet these people are able to get hundreds of others to follow them and believe in the religious nonsense they spew. A religious cult leader, who believes he is a Prophet of God, is a dangerous and scary thing and you don't have to look very far in our past to see that. In the past, we have had numerous mass-suicides, committed by these cult leaders, from Heaven's Gate in California, to the Order of the Solar Temple in Switzerland and we all know about the most popular mass-suicide in history, which was the People's Temple Mass-Suicide in Jonestown.

This crazy religious cult leader, Jim Jones, was able to convince 917 people, from young to old, to literally kill themselves by drinking a cyanide laced potion all because Jim Jones didn't want people leaving or fleeing his religious camp. Since Americans took our almighty God out of our schools and everything else, all hell has broken loose and America is being thrown into turmoil, which we may never be able to recover from. Remember the old saying "In God We Trust," maybe we need to focus on getting back to that because the way people tend to act towards one another these days; it seems like everyone is out for themselves and their self-interests.

To me, it's interesting that people hate on Americans for supporting our American Flag and our American National Anthem, only to turn around and call us white racist and white supremacists, for supporting our own country. These of course are people from all over the world who hate America and now these movements give these people a chance to display that frustration, although they themselves, aren't even American. I saw the perfect quote for this statement the other day, it simply stated that, "Only in America, will the United States President, be harassed by the American government, illegal immigrants and foreigners, all for protecting the American People".

We witness this everyday in politics because you have dozens of people in office and foreign political groups from all around the world, going after President Trump because he supports our American history and traditional values. These so-called State officials are okay with people destroying monuments and stomping on our American flag because they claim it's all in the name of minority equality, seriously? Democrats, along with these State and city officials, were hired to represent the American people and protect our American ways of life.

How can these American representatives allow people to disrespect the American flag or try to erase our entire American history or culture? Then again, we've already seen how much democrats and Nancy Pelosi care about Americans or the men and women who fought and died for this country, democrats and Pelosi gave a folded American flag ceremony to George Floyd's family. A known long-time felon and criminal, who robbed and pistol whipped a pregnant woman, was given a military ceremony, a ceremony that's reserved for the men and women who laid their lives out for this country.

This is a ceremony that is reserved for the families that have lost their love ones due to someone else senseless war and you disrespect the ceremony, by holding the ceremony for a well-known criminal. This is the logic democrats use though, this is the ideology that democrats pass on to millions and they do this because they want minorities to think they are their saviors, they want minorities and others to think that they are the only ones that can put a stop to all this chaos. What people don't realize is that, democrats really do this because they want all Americans divided because that is how they stay in control of the American people.

The proof is in the making, democrats, led by Nancy Pelosi, took it upon themselves to reject the American Stimulus package, not once, not twice, but three times, before they would eventually pass the stimulus package to help out the American people. Most of these democrats, especially Nancy Pelosi, have been exposed time after time trying to pass off their hidden agendas in new legislation bills that they bring forth to Congress. Then, when their new bills or packages are rejected from Congress because these bills seem to be to outrageous to even pass or these bills seemed to only help out democrats, no one else.

This is also where they use the blame game because since their bills tend to be rejected, it's all President Trumps fault, not theirs for trying to pass ridiculous bills of legislature. There's a double edge sword to this though because Americans are getting in trouble for supporting America and our American traditions, but the people leading this charge, are the people who we elected to represent the American people. American's waving the American flag and showing support for the American national anthem or even God, are labeled racist because in today's society, if you support America, you are somehow supporting white supremacy and a racist white President.

It's interesting that when each new U.S. President is sworn in to the Oval Office, every single President puts their hands on the bible and swears to God on it. Each of these Presidents swear on the bible to our nation, one nation under God; that they will protect and serve the people, but also help defend the Constitution of the United States of America. Finally after every new U.S. President's speech, they complete it with, "and may God Bless America", but it's funny how each new U.S. President does this and swears to our almighty God, yet as a nation we have literally taken God out of everything.

The puzzling thing about all this is, the people that have tried and succeeded in taking God out of everything are mostly non-believer's, atheist's and foreigners, who are led by State officials, that could give a damn about America as a whole. These are usually the same people, who don't believe in our God, instead, they believe in some form of devil or they believe in an Islam Prophet, who only loves you, if you kill everyone who doesn't worship him or his teachings. This is the fearful teachings of this prophet, this false prophet would rather you kill everyone who is different then you are, then kill yourself and if you do both these things, you will show him you love him, but he'll also grant you 72 virgins.

Wasn't that what Hitler wanted to do all along though, kill everyone who got in his way of creating a one race world, so his race would be the dominant and inferior race, seems to me, Allah, is preaching the same thing. I've honestly never read anything he's supposedly written,

126

but just take a look at the news from the Middle East, it's nothing but war and poverty, these people are destroying cities left and right and leaving their citizens with nothing. Since these people are non-believers and don't believe in our God, they berate and belittle our God, but still turn around and want Americans to change our beliefs, to better suit their beliefs because if we don't, they claim they feel left out.

Seriously, some of these un-American people go on record to speak out and even have State Senators speaking out for them, claiming that these people feel left out because Americans won't celebrate their traditions and beliefs. It honestly makes no sense because it would be like Americans going over to China and telling the Chinese they need to change their traditions to better fit Americans, you'd probably end up in jail. Americans choose not to celebrate these people's religion or beliefs because their religion is focused on killing all American infidels, so seriously, why would Americans want to celebrate a tradition that aims to kill us and has killed thousands of Americans in the name of a Prophet?

These also tend to be the illegal immigrants and foreigners, who come over to America illegally from their country, to try to find a better life because their own country, is filled with war and poverty. The crazy thing is, these immigrants come over here and demand that Americans change our traditions and beliefs to suit them and if we don't change our beliefs, its discrimination against these immigrants. The sad thing about all of this is, we have State governors, mayors and senators, fighting for rights and freedoms for these immigrants, rather than fighting for the American people.

These State Senators and Governors, have no problem with giving foreigners and illegal immigrants anything they want, especially money that is supposed to be going or is owed to the American people. We currently see this going on with a New York State Senator, who thinks that illegal immigrants somehow deserve a handout of over $350 million dollars from the government. Yes, I said that correctly, State Senator AOC, asked the government to give illegal immigrants over $350 million dollars because she claims that illegal's deserve the help.

The people she often wants to help are the same illegal foreigners and immigrants, who don't want Americans praying to our God, don't want Americans celebrating our beliefs, but they do want Americans to be okay with them wanted to kill all American infidels. It's crazy

127

because these foreigners want us to be okay with them praying to Allah, a Muslim Prophet of God, who hates anyone who doesn't worship the Muslim or Islamic religion. The thing I always come back to is the fact that, he's the prophet that tells all Muslim and people of Islam that, you need to kill all the infidel's, the infidels meaning me and you, Americans.

We all know how it is over in Asia and the Middle East, Russia could also care less for Americans, Iraq and Iran, are basically just waiting to probably get their revenge from all the stuff we put them and their people through. Muslims and people of Islam, run most of the Middle East and according to these Muslims and Islamist, `Westerners`, which means `Americans`, are the foreign enemy and all must die or be killed off. These immigrants and foreigners are even taught from a very young age that Americans are the enemy, yet were supposed to accept these people.

It's crazy to me because these Muslim immigrants, come over to America, try to change our American culture to their foreign culture, but if Americans don't accept this change, we are somehow violating their foreign rights, seriously? Muslims, are prime examples when I talk about this because these people come over from war-torn, poverty-stricken countries, that support these radical ideologies of Jihad and follows the teachings of Allah, only to turn around and expect Americans to change our beliefs and traditions over to the same beliefs they ran from.

The reality is, these foreigners feel that they have more rights than Americans do and they've proven it. How many times have we seen the news stories about Muslims, who went after their next-door neighbors, who owned pig farms because these Muslims could smell the pigs and pork, is a no-no. These foreigners felt like they had the right to go after their next-door neighbors and try to force their neighbors to move or close down their pig farms that have been there for generations because Muslims can't have pork and can't be near pork.

Pig farms that have been family businesses for decades, are being forced to deal with backlash from Muslim people because these foreigners feel they have the right to demand that these people shut down these pig farms, they've owned for years. It's crazy when you think about it because no one has the right to tell other people what to do on their own property, but Muslims think they can and since they think they can, they go complain to the city council members or State Senators because their neighbors choose to ignore their stupid requests. We are honestly left dealing with these people because of Obama, Barack Obama told Americans we needed to accept these people.

He was the one who first forced Americans to change our beliefs and traditions d accept the new change because Obama was a self-proclaimed Muslim himself. These people don't believe in our God or American values, but these people also tend to seriously hate our God, yet they complain and protest that Americans should change our values to fit theirs, even though they think all Westerners are infidels and should be killed off. Last time I checked, that's what makes them foreigners and immigrants and us American citizens, we were born and raised here, you're here as a foreigner, you're the one that has to accept our American values because you are over in our country.

This honestly keeps me puzzled daily because these foreigners are literally trying to change our American heritage, our American traditions and even our American beliefs, yet they know if these people tried to do this in their country, they would laughed at. Their countries would not change its heritage or tradition to suit a foreigner, so the same ideology should apply here in America, Americans shouldn't have to change our heritage or our tradition to accept a religion that believes we are already the enemy.

It's also funny because some of these people are foreign immigrants, over here in America illegally or on an expired visa, still, these people feel as if they have more rights than Americans. Muslims and other foreigners need to accept our American beliefs, our American history and our American traditions and if you don't want to, you can always go back to your unhappy Islamic war-torn country, so we can enjoy our Western way of life. One of the crazy things to think about is the fact that, the religion of Islam, has started more religious wars than any other religion in the world, but we're not talking about face-to-face wars, we are talking about mass-terrorism, mass-bombings, mass suicides, it's never face-to-face.

The other crazy thing about their religion and how they convince people to become suicide bombers is, some of these suicide bombers are mostly Muslim females, who usually had no choice in the matter because Islamic women are often forced to be suicide bombers after being convicted of some idiotic crime. Muslim and Islamic woman, are

129

stoned alive, beheaded alive and even burned alive, for crimes that would be considered minor in the United States, but some of these convictions wouldn't even be considered a crime in America. This is why I am always puzzled by State Senator Ilhan Omar and what she does as a State Senator.

She should be fighting for equality for Islam and Muslim women, let alone American women because that's what she was hired to do, instead she praises the Taliban and tells Americans that we should accept al-Qaida. In addition, you can correct me if I am wrong but, people who practice Islam have started more religious riots and wars in the name of Allah and Jihad, more than any other organization in the world, but they have also committed more mass-killings against others, than any other religion in the world. When it comes to religion and the role it plays in today's society, if I simply asked you what religious group has caused the most mass-bombings, mass-terrorism and mass-suicides for a God, but also their religion, the answer would be Islam.

Religious wars were fought centuries ago over Christianity, we've seen examples of this from reading about the rise and fall of the Roman Empire because the Roman Empire was thrust into religious war after religious war, all because they chose Christianity as their religion. The Romans got rid of Mithraism, a roman mystery religion that, was centered around the God, Mithras and took on Christianity as their religion, which made many other world leaders, very angry. Now within these God forsaken lands we call the Middle East, it's all about Allah, the Islamic rule and their propaganda of a one race world, where infidels, hence Americans, don't exist and are to be extinguished.

Over in the Middle East, North Korea and maybe even some parts of Asia, Americans are literally considered infidels, bad people teaching Western Propaganda and to these people, all Americans are unruly, untamed animals that are to be killed off. That's the crazy thing about Muslim and Islamic followers and believers in America, these foreigners come over to America, take part in enjoying our freedoms, only to turn around and demand Americans change our ways of life to better suit theirs.

Our God, is offensive to them because they prey to another Prophet, but these people complain to civil rights leaders that they feel left out because Americans celebrate our God, instead of theirs. The sensitivity of America has become so mind-boggling it's pathetic, millions of people have become sensitive to everything, now even YouTube, won't show blood of any kind because they assume it's too offensive to kids, like these kids haven't seen anything worse.

These foreigners are the same way though, they leave their own war-torn countries, countries that are filled with chaos, poverty and turmoil, then come over to America and instead of just accepting our way of life, these foreigners try to change our American faith because these foreigners are sensitive to our way of life. In reality, they are simply trying to change our American history, change our American traditions and change our American beliefs because like young kids that were raised on hate, these foreigners were raised from a young age to hate Americans.

I watched an interview where a South Korean wrote a book about the experiences she had in North Korea and in one statement she claimed that, "in North Korean schools, all Americans are the bad guys, all Americans are the enemy". Certain foreigners grow up hating Americans just like the people over here in America, due to this hatred, they try to change our culture. Let's also be clear, this doesn't account for all foreigners, there are legal foreigners over here in America, who appreciate their freedoms and rights and they, along with thousands more, are happy with their American dream and American way of life.

Freedom of religion, was an Amendment passed so all people, of all races in America, can practice religion freely, without any interference from anyone, so you cannot force your religion onto someone, who doesn't accept it because people have that right. This amendment gives a voice to all religions, but also gives people the right to choose what faith they believe in, but also what faith they want to follow, you don't make that choice for them. As if this wasn't clear enough, you can also learn about religious separation by looking up your history. In addition, the governments passing of, "Separation of Church and State" because you will see that people have the right to follow whatever religion they want too and don't have to conform to any religion.

Americans accept everyone, of every faith, even if your faith tells you to kill Americans, we still accept you for who you are, but don't try to stop Americans from praying to our God, definitely when you are praying to a Prophet, whose sole purpose is to kill and dismember anyone who doesn't conform to what he preaches. Plus, for a religion, no offense, it's just a terrible one to follow, you basically are following a Prophet, who teaches you too hate everyone that is not the same as you, but also kill anyone who says anything bad about him. If you do these horrible things to other people for him, then you will show your love and appreciation for him.

Don't mention the fact that, if you are stupid enough to be a suicide-bomber that kills yourself in his name, you are stupid enough to believe that when you die, you have 72 virgins waiting to please you in heaven. The thing that gets me about the 72 virgin's conspiracy though is the fact that, these people treat their woman like complete dirt, they keep Muslim women covered up, so why would 72 virgins be a good thing to these people? What most people don't realize is that, before Islamic rule took over, Muslim women lived normal lives, these women weren't subject to scrutiny 24/7, but they were able to wear the clothes they wanted to and do, as they wanted to.

In the Islamic practice, these men are taught to mistreat and abuse their women, women to these men, are nothing but child bearers, who are to be kept fully clothed and covered up, so the only thing that's seen is their eyes. Do I need to remind you that this is also a religion where the women and convicted foreigners are burned alive, stoned alive, buried alive, beheaded alive, literally killed or beheaded, for practically any reason, while the rest have the unfortunate job of being suicide bombers. I honestly believe that this is not a God or Prophet you should worship or even follow, no God should be teaching you that much hate, but also no God or so-called Prophet, should ask you to kill yourself to prove your loyalty and love for him.

I say this because if you have looked at the teachings of Allah and the dealings of the Islamic people that follow him, you will see that foreigners and enemies, who are caught by these people are instantly beheaded because these people simply don't believe in his teachings. People who don't believe in their Islamic faith, are called traitors and foreigners to their people and their lands and it gets worse if you offend these people in any way because they don't talk to you, they rather just bury you alive or simply line you up and behead you.

A crazy religion none the less, but Americans don't actually stop these people from worshipping or praying to Allah, so these Muslims need to stop trying to tell Americans we are violating their civil rights, when we choose not to celebrate their beliefs. Seriously, this leaves me confused especially when these beliefs tends to be focused on killing

132

Americans, but also destroying our American Westerners way of life. Loving and worshipping our God, should not be seen as a crime, nor should it be looked upon as a bad thing in any way, but it's crazy because in today's America, our American traditions and beliefs, are slowly being torn apart by these people and millions more.

We need to go back to loving our God and treating him the way he should be treated, you don't have to go to church to have faith in God, you just have to believe in having a purpose in life and that God has a purpose for you. Therefore, we need to put God back into our unbalanced, undisciplined schools and back into our traditions and beliefs and we need to stop trying to cater to everyone's feelings. We've tried the other way, we keep going backwards and keep having to deal with complaints about God and our American way of life.

Basically were being told to bend to these un-American, non-believers, who have no faith in our God, don't share our beliefs, but want Americans to be okay with these people trying to change our way of life. With people constantly killing others, homeless taking over, constant school-shootings, mass-terrorism and now a deadly virus that has infected millions, but also somehow can't be contained, I don't know if we can handle anymore, but we are going to need some serious faith to get us through these crazy times. I say this because you don't necessarily have to be a church person to have faith and believe in God, the almighty above, it's more of a feeling, but also just believing you have a purpose in life.

People think they have to attend church every Sunday or get on your knees and pray to receive the lords embrace, in reality, God is always with you, it's just a matter of having faith. You have to also realize that, the American church system, is not a place of faith because these churches have become corrupt money systems for preachers and pastors, that will allow you to pray to God, but only if you donate to them first. Like the State lotto, churches are corrupt money making machines, that focus on making money off of the American people, their just worse because pastors and preachers tell you to donate to their cause, then you will receive God's prayer.

Foreigners also tend to use their religion as an excuse, these foreigners come over from other poverished countries and enjoy being in a free nation, yet they still demand that Americans change our values, traditions and beliefs. It's crazy because it doesn't just stop with

133

American beliefs and traditions, these foreigners and immigrants have joined in on the movement of blaming police officers for killing their people. Now, all immigrants, foreigners, illegal immigrants or otherwise, living in America, have come forward to claim that they are also victims of major police brutality.

Let me also say this before we continue, for those of you who think there is a police brutality pandemic going on in America, just stop already because when it comes to police killing minorities and immigrants, there is not a police pandemic occurring. We can even look at the facts or what we've already discussed because the facts are, in 2019, police officers shot and killed 14 minorities and 27 white Americans. So this means that out of the over 7,600 minorities that were killed in 2019, 14 minorities, were shot and killed by police officers, while over 7,400 minorities were shot and killed by their own.

So seriously, ask yourself, is there really a police brutality pandemic occurring against minorities in America? Something that is true and concerning about this is, 14 minorities were shot and killed by police, which just so happens to add up to the same amount of children and teens that were murdered in one weekend, in one city in America. Children and teens, are being innocently gunned down or killed by stray bullets, in these crime and gang infested communities, shot and killed by their own.

Let me say that again so you heard me correctly, in 2019, there was an estimated 14 minorities, who were shot and killed by police, while over 7,400 minorities were shot and killed by their very own people. There is no evidence of police brutality, the media's narrative is to push police brutality because that's what they are told to push, but they are only calling it a pandemic because minorities are being killed at an alarming rate and they need someone to blame this on. The reality is, these people use the blame game just like everyone else, the media will lie and deceive you into thinking, what they've been told you need to think, they create news stories that are aimed towards people that they want to deceive because deception is the key.

This is why the blm movement has gained so much notoriety, the media has helped blm leaders push their false propaganda to the American people, even yahoo has got into the action because now they have a blm tab at the top of the page. Honestly, if it wasn't for the medias help, and the media fanning the flames, the blm movement

134

would not even be a movement, they would have never gotten their feet off the ground because think about it, their basic principals are based on the fact that, all white people are bad and should be erased.

We've already discussed before how these blm Marxists leaders are demanding that every white American living today, hand over everything we've worked hard for, over to minorities because these blm leaders claim these things were handed to white people simply because the color of our skin. The statements coming from these blm Marxists leaders could be considered racist to its core, they are literally demanding that all white Americans give up everything they own and will own in the future because all white Americans got it all through white privilege.

It's worse now because minorities, led by these blm Marxists leaders, are literally screaming racist chants at white Americans, tearing them down and calling them every racist name in the book because white people won't give in to their ridiculous demands. It honestly makes no sense to me, if these blm leaders and their followers are not demanding that white people give up their safety and security, but also their homes and communities, they are berating white people for being white supremacists and the ones responsible for supposedly oppressing all minorities. Seriously, how is this advocating for racial equality though, how does berating other people solve the problem of thousands of minorities dying in urban communities, how does demanding white people to give things up, better the lives of minorities?

I honestly don't think it does, in fact, I think it hurts minorities because instead of building up communities, minorities are rioting and destroying communities, looting grocery stores, but also burning down minority owned businesses, so I honestly don't think these destructive and chaotic methods, are really helping out minorities. If you were really fighting for racial equality or bettering the lives of minorities, you would be going into urban communities and getting rid of drugs and gangs. You'd be in urban communities trying to stop all these robberies and killings, you would also be in these communities helping kids focus on an education, you wouldn't be going into white communities, demanding that white people hand everything over.

When you think about it, these blm Marxists leaders, are the racist ones, they complain about groups like the KKK and others, only to turn around and show support for the Black Panthers, an organization built on the principal of taking over the world and ridding America of white people. You've seen occurrences of this on television daily, white Americans are having our history destroyed and dismantled by these blm Marxists leaders because their opinion is that everything white, is racist, but also represents white supremacy.

Therefore, since our entire American culture is supposedly built by racist white supremacist men, it needs to be erased and changed to better fit their idea and opinion of America. The logic they use makes no sense, their claims are based entirely on racism, it's the same idiotic logic used by San Francisco City Council members because these idiots are changing a school named after Abraham Lincoln, claiming that he did nothing for minorities. Like I said before, I couldn't make this stuff up even if I tried to, these people are just so stupid, it's pathetic, but you can see that it's also false propaganda that they tend to be pushing.

We all know President Abraham Lincoln didn't own slaves, but also represented North America in the Civil war to free all slaves, but according to these morons in San Francisco, President Abraham Lincoln, did nothing for minorities, so the school's name needs to be change. I honestly fail to understand why people would be making statements like these, especially when they know for certain that, President Abraham Lincoln, was the reason why minorities were freed, but also the reason why the Civil War was started.

It's just another baseless lie that these people push because they already deceived millions into thinking that the government and white people are oppressing them, so it doesn't take to much more to trick these people into believing that President Lincoln was the problem. It's kind of overwhelming and puzzling at the same time because these blm leaders and their millions of followers, have no problem claiming that all white people living today, including white children and teens, are responsible for slavery. Not only are we somehow responsible for the enslavement of minorities, since the color of our skin is white, were also responsible for spreading white supremacy.

The crazy thing about these blm leaders and the statements they make, is the fact that, most of the statements they are making, are all about white people giving up their homes and their financial security because minorities can't seem to get that on their own and white people only got it through their white privilege. So the house that you worked so hard to pay for over the past ten or so years, the security blanket that you created for your family, the safe community that you fought hard to protect, is somehow a privilege to these blm idiots and they want you to hand it all over to them. One of the things that makes me laugh about these blm Marxists leaders is the fact that, these idiots blame white people for moving into their communities and making them better, like that is somehow a bad thing.

We know for certain that minorities destroy their own communities because we've seen this occur for the past few decades, minority communities are often riddled with drugs and crime because no one cares about the real problem plaguing these communities, instead they blame other people, in other communities. The balls on these people have to be huge, although blm is led by women, there is so much racism being spread by these blm Marxists leaders, its freaking pathetic because they are the ones that claim to be doing it for equality.

But, like I've said many times before, I honestly don't think burning down numerous communities, burning down numerous minority owned businesses, but also killing innocent minorities, shows your advocating for racial equality. This is the mindset of blm Marxists leader's though, it's all about making their race superior to the white race, they think it's somehow a privilege for you to live in a nice house, that's in a nice neighborhood, doesn't matter that it may have taken you decades of hard work to get it. To me, it honestly sounds like a bunch of babies, crying over toys they can't have because their parents could never afford them.

Even something as simple as parents buying Christmas toys for their own children, is now being scrutinized. Parents that can't afford nice toys, are complaining and asking other parents to only buy their kids small amounts of toys because they can't afford to give them the Christmas, other parents can afford to. Seriously, people were complaining that other parents needed to buy their kids less toys because other people can't afford as much as they can, so their kids feel left out. Honestly, sensitivity has turned our nation into a bunch of whiny bi***es.

However, parents have no right to tell other parents not to spoil their kids on Christmas because you are too lazy to work so you can buy your kids toys, but this is the problem we have in America. People think they can tell other people what to do and how to live and if they don't agree with it, these people have no problem complaining or protesting about it. This is why the blm movement makes no sense at all, they are not fighting for minority equality, they are not fighting for minority justice, they are fighting to better their own lives, no one else.

I say this because I want you to think about something, honestly, stop and think about this for a second. There is a problem with minority profiling, there is a problem with minorities being profiled or judged simply by the color of their skin, but these are not the issues that these blm leaders are advocating for. Instead, these blm leaders want what the white man has, they don't want to work for it, they don't want to earn it, the white man has it and since the white man has it, these blm leaders want it. This is why issues like minority racial profiling, are pushed aside and ignored, but people need to realize is that, minorities are profiled more because minorities are the ones that are perceived to be more of a threat, when it comes to police encounters.

This is not because all minorities are dangerous, but because minorities are the ones that are seen to be more violent and threatening during police encounters. You have to also look at the facts because as we've discussed before, minorities account for more than half the crime committed in America. Now, before you say I am wrong, there are facts to what I am saying, go ahead and look up the crime statistics for America, you'll find that, although minorities only make up 14% of the population, they commit more than half the crime in America.

This is proof right here, why minorities are profiled more than anyone else because they are seen as the ones that cause more trouble when encountering police, not because the color of their skin, but because their character proves they tend to be more trouble than other people. As I said before though, this doesn't apply to all minorities, but a vast majority of them because this characteristic has been seen coming from minorities for generations. Minorities, are known to give police more of a problem when they are stopper or questioned, minorities are known to rob people when they walk into stores, this is not a white characteristic, this is a minority characteristic, that has been portrayed in the minority community for decades.

People can say what they want, but this is the reason why minorities are more involved with police, their character tells them that they should be watched, not because they are bad people, but because it's been proven time and time before, that they tend to be the people that start trouble. Then you always have those people, especially blm and their followers, complaining about being stopped by police more, yet they ignore the fact that they may have just committed a crime and are being questioned about it.

Change this perception and you change minority police profiling, but you can't change this perception by blaming someone else simply because they live a better life then you. People need to look in the mirror and figure out that the problem is not the police, it's not white people, it's the person staring at you in the mirror. The good thing is that, we are finally starting to see Americans, like myself, white Americans, minorities and even legal foreigners, ignoring the politics of blm and speaking the truth about who these people really represent. These Americans, have stepped out into the forefront and have exposed these blm leaders and their followers, for who they truly are.

Yes, black lives matter, but so does, white lives, Asian lives, Mexican lives, Filipino lives, Hispanic lives, Brazilian lives, South American lives, Canadian lives, European lives and even foreign lives. All lives matters, not just yours. These American speakers of truth are out there trying to spread the word of peace and unity, trying to get Americans to wake up and stop letting these ignorant people destroy our history or our culture. The main solution to the problem is for people to stop blaming everything on race or on other people; Americans need to start uniting more because all Americans bleed red, white and blue and if we don't unite, the people in charge will succeed at destroying America, seeing that they already started to.

The sad thing about Americans uniting is, uniting itself, is not what leftists and democrats want Americans to do, they want Americans divided and we've seen them push this narrative daily with their media platforms. It was the white cop, it was the white couple, it was the white bartender, it was the white protestors, these media outlets focus on pushing this narrative because this is the narrative that they've been told to push. In reality, the truth is very different then what they are claiming, the facts prove it.

It was three police officers, not all white, that pinned George Floyd to the ground, it was the white couple, who grabbed guns to protect themselves, after hundreds of protestors broke down their closed front Iron Gate. It was the white bartender, who shot a minority protester, after the minority protester jumped on his back, not once, but twice. These are the real headlines, these are the real facts about each of these incidents, but seeing that the facts and even the truth are something that these people tend to ignore, they change headlines to better fit their racial narrative.

Keeping with their narrative, no matter what the truth is, they'll change it, these people don't care if you know they've changed it either, they will still push their false articles and information, as long as the people will read it. This is also how these people in charge are able to push their false propaganda to people, they control the media airwaves and even the online media platforms, so they only show Americans what they want us to see and only tell Americans what they want us to hear. No one is united anymore; white people can't even unite anymore because if they do, they are seen as white people forming a white supremacist group.

Before, Americans would unite in times of need, unite when there was a national crisis or disaster, Americans would all stop to unite, but now, Americans could care less for each other. We say it's, `we the people`, but no one seems to think that way anymore, it seems like everyone is out for themselves and could care less about anyone or anything, unless of course it benefits them. This is also where the blame game takes hold of people, since they easily blame other people for their own problems, they have no problem only doing what benefits themselves. However, like I stated before, we all need to stop blaming our own problems on other people or other races, definitely minorities and yes I said it.

Minorities, not all, but minorities, are the worse when it comes to playing the race blame game, although they'll tell you otherwise. Minorities, are the only ethnicity group in America that will commit more racism and discrimination towards other people, especially white Americans, only to turn around and blame their racism and their racist act's, on other people, mainly white people because they have so-called White Privilege. Like I've stated before though, there is no white privilege, I'm white and I've worked for everything I've ever had, so has my parents, but there is the rich and privilege.

This also pertains to minorities too because don't discount the minorities, who themselves are millionaires and billionaires, living in the United States of America, that have more privilege then most white people. Let's be clear here, no matter what your opinion is, no matter what you've been told to think or believe, there is no such thing as white privilege. It is not a privilege to live in a nice house, it's not a privilege to live in a nice community, it's a right that these people deserve after years of hard work, years of working full time jobs, so they can make sure their families have a safe place to live in.

People can't just claim that it's all due to white privilege either, white Americans tend to have better houses, better cars or better lives, then minorities do because they tend to focus more on investments and hard work, this is not a privilege. The sad thing is, minorities also live in these so-called white privileged safe and secure neighborhoods and they choose to do this because to real Americans it's not a white neighborhood, it's a safe neighborhood that they can raise their families in. I say it's sad because the minorities that rather work for a better life, rather than complain for one, are now being labeled uncle toms and called sell outs for wanting a better life for their families.

This is because they live in these white privileged, safe and secure neighborhoods, instead of urban communities, so they are somehow sellouts to other minorities for doing this. This is also why the blm movement has lost so much traction with people, these blm Marxists leaders, are coming after white people for their homes and their jobs. Basically their entire lives, demanding that white people hand it all over to minorities, not asking, demanding. At first the concept of blm was accepted, millions of people were all in the agreement that minorities are often dying at a higher rate than other races.

Minorities also do lack an education and minorities do live in drug and crime infested communities, but the status quo changed when these blm rioters started going into communities and trying to destroy the lives of other white people simply because they claimed they lived more comfortable lives. These blm Marxists leaders lost Americans when they started demanding that all white people give up their homes, but also their fortunes and any further inheritance that they may acquire. To blm and their followers it's no longer about equality, it's about world domination.

Before you say I am wrong and write me off, just remember, blm Marxists leaders and their followers, are demanding that every single minority living in America, stop shopping at white owned businesses and grocery stores. Not only are minorities to instantly stop shopping at any so-called white owned store or company, minorities are also to further only support minorities and minority owned businesses, nothing else. Blm leaders have even went as far to claim that white people's lives don't matter, literally making these statements, yet, if white people did this, they would already be castrated and label racist, it's always a double standard.

If any white State Senator made this statement or even the U.S. President made a statement like this, they would be called racist, but since these blm Marxists leaders and their followers, are making the statement, it's accepted and okay. The black lives matter movement was never really about racial equality or fighting for racial justice for minorities, they want their race to have world domination and just like democrats, these people will do anything in their power to get it. These blm Marxists leaders, have proved this time and time again, they constantly focus on what advances their own agenda.

Like what many State politicians have done, they make statements and make bold claims, that are supposed to be for the betterment of their people, yet, they really only do it to better their lives and focus on their agenda of their new America. Besides, if these movements were really about racial justice, explain to me why, within the same week of these destructive blm protests that were being held for racial equality and racial justice, there were more innocent minorities killed by other minorities then there were by police officers? Seriously because you can't say this isn't true, we've seen it on television and seen the local news stories about the innocent minorities that were being killed at these riots and protests.

During just one of these protests, an innocent young minority girl was shot and killed because minority armed militants decided to shoot up the car they were riding in, after the mom was trying to get around their homemade makeshift barricade. Shouldn't this be concerning to blm and their followers, shouldn't this be something these blm Marxists leaders and their followers, are fighting against because armed minority men, took it upon themselves to shoot at a car filled with minority women simply because the mom tried to drive around their barricade.

The sad thing is, this is only one incident, there are dozens of more incidents just like this one, occurring at these riots and protests, where innocent minorities are being shot and killed by other minorities. No one, especially these blm Marxists leaders, wants to protest or talk about these innocent murders, they rather burn everything down and protest for criminals. However, this just leaves you puzzled because it's not white Americans committing these drive by's, it's not white Americans killing these innocent minorities, it's not white Americans behind all these shootings, its minorities.

The crazy thing about these so-called peaceful protests for minority justice is that, they don't make any sense because people are protesting and rioting for minority justice because their people are dying at an alarming rate, but they are the ones responsible for all the death occurring, not the people they are blaming. So protesting and rioting for minority justice, when you are blaming white people, especially white police officers for killing off your people, makes no sense at all. Definitely when you are destroying urban communities and burning down minority owned businesses in the process.

In addition, the proof is in the making, the facts and the truth are spread right out in front of Americans every day because every day in American cities, hundreds of minorities are either robbed, shot or killed by other minorities, this occurs every single day. Seriously, you can even look at this by examining the fact that we talked about before, where we discussed that there were at most, 14 minorities, who were shot and killed by police officers in 2019, yet in 2019, over 7,400 minorities were murdered by their own people.

These facts don't matter though, the truth doesn't even matter, blm Marxists leaders and their followers, ignore these facts and blame all the alarming death on police officers because police are the ones who are responsible for killing off their people, not the minorities shooting and robbing people daily. Let's forget about the killing for a second though and talk about what else these blm Marxists leaders won't, which is how minorities, are the ones who are responsible for the separation and division that is caused in America. Think of it this way, only in America can minorities have their own awareness month, their own minority only holiday's, their own minority only colleges and schools, their own minority only television channels and shows.

Doesn't stop there though, they also have their own minority only radio stations, their own minority only dating sites, their own minority only clubs and bars, but still turn around and blame white people for the division and separation. This is also where I fail to realize the concept of how one race is allowed to celebrate their heritage and tradition, while other races are not allowed to because their heritage is

143

somehow offensive to other people. Minorities celebrate their differences and embrace each other in minority only groups and this is fine because they're celebrating their heritage, but if white Americans celebrate their heritage, especially there Southern heritage and embrace each other in groups, it's considered racist and needs to be stopped.

Not only are white Southern Americans, not able to celebrate their own heritage, now the flag that they all love, the flag that was designed to represent fallen Americans, the Confederate flag has been labeled racist and needs to be taken down from all locations. The useless New York State Governor, even got in on this disgrace to the flag, the New York State Governor chose to ban the Confederate flag from anywhere and everywhere because it's his opinion that the Confederate flag, only represents slavery and racism.

In addition, if you haven't already realized, a lot of the excuses these people use, State politicians, blm Marxists leaders, democrats and their followers, they all use the same excuse, they want to destroy Americans symbols because all these American symbols represent nothing but slavery. This is the excuse used by millions of people, since it's the excuse that is used by millions of people, these excuses soon turn into millions of people's opinions and soon these opinions are enacted into laws by State Senators. This very concept was used by the New York State Governor because the Confederate flag is something that Southern Americans use to celebrate their heritage, to them it's not a symbol of racism.

Since millions of minorities claim the Confederate flag is racist, the New York State Governor takes it upon himself to ban it from the entire State. This is the same State Governor who told the people he would not get a covid-19 vaccination shot because he doesn't want people to judge him. As the State Governor, wouldn't you want to get the shot to show your people that they should not be scared of the vaccination shot? Besides, I don't think one shot would likely change the entire world, but since this idiotic Governor does, he blames not getting a vaccination shot on, not wanting the people to judge him.

The sad thing is, millions of people think like him, millions of people think this way, they think they can do whatever or say whatever they want, no matter if the people agree with them or not. The truth is something they know nothing of, the facts they distort into lies so it better fits their narrative. You don't have to take my word for it either, you can easily turn on your television and see it for yourself, minorities, led by these blm Marxists leaders, have come to the conclusion that they can talk crap about anyone and any race they want, while others can't.

It's become scary to even walk down the street because if people don't give in to these minorities' demands or if people have a different opinion then theirs, they'll literally attack you or just have you arrested for a hate crime. We've seen some of these horrible attacks occur in America several times, where we've witnessed innocent white Americans walking alone in grocery stores and minorities coming up from behind and sucker punching them or attacking them. The sad thing is, millions of minorities are okay with this behavior geared towards innocent white people, hundreds of minorities have even cheered these people on after they've committed these horrible attacks against innocent white people.

It's crazy to think of because these people have the opinion that, all white people are bad and because all white people are bad, innocent white Americans, usually the ones that can't defend themselves, are being attacked and sucker punched by minorities. What's really sad is the fact that, most of these assaults that have occurred, the white victims were doing absolutely nothing wrong that warranted the attack, they were simply attacked for being white. Seriously, these white people were attacked because they were white, each minority walked up to these people from behind and sucker punched them, not because they did something to them, but because the color of their skin was white.

It honestly makes no sense at all, just like it makes no sense how, no one can have a different opinion then someone else, it's seems you either have to be one way or the other, no one can have a different opinion then others. If white Americans or anyone for that matter, has a different opinion then democrats, blm and their followers, you are considered the racist one, but also a creator of white supremacy because you supposedly hate all minorities.

That's another thing that gets me, these blm Marxists leaders, are calling for racial equality, but they are destroying anything white or related to the color white because it's their opinion that, America needs to get rid of everything that represents "whiteness" because it's racist to minorities. However, isn't trying to get rid of an entire culture and history because you claim that it's offensive, racist itself? I honestly would think so, you are literally trying to destroy and remove an entire culture, based upon a racist opinion. The American culture, the culture that this country was found and built on, you are trying to erase and rewrite because you claim its offensive to you.

However, ask yourself, how is canceling someone's culture and heritage, fighting or protesting for racial equality? How is canceling and rewriting American history to replace it with your own version of history, advocating for racial equality? It honestly isn't a way to advocate or fight for anything, but it's just another hidden agenda coming from these people that want to change everything about America. These people want to erase our entire history and culture because these people claim it's all built based on white supremacy, but also by white supremacist men.

This is often why we've seen people fighting to take down our American national monuments and statues, but also why some people, are instantly destroying national State parks and even disgracing our fallen heroes' graves because they claim everything related to the color white, is offensive or racist to them. These people, are all just mind-less idiots because these national monuments and statues, are there for a reason, there dedicated to the people who dedicated their lives to influence a nation, but also dedicated to the people that fought to make sure every American living today would be able to enjoy the ability of being free.

These American national monuments and statues, do not represent racism, nor do they represent racist men, they represent American freedoms and values that were instilled by these people. People always forget, if it wasn't for these so-called racist white people, we would not be where we are today, they all helped in the advancement of America. Then again, this seems to be where these blm Marxists leaders opinions matter more than others because these people don't care about history, they don't care about the brave men and women that came before them, their opinion is that if they were white, they were all racist white supremacist, who did nothing for minorities or the minority community.

This is what tends to make you ignore these blm members and their movements because it's never fully about minority equality or justice, it's more about them wanting to be more dominant and inferior then other people, especially white people. We've talked about this a lot in the book because this is what blm's narrative is, it's all about trying to get white people to relinquish this so-called white control, but in reality, it's the people behind the scenes, that have the power and the full control.

This is the narrative and the agenda that these blm Marxists leaders need to push though, pushing this theory of white people being the racist ones, helps them convince their followers into thinking that all white people are to blame. We've seen the outcome when people hate others for the color of their skin, we've witnessed the hatred these theories portray onto other white people. You can clearly tell that these blm Marxists leaders and their followers, want all white Americans to suffer, just from the statements that they make.

It's crazy because these people demand that you lose your homes, lose your cars and even lose your community all because you have it and they don't. These people could care less that it may have taken you up to ten years to finally be able to provide a safe and secure home for your family, but they also could care less about you and your family having a house to live in or a roof over your head because were white, so this means were privileged. It's kind of like we as white people can't win, on one side, we have people coming after us because our skin color is white and on the other side, we have people coming after us because they claim were responsible for the crappy communities they live in.

Since these people feel that we are responsible, even for the alarming death rate of minorities, we should be the ones to suffer and hand everything over to minorities. They want us to do all of this although facts have proven that minorities, are the ones who are really responsible for the damage caused to urban communities. You can also see this opinion pop up when you look at the demands that come from these blm leader's, they want white Americans to give up everything, these people are too lazy to get a job, are to uneducated to have a career and are always looking for a handout.

I always refer to the alarming rate of death occurring to minorities because this one statistic, this one fact, is something that is ignored by millions, but the problem is not knowing whose causing it, the problem is these people going after other people who are not responsible for it. It's the same thing with the democrats, they blame the gun for the mass-murder, not the actual shooter, the one who pulled the trigger. There is a pandemic though, there's a huge minorities killing minorities pandemic because minorities are killing each other at a substantially alarming rate, but this is also occurring on a daily basis.

Just the other day in the Bronx, some poor innocent minority father walking home with his daughter, was shot and killed in broad daylight, after a gunman pulled up beside him and shot him straight in the head. This guy's daughter was walking with him, while holding his hand, yet these individuals didn't care one bit as they slowly pulled up beside him and shot him directly in the head. This happened in broad daylight, in a mostly minority area, in front of everyone, this is the problem we should be going after, this is the problem that is plaguing urban communities, not white people living in nice communities with low or no, crime at all.

The route to minority justice, which way is it again because I've seemed to have lost directions? Racism; the definition that explains it is, a prejudice, discrimination, or antagonism directed against a person or people on the basis of their membership of a particular race or ethnic group. This is exactly how blm and their followers, are treating white people all across the United States of America, these people are literally wishing harm and famine on an entire race, while at the same time claiming it's because they want racial justice and equality. It's their opinion really and it's all based on the assumption that our ancestors were nothing but white supremacist slave owners, who profited off slavery.

What most minorities tend to ignore, especially these blm Marxists, is the fact that, there were numerous minority property and slave owners that fought for the South because they didn't want slavery to end. It's sad because blm leaders and even minority State politicians, will go on television and berate white Americans, telling white Americans that we somehow owe them something, while they force all their ridiculous demands down our throats because they claim it's for racial equality.

In reality, everything these people are demanding, forces white people to give up what they've worked so hard for and simply turn around and give it to people, who don't actually deserve it, but want it because white people have it. Blm and their followers, are often seen committing racism or hate crimes against white American's and others daily, but that is not news, minorities attacking innocent white people, is not news, white Americans yelling racial slurs, while they raise their fist towards minorities, is news. Remember the narrative and agenda we talked about, this continues here and continues to be the downfall of Americans because we give these people the attention they seek.

What's worse is, if these people don't get their way, they destroy things, until we give them their way. I don't need to mention the white American couple, who kissed the boot of a supposed minority militant priest, who I think also claimed to be some kind of prophet because this white American couple had so-called white guilt and felt guilty for being white. No, you are not guilty of anything, you are white, that's all, you may be guilty for being stupid for kissing the boot of someone else, but you owed that militant priest nothing. You should probably make sure you brush your teeth 3 or 4 times a day, you know, to get that disgusting white guilt taste out your mouth.

The downfall of America, has already become evident because white Americans are getting in trouble for simply being white, the color of our skin is making people instantly judge us, but we are also getting in trouble for simply trying to protect our safety, our values and even our hard worked for way of life. To most minorities, mostly these blm Marxists leaders and their followers, white Americans represent nothing but white supremacy, therefore every white person living today, is responsible for the oppression of minorities simply because the color of our skin.

It's the pure definition of racism though, these people are literally attacking an entire race, but also berating and belittling, an entire race all because these people want to be inferior to white people, that's racism at its core. The crazy thing to think about and what's even more overwhelming to think about is that, the truth is long gone, what the media prints, has become the truth and these people only care about pushing their narrative. We see it daily on our local news, there are speaker's, democrats, blm leader's, minority State senators, white State senators, just about everybody, speaking these days, on what they see as the truth, what they belief is the truth, but their truth is what they created in their head and not the actual history that's occurred.

The one that seem to get me the most are all theses speakers trying to say that, "black on black crime isn't the problem to minorities, its police officers and police brutality". Where's your proof though?

149

Where is the evidence that proves you can honestly make this statement, especially when we discussed that there were only 14 minorities killed by police in 2019, compared to the over 7,400, that were murdered by their own people?

These people never show you the truth or the real data and statistics because that doesn't follow their agenda, that doesn't help them push their narrative. I've done study after to study for this book and all statistics and data reviews all showed the same obvious results, white people kill more white people, minorities kill more minorities, basically every single race, is their own worst enemy. There does show a level of police brutality against all races that we should probably be concerned with, but there is no police brutality pandemic going on in America. Contrary to what these people want you to believe, police officers are not out killing off minorities, this simply is not happening.

Minorities, are killing more minorities, than any other race in America, although there might be police brutality, police officers, are not to blame for all the death and turmoil occurring in minority communities and neighborhoods. This is what I cannot stress enough because minorities are not robbing and killing people, because of police brutality, minority gang members are not shooting at each other, because of police brutality and minorities are not selling drugs and killing people, because of police brutality. So seriously, how can you blame all the crime and violence occurring in these minority communities on police brutality?

This is where I get lost and confused when it comes to what minorities are claiming because we all know, minorities are the ones responsible for the crime, the violence, the death, the drugs and the gangs in urban communities, but minorities don't take responsibility for these occurrences, nope, to them police officers and white people are responsible. It's like seriously, how? You know for certain that minorities are killing people more in these communities, you know for certain that minorities are selling drugs and joining gangs in these communities, so how do you honestly blame it on people, that don't even live in these communities?

This is why I fail to understand anything they do because how can you honestly blame someone else for what's going on in your own community, especially when you know for sure that it's your own people that are the root cause of the problem? It just makes absolutely no sense at all, that's like blaming the ice cream man for not giving your kid an ice cream bar, but in reality, it's your fault because you didn't bother to give your kid money to buy the ice cream bar. It does help that we now have Americans slowly coming out from the woodwork, including rational minorities, who are speaking out, trying to get people to wake up to the truth and the harsh reality of what will happen if we continue to let these people do this.

It's sad because these are the philosophies and theories that are being pushed by these people, they could care less about the truth or what opinion you value, they have an agenda and if you are not part of that agenda, you are written off, just like the truth. It all starts from the top too because there are numerous State representatives claiming that, "white Americans are the only ones who can fix racism" or "white Americans are the only ones that can end racism, if they will only stop their racism towards minorities". My favorite one, "white Americans enslaved African people first, so white Americans owe minorities".

All three of these statements are straight BS, especially the last one and I've already proven that white colonialists didn't start slavery, North African Moors did, history and facts even proves it. Then again, like we discussed before, the truth is just something that's written off and facts are simply changed because these people don't care about the truth, especially if it doesn't coincide with their narrative. Think of the reality of these statements that they've made though because all three of these were actual statements, being made by actual State Senators and civil leaders.

You'll see that brains are something they may not have because seriously, white Americans alone are not the reason for racism, nor will we be able to fix racism. Ending racism, is a task that will take all Americans. Everyone has racist tendencies, it's just most of us can control these racist tendencies, but the people that are deeply rooted in hate, will always be racist, this will never change. Every race in the world, has racist people in it; the only factor that separates everyone else from these blm Marxists leaders and their followers, is that these people use their own racism towards others, as an excuse, it's always this persons fault or it's always that persons fault, never their own fault.

We see this coming from these blm idiots daily, they are constantly on television talking about, what white people have, compared to what minorities have and it's somehow always white peoples fault that

151

minorities have less. It couldn't be the fact that, minorities chose not to work or it couldn't be the fact that, minorities rather rob, loot and steal to get money, nope, white people have more because our skin color is white. This is why, when I ask most people if they think these riots and protests are for justice, but also ask them if they think these protests, are really about racial equality, they tell me I don't know anymore.

With everything we discussed, do you honestly think these people are fighting or advocating for racial equality and justice? Just to reiterate, these people are rioting and protesting for racial equality and justice, yet they are demanding white people lose everything they have. It honestly makes no sense when you think about it because they are also burning down businesses, destroying communities, and the saddest part of all is, innocent minorities, including minority children, are being shot and killed during these riots and protests for equality.

I would think reality would have set in by now for these people or someone with common sense from one of these organizations would step up, but that would be too assumptive of me. These people have to think though, hey we just destroyed our own community, we just destroyed dozens of minority businesses and we claim we are doing this for equality, maybe we should stop and think this through a little more. It's crazy because most of these blm rioters and protestors, were asked why they were looting grocery stores and they simply responded by saying, "why not, everyone else is doing it and it's free stuff".

Everyone is doing it and it's free stuff, this is the thought process of these people, this is the logic they believe in, they easily follow other people because other people are doing it and they see the ability to gain free stuff, so they will take it, it's their character. Just because everyone else is doing it, doesn't mean you need to and it's not free stuff that so-called free stuff, belonged to the storeowner, they paid for it, you stole it, so basically you are a thief. Blm Marxists leaders, could care less though, these are the ideas that they want millions to follow, they want you destroying the country, they want you burning everything down, they want you divided because than it's easier to rebuild their idea of their new America.

That's what it is really all about, total control and racial domination, democrats want to control the government, media wants to control the news and blm Marxists leaders, want to control the whole damn country, one nation, under their rule and their control. Americans often fail to recognize that Congress helps fund, the blm movement, if you bothered to look it up, you will see that blm Marxist leaders and the blm movement itself, receives funding through the LWCF funding program, which allows blm to receive money annually from Congress.

Congress of course takes money from our hard earned American taxes and gives it over to these hate organizations, who do nothing for the country, but cause separation and divide. I mean seriously, the blm movement, was started back in 2013, but these blm Marxists leaders, waited till the death of a minority criminal in the year of 2020, to actually start protesting for minority equality. I think it's interesting to find that these people started their blm movement under the Obama administration, yet blm waited until President Donald Trump took over the Oval Office, to complain about a systemically racist government.

However, it's funny because these people don't protest for innocent minorities, these people don't riot for innocent minorities, these people riot and destroy their communities for criminals and minorities that tend to be life-long criminals. It's crazy, we now have all this chaos and destruction occurring, under the pretense of the killing of a criminal and yes I'm speaking of George Floyd and yes I said criminal because like I stated before, George Floyd, had a long criminal past and was far from an innocent man. Not only was Floyd a known felon, before he was killed, by not one cop, but by three police officers, Floyd was just released from prison where he served time for armed robbery.

What people also fail to realize about this so-called hero is the fact that, Floyd was convicted of robbing a pregnant women, but during the robbery he held the gun to her stomach, then after he was done robbing her, he pistol-whipped her. He's a hero to your people, seriously? Honestly though, how do you see this guy as a martyr or hero, how do you justify giving him seven funerals and donating over 13 million dollars to his family? Thirteen million, this is what his families go fund me account received because people started a go fund me account in George Floyds name and millions of people donated. These people did all this, while the parents of the innocent minority child, who was just killed by a stray bullet, can't even afford to bury their own child.

People give some criminals family, millions of dollars all because they claim he was a hero to their people, but people don't realize that the thirteen million raised, didn't even go to his family, it secretly went to democrats. Look up Act Blue and the donations they received from this go fund me account dedicated to George Floyd. I get it though, the hero thing of course because Americans tend to worship criminals more than the people that actually should be worshipped. Think about it, Americans turn criminals into God's, Bonnie & Clyde, two of the most infamous and ruthless criminals out there, were worshipped among Americans, John Dillinger and Jesse James, two well-known bank robbers, were worshipped by Americans.

Frank Lucas, a well-known heroin dealer, made millions off the drug that killed thousands of his people, Nicky Barnes, the same thing, Rick Ross, the same thing, these drug kingpins were all worshipped by Americans. The sad thing is, all of these individuals were also kings of destroying their own people and only looking out for themselves. It's insane when you think about it because Americans easily turn these criminals into heroes, but also create movements and destroy national monuments for these criminals, people who have done nothing but destroyed lives and communities.

I am sorry but you have to be crazy to call George Floyd a hero, Floyd was a criminal, who had a long criminal record, but who also probably never did a good deed in his life, he was no hero. People ignore the fact that Floyd, was caught passing counterfeit money at a store and that's why the police were called on him, but when the cops arrived, he resisted arrest and had to be taken to the ground. While being detained, Floyd, who was on two major drugs at the time, decided to resist arrest and fight with the police, it took three police officers to pin him to the ground.

Maybe Floyd shouldn't have been killed, yes, that is true, but at the same time, every one of these minorities like George Floyd, all chose to resist arrest during the time they were being detained. They all fought with the cops, none of these criminals had their hands up, none of these criminals obeyed the officers and there is court documents and video that proves it. The sad thing is that, the minorities that are shot and killed illegally by the police are overshadowed by the criminals that rush police and are shot and killed.

There are innocent minorities being shot and killed by police for no reason at all, but this also includes white Americans, but no one seems to care about these innocent murders. This isn't something these people protest or riot for, these innocent murders, don't help push their agenda, so they only riot and protest for the criminals, who chose to resist

154

arrest, which got themselves shot and killed. The media and news wants you to follow their agenda and their narrative of racial police bias, they want you to believe that there is a police brutality epidemic; they want you to believe it was the single white cop, who killed Floyd.

That's the narrative these people are told to push, that's their objective they focus on, they want you to follow a certain criteria because if you do, it enables them to slowly guide you and bend you, to think the way they want you to. White on black violence, is dominating ghetto neighborhoods, white cops, are killing unarmed minority men at an alarming rate, police brutality, is the worst thing in America to minorities; these are the narratives they push, these are the statements they boldly make. Doesn't matter that these statements have no base or truth to them, it becomes more of, white Americans versus minorities because that's what these people want, there goal is to keep us divided.

This is because keeping Americans divided, allows them to keep their lies and deceptions going. Think about the push I am referring too, Barack Obama, was in the Oval Office for 8 years, from January 20th 2009 to January 20th 2017 and it just so happened that the blm movement was started on July 13th of 2013, just about four months before the November polls and four months before Obama would be re-elected. Movements like these, always tend to pop up during election years, today's blm movement, just so happened to start right after a failed three-year impeachment and an attack of a global pandemic.

Once reelected into office, Barack Obama would do nothing for the blm movement, a movement that slowly faded back into the background, only to somehow pop up seven years later, which just so happened to be re-election time in America. Think about it though, these movements usually tend to pop up around election time because in 2013, the blm movement had minorities protesting for a minority American President, yet Barack Obama, had already been U.S. President for four years. We also had minorities rioting for racial equality and calling for minority justice and supposedly the only person that could do this for minorities, was Obama.

Barack Obama won the reelection of course, but what did he do for minorities during their time of crisis, what sacrifice did he make for minorities and the blm movement? The answer is, nothing, Barack Obama chose to put his focus on gay people having rights, illegal immigrants and foreigners being able to come into our country freely

155

and telling Americans that we should accept Muslim and Islam people, even though their religion and even their own people, tells them to kill all American Infidels.

Now, it's 2020 and reelection year for President Trump, so of course once again numerous movements, are popping up all across America because democrats want President Trump out of the Oval Office and they will do anything to get him out, even if that means destroying our country in the process. The people in charge, mainly democrats, leftists and liberals, have already set the narrative for millions of people to follow, the sad thing is that, millions of people blindly follow it to a tee, while the media broadcasts what stories they want you to see, as they help spread the lies.

Want narrative, well, it's a federal crime to destroy or attempt to destroy any structure or national monument on public property, that commemorates the service of any person or persons in the armed forces of the United States of America. Yet, millions of people did it and got away with it, thanks to American State Mayors and Governors, who actually created bail reforms for these people, people destroying American cities. Destroying public national monuments and statues, is a federal crime, but democrats were okay with these people destroying and defacing our national monuments and statues. They were okay with it because these State politicians actually claimed and stated that, these people were expressing their rights and freedoms.

This somehow gives these idiots the right to destroy dozens of American national monuments and statues, but it's a constitutional law, Public Law 108-29, which is the Veterans' Memorial Preservation and Recognition Act of 2003, that was passed to protect these statues and monuments from ever being touched. I think the real question is, why are American State representatives okay with these people destroying our national monuments and statues, especially when there's a U.S. Constitutional law that protects them? There's always an ulterior motive behind what these politicians say and do, democrats deny the American stimulus package three times, then claim their responsible when one does pass.

These liberals and Democrats claim George Floyds a hero, so they take a 9 minute, knee of silence for him, dressed in African scarves. Democrats fail to impeach President Trump, so they pass a bill to investigate the way President Trump reacted to the global pandemic, every single move they make has a motive to it, just like these blm Marxists leaders. Democrats want President Trump out of office and they will try to do anything to get what they want, they'll even let their country be destroyed from the inside out.

Democrats, even liberals, could care less about the American people and they've proven this time after time, they constantly go after President Trump, a U.S. President, who wasn't voted in by the American people, but supposedly by white supremacists. According to democrats, blm protestors and their followers, all white people who follow President Trump, are white supremacists. Forget that President Trump, also has minority supporters because according to these people, we are all white supremacist and if you think I'm joking, PETA, the world health organization for animals, recently stated that, milk from a cow represents white supremacy.

Yes, milk from a cow, is related to white supremacy because it's white and since its white, that means milk is racist. I mean, how stupid can you possibly be, you are literally saying that a beverage is racist because it's white, not only does this make you look like an idiot, but it makes you a special kind of stupid. It just never stops with these people either, it's never enough because if it's not one thing it's another, if it's not schools having to change their names, it's food companies having to change theirs.

I fail to understand how you can say everything white, is related to white supremacy because this is your opinion, it's not the truth, it's not the facts, it's your opinion, so why are we changing everything and getting rid of everything, just because of one's opinion? It honestly makes no sense to me how we can come so far as a nation, only to be drawn back to the ages of slavery and segregation because people prefer to live in the past, instead of the future. You see these narratives taking place daily because we have State politicians, who are seen giving citizens and non-citizens the right to tear down our national monuments and statues, destroy our national parks and even disgrace our national anthem, all in the name of equality.

Forget about American rights and our basic law proof U.S. Constitution, to these democrats, these things don't exist, they ignore the Constitution and make their own rules. It's crazy to me because according to our democrats, the people in charge of our American rights, the State officials who are chosen specifically to represent the

American people, are okay with people destroying our countries symbols of freedom. We seen this ignorance on display this year in 2020, when it came to Americans being told not to celebrate the 4th of July, our very own American Independence Day.

Since these democrats shut the entire country down, State by State, these State politicians tried to literally tell Americans not to celebrate the 4th of July because gathering would be too dangerous. Our very own American Independence day, the day Americans fought and received our freedom, Americans are told not to celebrate because these politicians, are afraid of a virus that is 99.8% curable. It's also puzzling because thanks to this so-called uncontrollable, but curable virus, the American people have to suffer and can't celebrate our very own Independence Day. It doesn't stop there though because these democrats are literally seen on television, arguing with anyone who has a different opinion then they do.

They are also the ones, along with blm Marxists leaders, that are telling people it's okay to riot, loot and burn everything down, but it's not okay for Americans to celebrate our very own Independence Day. Now, this fool Colin Kaphisneck, a guy who just needs to disappear, but who also hasn't played in years, but somehow thinks he's still good, thinks that he has the right to talk bad about Americans celebrating our American Independence Day. According to Colin, our country and every white American living today, is racist and America was supposedly built on white racism, but the sad thing about him making this statement is the fact that, his parents are white, so he's calling his own parents racist.

Think about that for a second though because this just shows you what type of character this dude really has, he's calling the people who took him in, the people who adopted and raised him, racist because they are white. I mean, honestly, what kind of person would do that? It gets worse with this washed up guy because this washed up player is claiming that white people oppressed him, white people kept him down, although these so-called oppressing white parents, were able to provide him a pretty good life.

This life was so good for him, that it gave him the ability to become a football star, eventually being drafted into the NFL. To me it's also funny how, people that don't really experience racism, poverty or oppression, are the ones complaining about it, yet the minorities and white Americans that, are really experiencing oppression, are ignored because they don't have the same platform rich privileged people do. This is why people have the opinion that America is somehow racist, but it's also the reason why these people claim America was built by white supremacist men.

That was the way things were back then, minorities weren't around, until North African Moors brought them over to the Americas. Many minorities like Colin, don't care about these facts though, they call our American values racist and claim that our very own Independence Day, is a racist holiday because it represents a nation that was supposedly built by slavery and racism. It's puzzling to me how people that should not have a voice, are somehow given a voice and feel entitled, with this entitlement they think they can say whatever they want, although their voice should be drained out.

The interesting thing about the whole un-American movement, is the fact that, these people are clearly disrespecting the American flag. These people criticize our American national anthem, which is a slap in the face to the thousands of men and women, who died so all Americans could be free, not just some. Slavery, ended hundreds of years ago, so people of all races were allowed to join the U.S. military, most of them joined for a better life, but they were sent off to war and most of them fought for a purpose, which was freedom for all. These are the people you are spitting on when you disrespect the American flag by spitting or standing on it.

These are the people you are offending when you disrespect the American national anthem by kneeling because these symbols were created for freedom, not racism and especially not slavery. It's all nonsense because you have millionaire sports player's, white and black, who have never experienced any form of oppression, protesting and kneeling to our American national anthem because they claim their advocating for racial equality. But, everything they do tends to be rhetorical, these people claim they are kneeling during the American national anthem for racial equality and justice, but the American flag doesn't represent one single race, neither does the American national anthem, they both represent all Americans.

In addition, it honestly makes no sense when you think about it, you are kneeling to the American national anthem, the anthem of the free nation that you live in because you claim you are advocating against racial justice and equality. Seriously, how does kneeling during the American national anthem, stop the crime and violence from occurring in urban communities, please explain to me how these two things correlate with one another?

Do minorities see you kneeling on television and say, oh man, we should stop robbing each other, I think not. Do minorities see you kneeling and think, maybe we should stop killing each other, I think not. Do minorities see you kneeling and think, maybe we should stop selling drugs, I think not. So seriously, how does you kneeling during the American national anthem, take a stance against racial equality and justice? It honestly makes no sense at all and those doing it, need to have their heads checked because you are at a million dollar stadium, about to play a game you get paid millions of dollars to play and you think kneeling during the American national anthem, is going to solve the problems minorities have in their communities.

If you are kneeling during the national anthem, you are not solving any problems or are you even advocating against any problems. The only thing you are doing is disrespecting the thousands of American veterans and those who died, so you could be free to play a sport for millions. The disrespect that is occurring to our brave men and women, even our veterans, who fought and died for this country, is so overwhelming, it's pathetic. That's the narrative these people are pushing, these people in charge want you to believe these things represent racism because if you believe their lies, it's easier to push their narrative.

This is how it all works though, democrats and the media are using misdirection to make people focus on things that seem more important, it's because they have their agendas already laid out and anything that will help them push this agenda, they take full advantage of. That's why misdirection is so key for these people, you have to pull it off all at once because if you don't succeed at pulling it all off, someone is bound to find out what's really going on. This is honestly why it helped the democratic Medias narrative, when the police officer, who supposedly killed George Floyd, was white, this gave them the spark they needed to ignite the flame, right before elections.

Their narrative never really follows the real truth, so they always tend to ignore the facts, which in this case, the facts were that, the white cop wasn't the only cop on George Floyd. Yes, the white cop had his knee on his neck, which was ridiculous, but two other cops were also pinning Floyd down, they weren't white though, so that little bit of info is ignored and pushed to the side. This is because the real narrative doesn't fit the democratic Medias narrative, so they don't show the previously aired video, which shows the other two officers also pinning George Floyd down.

They can't do that, if they do that, it will destroy their narrative, the real version dismantles their version of the truth. These other two police officers , one black, one Asian, were laying on George Floyd, trying to pin Floyd down because George Floyd, was still trying to resist arrest, although he was already pinned to the ground by three officers. Rayshaad Brooks, not entirely the same case, but same after effect because Brooks was found passed out drunk in his car, while he was sitting in line at the Wendy's drive thru, with his car running.

At first, the officer simply wanted to let Rayshaad be and just asked Rayshaad to politely pull over to the side into a parking spot. However, after watching Brooks slowly drive over and still not park all the way, this police officer was concerned for his safety, so he parked his truck to the side, got out and went to make sure Rayshaad Brooks was okay. After a short period of time, when it was discovered that Rayshaad was obviously drunk, the police officers went to detain and arrest him for a DUI. Seeing what was about to happen Rayshaad resisted arrest and started instantly fighting with the two police officers on the scene, taking both officers to the ground.

While on the ground with both officers, Brooks was able to break free, grabbing the police officers tazer in the process, tazing one of the police officers. As Rayshaad Brooks, then started to run away, Brooks again shot the tazer at the other police officer, hitting him with the tazer, who then returned fire, shooting and killing Rayshaad Brooks. Unfortunately, it's simple for the media to change the narrative of both of these stories, just like they do with all the rest of their headlines because with one little twist, they can easily replace and distort the truth to how they see fit.

Since the media is trying to push their narrative, they switch the headlines of these stories, so they coincide with what they are pushing, we can see this with the Rayshaad Brooks case because Brooks was a child abusing criminal, who resisted arrest, tazed the cops and was shot and killed in the process. This is not the story line the media uses though, the truth is not the headlines that the media prints, instead they chose to print headlines like, "white cop kills unarmed minority man," but also", white police officer shoots and kills unarmed minority man". These are the actual headlines the news and media used for their stories, these are the headlines they used for their news articles, it's far from the truth, but since it fits their narrative, that's what they run with.

You don't have to go very far to see just how easily these people spread their false realities with lie after lie because Rayshaad Brooks, is prime example. Brooks, was far from an innocent man, but to fit their narrative, they change their headlines, so it describes Rayshaad Brooks as an innocent man. Like I said though, the media does this on purpose, the truth is that he was a child-abusing criminal, that was supposed to be in jail, but the media ignores the truth and they mold their headlines so it seems as if, Rayshaad Brooks, was just another innocent minority, shot and killed by police officers.

George Floyd and the other criminals were all the same, the media changed every headline so it seemed as if, innocent minorities were being gunned down by police officers, but the truth is, minority criminals were resisting arrest and being shot in the process. These headlines are also puzzling to me because even Rayshaad Brooks attorney, tried to declare that the tazer in Rayshaad Brooks hands, was not a lethal weapon, but the tazer in the police officers hand, was a lethal weapon. Therefore, these officers had no right to shoot Rayshaad for pointing the tazer at them or even shooting the police officers with the tazer.

The truth is that, all of these minority individuals, were long time criminals or were caught committing some kind of criminal act, they were all about to be detained and instead chose to resist arrest and fight with the police officers. Granted, no one should be shot and killed, especially shot in the back and killed, but at the same time, if you choose to fight with police officers or even shoot at police officers, the resulting outcome, is totally on you, no one else. I will not lose any sleep over criminals, who resisted arrest and got shot and killed by police officers in the process, just won't happen.

The media tends to always change the truth, but the simple fact is, minorities shoot and kill each other at a very alarming rate, more than white people, more than police officers, but according to the media and minorities, it's white people, especially white cops, that are responsible.

This is where the confusion starts to set in because minorities choose to resist arrest and end up getting shot and killed and the people blame the police for being the ones responsible for the minorities actions.

Minorities, rob each other and kill each other, somehow the police are held responsible, it honestly makes no sense and is very confusing to me because if minorities, are the ones causing all the chaos and violence, how are the police the ones responsible? I'm not here to be racist, although some might be calling me one because that's just how these people work but, I'm just trying to point out facts, but also what the real root cause of the problem is because it isn't white Americans or the police, it's minority gang bangers, drug dealers and thief's. It's also minorities, who are causing violent crimes towards others, it's minorities constantly turning their communities into drug and gang infested neighborhoods, it's definitely not a white thing.

I mean seriously, have you recently looked at Chicago because if you did, you would see that, in one weekend alone, there were over 90-recorded shootings. The sad part is that, 27 of these shootings resulted in the death of minorities and 18 of these murders, occurred in as little as 24 hours from each other. Eighteen, 18 minorities, were shot within 24 hours of each other and this was only one weekend in Chicago, this happens every single weekend, in multiple cities around America like Chicago, Atlanta, Baltimore, Philly.

The sad thing is, these numbers are often the same, hundreds of minorities and other innocent people, are being shot and killed, every single week, yet, no one is doing anything about these killings. According to yearly statistics and yearly data reviews, police officers are responsible for shooting and killing about an average of close to a 1000 Americans each year, but minorities only account for usually 23% of these police shootings. Seriously, out of the over 7,600 or so minorities that were killed in 2019, 14 of them were killed by police officers, while the majority of minorities, over 7,400 minorities, were killed by their own people.

It's facts also and the facts are simple, the truth is simple, the truth can't be ignored and if you bothered to look at actual FBI data and statistics, starting from 2016, the truth is that, more minorities have been shot and killed by other minorities then by police officers. The statistics are easily assessable and the FBI loves their data reviews, so you can easily look up just about any information that you need to or any statistic that you need to. The scary thing is that, minorities will swear up and down that this is not the truth, that these statistics are false, even that minorities are killed more each year by the police, but also white people, but they are wrong.

We know these people are wrong, data reviews proves it, but we also see the violence occurring in these communities every time you turn on your TV. Every day in America, someone is or has been robbed, shot or killed, and it's not police officers, who are responsible for these violence crimes towards people, minorities and other Americans are. What these blm leaders and minorities believe and claim is that minorities, are dying at a faster rate, faster than any other race and yes, this is very true, minorities are dying at a faster rate, but that doesn't necessarily mean they are being killed more.

Seriously, this only means that minorities are dying at a faster rate, faster than any other race is dying, this doesn't mean more deaths, this doesn't mean more people have actually died. Look at the statistics and facts, more white American's are killed each year, then any other race in America. White people will always suffer more deaths each year, not because the violence, but because the white population accounts for more than half the population in America. But, there is a huge difference between, dying at a substantially faster rate, then actually being killed because dying at a substantially faster rate, just means you are being killed faster, then others are being killed, this doesn't amount to more death, this amounts to you being more prone to violence.

Thinking this way is what helped these blm Marxists leaders, convince millions of minorities that, the crime and violence occurring in their communities, is somehow someone else responsibility, not theirs. This theory is also how the media scripts some of their headlines when minorities are involved, the media chooses words carefully and makes sure their headlines are geared towards those who fit their narrative, this is why you will often see the media use phrases like, "more prone to" or "more likely to happen". The media uses phrases like these because these phrases help them push their narrative, since minorities are `more prone` to crime and violence.

Minorities are also more likely` to have interactions with the police, this somehow makes them more likely to be victims of police brutality. The key words are, more likely, minorities are more likely, to deal with the police, but saying something like, more likely, doesn't erase the actual proof, which shows that white people, are actually shot and killed more by police officers, then minorities. This isn't something that is, likely to happen or more likely to happen, this is something that is actually happening, white Americans, are being killed more during their interactions with police officers.

Go ahead, call me a liar, call me an idiot, call me a President Trump supporter, call me a racist, call me uneducated, call me whatever you want, it won't erase the fact that, white Americans, are killed more each year during their interactions with police officer, more than minorities are. Also take a look at the different instances of minority and white homicides, which were committed by police officers. We can see examples of this difference by looking at the different cases between Tony Timpa and George Floyd, one was white, one was black, but both were killed the exact same way, yet only one was seen as a hero, the criminal of the two.

That's all thanks to the media and the government's narrative to only show Americans the news they want us to see and deceive us into getting us to follow their objective. For those of you that may have forgot, Tony Timpa, was a 32-year-old working class white American, that was killed by police, while the police had him pinned to the ground, while an officer shoved his knee into Timpa's back and shoulder. Not only was Timpa pinned to the ground with a face full of grass and an officer on his back, Tony Timpa, was handcuffed with his arms behind his back and his legs zip tied.

Like George Floyd, the police officer continued to shove his knee into Tony's back and neck area, even though Mr. Timpa, was already on the ground, cuffed and zip-tied, saying he couldn't breathe. The officer ignored him and continued to pin his shoulders and neck down, cutting off all circulation. Mr. Timpa pleaded for more than 30 minutes, even saying, "You're going to kill me, you're going to kill me". This of course was ignored by the police officers, who soon watched Mr. Timpa take his last breaths, but laughed as they simply thought Mr. Timpa fell unconscious.

Mr. Timpa fell unconscious, while the police officers continued to stand there and laugh at him, they never even bothered to check him for a pulse, although he laid their unconscious because they assumed he was sleeping. The crazy thing about the arrest is, these officers joked and laughed about waking Mr. Timpa up for school and making him waffles for breakfast as they stood by his side, watching him loose consciousness as he draw his last breath. As Mr. Timpa, laid there dead, these police officers did nothing to check his pulse, nothing to see if he was alive and continued to assume he was just sleeping.

The story changed when the EMT's arrived and after being loaded onto a gurney, Mr. Timpa was loaded into the ambulance and the 32 year old, non-criminal white American, was pronounced dead on scene. No riot's, no protest's, no media coverage, no justice for his family, no million dollar go fund me account for his family, no justice for him and all the other innocent people that have been killed for no reason. What gets me is that people will protest, burn everything down, destroy businesses, destroy communities, destroy their own neighborhoods, all for criminals, yet they do nothing for the innocent people being killed.

Remember, before George Floyd, was unfortunately killed by these cops, Mr. Floyd was a criminal, just released from prison for serving an armed robbery conviction, not only that, he had a long criminal record, Tony Timpa was an innocent white American, who was simply off his meds. Funny thing about the Timpa case is that it occurred in 2016, technically 4 years before George Floyd was killed, Mr. Timpa was even killed during an election year, yet nothing was done for this innocent American or about police brutality. This is the democratic Medias narrative, if it fits their narrative good, if it doesn't fit their narrative, change it until it does.

It's crazy because I honestly think doing this only hurts minorities, blaming other people for the minorities that are killing people in urban communities, hurts no one but minorities. Seriously, ask yourself, whose the ones being hurt by the crime and violence in all minority communities, minorities. That's the sad reality of what we are facing today, urban communities have become operation zones for death, gangs and drugs, but these communities have also become battlegrounds for robberies and shootings. Communities can start out good, but soon they become, gang and drug infested communities and some of these communities have been technically war zones for generations.

These communities have been dangerous communities for years, where innocent minorities, are constantly being robbed, shot and killed on a daily basis. What makes all of this no sense is the fact that, this isn't police officers or white Americans or even white gang members, committing these shootings or causing the trouble in these urban communities, these are minority and Latino gang members, who are shooting at each other for simply wearing a different color. I say it makes no sense at all because honestly it doesn't, minorities are being robbed, but also gunned down daily, for no reason at all and this even happening to young minority children.

Instead of minorities advocating for justice, they burn down their communities and attack the police officers in these communities because they blame police officers and white people for all their problems. This is where it really gets tricky because these are the very same people that claim, defunding the police, would help rid urban communities of crime and violence, but also stop all the violent encounters minorities experience in America. Think about that for a second though, the police that are keeping the streets from becoming total nightmares, are the ones you are protesting against.

Not the ones that are actually causing all the death and destruction to your community, but you also claim defunding the police would help. Do I have to say it or are you already thinking it because if you honestly think that defunding the police, would somehow stop all the crime in America, you are a special kind of stupid. These blm Marxist leaders and State politicians, say it's a race thing though, but the truth is, if you want to start a protest about minority justice or a protest for minorities to stop being killed, you need to start with your own race and realize that your own problems start from within.

Look at statistics and data reviews, from the time these riots, protests and looting started, there have been dozens of innocent minorities murdered during these protests, not just in Chicago, but in every city in America. Thanks to this pure hatred, people of all races, are now dying at a faster rate than ever because State politicians are choosing to defund the police, which gives criminals the right to do what they please, definitely in non-policed cities and communities. It honestly makes no sense that you would defund the police and think that crime would drop drastically in your community.

The phase of denial usually comes into play here and I'm sorry, but I'm just stating facts and telling the truth, the real root of the problem doesn't lie with white Americans or police officers, although most of you blame us. You constantly see racism aimed towards white Americans, coming from minorities, who often use excuses for their

167

own racism, definitely when it comes to this so-called white privilege; that all white people supposedly have. This is all because somehow all white people are former slave owners, who supposedly enslaved everyone because they only support white supremacy.

White Americans, should not be blamed for anything related to slavery and we should not be forced to feel guilty for things our ancestors participated in hundreds of years ago, especially when your ancestors probably had more of a part in slavery, then ours did. You, yourself, had nothing to do with slavery or were never a slave, your immediate family had nothing to do with slavery or were ever slaves, so seriously, how can you blame white people for something you've never experienced? The crazy thing is, like I've stated before, North African and Arabian Moors, who were powerful leaders and land bearers themselves, started slavery and the slave trade, way before the thirteen colonies, even existed.

These greedy, but powerful North African and Arabian Moors, traded their people to anyone who would pay for them and they basically traded whoever was valuable to them. Colonists and explorers, didn't just come over to Africa and steal people, your people were sold to them in the name of slave trades. Just a little more info about these monstrous African Moor leaders, North African Moors, started selling off their own people to trader's because they found that their own people were a better-valued trade commodity. Their people had more value than anything else these North African Moors had to sell and they didn't only sell their people to Westerners either; they sold their own people to anyone who paid for them.

Somehow, according to these blm leaders and their followers, this time in history transfers into white guilt and somehow white Americans are being pressured into feeling guilty for simply being white. You can see this by what's been going on lately, you can also see what I am referring to when we are forced to watch white people kissing the feet of minorities because they supposedly feel guilty for being white. Uh, what the hell is wrong with you, first off, were supposed to be in this so-called democratic pandemic, so that's not very hygienic, but you are apologizing and kissing their feet because you feel bad for being white.

Why is that though, what crime did you commit for simply being white? White Americans owe minorities nothing and minorities deserve nothing, unless you work for it, just like every other American, white, minority, Hispanic, doesn't matter, if you want something, you have to earn it. That's what these State Senators, civil leaders, blm leaders and other minorities are saying white privilege is, supposedly it's a privilege for you to work 40 hours a week, so you can provide a safe and secure home for you and your family.

We all work for a living to support and take care of our families, hard working Americans are not provided with any privilege, we are not given any free handouts, we work hard for everything we have. It all just speaks volume to the character of these people because even innocent hard working minority American's, just as tired of seeing this crap on television as white Americans are, are now being called traitors for speaking out against these other minorities. Seriously, these innocent minorities are being told they are sellouts to their own people, but also are being told that they hate their own race, but they are also somehow against their own race.

I'm serious too, minorities, who voice their opinion or stand up against this racist oppression movement, we call the blm movement, are now being told they somehow hate their own people, but are also being labeled as traitors to their own race. It seems to all come down to the fact that these blm Marxist leaders and their followers want racial domination, they don't want to be second, they don't want to be third, they want to be first and they will do anything to make it that way. You can look at the minority militant group who stormed Georgia's Stone Mountain Park because they wanted to destroy a national confederate monument.

It was about this confederate monument coming down, until the news was on them, then their demands changed very quickly. Then, this groups demands changed to white people, giving up an entire State, preferably Texas, to this black racist group. Just hand it over to these minorities and once all is said and done, white people, are not to enter these lands or enter the State because white people are simply not allowed. If this doesn't scream people wanting racial dominance, I don't know what does or what else would. It's all the same, it all comes down to slavery and how white people should feel guilty for something that happened hundreds of years ago.

Everyone forgets the fact that, a minority man from Nigeria, Anthony Johnson, was the first recorded slave owner in America, during the time of the 13 colonies and Mr. Johnson owned four white

169

slaves and one minority slave. White Americans, also most Americans living today, had nothing to do with slavery, nor did our parents or grandparents have anything to do with it, so we owe people nothing, you want something, go out and work for it. Tom Macdonald, a rap artist everyone should pay attention to, had a great expression of this in his song "white boy".

Tom Macdonald, stated that, "the white race as a whole isn't the enemy, theirs racist white people, but we are far from that collectively," the statement rings very true. Yes, there are racist white people, but there are also racist minorities, racist Hispanic people, racist Asian people and others, all these people are dead set in their ways and they feel they are superior to everyone, doesn't matter what your skin color is. You also won't ever change the minds of these people either, they will always be complete racist a**holes, but what screws Americans, is the fact that, most of these people tend to be freaking rich, so they do as they please.

As a whole though, not all white people, including myself are completely racist and we try to live normal lives like everyone else, but as white Americans, we are tired of being labeled racist. This is all because we are white and you feel we owe you something, when in reality, we don't. Minorities complain about not getting help, but it's a proven fact that, minorities and immigrants, receive more in government assistance and so-called help, then any other race, including white Americans.

White Americans are not, nor were we ever, the white slave owners of the past, so stop trying to act like we were, we honestly owe you nothing at all. Tom Macdonald, also stated in the song that, "you can't just label white people racist all because we are related to people that did some terrible shit, way before we were alive" because you simply can't and don't have a right to. All of our ancestors had slaves or participated in some form of slavery, there were even minority property and slave owners, who fought in the Civil War for the South.

We as white Americans, were not the only ones that kept slaves, the Americans up North, didn't even own slaves, but we also didn't participate in slavery, nor were we the ones that killed hundreds of American Indians, all for their free land and food. This is another sore subject when it comes to people talking about what people deserve and what they don't because there are people advocating for American

Indians, claiming that American Indians had all their land stolen by the white man. I am half American Indian, Iroquois, but what people need to realize is that, before white colonists came to and discovered America, most Indian tribes were living towards the West and were not bothered.

The only ones that were bothered were the ones that lived near the thirteen colonies, but most of these Indian tribes were friendly and worked with the American colonists, instead of fighting with them. Besides, most American Indian tribes living in the West, continually fought with each other for land, more then they fought with the white man. American Indians, only started to fight with white colonists after Americans started exploring the West and started taking over the land that they were discovering, which then started creating what we now know as, the United States.

American Indian's living today, have it worse than any other race because certain American Indian tribes, are still forced to live on reservations and are secluded to different areas of America, that's slavery, that's being enslaved, not you living freely in America, going and coming as you please. People of all races experience some form of racism, it isn't secluded to just one entire race, contrary to what you are taught to believe, everyone experiences racism and discrimination, just depends on how much you are forced to deal with as a person.

In addition, contrary to what minorities and others are claiming, white people do experience racism, they experience plenty of racism, there is also a huge difference when it comes to white racism, compared to other racism, although people may choose not to believe that there is. However, there is a huge difference between white racism because we now have people claiming everything that is the color white, is somehow racist. The difference is very clear and even evident, the hatred for white Americans, even the hatred for innocent white American children, is getting out of hand because now innocent white American's, including their children, are quickly being verbally attacked, even physically attacked, simply being white.

This is what I am talking about, this is why there is a huge difference, when it comes to white racism, innocent white people, are being verbally threatened and physically attacked, for no other reason, then the fact that they are white. We've witnessed on the news lately and we've even discussed this before, everything white, is now racist and represents white supremacy, everything from food labels to the color itself. Not to mention, if you support anything that's related to white, if you support anything with the color white, you are a racist white supremacist, who is secretly a white Nazi and KKK supporter.

It's crazy because white American kids, are quickly made fun of or beaten up, simply because the color of their skin is white. These hateful acts are not usually done by one minority kid, nope, these horrible acts tend to be committed by several minorities teens, jumping one kid. This to me is insane, these innocent kids are being beat up for simply being white and this is being done by minority kids, who think it's okay to beat up on innocent children because they've been taught this way.

It's crazy when you think about it because minorities are under the assumption that somehow, they have the right to call white people every racist name in the book, but also literally beat up innocent white kids simply because they are white. Unfortunately, to these minority kids and most other minorities, this is not racism or discrimination they are committing towards white people. If it was all reversed, if it was white kids in America, beating on innocent minority kids, it would be a different story, these white kids, would be committing hate crimes against minorities and all hell would be breaking lose right now. Since it's reversed and it's minority kids doing the beating and assaulting it's no big deal.

What's so puzzling about all these so-called racial problems that we are having is the fact that, minorities are not only racist towards white Americans, but they commit racism against everyone else, but still turn around and claim that, they are the ones being discriminated against. Today, it's getting worse though, now, we have these blm Marxists leaders and their followers, protesting and rioting for minority equality and justice, not only protesting for it, but demanding it or else. It makes no sense because these blm leaders and minorities themselves, are the ones killing minorities at an alarming rate, but also destroying minority lives in the process.

You always have to remember, these people started an entire movement, protesting and rioting for minority equality, but all they've really done is, destroyed dozens of communities, burnt down dozens of businesses and defund the police all around America, that's not advocating for racial equality. Not only are you destroying minority lives, but you are also burning down multiple businesses, looting and stealing from grocery stores and worse of all, you are the ones destroying your own communities and neighborhoods. Dozens of innocent minorities, are also dying at these blm riots and protests, other minorities, are getting into violent confrontations with each other and instead of talking it out, these armed minorities, are shooting each other and innocent minorities, are being caught in the crosshairs.

It's a constant scene of chaos and destruction, store after store, community after community because these blm Marxists leaders and their followers, are burning down neighborhoods and communities, one by one, claiming it's for minority justice and equality. This is where it starts to gets crazy because these violent protesters are destroying everything in sight, claiming it's for minority justice, when we all know the only people this is hurting, is minorities. Thankfully, we do have minorities who are starting to state their voice and these are people that are very highly respected by Americans and by fans all over the world.

Influential people such as: A$AP Rocky, Kevin Gates, Jericho Green, Officer Brandon Tatum, and many more because these minorities are helping wake the American people up. When you listen to these influential people, they don't take a side, they don't even force you to pick their side, they just tell you how they feel and how it really should be because it's the simple logic that we as a people used to think with. The mind-boggling thing about these influential people I mentioned is that, all these people were told that even they hated minorities because they chose not to take a side and take a stand by claiming all lives matter, not just black lives.

The truth is simple, all lives do matter, white, minority, Asian, Mexican, Latina, European, all lives matter, you can't just eliminate one race and say your race matters more than them because that's the real definition of racism and discrimination. White everything is racist, it supports white supremacy and discrimination against minorities, seriously, how though? Honestly, how is this statement allowed to even be said, these people are claiming that anything with the color white, represents white supremacy, that's race discrimination against white people, is it not?

I would honestly think it is, yet you see these blm Marxists leaders and their followers, tearing down white people and giving them a list of demands, that white people are supposed to adhere to simply because

173

we are white and we somehow owe them. It's honestly become one big joke and these blm Marxists leaders and their followers, are given to much power. If you think I am joking, I am not, think of this, recently a famous soccer player overseas was at practice with his team, when a group of blm protestors, came to the stadium and protested for him to be fired, and he was actually fired

Seriously, while this soccer player was practicing, hundreds of blm protesters showed up to the stadium requesting that the team fired him, although he did nothing wrong to them personally, the team fired him. However, you know why he was fired, you know why these blm protesters came asking for his head? These blm protesters came to the stadium asking for this soccer player to be fired because his wife posted something online, in her native language, that said something about these blm protestors, something about how these blm protesters are getting to crazy and out of control.

Blm protestors, seen her comments online and took it upon themselves to leave the wife alone, but go after the star soccer player, who did absolutely nothing wrong, but was guilty by association. This soccer player's wife also did absolutely nothing wrong, all she did was give her own opinion, but too these people, you have no opinion and since hers didn't match their opinion, these blm protestors took it upon themselves to ruin this couple's life. The fact that the soccer player's team actually went through with the firing, is a joke in itself, they owe this soccer player and his wife something because you fired him based on other people's opinions.

People told you to fire this guy, just because of the opinion that his wife shared online and you did. Not only that, I can't believe the team gave in to these little cry-babies and lost a star player because these blm protesters believe that no one can have a different opinion then they do and if you do have a different opinion, your opinion don't matter, also your life doesn't matter. Now, we have city after city, burning and communities simply destroyed, even the streets of D.C., are being destroyed and vandalized by these blm protestors, who really could care less about minority justice and more about their own agenda.

In a June 2020 interview, blm Marxists leader's, were on record for saying some of the most craziest, racist statements ever. One of these statements was said by blm Co-founder Patrisse Cullers, when she stated that, "we are trained Marxists". For those who are not familiar with Marxism, Marxism, is the political and economic theories developed by Karl Marx and Friedrich Engels, who wanted to create the basis for the theory and practice of communism. These people are trying to push this very theory and opinion, demanding people listen to them and they hate anyone who does not listen to them.

You have to remember though, these blm Marxists leaders and their followers, also stated that, "George Floyd's past, is the past and it didn't make him". So a guy, who had a very long criminal record, who was also a two-time convicted felon, but also just released from prison, all this doesn't matter because George Floyd, was a hero to these people, although his real life actions, proves otherwise. Nevertheless, thanks to their highly rated opinion and thanks to the fact that, these people can't stand white people, all white Americans, are easily being labeled racist, especially the ones that speak out.

Even asking a simple question, like I have done many times in this book, can get you in trouble with these people, it honestly makes no sense to me, but it's taking place right before our very eyes. This is the way of the world now and the kicker is, when minorities raise their fist to show support for black power or the black panthers, it's okay and accepted, but if white Americans raise their closed fist, they are white supremacists and Nazi's. Like we discussed before, we all know who the Black Panthers are because they are a well-known hate group, who feels that minorities are superior to everyone, definitely white people.

The worst is what's happening to innocent white Americans, who are being fired from their jobs and castrated online all because they were caught behind doors or on tape, saying something racist or offensive to someone else. Yet, you can turn on your television and easily see about 10 people from other races, saying the exact same thing that these white Americans said, but they face no repercussions, no consequences. Racial equality, for who? It's sad because due to these offensive and racist remarks towards others, these white Americans, also are blasted as racist people online by hundreds, if not millions of others, who don't even know them.

That's another thing with how bad America has become, people online think they know better than everyone else and they will literally tear you down and tear you apart because they feel they are entitled to do so. Unfortunately, since this trend has become the norm, the victims of these peoples wrath, tends to be innocent white Americans and innocent white kids, who have done nothing wrong, but have to deal with this racism, simply for being white. These blm leaders and their followers, seem to have a Hitler complex, if you ask me, they raise their fist the same and when it comes to their own race, if it doesn't benefit or help the minority race, they could care less.

The fact of the matter is, we are exposed to racism on a daily basis, on television shows, on the news, even at our music concerts because you will often see minorities berating and discriminating against white people, every chance they get. You don't have to even take my word for it, you can easily turn on your television right now and witness it for yourself. Even white American television shows and movies, are being canceled or taken off air because minorities said these television shows and films, were racist and somehow represented white supremacy, so these shows and movies literally needed to be canceled and cut from production and air play.

Doesn't work the other way though, minorities have a television show called Black-ish, very offensive to white people, still on television, minorities have BET, Black Entertainment Television, where they show only black cinema films and have only minority television shows on their channel. It doesn't stop their though, minorities have their own black only schools and colleges, black only holidays, black only everything, but if white Americans do any of this, they are racist and supporters of white supremacy.

Think if we had a television show called, White-ish or a whole entertainment channel dedicated to only white people called, White Entertainment Television, they'd all be labeled racist and offensive, just because it's all white people. Both of these would be marked racist and wouldn't be allowed on television because they'd be deemed discrimination against minorities. Gets worse though, minorities form black only groups, create black only support organizations, but also have black only schools and colleges and this is seen as okay, but if white people, are seen forming support groups or supporting their own community, they are quickly labeled as Nazi's or clans members.

If white people talk about our history or have shows only dedicated to white people about our history or our heritage, these shows are quickly canceled, the actors, labeled racist and called for committing race discrimination against minorities. If white Americans have white only colleges or schools, not allowing any minorities or colored people,

176

it's quickly labeled a racist school and people actually try to get the school canceled. Yet, like we've discussed before, minorities can form support groups, support the Black Panthers, a known hate group, have the NAACP, a civil rights support group only for minorities.

But it doesn't stop there, they also have BET, Black entertainment television, a whole television channel dedicated only to minorities, have schools and colleges only dedicated to minorities and even television shows only dedicated to minorities. What is so annoying about this is the fact that, if white Americans are seen doing the same thing as minorities, hence, supporting each other, celebrating our history, celebrating our heritage, white Americans are labeled racist, white actors, are quickly fired and television shows, are cut and canceled, yet, minorities do it with no repercussions.

We have already witnessed this travesty unfold in front of our eyes, we've been subject to seeing several white Americans lose everything they have, for simply saying the n-word, whether it was to friends or in private. A single word that is constantly used, said and objectified by minorities all around the world, on television, online and in real life, but since these white people said the n-word, they literally lost everything and I mean everything. Like we discussed before, recently a white NASCAR driver said the n-word online to his white friend and no one else, while they were playing a video game, but since a minority NASCAR driver heard about this NASCAR driver saying this word, the minority NASCAR driver claimed that he felt offended, although he wasn't even there when it was said.

The white NASCAR driver said the n-word to his friend online and only to his friend, while they were playing a video game because the friend wasn't acting right and the white NASCAR driver asked his friend, "What are you doing n-word?" Now, to me this is not racist because this has probably been said between friends, online gamers, white and minority, to each other more than any other word in the world, but since this minority NASCAR driver heard the story of the white NASCAR driver saying it, the minority claimed he was offended. It's crazy because the white NASCAR driver was fired from his team and lost his whole career.

It's crazy because the word was never said to the minority NASCAR driver, but since he was offended by what this white driver said, the minority NASCAR driver gets the white NASCAR driver fired, basically ruining his entire career. I think the crazy part is that we allowed this to happen, the drivers company, is the one who had the final say and what did they do, they fired him and killed his career all because he said an offensive word online to his friend.

It's the new reality of America, in a world where thousands of white Americans have fought and died for this country, everything white is now considered racist, all the way down to the milk we drink. You would think it would stop there though, but it doesn't, unfortunately we are also seeing innocent white kids picked on, but also attacked by groups of minority kids, not one or two, but by groups of minority kids all because they are white and in today's messed up society, being white is crime. That's some good parenting skills though, but the sad thing is, the parents sometimes have no clue what their kids are actually doing out on the streets because most parents tend not to be in their kid's lives, so these kids tend to raise themselves.

That's the sad thing about what's going on though, innocent white kids, who have done absolutely nothing wrong, are being beat up and attacked by groups of minority kids all because these minority kids say they are offended by the color of their skin. Like I said before, who cares if their parents are okay with this behavior because these minority teens could care less, most of them don't listen to their parents anyway and they tend to do what they want, whether they are told not to do so or not. Honestly though, how does someone justify beating on an innocent kid, definitely when your reason for beating on the kid is because the color of their skin is white?

It's sad because like we discussed before, if this was reversed and it was a group of white kids beating on one minority kid, it would be considered a hate crime and race discrimination against minorities and the white kids would be jailed for causing major physical harm or injury to someone. The interesting thing about all of this is, minorities discriminate against all white Americans constantly, but are also seen calling every white American they come across, every racist name in the book, but minorities don't consider this racism, they don't consider this discrimination either.

It's like seriously, you're the ones who are seen being extremely racist towards others, you are the ones who are calling other people offensive names, you are the ones saying the n-word to each other and calling all white people cr****rs. Minorities are also the ones who constantly berate innocent white people and attack them if they don't like em, all because they think they can. So seriously, I want to know what gives a person the right to offend and belittle or even attack someone simply because their race or skin color is different than yours? It's like the old saying, 'you are a walking contradiction" because you ask for racial equality, but you don't offer the same equalities to white people.

Instead, you want to be superior to white people, so you claim everything white represents, "whiteness". Blm leaders, their followers and leftist, aim to destroy American history and they have already started destroying our public national monuments and statues, tearing these numerous monuments down because they claim they represent people, who were racist white men. Forget about all the good things these Americans did for our country, forget about all the liberties these people fought and died for because according to these people, our American heroes from the past, are nothing but white racist slave owners, who represent nothing but white supremacy.

This is why blm Marxists leaders, their followers, liberals and democrats, demand Americans change our entire history or erase our entire history and rewrite it, so it better suits their idea of American history because our current one is supposedly all built on racism. These liberals and protestors are committing federal crimes and getting away with them and I say federal crime because it's a federal crime to destroy and deface any American public national monument, standing in a public place, yet these people are doing it left and right.

These are American statues and monuments of our four fathers, the brave men and women who fought and died for this country. The American influencers, who paved a way for a better life because if it wasn't for these American heroes, we would still be stuck under British rule. It's crazy because according to blm Marxists leaders, their protestors, democrats and liberals, our American heroes were all white supremacist slave owners, who hated minorities and fought to keep them enslaved. The worst is when these people destroyed a statue of former President, Abraham Lincoln, the U.S. President, who was shot and killed by a Southerner, for freeing slaves.

Still, according to these people, President Abraham Lincoln, was a white supremacist, who hated minorities and wanted slavery to continue. The real facts tell you that, President Abraham Lincoln, started the Civil War because he felt that all men and women were created equal, but President Abraham Lincoln wrote about his thoughts in a national doctrine called the, Emancipation Proclamation. President Lincoln, wanted all people to be free, not only minorities, all people who were enslaved.

Once he succeeded in doing so, he passed an amendment to keep it a law, due to the passing of this amendment to free all slaves, President Lincoln was shot and killed. We can also simply look at the destruction and defacement of Ulysses S. Grant statues and monuments because this was a general who served in the Civil War and fought for the North, then became the U.S. President, after Grant did such a good job in the war. You can ask most people and they will usually tell you that, if it wasn't for Ulysses S. Grant, the Civil War would not have been won by the North and America would not be where we are at today.

Ulysses S. Grant, took over the U.S. Presidency, after the Civil War because Grant, was asked to do so by the American people and he became the U.S. President, during one of the worst times in American history. Ulysses S. Grant was also credited for pulling Americans out of a deep depression, something people thought would last for decades. Still, according to these blm Marxists leaders, liberals and democrats, these two men were traitors to the American people and should not have statues and monuments in their honor because these men represent white supremacy and so-called "whiteness", but also supposedly did nothing for minorities, only white people.

That's what's funny to me, blm Marxists leaders and their protestor's, which are not only minority, there are white ones to, claim that these American national monuments and statues represent racism. Therefore, they take it upon themselves to destroy and deface these national monuments, although it's a federal crime to do so. These people are not worried though, they tend to easily commit these crimes without hesitation because democratic Mayors and Governors, are bailing out protestors, who are being arrested for these federal crimes. A prime example of this, blm protestors and rioters, were protesting and rioting in one city for almost 50 days straight and wouldn't move, just continued to destroy the city.

So President Trump, tired of the destruction, sends FBI personnel to start rounding protestors up and what does the city's mayor do? Instead of being happy that President Trump, has helped him out and sent these men to get his city back under control, this mayor sends a request to President Trump to remove the FBI personnel, instead of the people destroying the city. That's right though, instead of the protestors being rounded up and taken away, so the destruction being caused to the city would stop, this liberal mayor sends a request to President Trump, to get the FBI out and leave the protestors alone.

These liberal mayors are okay with their cities getting destroyed and national monuments being burnt to the ground, they want this to happen because then it's easier to continue to blame all the crime and violence on President Trump. These liberals and democrats want you feeling oppressed, they want you to feel that you are being held back, they want you to feel that you need them because it's all about the election and who's side you are going to choose. Their plan doesn't work without you and they will do everything in their power to get you to be on their side, whether that's destroying their country or not.

It's kind of like debates and the process before election, it's always a popular question, who you going to vote for, what side do you want to choose. In reality, half these people don't do what they promise and you can correct me if I am wrong, but President Donald Trump, is the only U.S. President, that has done everything he said he was going to do, while fighting an onslaught of liberal and democratic bull crap. It doesn't stop with them simply destroying our country though, no, these blm Marxists leaders and democrats, now claim that everything white, from food labels to names on buildings, somehow represents white supremacy, anything colored white or named after a white person, represents nothing but racism and white supremacy.

I wish I was exaggerating on this one, but like we discussed before, we are currently seeing several displays of this in recent news, currently several food labels and product names are being forced to be changed or redesigned because these food labels or company labels, supposedly represent white supremacy and are offensive to people. Seriously, have we become so soft as a nation to where we are offended by what food label looks like? A food label that has nothing to do with us at all, other than eating or not eating the food?

Where did we lose common sense in America, people are literally claiming that the syrup bottle of Aunt Jemima, is racist, Uncle Ben's Rice, is racist, Land O' Lakes Butter, is racist and I am thinking, seriously, I mean, seriously? What do you people possibly think of when you think of Aunt Jemima, if it's slavery and racism, then you are racist, I think of wholesome goodness on my pancakes, just like most normal human beings. Uncle Ben's Rice, Land O' Lakes Butter, these foods have nothing to do with racism or even can be considered racist and just because you say they are, doesn't make it true.

That's the kicker though, that's the part that is destroying America, these people are tearing our country apart and forget about any debates, forget having a debate about whether these things should be happening or not. These people don't care what the other side has to say, it's their opinion, their way and they'll burn everything down, until you give in to their demands. Famous statues of people, also famous names of national monuments and buildings, have to be changed because these blm protesters are claiming that these statues represent racism.

It makes no sense to me, but destruction is key to these people, that's why blm leaders and minorities, use it as an excuse. It's easy to see this because these blm Marxists leaders and their followers, love to tell everyone on the news, just how they will destroy everything they can, unless you give in to their demands. We know these people love doing this because we've seen these blm Marxists leaders and their followers, tear another race or culture down, destroy their own communities, destroy minority owned businesses and they've done this, all in the name of racial justice and equality.

It all makes no sense because these people do this because they claim that minorities, are dying at an alarming rate and yea, minorities in America, are dying at an alarming rate, but this alarming rate of death, does not fall at the hands of white people or police officers. What these people hate is the truth, minorities are dying at a faster rate, but these people are dying at a faster rate because they are being robbed, shot and killed by their very own people. This is why they are dying at a substantially faster rate, not because police are killing them or white people are oppressing them. Like we talked about before, one weekend in Chicago, there were over 90 shootings, 24 of them being fatal and most of these, if not all of these shootings, were committed by minority men and women, not white people.

The facts and the truth, are easily ignored these days by blm Marxists leaders, liberals, democrats and even the media, but the sad thing is, these people want normal Americans to be okay with them destroying our country and erasing our entire culture. This isn't limited to just American cities though, no, unfortunately innocent minority children, are being shot and killed, during these blm riots and protests because these armed men are taking it upon themselves to police the streets. This is what's crazy about some of these shootings, innocent people, men, women and children, are being shot and killed. Parents chose to ignore makeshift barriers and try to drive away from these protests, only to be shot at or fired upon.

A perfect example, is to look at what happened recently during the blm protest for criminal Rayshaad Brooks, where innocent Secoriea Turner, was shot and killed, while riding in the back of her mom's jeep. Secoriea's mom accidently drove towards the protest and wanted to leave the area, so she tried to avoid a makeshift barricade and drive around it, this offended the armed minorities, which were standing near their fake barricade. As Secoriea's mom tried to drive around the makeshift barrier and away from the armed men, the group of armed minority men, instantly opened fire and shot at her jeep, killing innocent little Secoriea Turner, who was sitting in the back seat.

Now, these weren't armed white men who killed her, this wasn't the police that killed her, these were armed minority men, who took it upon themselves, to shoot at a jeep with women and a little girl, who were simply just trying to drive away. These mindless minority armed thugs, took it upon themselves to become judge and executioner and chose to shoot up this jeep, that they knew consisted of only two women and a little girl, firing multiple shots at the back of the jeep, killing innocent little Secoriea.

The sad thing is, these armed minorities, didn't even care it happened, they didn't care they killed a little girl, they showed this by continuing to protest, while the mother rushed to save her daughter's life, only to have to watch Secoriea, slowly pass away. None of these protesters stopped these armed men from shooting at these innocent females, none of these protesters even ran to their aid. What's even more sad, is the fact that, these protestors actually cheered these armed minority men on as they continued to shoot at the jeep from behind, killing innocent Secoriea Turner and injuring her mom.

Minorities cause these huge riots and protests and if they think you have offended them in any way, they have no problem, turning to violence, we seen this here because Secoriea and her mother were innocent, they did nothing wrong, but they were still shot at by these armed minority thugs. The crazy thing is, you can honestly blame the recent rise of crime in this area on the recent killing of Rayshaad Brooks because it was thanks to this criminal resisting arrest, which led to Secoriea Turner being killed.

I say this because you have to look at the case of Rayshaad Brooks, the media spins every news story they can, his was one of them and as a result of that, people started rioting, looting and protesting in his name. Rayshaad Brooks sister, who calls herself, Lady A, is prime example of the medias narrative because she formed her own blm movement group and her first mission was to burn the Wendy's down. Lady A, gathered a group of hundreds of blm protestors and leftists liberals, then went down to the Wendy's, where her brother Rayshaad, was shot and killed and actually burnt the Wendy's down.

Not only did they burnt it down, Lady A and her cronies, formed a ring around the Wendy's as it burned, so no one could come save the place from burning to the ground. Yup, this Marxist, took it upon herself to lead hundreds of minorities in burning down the Wendy's. This was because you know, it was Wendy's fault that Rayshaad Brooks, was drinking and driving, but also chose to fight with the police, who eventually killed him after he shot them with a tazer. Lady A's doesn't really care about minorities though because if you look at the previous example of the death of Secoriea Turner, you will see that her death occurred at this exact Wendy's blm riot that, Lady A, was controlling and leading.

It's crazy because Lady A , was even asked about the innocent killing of Secoriea Turner, but instead of calling for justice for Secoriea, Lady A simply stated, "what happens on the other side of the street, we can't control". No sympathy shown for this innocent little 8 year old minority girl, no quest for justice, for little Secoriea, no care given about this innocent little girl, who was shot and killed for no reason at all. Instead, she burns down an entire Wendy's building and lets it burn to the ground for her brother, who was a convicted child abuser and was only out on release, because of COVID-19. After all the killings and injuries occurring at this Lady A rally, the police finally moved in and was able to remove the crowd of blm protestors.

The protesters, including Lady A, still fought with police as they left the area, only to come back to try and retake the area from the police. These people actually started a, "take back the Wendy's" campaign and marched back to the Wendy's to try and take it back, from the people who were trying to clean the area up. Lady A, the blm instigator, then bellowed out with a microphone to the police, "we are here because we demonstrated peace and we were pushed out, I don't understand, how you can be so against peace?"

Seriously, she literally asked the police officers this, the ones that were trying to stop these people from destroying the place even more. So, forget the fact that her and her followers personally burnt the Wendy's down to the ground or the fact that, there were dozens of innocent people injured, but also shot and killed at this protest. According to Lady A, this protest was peaceful and she just can't understand why the police are so against her ways of peace. This is the ignorance of these blm people and their followers, not only do they think they have the right to destroy public property, they make the idiotic statements that have no base or sense to them.

You see it daily, liberal and democratic State mayors, are constantly on television telling Americans how bad President Trump is for our country, but also how bad crime is because of police brutality. This is the democratic propaganda, this is the media and liberal's narrative, they want you kneeling to them, they want you to think you've been a slave to the system because once you think that, they can deceive you into thinking their way. These people in charge use this deception because its key to their narrative, they want you to feel oppressed, they want you to feel as if you have no chance to succeed in life because if you do feel this way, they can easily deceive you into thinking they are the solution.

The scary thing is, the deception has already been in play, we are constantly seeing everyone from sports players to famous actors fall in line with these theories and ideologies, if they don't fall in line, they are scolded until they do. If any one of these stars or actors, says anything wrong or something other then what they are supposed to say, they have to spend the next month or so apologizing because they supposedly stepped out of line by saying what they said. In America, we no longer have freedom of speech, we no longer are able to speak freely because people have given words tremendous power.

Simple words went from being letters strung together to make a word, to somehow being something that can't be said. It's weird though because saying the word makes it offensive to others, but those other

185

people, can say it. Think of it this way, take a look at the n-word, if I say it and other white people say it, it's racist and offensive, minorities say it to everyone and anyone, but also to each other daily, it's accepted and not racist. It's crazy how we as Americans give power to these words because they are just that, words, if you give them the word to offend you, then that is your own fault for being so sensitive.

I honestly believe that people are sensitive to words because people are uncomfortable in their own skin. It's like millions of people have all become sensitive little kids with insecurities that others have to baby, so their feelings don't get hurt. Words have to be sugar coated for this newer generation, so these people don't get offended, this even goes for debates because certain words are not to be said during these debates, if these words are said, they're seen as offensive to the other side. This is often why there are no more debates in America, debating is now off the table, you can't debate with anyone anymore because people value their opinions more than others or sometimes just don't listen to what others have to say.

It tends to make no sense because these people can be close friends or even family members of yours. It doesn't matter, if you say one thing that offends these sensitive people, you are no longer a friend or family member and they now despise you. Forget all the separation and divide, we all need to stop letting these blm Marxists, liberals and democrats, separate and divide our country because the only way we can succeed as a country, is if we unite and come together, racism, is based on ones judgment of another, so once we can change that judgment, we can change racism.

White American's, all have different ancestors, we come from all different backgrounds and cultures, our ancestors were all treated differently, depending on where your family originated. Like I've stated before, white Americans, should not be blamed for what our ancestors did, hundreds of years ago, especially seeing that we are people living paycheck to paycheck, just like the rest of em. We are also not all just white Americans, there are a lot of white Americans with mixed ancestry, take a look at myself for example, my dad is German and Irish, while my mother is American Indian.

So most of my ancestors had it worse than yours did. Between the thousands of American Indians, who were slaughtered and stripped of their lands, to the Irish, who were also brought over to America and

186

sold as slaves, to the Germans that were stripped of everything and sent to concentration camps to die, my ancestors had it worse than yours. Today, you will see most of our American Indian Natives, kept on reservations or forced to live in secluded communities, to me that's slavery, that's a culture that is being enslaved, these people have already had their land taken, yet they are still forced to live in secluded locations.

Minorities, honestly have no right to complain about slavery, the fact and truth is, they were never slaves, their parents were never slaves and even their grandparents were never slaves, granted, their grandparents probably did have to deal with segregation. Still, these minorities were never slaves, don't even know what real slavery even looks like because they only know what they've seen in pictures and in movies, yet they still claim they are victims of slavery. In fact, when you read your American history, you will see that minorities often fought in the Civil War, for the Southern Confederate side.

This was all thanks to their minority American slave owners and minority American property owners, who didn't want slavery to end. Now, I know there will be people reading this book and will declare me a white racist, who supports white supremacy because besides everything white being racist, these people hate when others state the obvious or defend facts and the truth, which I am doing. But, no, I'm not a racist, I accept all and hate all races at the same time, well, except Muslim and Islam people because these people are taught to hate and kill me and my family, so these people I do not accept.

I accept people by the character they show me, if you have bad character, I don't usually talk to you, that doesn't make me a racist., that doesn't make me some kind of phobic person, that doesn't make me special, it makes me normal. I also hate people that think, being gay is normal and should be accepted and I hate people who add on the word phobic to everything, simply because people don't accept them or their opinion. I hate people, who use other races as an excuse to berate and belittle these other races, but I also hate people, who falsely accuse others of discrimination because most of the time they are the ones committing the discrimination.

Moreover, I hate anyone who thinks my life isn't worth much simply because of my skin color. I am a huge fan and supporter of numerous minorities, besides these awesome influential people,

Brandon Tatum, Candace Owens, Jericho Green, ABL, The Conservative twins and if you are not too sure who any of these people are, I suggest you might want to look these people up. These individuals will blow your mind with the truth and they will expose to you the false realities being portrayed by this corrupt system, you'll learn more truth about the real lies behind these movements, then anywhere else, they are smart, intelligent, oh yea, they are also all minorities, who I tip my hat too.

Like them though, I am tired of seeing innocent white people and even innocent minorities, having their lives being torn apart l because the color of their skin or because they believe in saying, all lives matter, not just black lives matters. I am also tired of seeing innocent white older men and innocent white children and teens, being attacked and beaten by minorities, for simply being white, this doesn't make me a racist, this makes me a realist because I don't believe any of these actions help's minorities advocate for equality.

I am a person that believes in pro-life, so my view on life is different than these blm Marxists, democrats, leftists and liberals, since I have a different opinion, this offends these people, so therefore my opinion offends these people. This is also where the confusion starts because why are Americans not allowed to have their own opinion, why are we not allowed to think and speak freely anymore? Do Americans not have Freedom of Speech, are we not allowed to be free independent thinker's, why are you forcing people to conform to your opinion or your ideology, when Americans have the freedom to choose?

In addition, what happened to being able to come up with our own ideas and having your own opinions, when did that go out the window? These are the questions that play on the minds of many Americans because in today's crazy world, leftists, liberals and democrats, are twisting people's words around, like their making cotton candy at a State county fair. Americans, white and minority, are no longer able to have an opinion that differs from these people.

If you do have a different opinion that doesn't jive with this leftist un-American ideology, to these people you don't matter and need to erased, so you can't cause any friction. This is the harsh reality of the internet and the media narrative today, these blm leaders, liberals and democrats, push an agenda they want you to follow. If any American tends to have a different opinion about this agenda, these people try to smear your name and dig up dirt on you, simply so you can't cause any derailment to their agenda. The real enemy to minorities, is not white Americans, it's these so-called minority leftists civil rights leaders, rich white liberals, democrats, these useless elected State Senators and even more useless elected State Mayors and Governors because these are the people that are really holding the minority community back.

Think about it, these civil leaders, democrats and State politicians, have been preaching the same agenda for decades, not just years, decades, preaching year after year, that they are fighting for better opportunities and equality for minorities, yet the opportunities they speak of, never seem to come. The opportunities, are only given when minorities themselves step up and decide they want a better job and community for themselves and their families, so they work hard on their own to provide a better life, since no one wants to help them.

This destroys these liberals and democrats narrative because like I've stated before, there are plenty of successful minorities, living in America, but to the leftist liberals, they can't run with this information, so they suppress it, so they can push the narrative of a racist America. It's crazy because you constantly see these liberals and democrats getting exposed for pushing their hidden agendas, they really only care about their legislation and power, but also getting President Donald Trump out of office, while they protect their own riches and wealth.

Look what the main purpose was for, at first these blm protesters had a good purpose and mission, stop the innocent killing of minorities, but also to stop the destruction of urban communities. Instead of fixing the root problem, blm leaders, liberals and democrats, forced minorities to think it was police officers, especially white police officers, who were responsible for the problem, not themselves. So what happens, they start a movement for police brutality and for police to stop killing innocent minorities, when in reality, minorities are killing each other at a faster and alarming rate, faster than anyone else.

You see the outcome of this so-called democratic help because we still see low-income neighborhoods full of poverty, full of drugs and crime, yet these civil leaders, liberals, democrats and even State Reps, still preach they are fighting for equality for minorities and these politicians still promise they are here to help, but yet the help is never there. It's easier for liberals, Senators and even democrats, to blame all

189

their faults on white Americans and President Trump, rather than facing the truth because the truth hurts their narrative. Blm leaders and mainstream leftists, are a huge part of this because these people are constantly blaming everything on white Americans and the main person they blame, President Trump because according to these lunatics, President Trump is racist and supports white supremacy.

It's their well-known logic at play again because an American U.S. President, who was elected by the American people, who also stands up for the American people every day, is being called a white racist. It doesn't stop there because along with being a racist, they also claim that he's a white supremacist, who supposedly used his white supremacist friends to get into the Oval Office. That's the thing about President Trump and his time as President, President Trump has actually done more for the American people, more than any other President of the United States, besides Abraham Lincoln.

This includes helping out minorities, the democrats and liberals know this and they hate it, this is why they try to smear President Trump's name every chance they get. In fact, they hate it so much that democrats are trying to do everything in their power to win the election, including stealing the election through mail-in voting. So they can get President Trump out of the Oval Office, they are willing to push for mail-in voting, instead of in-person voting, so they could steal the election a little easier.

Think of what President Trump, has already had to face for the first four years, it first started with a fraudulent democratic impeachment, then it went to a global virus pandemic, then it went to police brutality and the blm movement, while the whole time democrats are screaming racism and Russian collusion. As if this wasn't already enough for President Trump to deal with, now Sleepy Joe Biden, is claiming that Americans need to watch out for Russian interference and tampering because Trump will use it to steal the election. What you have to realize is, these leftists, liberals and democrats, want President Trump out of the Oval Office so bad, they will ignore people tearing apart their own cities and communities.

It doesn't stop there though because they will also ignore the crime and violence that is skyrocketing in their cities, simply because it's easier for them to just blame it all on Trump. It's crazy because once President Trump tried to stop these people from causing this chaos to

American cities, these politicians claimed that President Trump, was the one who was wrong. This of course was supposedly because President Trump was the reason why there was a rise of crime and violence occurring in major cities.

Major U.S. cities have broken out in violence all around America and some of these cities crime rates have skyrocketed, especially in the cities that have had the police defunded. Murders and homicides have skyrocket into the hundreds, all in one weekend, yet these liberal and democratic mayors are more interested in blaming President Trump, rather than stopping the rise of violence. These State political leaders, are okay with people destroying our country; they are okay with hundreds of people being slaughtered daily, this is the narrative they want to push, they want you to think our country is in turmoil and they're the only ones who can help.

They want you to think this way and have already tried to push this theory because according to these State politicians, everything going on right now, the crime, the violence, the protests, the death, the chaos, the destruction, it's all President Trump's fault and if you vote democrat, all this chaos will somehow all go away. These political leaders, often forget to mention that they are the ones letting all this chaos and destruction occur, they are the ones letting people commit federal crimes by tearing down national monuments and statues, but they are also the ones who strives to keep our country divided.

We've seen examples of this constantly on television because these liberal and democratic Mayors, choose to ignore the chaos and instead castrate President Trump, for just about every move he makes, while they ignore the violence that's destroying their cities. Prime example of these State Mayors, is liberal mayor Lori Lightfoot, who hates President Trump and personally went on record to tell President Trump that, he isn't allowed to send federal troops to her city to stop the violence because he's the one responsible for the violence. Mayor Lightfoot said that President Trump sending in his federal troops is an abuse of power and she doesn't want his white troops in her city.

Yet, her own city, Chicago, has had more shootings and homicides recorded in one day, then any other city in America. That's also one of the mind-boggling questions that sit's there on your brain, why are we having to send federal agents to protect our national monuments and statues in the first place? Especially when these monuments and statues

191

are not to be touched or defaced because it's a federal crime to do so? Seriously though, how does this make any sense, how would a State Mayor be okay with people taking over their city and sending their city into chaos, but they are not okay with President Trump offering help to rid their city of the violence?

The sad reality is that, this liberal mayor should not even be a State mayor, democrat Lightfoot's city, Chicago, has the worst crime rate in America and instead of taking care of her city, she lets it sink into chaos, while she blames it all on President Trump. She is also the democratic Mayor that gave in to rioters and protestors, who attacked the police officers, who tried to protect a Christopher Columbus statue, from being torn down. What does Mayor Lightfoot do, after having tons of officers wounded for doing what they thought was right, this un-American Mayor stabs these officers in the back.

This idiotic mayor gave in to these rioters and secretly has the national monument of Christopher Columbus taken down in the middle of the night, consulting no one. Jericho Green, a guy we should all listen to and I hope is not mad I am using his name or quote, but Jericho Green said it perfectly when he stated that, "if it affects one part of our society, it really does affect all of our society". This is true because we are seeing the outcome all across America, our country is being torn apart by these simple-minded brainwashed people, who believe America is racist.

This is the logical thinking that comes from these people though, true Americans know that the logic thee people use is wrong, but there are millions of people following the lead of these uneducated illogical thinker's and it's affecting all of society, not just parts of society. Forget about the real truth, which they tend to ignore because President Trump is the only sitting U.S. President, that has ever did what he promised the American people he would do, although democrats will say otherwise. President Trump, is an amazing President and far from a white racist, but these people don't accept the truth, they see Donald Trump and not President Donald Trump and to these leftists, President Trump, is an evil white lunatic.

Doesn't matter that President Trump, just passed a bill to invest over 100 billion dollars in a program for minority urban development. President Trump granted the 100 billion dollars to be spent on urban neighborhoods to help develop their community and give them a better chance at life. Obama never did one thing for minorities, especially never passed any bill to spend over 100 billion dollars on minorities and he was a so-called minority, supposedly our first minority U.S. President, who represented all minorities, yet, Barack Obama never once bothered to help out minorities or focus on redevelopment in urban communities.

That's these politicians specialty though, liberals and leftists, love to judge people on who they think they are, not who they really are, you can even forget about the real you, to these politicians, the only you that matters, is who they assume you are. This is why these liberals and democrats see white racist Trump and not President Trump, forget about him being a successful businessman, who built a billion dollar empire. Forget the fact that as U.S. President, Trump donates his entire Presidential salary and only takes $1 dollar because he's forced to.

The real truth is, President Donald Trump, is one of the only President's to ever give a damn about the American people in a long time. President Trump has gotten us out of bad deals and even wars, but this doesn't matter to these liberals, democrats and leftists, President Trump, can do no right. These politicians show how much they care about America by letting people get away with trying to erase hundreds of years of history all because these people claim it was all built on the basis of white supremacy and should be erased. The politicians that we elected into office to represent Americans, have taken it upon themselves to let people destroy our American traditions and our American values.

Now, these people are trying to make Americans feel bad for what our four fathers did because according to these State politicians, our four fathers, were supporters of white supremacy and did nothing for our country, yet these are the people that influenced our great nation. The thought process of a liberal and democrat, is just overwhelming to say the least, there is no common sense anymore, there is no devil's advocate of what's right and wrong, there's only their way and the way they see things.

You have to also remember, these are the very same people that claimed, "living in a nice home and having a safe and secure community to live in, is a white Privilege". We've discussed this before because according to these leftists, liberals, blm Marxists leaders, democrats and others who follow their lead, safety and security is, a

193

white privilege and since it's a white privilege, white Americans, are to stop it at once and hand over our hard worked for homes and lives, to a minority or brown family.

It just seems to get crazier and crazier because these people even claim that white Americans have certain, "attributes of whiteness," to them and because of these, "attributes of whiteness," white people are more privileged then others. Prime example of this is when the National Museum of African American History, released an entire chart about the differences between white Americans and others, but also how white people have so-called, "attributes of whiteness". It's crazy when you think about it because these African American museum directors, thought it would be okay to release an entire chart, that describes what qualities are to be considered white qualities and how all white Americans have, "attributes of whiteness".

I think all of this is non-sense, but the really messed up part is when these museum directors labeled, things like, "family values", "hard-work" and "rational linear thinking", as form's of "whiteness". It's insane because these minority museum directors, went on record to claim that, minorities don't work hard and can't seem to think on their own, but the ones who are successful hard working Americans, the ones who are able to think and solve problems on their own, are only able to do this because they themselves have, "attributes of whiteness".

This is a huge reason why discrimination and racism will never end in America, but also why there will always be a constant divide between white people and minorities, not because of white Americans, but because these people are creating a constant divide between Americans by spreading lies and false propaganda. These people in charge, also the minorities that have influence, want the country divided; they want it to be white Americans versus minorities because if we are at each other's throats, it doesn't take much to push one side over the edge. Take the great State of North Carolina for prime example because just recently in Ashville, North Carolina, these council members have somehow found a way to bring minorities all the way back to the days of slavery.

The City councilman for Asheville, North Carolina, just recently passed and approved a bill to approve to give their minority population or minority community members, reparations. Not only did they approve reparations for minorities, they agreed to apologize to

194

minorities for their participation in slavery, and even segregation. That's right these City councilman, took it upon themselves to apologize for something they have never took part in, which was slavery and something that their community has never been part of, which is segregation and apologized for it.

Of course this all started because two minority council member's sent in a new bill to pass and they claimed that, "they come from a lived experience, the trauma that was experienced by our four father's, even though you haven't experienced it, you still carry it through the bloodline". To me, this is just crazy, how can you even justify making a statement like this, when everyone living in the United States today was never a slave, nor a slave owner and it's been proven that your own people started slavery.

What you are basically stating, is that your people are lazy and you want free handouts and instead of working hard for things, you are going to use your ancestors as an excuse to get it for free. Also, you claim it's a lived experience, but a lived experience is experiencing something that is affecting your life right now, not something you, your parents and even your very own grandparents, have never dealt with during your entire lives. Moreover, you are members of the Asheville, North Carolina City Council, how are you suffering from the trauma of slavery? In addition, when they said, "you still carry it through the bloodline," it's like okay, so that means American Native Indians, still being secluded today, are to be given reparations.

The Irish, who were some of the first slaves to be recorded, but also some of the last slaves to be recorded, are to receive reparations, the Germans, who were subject to genocide, are to get reparations, so why is it only minorities, who are receiving reparations? I honestly think if you are claiming that the trauma your four fathers experienced, is the reason why you and your people deserve reparations, you shouldn't be a city council member because like many others, you choose to live in the past, instead of bringing your people into the future.

It makes no sense when you claim this, but then you leave out the other people in your community, whose ancestors probably suffered far worse, then your four fathers did. It's crazy to me because these people act like slavery was the worst thing in the world and only occurred to minorities, when the fact is, slavery occurred to every race in America, not just minorities and some of our ancestors had it far worse than

195

slavery. The sad reality of it all is, the truth really doesn't matter, these people will always use slavery as an excuse, they will always live in the past and they will always use their ancestors to try to get ahead in life.

The narrative for these people never changes, they don't care who they hurt, they don't; care if they are seen as idiots because everything these people do is questionable, and the sad thing is, these people are okay with it. One thing that people seem to also forget is the fact that, every American living today in the United States of America, is a free individual, there is no separate law for white people, there is no separate law for black people, there's the United States Constitutional laws and they apply to every American the same.

It honestly makes no sense because from 1774 to 1804, the Northern States in America, abolished slavery and didn't participate in it, although slavery was still vital in the South. Seriously, in 1780, Pennsylvania, became the first State to abolish slavery, followed up by Massachusetts in 1783, which officially abolished slavery for the entire State. This was because the opinion back then was that slavery, hurt the U.S. economy, rather than build the U.S. economy. Most Americans in the North hated slavery and wanted the entire United States of America to be, "free states", as they called them.

These people wanted slavery to be abolished, so most Northern States outlawed slavery and made it a crime to enslave people. These Americans from the North, did not profit from slavery, these people from the North, did not succeed, because of slavery, so how can you claim slavery built America, so white people owe you something? This is why it all makes no sense when you see minorities kneeling during the American national anthem and disrespecting the American flag because these people, are spitting on their ancestors graves.

The fact of the matter is, we are all different, we all come from different backgrounds, Americans should have one goal in mind and that goal is to unite against these un-American State Senators, blm leaders, politicians and their millions of followers, who want to see the America we all love, destroyed.

-- Chapter 4 --
What's ours is ours, you don't just
get it because you want it.

Let this statement sink in for a second because it's what most people in America tend to forget, what's ours is ours, you don't just get it because you want it and you think you are entitled to it, especially when we worked hard for it. People don't work hard to provide a life for you; they work hard to provide a life for themselves and their families, so this entitles you to nothing we have. This is a statement that seems to be lost in translation because now we have a whole generation of teens and minorities that think, because of their skin color they are entitled to everything, even if they didn't work to get it.

It's a totally insane way of thinking that was brought on by democrats and blm leader, seriously, why would you think you deserve something when you never worked for it simply because of your skin color? The funny thing is, if you look at platforms like YouTube and face book, even online news websites, you will see other minorities standing up for what's right and are coming out to talk about the ignorance these young teens and adults are showing. Still, it doesn't matter though, these minority youths and others, could care less about what others think or say, they all think everything should be handed to them and they will riot, loot and protest, until they get what they want.

That's the scary thing about these youths and their elders, they don't care whether they are right or wrong, they will still destroy communities, burn businesses down, loot every store in sight and claim the reason they are doing all of this is, they want racial equality and reparations for the past. Think of it this way, the Marxists leaders of the blm movement, supposedly claim that the organization is not about racial dominance, it's about racial equality, yet, they've created an entire list of demands for white American's. It's puzzling because the very first demand is for all white American's to give up their own hard worked for homes to minorities or brown people because your white and since your white, you don't deserve it; they do.

Seriously, I wish I was joking, but these blm Marxists leaders, brought forth a fully typed document, that clearly states that all white people, not just some, but all white people, should give up everything they have worked hard for, to minorities or brown people. This is of course because white people, supposedly got everything they have through privilege, not actually working hard for it, like most of us did, and continue to do. Forget the concept of working hard for something, these people could care less about working hard for anything, they automatically assume they are entitled to what other people have simply because their skin color.

Think of the irony in that logic though, minorities, led by these blm leaders, hate on white people so bad because they claim that all white people have so-called white privilege thanks their skin color. Yet, minorities riot and protest that, they deserve everything handed to them simply because of their skin color. It makes no sense because these people berate and belittle white people thanks to the color of their skin, then turn around and demand that, they are to be handed everything that white people have because the color of their skin.

It's sad because these blm leaders or trained Marxists, as they so claim to be, actually created a list for white people to adhere by, but the whole list is racist and is basically a message telling white people that they should be ashamed for simply being white. It's crazy; the list basically ignores all the hard work white people have done to get where there at because these people or idiots, claim that, everything white people have, they got through the privilege of being white. It honestly makes no sense because ; these people have inspired others to follow their idiotic ideologies. We can take influential television host Ophra for example because ; she created an entire television show about how white people should feel guilty for being white.

These peoples actions speaks for itself and to have an entire show about how, white people should feel guilty for being white, just shows you how much character you lack, seeing that it was white people, especially white women, who made you rich in the first place. The list these blm idiots created is absolutely ridiculous and we can see that by examining some of the demands, but it's also funny how most of their demands start out with, "white people". This is even the way these blm leaders worded some of their demands, starting with, "white people, if you're inheriting property you intend to sell, give it to a minority or brown family, and you're bound to make that money in some other white privileged way".

These demands got worse, "white people, if you can afford to downsize, give up the home you own to a minority or brown family". Then you have the most racist one of all, "white people, especially white women, rat out and turn in white people who say racist words to you and this should be easy but all those sheet less Klan, Nazi's and other lil' dick-white men who will all be returning to work, get they ass fired, call the police and say they look suspicious so they will get arrested."

Seriously, this is what some of these demands were, I honestly feel like these people have a few screws loose because how could you make these racists demands, then turn around and ask for equality? I am sorry but, I didn't know me and all my friends were white sheet less Klan, Nazi lil' dick men, who commit racist acts and discrimination against women daily. I mean, that's news to me, but to tell these blm leaders that the statement they are making is racist, makes you the racist one, imagine that one.

The whole list of demands that these blm leaders created is one long list of racist demands, but is also very discriminating towards white people, especially white men, who they literally called Nazi's and something I won't repeat. If this was reverse though, if white people made a list of demands like this or said anything as remotely offensive to them as they did, it's discrimination and a hate crime. It's a double standard, just like these democrats with their, "Rules for thee, not for me". The thing that really makes no sense about all of this is the fact that, minorities protest and riot for racial equality, yet, when it comes to racism, they commit more racism towards others, than anyone else.

These ridiculous statements made by these blm Marxists leaders are racist to the core, they all lead to the same solution for these people, they want to take everything away from white people, and they won't stop until they do. You can see the difference in something as simple as a fist raise, white people get in trouble for raising their fist because when they do it, their considered to be supporting Nazi's, yet, when minorities raise their fist it's okay because it represents black power and the Black Panther's. Although the black panthers, are a well-known hate group, that not only hates the white race, but these people also believe that white Americans, every last one of us, should be killed.

Seriously, how is it racial discrimination when white Americans are the ones committing the so-called racist acts, but it's not considered racial discrimination against others, when minorities form hate groups and commit hate crimes against white American's? This is the major question that I would love an answer too, but will never receive one

199

because these people don't believe in answering questions, they don't believe in discussing things. These people only see things their way, that's it, they don't want to negotiate with you, they don't want to converse with you, they want to dominate you, plain and simple.

These people use fallacies and fallacious arguments to push their false ideologies onto other people, they take the truth and bend it to their will, so the truth becomes the lie and the lie becomes the truth. Truth is something that has long been forgotten, nowadays people base their opinions and arguments on assumptions, instead of waiting for the truth or even the facts, they act on what they assume and believe is to be true. These beliefs are what have caused so much animosity between Americans; these people are destroying communities and burning down businesses, all in the name of criminals, who never did anything for anyone, except be a criminal.

Dozens of riots and protests started because of assumptions, people assumed it was another innocent minority being shot and killed by a police officer, but in reality, there were many factors that led up to the death of George Floyd. Unfortunately, to these people and blm leaders, fact's don't matter, the truth doesn't even matter, these people see a situation that helps them push their agenda, so they take full advantage of it, whether they know the truth or not. Prime example of this is, these blm leader's on television claiming that their people are looting jewelry stores and clothing stores because to them it's a form of reparations.

In reality, they are all thieves and they are stealing from these companies, they should be put in jail because they are not due any reparations, they are breaking into businesses and stealing from them, that's robbery. That's also another thing that is puzzling to me, people are talking about minorities receiving reparations because blm leaders, State Senators and other civil leaders claim that they deserve reparations, yet, they are basing this prediction on the fact that their ancestors were the only ones who were slaves. These people did not work for anything, they did not bother to focus on a career, and they sit at home and live off the government, then turn around and claim that they deserve reparations, because of what their ancestors went through.

The blm and democratic logic that seems to play out with these mindless people is amazing to me because they believe that since their ancestors were slaves, they deserve reparations. You can also forget the fact that everyone, this includes white people, had slaves as ancestors,

200

especially the Irish. This doesn't matter though because minorities still claim that they deserve reparations simply because of what their ancestors went through. The fact of the matter is, your ancestors had to deal with slavery, not you, your ancestors had to deal with segregation, not you, so how do you seriously think you deserve anything for free, if you have not even bothered to work for it?

What's sad is, these people that are complaining and protesting about reparations, are spitting in the faces of all the minorities that came before them, people like Martin Luther King Jr., and even Malcolm X because they fought for rights and equality for their people, they didn't riot and loot to get thee rights. Instead of working hard and inspiring your people to do better like they did, you are rioting and looting stores and even grocery stores for racial equality and claiming that it's for reparations.

The crazy thing is that these young minorities will look you dead in your face and tell you they hate you, just because you are white. There is no quest for real unity like there was back then, these people thrive on hatred and this hatred fuels their actions and due to this deep hatred for white people, they try to destroy white communities and businesses because these people blame white people for all their problems. Not everyone is raised to hate, but when you are raised by the false media and these so-called people loving democrats, but also these race dominating blm Marxists, you tend to develop reasoning on your own, but you also tend not to care about what other people think or believe.

It's sad because things like an education, having a job, having a career or even having a family, are all being displayed as bad characteristic traits, by people that hate our American traditions and will do anything they can to change and erase them. According to Education Weekly, one of the major problems with education when it comes to today's youth, is the fact that parent's are not involved enough in their children's lives, so they are not involved enough in their education or their schooling. This could come down to the fact that parents are not at home like they used to be, which tends to hinder the children from learning and developing, which in turn, turns them into racist little uneducated brats, following their own discipline.

Now more than ever we need to teach and educate our children, we need to teach them how to use common sense in their decisions, how to properly deal with racism and discrimination, but also how they should not believe everything they see or hear online or on television. Learning from a young age helps children develop and grow into better and smarter individuals, but it also helps them learn valuable lessons such as; learning right from wrong, learning how to deal with criticism, learning how to be polite and use manners, but also just how to be a decent human being.

That's a major problem in today's new America, there are too many children growing up not knowing how to react or deal with situations or problems on their own because they've never been taught how to deal with them. Americans hide violence from children and even teens, on television and the internet, then turn around and let them play the most violent video games ever, seems like the logic is missing. Then you have the other half of the equation where parents keep their children secluded from anything and everything offensive, then turn around and wonder why they are so shut off or afraid of the world.

These children and teens are so hidden and secluded from anything dangerous, harmful, or hurtful, that it is making them soft, fragile, and sensitive. These kids tend to get frustrated with simple things because they cannot handle the disappointment, they cannot handle being told no, and they cannot handle dealing with any form of pressure; so they act out and destroy everything in sight. Take the kids of the 90's for example, when we were younger, I am 40 now, but when we were younger, we were outside playing, for us getting scrapes and bruises was an everyday occurrence.

We were taught about everything and we were not just handed everything, if we wanted something, we actually had to be good or work for it, and we could not just act out to get our way. Most of the time, if you were good, you got to go play, if you were bad you were grounded and were whooped, but you learned your lesson, simple as that, this is what's missing in today's generation. If you hurt yourself while you were playing, you would get bandaged up and go right back outside. Today, if you ground a kid, they cry and wine so much that you literally ungrounded them, just to stop them from crying so you can get some peace and quiet.

American teens, white and minority, are the worse because they all feel they have some sort of entitlement and if you don't give in to this self-entitlement, they throw major temper tantrums, which usually ends up with something being destroyed. Sometimes it's our fault though

202

because it's our generation of parents, that kept children and teens secluded from anything that they deemed too offensive, due to this, most of the children grew up guarded from just about everything. These secluded and fragile kids are now the generation that are controlling the nation and they are simply offended by everything, we now live in a generation of emotionally weak people.

Due to this sensitivity, everything has to be watered down so it's not to offend anyone, this includes the truth. You have no more freedom's, you have no more right to freedom of speech, you have no right to have an opinion of your own, you have no right to do what you please anymore, unless of course you are gay, lesbian, a feminist, a blm protesters, a foreigner, an illegal immigrant, a democrat or a minority, then you somehow have the right to do whatever you want. In today's new America, you literally have to watch what you say, even to some of your closest friends and family, but you also have to watch what you do because people you don't even know, will easily get offended by your actions or what you say.

Since these people feel offended by you, they will take it upon themselves to castrate you, your family, and anyone who likes you, online because there to scared to do it to your face. It's crazy because they castrate you online because they know this castration will soon be followed by hundreds, if not millions of people, who don't even know you. That's what it has become today, it's not a debate anymore, people don't argue about anything anymore either, they assume their right and your wrong.

This assumption that they have, follows their actions as they will easily ruin you and your families lives on social media, simply because they rather spread lies, rather than have an actual conversation with you. Some of these people now on the front lines of this, are the same children and teens, who were forced to grow up quick because their parents weren't really parents, which left these teens taking care of their siblings. Now they've grown into people that think they are grown and entitled to everything because that's the way they raised themselves and their siblings to be.

Even children and teens have to be watched carefully these days because sometimes hatred runs deep and when it starts at a very young age, these kids can't take the pressure when they are forced to deal with it, so they act out with violence. We've seen these horrible acts of violence committed by young kids when it comes to school shootings, young kids and teens are bringing weapons to their schools and taking their frustrations out on other kids. Let us also start this off by honestly saying, "Guns don't kill people, people kill people, a gun can't pull its own trigger" because somehow in America, politicians, are blaming the gun for the mass murders and not the person pulling the trigger.

Not only is this a slap in the face to the shooter's victim's, this also in turn helps the government pass their hidden agenda and we all know what that is, which is the fact that these State politicians, are constantly trying to take your guns away. Do you realize in the past 5 years alone we have had more teen school shootings than any other form of teen murder. Yet the government shows you that they could care less about the victims and more about getting rid of the Americans guns.

According to Wikipedia and other sources, in the last 5 years from 2015 – 2020, in the United States alone, there have been a total of 139 school shootings, where the main perpetrators were children and teens. These children and teens are usually subject to major mental and physical abuse and eventually can't take the abuse anymore, so they flip out, eventually killing most, if not all of their family members, then turning their frustration to their fellow students. One of the scary things about all of this is, it's been stated that most of these kids start their killing sprees at home, murdering their entire family, before they continue on to their schools or objective.

What it comes down to is, we need to sit down and talk to our children, asked them how there day is going, spend more time with them, before they go off on a killing spree. We also need to take the time to teach them about history and how it paved the way for us Americans today because if we don't, our nation will soon be destroyed by these history erasing, self-entitled, uneducated un-American teens. This all does kind of circle around to home is where it all starts because parents are the ones that these children often look up to and inspire to be like, but tend to go off the loop, when that inspiration is not there.

We as parents want our children to be able to dream big and grow up to be whoever they want to be, but if we lack in raising our children, they are often left unsupervised and tend to do whatever pops into their head because they know they will not be held accountable. Unfortunately, it does start from the day that these children are born because these newer generation of parent's claim that their children

204

don't have an orientation when they are born. This is where the mind screw starts because these children grow up thinking their one orientation, only to find out their the opposite orientation of what they were raised as.

These ridiculous trends have to be stopped, people need to realize that following trends like these, honestly makes no sense at all, you are following people that have created something because they think it's a cool thing to do. Seriously, you wouldn't jump off a bridge if other people were doing it, would you or you wouldn't jump in front of a car just because your buddy thinks it's a good idea, would you? People need to stop following people and start thinking on their own again, we used to do it in the past, we should be doing it now because we as Americans do have the ability to make up our own decisions about something.

Something like declaring the orientation of your own child because seriously, there are only two genders for children to be declared when they are born; two orientations, you are either having a baby boy or baby girl, no exceptions. This also goes back to American's having common sense and common knowledge because conmen sense tells you, you are either having a baby boy or baby girl. Common knowledge of anatomy, tells you that you are having a baby boy or baby girl, so why wouldn't you claim the orientation of your child?

Seriously, do you think this helps children in the long run, do you think kids benefit from your unwise decision, we already know that everything has to be watered down for kids these days, do you really want to set kids back further then they already are? Children tend to already be intrigued by just about anything, when they are growing up because they are introduced to a world that is filled with mystery and intrigue. The crazy thing is, growing up in our generation, you were always being taught about life, people raised you like you were one of their own, treated you the same way too, but you learned valuable lessons about common sense and doing what's right, rather than doing what's wrong.

That doesn't occur today though, everyone hates everyone so the world is separated and divided, therefore people treat others the wrong way, but race plays the biggest role in all of this because separation and division fits the democratic narrative. It's crazy because the narrative being pushed by these people, keeps Americans separated, we've seen this push by watching people, who show love for the American flag being labeled racist for supporting it. Not only that, according to these very same people, if you don't kneel during the American national anthem, you are a supporter of white supremacy and part of our systemically racist government.

This honestly makes no sense because the American National Anthem was created and designed to be an American symbol of freedom, back in 1931, but since this newer generation has no clue about history, they believe the delusions passed on by these people who want to erase our entire American culture. It's really because democrats and these Marxists blm leader's, have convinced millions of people to believe that these American symbols represent hate and white supremacy. We know, these American symbols represent the thousands of men and women, who have fought and died, to give you the right to be free in this country.

When you are kneeling to the American national anthem, you are not advocating for racial equality, you are not advocating for racial justice, you are spitting in the face of the thousands of men and women who came before you. These men and women laid their lives on the line every day, so you could enjoy the choice of being free, but people don't care, they follow idiots like Lebron James and other basketball players, who kneel during the American National Anthem because they claim they are advocating for equality.

It honestly just shows you how dumb these people really are and how brainwashed they have become because to honestly think that the American National Anthem represents white supremacy, just makes you a special kind of stupid. Seriously, where is the correlation between the American National Anthem and white supremacy? Hundreds of minorities are being robbed and killed in urban communities all across America, not by white people, not by police officers, but by other minorities, how is kneeling to the American national anthem taking a stand against that deadly violence occurring daily in urban communities?

Then you hear these same people claim that they are kneeling to the American national anthem because they are advocating to get rid of systemic racism, yet is it really systemic racism, when you're the one responsible for the chaos and violence that has occurred in your community for decades? I honestly fail to understand how kneeling to the American national Anthem helps you advocate for racial justice and equality, when your own kind is the one responsible for all the violence occurring to your own people?

Seriously, is kneeling to the American national anthem going to stop other minorities from robbing and killing people in urban communities, is kneeling to the American national anthem going to stop drug dealers and gangs from dealing drugs in urban communities, I think not. I'm surprised this dude even graduated high school because he is a straight idiot and yea I said it, Lebron James is an idiot, anyone who claims that their own people are being hunted down like dogs by police on a daily basis, is clearly a senile idiot.

The sad thing is, this idiot has millions upon millions of followers on his social media sites, yet, he uses his influence to push hate and make these outrageous statements that he should obviously think about before he makes them. Before we move on, think about this for a second, Lebron James, makes more money off of endorsements from China, then he does in America, yet, he's complaining about a systemically racist government, who is oppressing him and his people. This is a major problem we have today, millions of people are following the lead of people who don't care about other's and these people have proven that they only care about what benefits themselves or their so-called narrative.

I say this because as we discussed before, Lebron and others, were made rich by the very people they are berating and belittling, yet they could care less as they continue to push their theory of hate, every chance they get. Back in the day, everyone from your parents to your neighbors, everyone was teaching you about life choices and knowing the consequences of a bad one, not anymore though, according to people like Lebron, blm and their followers, if you make bad life choices it's okay because you can just blame it on other people. This is what I fail to understand about this so-called systemic racism against all minorities, it honestly makes no sense because minorities claim to be oppressed, yet, they control their own destinies, just as everyone else in America does.

But you have to think of it this way, minorities,, are the ones who choose to let gangs and drugs infest their communities, minorities, are the ones who are responsible for the decades of crime and violence that has plagued their communities, no one else is responsible. No one else is responsible for the chaos and violence that has fallen upon urban communities, except for the people living in those communities that are allowing it to happen.

Lebron, blm leaders and their followers don't care about this fact though, they don't care that this is true, their agenda is to push for white hatred and they will do anything to push that narrative. This is often why people saying our government is systematically racist towards them, tends to make no sense because minorities don't even like or let white people into their communities. White people are not in urban communities causing crime and increasing violence, minorities are though, minorities even tend to control these communities, letting in who they want to let in. So seriously, how are white people to blame for the crime plaguing urban communities, how are white people responsible for the violent deaths occurring in urban communities?

White people are not and cannot be responsible for someone else actions, other than their own, but millions of minorities believe they are, which to me is crazy. These minorities, led by blm, honestly believe that even though minorities made all these bad life choices, it doesn't matter, it's still white peoples fault they are in the situation they are in. Their education and schools are the same way, since white children are said to be doing better than minorities in schools, certain schools have chosen to lower their own standards and dumb down school, so minorities have a better chance of being passed.

One example to look at is school teachers because most of these teachers are quick to pass minority teens just to get rid of them, so they did not have to deal with these misfits in their classes, which is often because these teens themselves are uncontrollable and listen to no one. People blame these teacher's, but when you think about it, is it really the teachers fault that these kids act the way they do, is it really the teacher's fault that these kids have no discipline? The answer would be a strong no because the fault falls on their parents. Discipline and self-control, are really characteristics or traits that seems to be missing these days because without these behavioral traits, these kids have become uncontrollable little destruction makers.

These kids tend not listen to anyone because they have no authority figures in their lives, there's no one telling them what's right and what's wrong, so this decision is made by them. Most of these teens may have parent's at home, but their parents aren't real authority figures or people that take charge in their lives, so even their parents have a hard time controlling them. The only break their parents get is when they are sent off to school for the day, but since democrats and liberals have taken that away, these parents are stuck trying to control kids that just don't want to listen.

That's another sad thing, besides what COVID-19 has done to our country, we are now seeing public schools being closed left and right, all thanks to our State mayors and governors, who claim that there is no money available in the state budget for public school systems. Closing public schools is crazy because how does the government justify closing public schools, especially when these schools are mainly available to the public. Due to lack of funds, these State officials have chosen to close public schools, yet most of these politicians are seen fighting to keep private schools open, which are schools designed only for profit.

The weird thing to think about is, the government spends more money on war and foreign aid, then it does on our education system, so it would seem as if they don't seem to really care about Americans receiving an education. Thanks to a mismanaged budget and the closing of public schools, the government is forcing parents to try and provide an education for their children by sending them to private schools, schools parents can barely afford. We already know that parents are not involved enough in their children's education, but seriously, how are parents supposed to provide an education for their children, when there is no education to be had?

Private schools cost a fortune, but since public schools are being closed left and right, private schools are the only ones available to the communities, which make it harder for parents to educate their kids. That's right though, in America, State officials like to make money off of our children, so they close public schools and open private schools, not really caring whether parents can afford it or not. Just like the U.S. Prison system, it's all designed for profit, doesn't matter that the American middle class are the ones who has to pay for everything, it's all about making other people rich, especially city and State Officials.

To break it down in a much simpler way, we can look at reviews of these Profit Schools because according to Private School reviews, it's been stated that the average cost for a private elementary school is close to $12,000 dollars a year and private high schools average out at about $17,000 dollars each year. So, you can just imagine how expensive it is for the American middle class, especially if you have more than one child because then you're paying double, sometimes triple, which is often more then you even make in one year, all this just to keep your kids in school.

When you think about it, you see that it will literally cost you close $40,000 a year for your child to receive an education. It doesn't stop there, this is just one year, you would honestly go broke if you had to send your children to both a elementary school, then a private high school. This is what America has become though, the rich get richer, while the poor get poorer, politicians do anything for power and this includes taking advantage of the American people because for them it's all about keeping power, while they fill their pockets.

These State politicians never have enough of both, so they do whatever it takes to get more, this includes lying and deceiving the American people, to further deepen their own pockets. Children should have an education to look forward too, whether their parents can afford it or not, parents shouldn't have to go broke trying to provide an education for their kids. Public schools should never be forced to close, especially when they are available specifically to the public, also the fact that the American people pay a school tax every year to keep public schools open.

This yearly school tax is even paid by citizens of the community that don't have kids attending the school system, but since they are in the school district, they have to pay a school tax. It honestly makes no sense to me because our government spends billions of dollars on foreign aid, so they can help third-world countries and their people, yet at the same time, they budget only a few million to invest into our children and our American education system. So seriously, why does our government spend billions of dollars on foreign aid to help out other counties, but when it comes to the American education system, they only spend a few million?

It's not the same in America anymore, education is not the same anymore, learning is not the same anymore and now thanks to a 98.6% curable disease, instead of learning in a classroom, these kids are at home learning from computer screens. No one focuses on the importance of an education anymore, these people rather teach their children to use their race and their hatred for other's as a way to get ahead in life, which to me is crazy because raising children this way provides them with no future. Unfortunately, this is often why these kids grow up with no guidance, no one shoving them in the right direction, but also no one guiding them on what's right and what's wrong. As we all know, online social media platforms are dangerous places for anyone, we've already discussed that people will easily go online and tear down you and your family, although they have no clue who you are as a person.

This verbal assault doesn't stop with adults though, children and teens are also going online to berate and belittle people and other kids and these are children, doing it because they seen their elders doing it. We've seen the unfortunate outcome of this hatred play out several times, one thing every parent should never have to experience, young kids taking their own lives because kids from school continued their hateful verbal assaults online in front of hundreds. This tragic event has played out with high school students all across America, teens are killing themselves because they can't handle the hatred or verbal abuse that they are exposed to daily.

Unfortunately, we now have kids learning, preaching and teaching hate, their parents never guided them to what was right, so they chose their own path and they see hatred as a way to justify their actions. This deep hatred for white people and true Americans, is stirred up online, on social media platforms and unfortunately, innocent teens are caught in the crosshairs, which then makes them the target of thousands of teens, who don't even know who these victims are, but since other teens are doing it, they join in on the verbal assault.

That's one of the major problems we have in America, we have too many people, even kids that easily follow the lead of others, they easily follow the lead of people who use hate as an excuse for their horrible actions. It falls on the behaviors they learned from home, also how these parents are hardly there to raise their children, there is no discipline, there is no guidance, so these teens are left raising themselves.

Don't get me wrong, there are parents out there that are amazing with their kids, the parents that are doing the right thing, spending the time with their kids, teaching them, raising them right and to these parents I applaud you. I'm referring to the other parents, who are so involved in their own lives, they tend to forget they even have kids, which then forces their own kids to grow up faster, so they can take care of themselves, but also their siblings. With this lack of parent involvement or lack of simply acting like parents, these kids are forced to grow up quicker than they should, which also forces children to deal with adult situations, at a child's level.

This could be why most of these teens grow up with so much hatred towards other's, they are tired of the situation they are in, since they are stuck in this ongoing situation of no hope, they release their frustrations the only way they know how, which is to take their frustrations out on other people or other property. Their parent's authority is no longer there because the discipline was never there from the beginning, so they tend to live by their own rules, disciplining themselves for the actions they commit towards others.

The interesting thing about all of this is, this is just half the problem these teens deal with, today's parents seem to be so wrapped up in their own lives, that they tend to forget about anyone and everyone else around them, this includes their very own kids. I think this is where I really start to worry about our species because people are literally forgetting their own kids in the back seats of their vehicles, forgetting them long enough to where these poor kids are being killed due to suffocation or heat stroke. Just imagine that though, you just had a baby that you carried for 9 months, one day while going to the store, you were so caught up in what you were doing that you left your own baby in a hot burning car for hours to suffocate and die.

I think when I talk about this stuff, my mind just wants to say, this can't really be happening can it, but the stories I see on the daily news tells me, yes it can and the sad thing is that this isn't just occurring once or twice, its occurring way more than it should be. It's just insane to think about because these innocent children are being killed all thanks to their parent's stupidity, all thanks to their parents that are so involved in themselves, they forget about the kid sitting in the back seat. Seriously, how do you forget your own child in the back seat of your car, a child who you carried for 9 months, the same child you buckled in for safety before you left your house to take your trip to the store?

That's also what is very worrisome, these parents are not just leaving their babies or children in the cars for a couple minutes, these parents are leaving these babies and children in their cars for hours, sometimes longer. This to me is unjustifiable, you should be charged with premeditated murder because you literally left your child in a hot car long enough to where the child died from heat exhaustion. That's another sad reality occurring today, some parent's are so wrapped up in their own lives, they tend to forget they even have kids, so their kids are left fending for themselves.

In reality, these parents shouldn't be parents, they should not be in charge of the care for other's because they don't have the time or devotion it takes to care for anyone but themselves. Seriously, how could you honestly be so wrapped up in your own life, where you forget about your child sitting in the back seat, the child you buckled in for safety? Not only is this happening with kids, but this is even happening with peoples animals too, so just imagine if these people killing their animals had children, I think we'd all be in big trouble.

Americans have a lot of problems right now, problems that are slowly taking over, but if Americans just stopped and thought things through before they acted, we could probably fix most of the problems we have and start rebuilding our great nation. Present day in America tends to speak for itself because our country is filled with turmoil, destruction and chaos, minorities have been tricked into thinking they are suffering from systemic racism, but it's really their own bad life choices that got them where they are today. People don't want to hear this though, they don't want to hear the truth, they don't want to hear that their bad life choices put them in the situation they are in.

Instead they want to listen to people like the Obama's, Ophra and Lebron James, who basically wants minorities to feel like they are oppressed and enslaved by our systemically racist. There is no end to their lies or their deceptions because these very same people are the same ones claiming that the American Flag and the American national anthem are not symbols of freedom, but symbols of white supremacy. Like we discussed before, State politicians and influential people have tricked millions of Americans into thinking that both these symbols of freedom are actually symbols of racism.

It's insane and the logic of course makes no sense because you are claiming that if you are in America and support the American flag and the American national anthem, you are racist and a member of white supremacy. I am not making this stuff up, these people have instilled these ideas into millions of people, millions of Americans are being told that, to be American, is to be a traitor. It's puzzling to me because

213

if you are in America, you are American, you may be white, you may be minority, you may be of other origin, but if you are a citizen of the United States, you are American, no exceptions.

The logic and ideologies that these people use is just mind-boggling, you can see this by examining the minds of this newer generation, whose currently out protesting to take down statues of Abraham Lincoln because they claim that President Abraham Lincoln, was a white supremacist, who hated minorities. I wish I was making this stuff up, but it would honestly be to hard if I tried, but like we discussed before, these people are complaining that Abraham Lincoln, the U.S. President who was killed because he freed all slaves, was a white supremacist, who hated minorities.

I think Ron White said it best when he stated, "You can fix just about anything you need to, but folks, you just can't fix stupid" and he was right because you simply can't. The sad thing is, blm, minorities and minority civil leaders, used this excuse as the reason they wanted President Lincoln's Statue taken down. Lincoln's statue whose statue has stood there for decades, needs to be taken down because President Lincoln represented white supremacy. I mean honestly, the ignorance runs deep with these people and they show it every single day. Forget the fact that President Lincoln started the Civil War to free the slaves, forget that President Lincoln passed an amendment to free the slaves and I guess you can also forget the fact that President Lincoln was shot and killed for his so-called hatred of minorities.

That's the crazy thing about what these people are claiming is, President Lincoln would have never been killed if he didn't free the slaves, if President Lincoln would have never started the war, minorities would still have been enslaved and President Lincoln would have still been alive. Honestly, President Lincoln started the Civil war because he was tired of seeing people enslaved in chains, this is why he started a war and passed an amendment to make sure these people stayed free. It honestly makes no sense, but their statements only seem to get worse because according to these people, President Lincoln, was a white supremacist, who hated minorities, but wanted to keep slavery.

This was all supposedly because Lincoln wanted white people to be inferior to minorities. I mean, what kind of logic is that, what in our American history tells you that President Abraham Lincoln hated the entire minority race and wanted white people to be inferior? You really just want to look at these people, grab them and ask them what the hell is wrong with them. Seriously, President Lincoln started a war to free everyone who was enslaved because President Lincoln himself, hated seeing minorities suffer and in chains, what in history tells you or proves to you otherwise?

In fact, what people don't realize is that President Abraham Lincoln never owned a slave in his life, President Lincoln was against slavery from the very beginning, not because Lincoln supposedly hated minorities, but because President Lincoln thought slavery was not only wrong, but cruel and unusual punishment. President Lincoln even wrote to his friend Joshua Speed, a former slave-owner claiming that, "I confess I hate to see the poor creatures hunted down and caught and carried back to their stripes and unrewarded toils; but I bite my lip and keep quite.

In 1841 you and I had together a tedious low-water trip, on a Steam Boat from Louisville to the mouth of the Ohio, there were, on board, ten or a dozen slaves, shackled together with irons. That sight was a continual torment to me; and I see something like it every time I touch the Ohio, or any other slave-border. It is hardly fair for you to assume, that I have no interest in a thing which has and continually exercises, the power of making me miserable." This came directly from a letter President Abraham Lincoln wrote to his friend, Joshua Speed, explaining that when he sees slaves being treated the way they are, as a continual torment that makes him completely miserable.

Now explain to me, how a U.S. President that felt and thought this way about slavery, who fought tooth and nail to abolish slavery and even started a war to end slavery, would be a supporter of slavery? The fact of the matter is that, President Abraham Lincoln was never a supporter of slavery or the enslavement of anyone, Lincoln always fought against slavery and his letters prove so, his statues should not only be left alone, but they should be worshipped because without President Lincoln, this world would be a lot different.

This idiotic ideology of course is pushed by the people in charge, but also by these blm Marxists, who believe in changing our history so it better suits their ideas of history. These people want to keep our country divided, they want to keep our country separated and they'll claim anything they can, no matter if it makes sense or not. People need to stop ignoring the truth, minorities were not the only slaves in

America and white people didn't start slavery, African Moors did, so stop claiming otherwise because if you are, you are wrong. If you don't believe me, please feel free to look up your history, your real history, not the one made up by these idiots.

If you do, you will see exactly what I am talking about, your so-called enslaved ancestors sold your real ancestors to just about anyone who would pay them. White American colonist thought of you as people, your ancestors thought of you as a trade commodity, there's a difference. This kind of thinking really start's from home because these kids are not taught about their own history, they are not educated on what the country has gone through to become the great nation it is.

These kids are not taught about the thousands of American soldiers that gave their lives so other Americans could enjoy freedom, instead, they are taught to think that past American wars like the Revolutionary War, was started because of slavery, but also that slavery built America. Contrary to what these people claim, slavery was not the reason the Revolutionary War was fought and slavery did not build America. The Revolutionary War was started because American colonists from the first 13 Colonies, wanted their freedom from Great Britain, who still controlled them. American colonists were tired of Great Britain's Parliament taxes and lack of representation of the American people, so they wanted their own independence.

In fact, if you look up the Revolutionary War or the American War of Independence, you will also notice that slavery, was not even one of the main key causes for starting the Revolutionary War. Making bold statements like these, just shows you how ignorant these people, including teacher's and professors have become, but also how uneducated these teens really are. Due to people thinking and believing this way and passing this thinking onto their kids, we are left with undisciplined, uneducated and uncontrollable children, teens and young adults, who are being taught the wrong way by other people, who follow these ideologies of hate and entitlement.

Thanks to this idiotic ideology, but also blm Marxists, democrats and liberals, pushing their ill-minded philosophies onto others, self-entitlement has now become a justifiable claim. Self-Entitlement, has become a huge factor when it comes to people using their skin color as an excuse because these teens and young adults are under the assumption that they are entitled to everything, whether they've worked

216

for it or not. This wrong way of thinking was provoked by these blm Marxists, then pushed by democrats and liberals, who have tricked millions of people into thinking that they are still facing enslavement and oppression from white people and our government.

Thinking this way, helps these people use the color of their skin and their race, as an excuse, claiming they deserve to be handed everything simply because of their skin color. This tends to keep me puzzled because minorities berate other people and want to take away what they have simply because of their skin color. It honestly makes no sense when you think about it, not because everyone supposedly hates minorities, but because minorities keep themselves separated and divided, then turn around and blame white people for this division.

I honestly get lost when I tend to think about it, but I always come back to the very same question, if minorities are the ones responsible for all the chaos and violence occurring in urban communities, how does the blame fall on white people? It's honestly something that I can't seem to wrap my head around, I honestly fail to understand how people that don't live in the community or people that don't even live near the community, can be responsible for the crime, corruption, violence and death, occurring in the community. The latest thing I've seen is, news writers on yahoo writing about how people don't see the bigger picture, people complain about the violence in Chicago, but ignore the bigger picture.

I'm left sitting here like, what bigger picture are you referring too? In Chicago, minorities rob and kill each other daily, same thing can be said about cities like Baltimore and Atlanta. Therefore, what's the bigger picture were supposedly missing because all I see is violence occurring by minorities against other minorities? The fact that all of these people tend to forget is, people who live in urban communities tend to do what they want, they live how they want, what they don't do is, let white people or the government into their urban communities. This is a fact, white people cannot be held responsible for your terrible community or the bad choices you've made your entire life, the only one responsible is, yourself.

What's also proven to be true is, white people are barely living in these types of urban communities because they are mostly dominated by minorities and Hispanics, but they are also usually ran by minority city council members. This is really where all the white blame started,

217

like we discussed before, these democratic city mayors and governors blamed President Trump for all the violence occurring in their cities. Since these people claimed President Trump was nothing but a racist, which we all know is far from the truth, but these people claimed this opinion was true, since it's true, the blame gets turned to white people.

This is also the insane democratic logic that created all this white hatred, white people are supposedly responsible for all the horrible decisions minorities have made their entire lives, while the U.S. President is responsible for all the crime and violence they've committed in their communities. Minorities, don't focus much on an education, white people are to blame, minorities, don't focus much on jobs or a career, white people are to blame, minorities, have crime and violence running rampant in their communities, it's white peoples fault.

Knowing that, let me ask you something, if minority education is so bad and has been for generation after generation, why isn't all minority schools and colleges, being held responsible, why are white people and so-called white schools only being blamed? This to me is the ultimate question and double standard because minorities all over America are complaining about receiving a bad education, but at the same time, minorities have separate schools and private colleges that are only available to minorities. These minority only schools and colleges have been around for generations, not just decades, so why are these minority teacher's and professors not being blamed for the reason why minorities have no education?

The puzzling part is the blame and excuses these minority students use because it's not that they think the education system in a white school is unfair, no, it's because minority students want to only be taught by minority teachers. Seriously, these minority students claim that white teachers can't teach them because they are minority, so white teacher's can't relate to them, therefore they somehow can't be taught by white teacher's. If I am not mistaken, the only difference between teacher's is, the time they've been teaching, every person wanting to become a teacher goes to college and learns the same curriculum that everyone else learns to become a teacher or professor.

There is no racial course for teacher's to study, teachers are not taught to teach you, only if you are a certain skin color, they are taught to teach everyone the same. This again is why racism will never die in America, to many people use their race as an excuse, they don't care about other people or making mistakes, society has taught them that they can easily blame their problems on other people, rather than take responsibility for their own actions.

The statements that come from these minority students alone should be considered racist and discriminating against white teacher's, but according to democrats, liberals, blm leaders and minority students, it's not racist if the statement is coming from them, but it's racist when it's coming from white students. This way of thinking should sound familiar, blm leaders, started this very theory, they claimed that they can say anything racist to white people, while white people can't say anything. It didn't stop with just the racism though because these blm leaders and their followers told and pushed people to destroy communities and businesses.

This was of course because it all supposedly belonged to the white man, yet over half the businesses that were destroyed, were minority owned businesses. This is the logic these minority students tend to follow, this is why we have teens destroying our communities, neighborhoods and businesses because they are not the ones that have to rebuild everything after it's been torn down. These people are not the ones that have to suffer and pay the cost for what they did, none of them are held accountable for their actions because they are under the assumption that it's not their fault.

What scares me is, these are younger adults, also teens, who are running around burning everything down and destroying communities, not the minorities, who are out trying to provide a life for themselves and their families. No matter what you try to say to these younger adults, they will always be dead set in their beliefs, which is crazy because they fight for equality, but their advocating and fighting; is burning down minority owned businesses and destroying dozens of urban communities. This is why I fail to understand the purpose of the blm movement, they protest and claim their doing it for racial equality, yet, dozens of innocent minorities are being shot and killed during these riots and protests.

This is also a fact, there have been more minorities, children and adults, murdered during these riots and protests, more than the minorities that were killed by police officers in the past two years. Innocent minority children and adults, are being innocently gunned down during these so-called peaceful riots and protests, yet their lives do not matter because if they did, these minorities wouldn't have been killed in the first place, seeing that they were all killed by other minorities, not by white people.

With no discipline for these kids, it's turning young teens into uncontrollable, self-entitled crybabies, who don't contribute anything to society, but will destroy society instantly, if they are not given what they want. Destruction is the only way they succeed in life, so that's the route they tend to choose, but without anyone guiding them in the right direction, the only thing that ensues is, chaos. If you haven't already noticed, America tends to have more follower's then real actual leader's, you can clearly see this by all the destruction occurring to our American national monuments and statues because once one person started to follow the chaos and destruction, millions of others followed and intensified the chaos and destruction.

The other harsh side of what we've been exposed to is, millions of people trying to cancel an entire culture simply because these people claim it's offensive to them and their people, yet it's an entire race. Think about that for a second because these people firmly believe that instead of representing American freedoms, our American national monuments and statues, represent white supremacist men, who hated minorities and fought for the enslavement of all minorities. The sad thing is, this is not a thought these people came up with, this is not their logical way of thinking, this was a thought pushed onto them by democrats, leftist and liberal's, who want to secretly change our great nation into their version of America.

Honestly, who else would believe in the destruction of American national monuments and statues, but would also use the race card as an explanation as to why they should be removed, people that secretly want to destroy America and erase our American values. A few things that are interesting to think about are the facts that, we have American State mayors and governors, letting their cities be overrun by criminals, we have American State Representatives and politicians fighting to give illegal immigrants our money.

We also have an American Speaker of The House, that claims American national monuments and statues, also the U.S. President, are racist. You honestly think these people care about America, especially when they've pushed for the chaos and destruction of America? The key word I used was American because the only one talking about the

American people, fighting for the American people, supporting the American people, passing laws for the American people, is President Trump. This is also what makes every single statement that these State politicians and city officials make, puzzling.

These politicians always claim to be doing it for the American people, they always claim their fighting for the American people, yet their actions always proves otherwise. These are the very same people who tend to be responsible for the separation and divide being forced upon Americans because that's what these people want. They want Americans to be separated because when Americans are separated, it's easier to spread their lies and deceptions to the few, that way, the few, can then spread the false information to the many.

What these people really crave is control and power, with control comes manipulation, with power comes coercion, so they tell us what they want us to believe and only show us what they want us to see. Like we discussed before, these are the very same political people and influential individuals that own and control most of the platforms that brings Americas our news and information. Unfortunately, the fallacy that people are tricked into believing in, helps these political figures pass there fallacious arguments onto everyone who will listen, because they all claim this is the democratic way.

These arguments are just that though, fallacious because their arguments always appear better than they actually are, this is what they want, they want to mislead you, this helps them push their lies and deceptions. These people even start with our children, we know this because these very same State politicians are pushing to teach children in Elementary about their civil rights and civil rights movements, instead of teaching them about their ABC's. I honestly believe it's because children are very acceptable to new things, they easily accept something when told, they easily accept something other people tell them to or easily do what they see other people doing.

Teens on the other hand, are a little more difficult to deal with, but they are also easily deceived, especially the ones that were raised with hatred because when someone hates you, it doesn't take much to push that hatred further. Like we talked about before, this behavior often starts from home, when there is no discipline or some kind of authority at home, teens tend to follow who they admire, with this admiration comes destructive movements, movements that are often based on lies

221

and fallacious arguments. I remember when we were younger, if you stepped out of line, you were spanked and disciplined, sometimes with a paddle. This was not child abuse, this was discipline and you learned as a kid or teen not to do it again, simply because you didn't want another spanking.

Like I also stated before, spanking your kids to discipline them is not child abuse, people need to stop claiming that it is child abuse because that's the only way these kids are going to learn and be put on the right path. You don't have to take my word for it because we've been exposed to this bad behavior time and time again, we've seen the undisciplined kids who are driving their parent's nuts, but their parents are stuck between a rock and a hard place. These parents want to discipline their kids, they want to educate their kids on what's right and what's wrong, but since discipline is seen as a bad thing, they are stuck dealing with unruly kids that grow into unruly teens.

Thanks to millions of people that claim disciplining your children is abuse, children and teens could care less about authority because they've never had any form of authority in their lives and the people that do try to discipline them, are easily brushed off. In reality, child abuse along with child enslavement, are huge problems that go unnoticed in America, people assume that when they see parents disciplining their kids, it's child abuse. It makes no sense because these same people ignore their own neighbors, who are secretly abusing children, who they've abducted or kidnapped from their own families.

You can easily see what I am referring to when you look up, "Operation not forgotten", where the U.S. Marshals were able to find and save 39 children, who had been previously abducted or kidnapped from their families. An amazing feat for the U.S. Marshals because thanks to them 39 children get to live free of enslavement, but the sad thing about this is, all these children were found in communities and neighborhoods all around Georgia. This is something that should be a concern to all Americans, these children were found in the United States of America, they were found in communities and neighborhoods, which normal people like you and me live in.

It's crazy because this is taking place daily in the United States, children and kids are being kidnapped and abducted, but that's not our focus. Instead Americans and our State politicians focus on people that are merely trying to discipline their kids. It's crazy when you think

222

about it because there have been more recorded incidents of children being physically abused, tortured and killed, by their own parents and step-parents, more than any other form of child endangerment, but all these cases are ignored until it's too late.

Spanking and disciplining your children because they act like retards, is not child abuse, those who claim it is, really need their heads checked, but also need to just stay out of business that isn't any of theirs. Real child abuse and child endangerment is being ignored, while parents trying to simply raise their children, are being labeled as criminals committing crimes all because they were seen spanking or disciplining their own children. You think any of us 80's, 90's and early 2000's kids would talk back to our parents like these kids today, you got another thing coming, a paddle on the behind would be the only thing you would receive.

Today's kids, wouldn't know what to do if they were spanked, they have no idea the fear that is instilled by your mom saying, "Wait till your father get's home". The fear that was once instilled to discipline and keep kids in check, are no longer there, this is because everyone seems to think they can raise your children better then you can, they will even act as if they have the right too. Thanks to millions of people shoving their noses where they don't belong, children and teens are growing up without restrictions, without discipline, without direction and because of this, these kids easily follow the actions of people they watch on television, which usually starts with chaos and ends with some form of major destruction.

These teens have no authority figures to tell them otherwise, they have no forceful parents telling them that it's not the right thing to do, instead they follow people, who see a benefit in only helping themselves, not others. It's crazy because this newer generation of parents are no longer acting like parents, they are never at home enough to care for their kids, but they also never bothered to educate their kids on right from wrong, so now their children are chaos causing, damage inducing hoodlums.

Due to this lack of parent involvement, you have children raising themselves, then as they get older, they themselves turn into the parents because now they are raising their own siblings with the same hatred they were raised with. This is also where the hatred for other people comes into play because if these young kids were born with hate, grew

223

up with hate, hate is all they know and hate is all they learn. This important factor, besides other factors, could be the reason why we are now surrounded by uneducated, undisciplined, self-entitled children and teens that tend to do what they want, whenever they want.

Back in the day there was discipline, we acted out and guess what, we were disciplined and never did it again, but we also learned from our mistakes and learned right from wrong, but we also had common sense. Today's younger generation tends to act like they have no common sense, they only believe their opinion or the opinion they've been told to believe matter's, they don't believe in history, they don't believe in fact's, they believe what other's have told them. The crazy thing to think about is the fact that, these teens are killing people if you don't agree with them, it's no longer a debate, it's no longer a conversation, if you offend these teens in any way, they will easily shoot you without any hesitation.

This has become an outlet for misfit and misguided teens because they use this as a form of revenge for the people who have wronged them or the people that won't give in to their demands. We often see this gun violence play out in family situations between teens and their parents, these teens parents don't give in to their demands, so these teens act out with violence towards their own parents. What makes one person snap and kill people, we will never know, but teens are getting into violent confrontations with their parents and they are turning to murdering their own parent's as the solution to the problem.

These often-violent confrontations tend to start rather simple and are intensified by some form of hatred or frustration, we can see this by taking a look at the story of the couple in upstate New York, who were killed by their very own son. The story coming out of upstate New York, is about a 17 year old, who shot and killed his parents with a shotgun, not because they were bad parents or they did something wrong to him, but because his parents told him that they would not go to the store and buy him more beer. Since they denied him the beer, the son literally took a shotgun, loaded it and shot both of his parents in the back, not once, but 3 or 4 times each.

So that is shooting, loading, shooting, loading, shooting, loading, simply because his parents told him they wouldn't buy him more beer. His poor innocent father, was found face down in the kitchen and his poor innocent mother, was found face down in the master bedroom, both were found dead, shot several times in the back by a shotgun. I am not too sure what would possess someone to kill someone, especially when it's their your own parents, but if it's because of the reason described by prosecutors, it's mind boggling to me that a son would kill his parents without any hesitation simply because his parents would not go get him more beer.

Unfortunately, these brutal murders are not only happening in New York, throughout the years, there have been numerous young teens, ranging from 7 to 17, who are out committing premeditated murder, out shooting school's up, assaulting people and killing people without any hesitation. These murders usually occur after argument's or confrontations go horribly wrong or they've been offend in some way, these teens let their frustrations lead to hanger, which then leads to violence. The interesting part is, no one wants to discuss these issues, no one wants to discuss the fact our children are no longer safe on the streets or even in school.

Nope, these people are more concerned with illegal immigrants and the effects and damage plastic straws and bags, are having on our country. You can see this by examining the recent ban on plastic straws and plastic bags in New York, but also how illegal immigrants can now obtain drivers licenses, we focus on unimportant issues, not the real issues we should be more concerned with. This is funny to me because you think to yourself, how in the hell are plastic straws and bags so bad for the economy that they are banned, yet everything in the world, every product we see in America, contains some form of plastic in one way or another.

These people in charge act like plastic bags are the biggest problem in the United States, but the fact is that, everything we buy comes in plastic, is wrapped in plastic and even contains plastic, but plastic is the problem, so these people put a ban on it. It honestly makes no sense because these people are basically claiming that plastic is more of a problem then homicides, suicides, homeless veteran's, poverty, school shootings, mass-terrorism, pandemics, diseases, enslavement, kidnappings and even illegal immigrants.

Think about their solution to plastic bags though, paper bags, that's right so now instead of using something we can make, we decide it's better to tear down forest and trees, so we can make more paper bags and paper straws because plastic bags and straws are too dangerous. I would think killing the environment to make more paper bags would be more dangerous to the environment, but that would just label me as a free individual thinker, thinking on my own again, so my opinion would be wrong to these people. I honestly think that it's just another way for grocery stores to make money off the American people because it's almost just like another tax, the only thing that is different is that, this tax is just a dollar or so.

Which in all reality is one big joke because you expect Americans to shop at your grocery store, buy tons of groceries, but when it comes to bagging our groceries that we have to buy and pay taxes on, you are going to charge us an additional fee for the bags we need to carry our groceries in? Not much sense to me there, but it's also puzzling because some stores have resorted to not using any bags at all, paper or plastic, these store associates scan your items and put them back into the cart, so you are left to bag up your own groceries using whatever you have available.

It honestly makes no sense, like a lot of things three days because people focus on problems that are not really issues, which then forces the real issues to be swept to the side. People tend to do this a lot in America, real issues, real problems, are often ignored or pushed to the back, while problems that really shouldn't be considered problems, are brought to the forefront. This is exactly what helped the blm movement get off the ground, after 7 years of doing nothing, these blm Marxists leaders, received a fresh start after they took the problem of police officers killing minorities and turned it into a nationwide problem of police brutality.

The real issue at hand here is that minorities are dying at an alarming rate, the problem is that minorities are the ones responsible for this alarming rate of death, yet minorities claim that the ones responsible for their problems, are white police officers. Now because this opinion is shared by millions of minorities, especially minority youths, everything related to the color white is labeled racist and anything that deals with white people or white history, is claimed to be related to white supremacy, so it is to be changed or rewritten.

The sad thing is, we have already seen this play out in our schools across America, professors have rewritten their own version of American history, which they based entirely on slavery. It's only because of President Trump, that this idiotic way of teaching was stopped and teacher's are no longer allowed to teach their recreated non-American, non-sense to our children. This is something that democrats and liberals were responsible for because it was the democratic State senators and governors that claimed that our history is racist and built on white supremacy.

Since these American State politicians have the opinion that America is racist, but also being led by a racist U.S. President, they try to pass laws that will change and erase our entire history. We see this coming from democrats and liberals all the time, they don't believe in the American way of life, they don't believe in American history or our traditions, since they don't believe in American history, they want to erase it, so they can rewrite their own version. They used this theory to start the movement of tearing down American national monuments and statues because democrats and liberals deceived millions of minorities into thinking that all these American heroes, were racist and only looked out for white people.

This was the ideology pushed by democrats, liberals and leftists, not President Trump, yet they all blame President Trump for the problems they've caused. It honestly makes no sense because these politicians and influential people have convinced millions of minorities that these statues represent white supremacy, even statues of Abraham Lincoln, the U.S. President who started a war and passed an amendment that freed all people that were enslaved. What makes absolutely no sense at all is the fact that millions of people act like the entire United States of America, was involved in slavery, which we know is not true, if it was true, the Civil War would have never been fought.

The Civil War, was started because President Lincoln, wanted to free the people that were being enslaved in the South, the North did not have slavery, the North hated the idea of slavery, President Abraham Lincoln was one of them, therefore him and others in the North, never participated in the enslavement of others. African leader's did, African leader's, started, participated, profited, anything you can think of they did it and the sad thing is, most African slaves were sold for small things like blankets and bread.

So to see dozens of minority teacher's and professors, even school president's, claim that former U.S. President Abraham Lincoln was a white supremacist, who only supported the progress of white people, makes you question their credentials, not to mention their character. If

227

these statements were being made by white teacher's and professors, about minority statues and how they might find them offensive, the results are not the same, nothing would be done because it would still somehow turn into white people discriminating against minorities.

Isn't that technically considered discrimination against an entire race, though? It's puzzling because these minority leader's, are literally trying to erase and dismantle our entire American heritage and history because they claim it's racist and offensive to their people, so it needs to be changed, not should be changed, but needs to be changed. It doesn't make much sense because the history these people are trying to erase, is the same history that these people share with everyone else. All Americans share the same history, there is no separate white history, there is no separate black history, there's American history.

You can't rewrite something that has already been studied and written by hundreds of people for hundreds of years simply because you don't like it and think it badly represents your people. Remember, early minority property, land and slave owners, fought in the South for the right to keep their people enslaved, unlike President Lincoln and the Americans to the North. These people are literally trying to destroy our entire culture, destroy the entire legacies of the founding Americans, who fought and died for the freedoms these people take advantage of, but what's crazy is, they are trying to replace American history, with history that has no relevance to what Americans have been through as people, not just as a race.

Parent's already have a hard enough time as it is when it comes to trying to raise their kids right, but with everything going on right now, if we let this way of thinking continue, we'll be left with nothing but burnt down cities, burnt down communities, destroyed neighborhoods and people struggling to rebuild. We need to all honestly just sit down and talk about, who is really responsible for all this chaos and destruction occurring in America, but we also need to send these teens home, so they can be taught about history and the real problem they should be facing.

Seriously, white American's are not the problem, it's these State politicians and city leader's, that have been in the government for years, if not decades, claiming they are here to help minorities, yet the help never comes. Instead it's just more lies and deceptions, that comes from these State politicians, they lie to these people to get their vote,

228

but they never actually do what they have promised or said they were going to do. Honestly, think about it for a second, year after year, these State politicians and city leaders, have promised greener pastures, they've promised changed, but what has really changed, what have these people done to better the lives of minorities?

Nothing, nothing at all, they've honestly used the blame game this entire time, all the money they've ever received from the government to better their cities and communities was somehow diverted to other areas. It honestly keeps you questioning everything because millions of minorities blindly follow these State politicians and city leader's, yet these are the very same State politicians, that have let their cities, communities and neighborhoods be destroyed. These people are the sole officials, that are responsible for the progress of the community, they are the ones that are supposed to focus on the progression d advancement of the neighborhood.

These are the city officials, that should be out telling these young minorities that they need to stop burning down businesses and destroying neighborhoods because these are also businesses owned by minorities, so all your really doing is destroying what took people years to build. Also, something important people need to start doing is, people need to start minding their own business, young and old people, need to stay out of other people's business. Let people live their own lives, but also let parent's discipline their own children because everyone is allowed to have an opinion, even you, but that doesn't make your opinion matter more than anyone else.

That's the harsh reality of online social media, anyone can get online and spread their opinion about you, whether they know you or not. With hundreds of following every word they say, people soon take it upon themselves to castrate you and even your family online because you chose to have an opinion that differs from theirs. Don't bother to have a conversation or debate with these young minorities, democrats or liberals because according to these people, if you don't agree with their opinion, you hate your country and you are un-American, although most of these people themselves are un-American.

We've talked a little about this before, there are national protests and movements, that have been created because people want to get rid of the American flag and the American national anthem, claiming that it's because they both represent racism. This ridiculous opinion has led millions of minorities to advocate against these so-called racist symbols by kneeling to the American national anthem and those Americans, who chose not to kneel to the American national anthem, are labeled traitors to America. Seriously, how does kneeling to something that represents American freedoms, advocating for minority justice?

We've talked earlier about people focusing on the wrong issues, the same thing can be said here, these people focus on advocating in ways that really do nothing for what they are advocating for because they advocate by kneeling to the American national anthem. Yet, they do nothing about the dozens of murders occurring daily in their communities. Just imagine how much change these millions of minorities could actually make to their communities, if they only invested the time in their communities, instead of kneeling to the American national anthem at a sports game.

These people call for minority justice and even have millionaire sports players, calling for racial equality and justice, which to me is funny because most of these sports players are rich, but also tend to be racist themselves and only want to better the lives of their own race. The whole thing with minority justice is the crazy though, 9% of minorities are killed by police each year, 9%,and the fact that minorities are yelling, "hands up don't shoot", leaves you wondering, who's hands were up? Trayvon Martin rushed a police officer, while resisting arrest, Erik Garner, resisted arrested and started struggling with police, George Floyd, resisted arrest and fought with the police.

Rashaayd Brooks, resisted arrest and fought with the police, even tazed a police officer, so please, tell me again which one of these criminals had their hands up? The fact is, none of these individuals or the other 9% of minorities that were killed by police had their hands up, they all resisted arrest, fought with the cops and ended up dead in the process. In my book, whether you are white American, minority, Asian, whatever, you resist arrest and put the police into what they think is a life or death situation, you are going to be shot or killed because police officers are taught to diffuse threats against themselves, by any means necessary.

Police officers don't just shoot at you once or twice, they are taught to shoot until the subject is neutralized, so if you resist arrest and fight with the police, your choosing to put your own life on the line. That's why it makes no sense that minorities are protesting about police brutality, they are rioting and destroying communities claiming they have a police brutality pandemic, but 14 minorities killed by police officers, can hardly be called a pandemic.

Another thing that is ignored by minorities is the fact that, white Americans and Asian Americans, are actually shot and killed more by police each year, then minorities are. You won't hear about these statistics though, you won't hear about these facts, minorities will ignore the truth because they only focus on what helps them push their agenda, the truth is not something that helps them, so they ignore it. This has already been proven though, white Americans and Asian Americans, are literally shot, and killed more by police each year, then any other race, these people are also guilty of doing the same thing as minority criminals, they resist arrest and get shot.

It's not the same though, the outcome isn't the same either, white Americans get killed, no one bats an eye, minority criminals get killed, millions of people burn down their own communities. Just so you can see what I am referring to, we can take a look at the case of Tony Timpa, a white American, who was killed almost the same way George Floyd was, but was killed several years before George Floyd was. Tony Timpa, a white American, was handcuffed and had his hands zip-tied behind his back, while he was on the ground a police officer had his knee jammed into Tony Timpa's back and shoulder area, cutting off all circulate on after several minutes of complaining that he couldn't breathe, Tony Timpa eventually drew his last breathe.

The police officers around him, thought he was asleep, so they left him lying there handcuffed and zip-tied, they didn't even bother to check to see if Tony was breathing or not, which he was not because he already drew his last breath. When the EMT's finally got Tony onto a gurney, a few minutes after they loaded him into the ambulance, Tony Timpa was pronounced dead on the scene, this was in December of 2016, years before George Floyd was even known to Americans. It was also declared that Tony Timpa called the police for help, but also did not even resist arrest or fight with the police, yet no riots, no protests, no city wide destruction, no justice for him.

Think about this for a second, it was 2016, Election year, yet no riots, no protests about police brutality, but fast forward four years and in 2020, the next Election year, a minority criminal gets killed for resisting arrest and all of a sudden the world has a police brutality pandemic. This is another thing people need to think about because if Europeans are protesting about police brutality and yelling, "Hands up, don't shoot", how does that work, European police don't carry guns?

Guns are outlawed in European countries, so European police do not carry them, so seriously, how does that work, how can they be blamed for shooting people, when they don't even carry guns? A lot of things people are doing now makes no sense at all, this is one of them. It's not just minorities that deal with police brutality, minority injustice is broadcasted more by the media and democrats because that's their narrative, that's their agenda, that's what they want people to focus on, when people are focused on one thing, it's hard to turn them away.

Look how long these protests and riots occurred for, some are still occurring today, but it's crazy because these should have already been stopped by State senators, mayors and governors, but they sit back and do nothing as they play the blame game. Millions of young minorities took this same stance, except instead of doing nothing, they destroyed their own communities and killed their own people, while they blamed it on everyone else. We can blame this behavior on stupidity because we need to start teaching these teens and young adults, that this behavior is not acceptable, destroying your own neighborhood, only hinders yourself and your community, no one else.

Minorities are destroying everything in sight because they've been lied to and deceived into believing that their own problems fall on other people, since the life choices they have made, haven't gotten them anywhere, they see an outlet in blaming other people. These people can't accept the fact that they chose the life they are living, they chose not to focus on getting an education, they chose to join gangs and sell drugs, no one else made that choice for them. It honestly keeps you puzzled because these are the very same minorities and many others, who claim people are living comfortably, especially white Americans, simply because of privilege, not because they worked for it.

People are not just living comfortable lives because they've been handed it, no, contrary to what democrats and blm leaders want you to believe, all American's, white, minority, Asian, Latino, all Americans, work for what we have. Hard working Americans are the ones who work to keep their mortgages paid, are the ones who work to keep their families and others fed. Hard-working Americans are the ones who work to have nice homes and nice communities, so seriously, why should hard-working Americans give up everything to minorities because you claim your race and skin color allows you to receive, what everyone else has worked hard for?

I got news for you millions of followers, there are hundreds of minorities that have good lives, not because they chose to use their race as an excuse, but because they chose to focus on a career and providing a good life for their families. These people don't think their people are being oppressed, like democrats and blm leaders claim they are and most of these minorities believe that the blm movement, hinders their entire race. The sad thing is that these minorities are called traitors and uncle toms because they chose to move their families to a safer community and uncle toms because these communities tend to be white communities.

Seriously though, like I asked before, how can you hate on a person for wanting their family to have a better life, along with living in a safer community? Minorities have every right to live in white communities, just as white people do, but it's not the white people, who are labeling them as traitors, it's minorities living in urban communities. We've seen this occurring on the evening news, young minorities are going into white communities and interrupting the lives of these people because they claim these people stole their neighborhoods and forced them out of these nice communities and into urban communities.

It's just total non-sense when you think about it because how could you honestly tell someone else, that the community or house they live in and pay for, was once owned by you, so they need to leave and give it back? I just feel bad for my fellow Americans because the logic is just insane, no one should think this is the right thing to do, no one should think this is even okay to do, but hundreds of young minorities are doing it every day to innocent people. You can see this display of ignorance a lot on face book and YouTube these days, these minorities are coming out in droves, protesting and rioting for criminals.

While at the same time, there's more injustice occurring in urban communities by minorities themselves, then any other community in the United States of America. There are innocent 3-year-old minorities being shot and killed by stray bullets, minority teens dying from sitting on their couches, while they are inside their own homes, watching cartoons. You also have young minorities being killed by stray bullets because they were simply playing in their front yards when gang members saw each other and decided to shoot it out. Where is their justice, where is the justice for the 18 minority individuals, who were murdered during one weekend in Chicago or the dozens of minority individuals, who were gunned down or murdered in Baltimore and Atlanta, over one weekend?

This isn't white American teens pulling these trigger's, this isn't white American teens doing these drive-by's, this isn't white American teens robbing and killing people, these are young minority teens, who could care less about who they hurt or who they kill, including their own. We need to stop the killing period, we need to stop blaming people for our own problems because if the people responsible for the problem will not take blame, it's kind of hard to develop a solution.

The problem is, good Americans, are being seen as bad Americans because we believe in our American history and American tradition because of these beliefs, minorities have been deceived into thinking, that all white Americans living today are former slave owners and racist white supremacists. Millions of minorities no longer see white Americans as people or their neighbors, they no longer see us as equal's, now minorities judge white Americans by the color of our skin, not because this is what they believe, but because this is what they were taught to believe. Conduct of character, is no longer a thing, people don't judge you on your character, people don't judge you on your actions, they judge you by the color of your skin.

Now let me also clarify, although I am referring to minorities and minority teens, white American's are not completely innocent here, white American teens and young adults, are also standing side by side, with these blm cry-babies, complaining about a systematically racist government. The thing that is questionable about the whole blm movement is, if you say, "All lives matter", to these people, you are labeled racist, but you're also discriminating against minorities, but when you say, "black lives maters", it's okay because your supporting the lives of minorities, seriously? It makes no sense because doesn't, "all lives matters," mean that all lives matter, which include the lives of minorities, I might be wrong, but I would think it does?

How do you honestly justify that saying, "all lives matter," makes you a racist, but screaming, "black lives matter," isn't racist, when in reality, all lives matter, all races are just as important as yours. The sad thing is that, these ridiculous claims and statements, are not just coming

234

from blm leaders and protestors, nope, dozens of Americans are getting in trouble and being called racist for saying, "all lives matters", instead of saying "black lives matters".

This is of course our democrats and liberals hard at work here because they tend to be behind most of these movement's, these politicians claim it's all for the American people, but if it's all for the American people, how could people get in trouble for saying, "all lives matters"? Seriously, how is it racist to say, "All lives matter", when you are referring to all American lives and all American races? All lives do matter, just because you claim it's a racist statement, doesn't make it any less true, but that's your opinion, not ours, people are allowed to have a difference of opinion, you can't ignore our opinion all because you don't like what we have to say.

That's what is wrong with us as a country today, we celebrate the bad and castrate the good, we turn criminals into heroes and heroes into criminals, we take care of illegal immigrants, while we leave our veterans homeless. We've seriously gone wrong as a country and the fact that Sleepy Joe Biden claims that he will being giving U.S. citizenship to over 11 million illegal immigrants, if he's elected, should scare all of us. The fact that there is 11 million people over here illegally, is mind-boggling itself because these people are over here illegally and the government knows it.

Still, the government does nothing about it and now, democrats are talking about giving these illegal's immigrants instant citizenship. I thought illegal means illegal and if you are known to be illegal, you are deported back to your country, so seriously, how do we have over 11 million illegal immigrants living in the United States? Like I said before, if we only focused on the real issues Americans face, we'd be better off, instead other Americans blame their problems on people that are not even remotely responsible, the people who are actually trying to make a difference in the world. This even includes the parents of this newer generation, the good parent's trying to raise their kids right, are somehow seen as bad parent's, while the parent's that don't bother to educate or raise their kids, are seen as the good parents.

Now these so-called bad parents, are forced to deal with the backlash from hundreds of people online, who don't even know them, including the media because yahoo and other media outlets, love to publish fake online news articles about others that have no truth or facts behind them. Lately, our very own news media outlets have just become terrible, they spread more fake news and false information, then anyone else, the truth is something they don't concern themselves with, it's sad because this is how we are supposed to know what's going on in the world.

The proof is in the making when it comes to online news because yahoo will easily post an article about a white bartender, who shot and killed a young innocent unarmed minority protestor. They won't bother to mention in the article that, the so-called innocent unarmed minority teenager jumped the bar tender, who was only trying to protect himself. The real truth of the situation isn't what these people write about, this isn't news to them, the news is that a minority was killed by a white man, so that's the story they push and publish.

It's always fake news because they only publish what they want you to hear, they only talk about what they want you to believe, we can see this in the same article because they fail to mention that the protestor that was killed, was the second person to jump onto the bar-tender's back. I can do you one better too because they make up issues, but will ignore the real issues, like the one where a minority teen, broke into a woman's house, shot the woman in the leg, then shot her infant baby right in the face. That's right though, this minority teenager broke into a house and shot a poor innocent defenseless baby right in the face, but this is not news, this is not what these people cover in articles.

Instead they write stories about how blm leaders are looting grocery stores for reparations and how American national monuments and statues are racist. It's kind of crazy when you think about it because death is occurring at an alarming rate in urban communities, minorities are being robbed and killed by their own people on daily basis. No one wants to do anything about it, they rather advocate about systemic racism and how police officers are supposedly killing off their people. All this violence is ignored, while innocent people like retired minority Police Chief David Dorn, are innocently gunned down for no reason at all, other than trying to stop minority teenagers from looting and robbing his friends pawnshop.

No post or articles about his story or the dozens of other minorities being murdered, but of course a white bartender protecting his bar from looters and getting jumped, not once, but twice, is more important, then dozens of minorities being killed. I do agree with certain minorities, the focus should be on ending the death occurring in urban communities. I think every American is on board with that, but what we can't do is convince millions of people that it's their fault, when they are hell bent on blaming other people.

I think Americans would love to live in a world that has less crime and violence, everyone would and everyone has the right too, but you don't have the right to what other people already have, definitely when your reasoning is that it's because you deserve it. Problems need to be solved the right way and as much as minorities might not want to hear it, the only way crime and violence is going to stop in your communities is, if you guys put a stop to it yourselves. Don't get me wrong, other Americans like myself will help you, but you have to stop blaming our race for your problems and start realizing that the only one whose responsible is you.

Minorities have to make the choice to change, no one can make minorities living in urban communities change, the change has to come from minorities, especially when it comes to getting rid of drugs and gangs in these urban communities. This might be why parents in these urban communities sometimes have a hard time raising their children right, their children are exposed to nothing but crime and violence, this is all they know because this is all they've seen growing up. Since this is all minorities have known and seen growing up, minorities easily follow people that deceive them with fallacious arguments, these people make their arguments seem rather good, but in reality, these are deceptive arguments that have been made to appear better than they really are.

This is the reason why we have so many people following the lies and deceptions of others, these people use their fallacious arguments to pass judgments onto other's and have somehow convince millions of people to agree with them. This is also why we have so many people that think they know better than everyone else, they assume their opinion is the only one that matters. If you don't agree with these people, if you do have a different opinion then they do, you need to change your opinion or they'll never talk to you again.

It goes back to assumptions and how millions of people all around America, literally can't stay out of other people's business, they always have to add their two cents where it doesn't belong. We need to bring back the old saying, "stay out of business that isn't any of yours" because the concept is fairly simple, you should mind your own business, but also deal with your own problems, before you tell other people how to deal with theirs.

Our moms would always tell us, "if you can't say anything nice, don't say anything at all", this statement still rings true, people have no right to put other people down simply because they have a different opinion then they do or weren't raised the same as them. It really comes down to people needing to mind their own business, we have too many people that feel they have the right to interrupt other people's lives, even if they don't know them. The sad reality is, these are the people who go online and socially murder you because you chose to have a difference of opinions, since they believe your opinion is wrong, they have to make sure millions of people know it.

Like I stated before, everyone is allowed to have an opinion, but your opinion is your opinion, it doesn't mean other's have to accept it or other people are wrong for having a different opinion then you do. It's crazy because these people honestly believe that they have the right to tell other people how to eat, breathe and live, yet they can't seem to figure out the problems in their own lives, still they try to tell other people how to deal with theirs. The crazy thing that puzzles me is the fact that, if you don't bend to these people, if you don't give in to their opinion, they instantly get mad at you and try to destroy you in every way possible.

What also should be worrisome is the fact that, teens are participating in these online social media attacks also, teens are going online to verbally attack other teens because they are different. These teens assume it's okay to verbally attack these other teens, who are not like them because this is what they've been exposed to, they've watched their role models make fun of people online, so this inspires them to do the same. This can also bring us back to teens needing discipline because without it, you are left with teens, who not only think they have a right to verbally attack people, but they don't stop with their online attacks, these teens continue their vicious and hateful assaults at school too.

School shootings for example, are on the rise and have increased dramatically in the last 5 years, they only seem to be rarely occurring now because we are dealing with a national pandemic, that has shut down the entire country, although the virus is 98.6% curable. When you look at these violent incidents, you see that these teen killers usually start their killing sprees at home, where they've either been ignored or physically abused, so their family members tend to be their first victims. Children and teens can't handle the pressure or the verbal abuse, so they do what they have been taught to do, which is to use violence to solve their problems.

School shootings are bad, but what's worse is these young minority and white American teens, who are out running the streets, running with gangs, but also robbing and shooting people, who they see as targets. Violence tends to be key for these young teens, they use violence to solve every problem they have, this could be why gun violence is so bad in America, these teens use guns and violence to solve their problems. We think about these teens and the violence they commit towards others, but the government and State officials use these incidents to help push their agenda.

They try to pass laws and new legislature to lessen these incidents, but every one of these new laws ignores the broad spectrum of gun violence. With that, I am talking about we have innocent children living in bad neighborhood's and communities, that are getting shot and killed by stray bullets because these teen gang bangers see each other and shoot to kill. These aren't school shootings, these are murders occurring in communities' daily, innocent children and teens are being gunned down by other teens, who are using illegal guns, but they're not the problem, legal gun-toting Americans are the problem.

Democrats and liberals, want you to ignore what's going on in these communities because only certain incidents help them push their agenda, since they are blaming all these killings and murders on guns themselves, not the people pulling the trigger. Let's be honest though, guns don't kill people, people kill people, a gun cannot pull its own trigger, even a robotic gun has someone behind the button, so stop trying to blame it on the gun because this gives no justice to the victims of these violent homicides.

Gun laws are retarded and really useless, Americans have the right to own and use guns, but these State politicians want to disarm legal gun carrying Americans, claiming that guns are the reason why we have so much violence in this world. Yea, this may be partly true, but it's only partly true because the gun is only half the problem, the person behind the gun, pulling the trigger, is the real problem. Trying to pass gun laws to ban certain assault rifles and other guns, will not stop illegal guns from flowing into the streets, seriously, if gang bangers and drug dealers want a gun, you think they go to Wal-Mart?

Criminals don't give a damn about your gun law's, they can easily get an illegal gun off the street, probably quicker than you can finish your morning coffee. The only people these gun laws affect is legal gun-carrying American's, don't you think you guys have take enough from Americans, now you want to disarm us and leave us defenseless against intruders and thieves. Forget freedom of speech, forget the right to bear arms, forget having an opinion or having the freedom to raise your own children, we no longer are allowed to enjoy our freedoms because other people think Americans are too privileged and these people are the State Senators running our country.

We've seen what these State Senators are trying to teach to our children, we've seen the lies and deceptions that these State Senators have pushed daily, so we should expect it when they try to control just about everything else. They've controlled the minds of millions of minorities because these State Senators and leaders, have convinced minorities teens that history isn't something they need to be taught. It's interesting how these State Senators have come to the conclusion that everything with the color white, somehow reminds people of white supremacy, so if you support anything white or related to the color white, you are a racist white supremacist.

Seriously, how can millions of people blame a single color for their problems, it's a color, so what your saying is that, a color offends you because white rice offends you? Do you honestly know how stupid that make you sound, you are claiming that something is racist simply because it's white? Thanks to these State Senators pushing this ridiculous theory, we are stuck with self-entitled, self-centered and self-opinionated teens, who firmly believe everything should be handed to them, they shouldn't have to work for it, everything in the past was racist to them and their people, so they deserve everything because it's owed to them.

The sad reality is, these State Senators and their followers, are getting their way, if you look at recent news articles and news headlines, there are several food companies that are being forced to change their names or food labels because their labels somehow represent white supremacy. Dozens of companies and even schools, are being forced to change their names, names they've had for generations all because these State Senators, civil leaders and their followers, claim that these names represents white supremacy.

Movies that have been around for decades, are being canceled and taken off air because they somehow represent white supremacy, television shows, that have also been around for decades are being stripped off air all because it supposedly represent's white supremacy. Millions of minorities, are blaming everything white people, but also blaming everything that's the color white for their problems because these State Senators have somehow convinced these minorities that, the color white is related to slavery.

What's really hurting this country is the white Americans that think they somehow owe minorities an apology, an apology for something they've never done to these people, but it's crazy because some have apologized for simply being white. It's sad when Sports players are getting in trouble for standing up saluting the American flag and American national anthem because it's their tradition, but since they did not kneel and instead showed their support for the American national anthem, they are bashed and told to apologize. One apology is never enough though, they apologize and it's never enough for these people, but the fact is, you should never have to apologize for supporting these American symbols of freedom, if you are, the people doing it should be kicked out of America.

Seriously though, we've talked about this before, how can people supporting American symbols be bashed, especially when we are in America, not Africa? It makes no sense because this is America, why do sports players have to apologize for supporting America, it's their own country and it's the flag of their nation? Thousands of soldiers fought and died to provide the freedoms that all Americans get to enjoy, if it wasn't for these men and women, we wouldn't be where we are today, this is what these American symbols represent, not what you made up in your head.

That's the crazy thing about this whole situation, these players are getting bashed for supporting America by people all over the world, who are bashing these players for showing support for their own country. These days, parents of all races, are teaching their children that it is okay to hate the American flag and it's okay to disrespect the American national anthem. In reality, no, no it's not, when you do what you are doing, you are disrespecting the thousands of men and women, who fought and died for this country, the people that fought for the right for you be free. So seriously, how do you honor these people by kneeling to the national anthem?

These uneducated, unknowledgeable teens are destroying American history, they are trying to erase everything they can all because they were never educated about history, but their parents also never took the time to teach them about history. The proof is in the making when we see our American national monuments and statues being destroyed and defaced by these ignorant youth's simply because these monuments and statues all represents slave owners and white supremacist, nothing else. It's not the fact that, these are heroes and leaders to our nation, but also Americans who paved the way for the American people today, nope, not at all.

According to minority State Senators and minorities, these statues and monuments all represent white supremacy and slavery, so they need to come down or be destroyed. Thanks to all the hate and destruction going on in America, parents are now forced to keep their children inside, stuck indoor's, giving them tablet's, phones and computers to play with because it's become too dangerous to play outside. Unfortunately due to this, online and social media has become increasingly worse, all thanks to this crazy pandemic, everything we do is now online, watched by hundreds, if not millions of people.

For example, parents that post pictures of photos with their children are really just sharing them online for people to see, but these photos soon become scrutinized by people online, who think they know better than them or feel they have a right to make rude offensive comments. Take the beautiful country singer Maren Morris, her and her husband recently had a baby and she recently took a photo with their newborn, in the photo she is sitting in a pool on a pool float, while she's holding the newborn, people saw this photo online and went completely nuts. Doesn't matter that Mrs. Morris was holding the baby, or that Mrs. Morris was surrounded by people or the fact that the pool was like 1 foot deep.

All that mattered was the fact that, people online assumed this baby was in danger, so they took it upon themselves to post bad comments about Mrs. Morris and her husband. It's sad because this tends to happen online all the time, people look at pictures that were posted

242

online or they watch videos that were posted online by other people and they scrutinize every little detail about the video or the picture. The crazy thing about all of this is, these people don't even know the people they are verbally attacking online.

They don't know these average everyday Americans personally, they don't know these actors or singers personally, they've only seen them online. Another thing that's wrong with our country, that I can't reiterate enough is, people need to mind their own business and stop getting involved in business that is not theirs or has nothing to do with them. People need to stop assuming they know better than everyone else, everyone is entitled to their opinion, just because someone has a difference of opinion then you do, doesn't necessarily make them a bad person, makes them human.

This is where a lot of our problems seem to start, people in America think they have a right to butt into other people's business, but also seem to think they have the right to tear people down all because these people do things different then they do. You can see examples of this by examining the recent boom of online YouTube stars, these people are making money online, sharing their lives with the world, but it has a reverse side to it because these people are also left dealing with followers, who verbally attack them in their comments. Making money online is not a bad way to make a living, but it tends to get crazy sometimes because if people don't like something you did or something you said, they instantly attack you with hateful comments.

Since these people feel you offended them in some type of way, shape or form, they take it upon themselves to verbally attack you, your life and your family on social media, simply because something you did, rubbed them the wrong way. People that think like this, automatically assume they have a right to attack others online, they assume they have the right to post hateful comments, but in reality, they should not be worried about these people they are verbally attacking, they should be worried as to why they are so offended by everything.

I bring up people on YouTube when I'm talking about this because there have been dozens of online content providers that quit posting their lives online, due to the hateful backlash and hateful comments that these people post about them on their channels. It's also interesting that, there are a lot of teens that start out as You Tuber's, their videos are being watched by hundreds of people, but even these teens have to deal with hateful and threatening comments, that comes from other teens and even other adults. Think about that for a second, adults, grown men and women, think it's okay to verbally berate and belittle teens because these teens offended them or said something they didn't like, seriously, they are teens, you're the adult, grow up.

The funny thing is, I talk about all this starting from home because that's usually where these people are, these people are all at home sitting behind computer screens, posting hateful discriminating comments about people they hardly know, including children and teens. Everyone complains about the government stealing our privacy, but they are only partly responsible for the problem, millions of nosey neighbors, who watch and report everything Americans do, is the real problem. We've seen cases of this before, innocent people have been shot and killed by police officers because some nosey neighbor was at home, thought they saw something suspicious, so they took it upon themselves to call the police and report what they've seen.

This should be an issue we talk more about, innocent Americans, white and minority, are being shot and killed by police officers in their own homes because they were mistaken as intruders or robbers. The sad thing is, some of these cases where innocent people are being shot in their own homes, started when these people called the police for help, they thought they had an intruder in their house, so they called 9-1-1 for help. When the police arrived, they mistake the homeowner for the intruder and shoot to kill, this should be something we protest about, this should be something we are concerned about, but it's not.

Now, innocent people have to deal with police officers simply because they were labeled suspicious characters, who were acting suspiciously, by their own neighbors. State politicians talk about they want to ban American guns, in reality, they need to ban people from opening their mouths, they need to bad idiots from the internet and they need to stop letting people verbally attack others online just because they think they have the right to. It's interesting how millions of people can easily go online, discriminate or belittle other people, who have a different opinion then they do and be okay with it.

It honestly makes no sense to me because if you don't take their side or share their same opinion, you're the bad person, you're the one who is un-American, you're the one who hates America. It's crazy because like we talked about before, according to these young adults, anything American is now un-American, if you show support for America, our American flag or our American national anthem, you are a white supremacist that participated in slavery.

The reasoning these people use is so mind-boggling it's really unbelievable, they assume they know about slavery, they don't, they assume they know about history, but they have no clue. If these people did read about their history or if they bothered to learn about their history, they would realize that slavery and the slave trade, was around long before white colonialists participated or profited in it. History not only shows this, but it proves that North African and Arabian Moors, were the first people to sell people as slaves to anyone who would pay for them.

I know minorities want to believe that white colonist started slavery, but also sailed to Africa to somehow steal their ancestors, but I am afraid not. According to history, something that has been studied for hundreds of years by millions or people, slavery was started in Africa and the Middle East, by African and Arabian Moors. Contrary to what these people tend to claim, the Atlantic slave trade, was not the only slave trade occurring at the time, nor was it the first ever slave trade, there were many slave trades that had been created before the Atlantic slave trade.

African and Arabian Moors, wanted more ways to sell their people, since they wanted more ways to sell their people, they created numerous slave trades and slave trade routes, but once the New Americas were found, South America became their best customer. Millions of people tend to forget about that fact too, it's been recorded in our American history that, there were more slaves and slave owners living in South America, then there were in North America. South America was booming and on the rise because of slavery, since these South American cities were the first stops for African and Arabian slave trade ships, South Americans often profited the most from slavery and the enslavement of others.

Like over in the Middle East and Africa, some South American countries are still participating in some form of slavery, they still participate in some form of people enslavement, yet we have millions of people in America, claiming that they are subject to slavery. Since these minorities and others feel as if they are somehow still facing slavery, minorities take their frustrations out on white Americans and others because they blame white people for their ancestors being enslaved and kept in chains. What worries me about all of this is, not really that these people think this way because we've talked about the lies and deceptions these people believe and follow, but what worries me is that these people will easily use violence to get their way of if they think you offended them in some way.

This isn't just millions of minorities committing this violence towards others either, people from all races, are using violence against others as their solutions to their problems. Unfortunately, due to this mind-set of using violence as the solution, we now live in this crazy world where we have numerous city bombings, numerous mass-murders and numerous school shootings. It's gotten worse because numerous children and teens are killing their parents because children are offended by everything, which includes being told no, rocks, monuments and statues.

If you look at statistics and data reviews from today's researchers, you will easily find that our youth are using violence as their answer, you would honestly be shocked and surprised, to see what these teens are responsible for doing. You would also probably want to close the book because the horror some of these teens can inflict onto someone, even their own families, may keep you up at night. From children and teens killing people, to people killing people, America is now filled with constant death, with no clear end in sight.

Sometimes it's because these children and teens, were never taught how to accept rejection, they were never told no, so when they finally do get rejected, they can't handle it, so they act out the only way they know how, which usually means causing violence to others, with plenty of people being hurt in the process. This also brings us back to what we've talked about before, which is disciplining children and teens because this behavior often starts from home and without discipline, children, especially teens, use violence to solve everything. These young teens, no longer talk through their problems or bother to have a conversation with you about how you offended them, instead these teens are quick to resort to violence.

Behavior like this is often learned or taught from home, these teens act this way because that's all they've seen growing up, whether it was something they've seen on the streets or something they've seen at home, it's really all they know. Everyone needs to focus on raising these children and teens right because if we don't, they will continue to grow up thinking they can do no wrong, but also that their opinions matter more than anyone else and their skin color entitles them to use violence towards others.

Unfortunately, I believe these trends will never go away, some people will never be happy, they are always pissed off at everything, so since they are miserable, they like making sure others are miserable too. I'm also starting to believe this is why people verbally attack others because these people tend to be doing better than they are or they seem to be living better lives then they are. It honestly makes no sense to me because this is one of the lies and deceptions coming from blm and its Marxists leaders, they claim that since white people live better then minorities, white people should give up their lives to minorities, so minorities can have better lives.

Let me ask you something though, do you seriously think that's the solution to ending crime and violence in your community, do you honestly think that blaming white people helps minorities? I seriously don't think it does, but I also think this would only hinder minorities because you are not taking care of the root problem, which is minorities robbing and killing their own in urban communities. Instead of fighting to rid their communities of crime and violence, minorities, led by these blm Marxist leaders, are going into white communities, disrupting the lives of white people because like we talked about before, these blm Marxists leaders, have convinced millions of minorities that white people are the ones responsible for their problems.

That's another thing that minorities do that makes absolutely no sense at all, minorities go up to white Americans that are eating outside at restaurants and messing with them and their food, some even have stooped as low as to drink this white couples drinks. Seriously, what's wrong with you, these white people have done nothing wrong to you, they are simply minding their own business, eating the food they paid for? I mean seriously, you have to be a special kind of stupid to go up to a white couple and eat food off the plate they were just eating off, but also drink from the same cup they were just drinking from.

It's pure insanity because to actually drink after someone else that has already been drinking from the same cup, when there is a worldwide pandemic in the country, just shows you how stupid you really are and these people can't deny they didn't do this because we seen them doing it on national television. It really makes no sense at all because millions of minorities, following the lead of blm, are blaming white people on the reason why urban communities are filled with crime and violence.

There is no logic behind these ridiculous statements, there is no truth to what these blm leaders are claiming, still, it doesn't matter because millions of people follow these blm Marxists leaders and help them pass on their fallacious arguments. These are also the same people that can't seem to stay out of other people's lives or business, but also can't seem to take care of their own lives, yet they have the need to tell other people how to live theirs. It's mind boggling to me, how certain people think they have a right to instantly butt into other people's lives or business, business that has nothing to do with them, especially when the people's lives they are disrupting, they tend to not even know.

This is even occurring to our children, we can take a look at the case of a young minority 13 year old, let's call him J.F. from Minneapolis, who had a genius idea that he would open a hot dog stand, so he could get him some new clothes. Young J.F., wanted some new clothes for school, so he does what every little kid seems to do and that is, young J.F. opens his own stand in front of his very own house, in his own front yard. Now granted, this was not an ordinary stand, it was a hotdog stand, which I think was a great and genius idea because who doesn't love a good hotdog.

Young J.F.'s hotdog stand grew a little more popular in his community, so he had people coming from all over to see him, so all seemed to be good and he was on his way to getting new clothes. Unfortunately for young J.F. though, misery loves company and seeing that he was doing so good and minding his own business, trying to make money, someone or some ungrateful useless person didn't like this, so they actually reported this 13 year old to the city police for selling hot-dogs from his lawn. This was of course all due to young J.F. not having a permit for an actual hotdog stand, but still, it's a 13-year-old kid trying to make money to buy some new clothes, how could you call in to report him?

Let me say that again though, someone or some dumb**s, called the city and the cops on this young minority for not having a hotdog stand permit, a 13 year old kid. Does any of this stuff make sense to you people, seriously, why are things like this occurring, can people really be that stubborn and ignorant to where they get mad at a 13 year old for trying to make money for school clothes? The only thing young J.F. was trying to do is better his clothes situation and you call the police on him for not having a permit, he's a 13 year old kid, of course he didn't have a permit, he's a 13 year old kid with a hot-dog stand in his yard.

Honestly though, does that make any sense at all, you ratted out a 13 year old kid because he was selling hot dogs from his front yard? I honestly don't think it does, but after all was said and done, young J.F. made out in the end because instead of shutting down his hot-dog stand, the police and city, helped young J.F. get the permits he needed to start his own little hot-dog business. Thank God for decent human beings, but that's the problem, even kids can't do anything these days without someone else crushing their dreams, the first moment these kids develop some form of success, someone else steps in to try and shut them down.

Seriously, when we were younger, as kids we used to dream big, I mean really big, but we did this because our parents inspired us to dream big, our parents told us that we could be anyone we wanted to be. This is something that doesn't occur anymore, some parents, not all, but some parents are not inspiring their kids to do anything, but it's not only the parents, people that see kids succeed often try to interrupt in their success because they assume they know better. With other people interrupting in the process of raising your children, but also thinking they know better than you, the actual parent, children are left wondering if they are doing the right thing or not.

This often falls on the realization that children no longer dream about anything, they no longer are inspired to grow up to be anyone and the ones that do dream and inspire to be someone, usually have their dreams torn down by other people. The result of people doing this to kids all over America, has scarred these kids tremendously, kids these days don't know what to do because everything they try to do is seen as bad or something other people assume they should not be doing, so they are now more confused than ever.

It honestly makes no sense, why people would keep kids from having dreams or put kids down because they assume the dreams they have are just too big, but this is the world we live in now, even dreams are held back. This falls in line with what blm leaders, liberals and democrats, are pushing to minorities, they are trying to tell these minorities that, we know you can think on your own, we know you are just as smart as white teens, we know you can solve your own problems, but were going to focus on giving you special treatment and lowering standards for you.

It's puzzling to me because there are a lot of minority teens that grew up with white kids and have no problems with them. These minority kids, are also just as smart as the white kids they grew up with or went to school with, but since someone else is in their ear telling them they need special treatment, these minority kids are confused as to what is the right thing to do. Some minority teens tend to do the right thing, these teens tend to focus on what's right, but the other half follow these blm Marxists leaders, who are only in it for themselves because these people have deceived millions into thinking they want racial equality, but in reality, they want racial dominance.

It's funny because blm founders could honestly care less about racial equality and more about taking things away from white people, this isn't just coming from me either, these idiots are always on news or in news articles, talking about how white people owe minorities everything under the sun, all for what their ancestors went through. Remember, these are the very same people that created an entire list of demands for white people, which basically was a list demanding white people to hand over everything they have ever received or are going to receive to minorities simply because these people claim they deserve it, instead of the people who actually worked for it.

This is blm's ideology though, this is what these blm leaders believe, they don't care about having an equal opportunity, just like white people, they want to dominate white people because they feel white people have somehow kept them oppressed for their entire lives. Since they claim that white people are to blame for all their problems, they feel that all white people should somehow suffer because white Americans live in safe and secure neighborhoods, unlike minorities. Seriously, how can you honestly blame white people for your f***ups, you blm Marxists leaders claim it's our fault, yet most white Americans don't even live in these urban communities?

Like I stated before, it's not white people out looting and damaging grocery stores in urban communities, it's not white people that are out robbing and killing people in urban communities, so seriously, how can

250

you blame white people for the chaos you cause? This is another reason why racism will never end in America, not because Americans don't want it to end, but because people like these blm Marxists leaders, only focus on helping their own people, not others and especially not white people or the white culture.

Unfortunately, this doesn't apply to all of their people, we've seen examples of the chaos that occurs at these blm riots and protests, innocent minorities are being killed during these protests, but these blm Marxists leaders, seem not to care about these deaths. Even when questioned about these deaths and innocent killings, they shrug them off like they got nothing to say, yet let a long-time minority felon get killed and they will go off on you, like you never seen before. This is why you question everything blm founders say and do because they claim it's to better the lives of their people, yet, it's their very own people that are suffering from the chaos and destruction they have brought upon the nation.

The way America is heading, should scare us all, but we do have time to stop the chaos and the madness, but to do this, Americans need to come together and unite, so we don't continue on this path of destruction that other people want us to head towards. Separation causes nothing but division, division causes nothing but tension, tension causes nothing but hostility, hostility causes nothing but conflict and conflict causes nothing but disunity and dissension, between Americans.

If it isn't millions of Americans mad at each other or being at each other's throats, you have the other side of the spectrum, where millions of Americans are secluding themselves and their children from anything and everything they deem offensive. People doing this, doesn't make much sense to me because these people keep their children secluded from everything, then turn around and wonder why their kids turn out so sensitive. This sensitivity is even occurring in our schools, schools are cancelling sports programs and even p.e. sports activities because they say some sports are to violent for our young kids to participate in.

One sport that they banned is football, which is crazy because kids love football, but they banned it because these people claim football is to violent for kids to play because your chasing another person down and tackling them. It's crazy because with this new world of kid

251

sensitivity that's been created, we now have kid's sports games and competitions, where there is no declared winner's, every kid gets a trophy for participation, just so these kids don't have their feelings hurt. I mean, seriously, what's the purpose of practice makes perfect, or kids becoming all they can be, if all you are going to do is hand out trophies or awards for participating in the game, just so you don't hurt these kid's feelings?

It doesn't stop with the sports in schools though, we now have teacher's all over America, passing kids that definitely shouldn't be passed, these teacher's and their parents, don't want to hurt these kids feeling's, so they pass them on to the next grade. This teaches these kids nothing about life, nothing about becoming a smarter individual, nothing about even becoming a better individual, all it does is puts the theory into their head that, as long as you tried to do it or read it, that's good enough.

We need to start going back to the way we were all raised, contrary to what others say, we need to step back into our parents of the 80's and 90's footsteps, we need to do things the right way because if we don't, we will fail these kids, which will leave them with no future in sight. We need to start focusing on fixing our problems from within, this starts at home, it all starts from home, if we don't start spending more time with these children, the more lost they will become. Democrats are the worst when it comes to promising things to Americans, especially when it comes to minorities because these are the same politicians that have been promising help for the past 5 decades, yet, they never really actually help out urban communities.

Instead they line their own pockets, while crime tends to run rampant. These people don't care about your children, these people don't even care about your children having a future, but they will swear up and down they do, but only if you take their side and give them your vote. These politicians really don't care about the American people, these people only care about their self-interests and their rich friends, power is key to these people and they will do anything to keep it.

These State politicians will also use any movement they can to spread their lies and deceptions on the American people, this includes a national pandemic, which is affecting the world. You can see what I mean by taking a look at these current State politicians, who are trying to use this so-called deadly Corona Virus, COVID-19, as an excuse to as why the virus is killing their people more, claiming that the government, led by President Trump, is somehow using covid-19, to get rid of minorities. If you look at these ridiculous statements that are being made by most of these State politicians, the claims alone honestly make you shake your head, now it's worse because these politicians have the audacity to claim that illegal immigrants somehow deserve money and help from our government during this COVID-19 pandemic.

It's crazy to me because I've watched State politicians go on national television and tell the government that, illegal's immigrants deserve more help than Americans do, people who are over here illegally, deserve more help than the people who these politicians are supposed to be representing. It's shocking to see some of these State politicians, claim that illegal immigrants somehow deserve more help than Americans do, it's shocking because I didn't know illegal immigrants had rights.

I mean, illegal means illegal, therefore you are over in America illegally, so you are to be instantly deported back to whatever country you came from, no exceptions, illegal people don't share or even have American rights. One thing that tends to worry me is the fact that, these State politicians fight more to give illegal immigrants free healthcare, while most Americans currently living in America, go into a hospital to get help, only to leave with a huge amount of debt because they have no healthcare insurance.

Free healthcare or cheaper healthcare, would be something Americans would love, but these State politicians, are not fighting for Americans to have free healthcare, nope, they are fighting for illegal immigrants, people who are over in America illegally, to have free healthcare on the American peoples dime of course. So, not only are Americans paying for our own expensive hospital bills, if democrats and liberals have their way, Americans will now also be paying for the hospital bills of illegal immigrants and foreigners, who won't have to pay a dime.

Once again, here is the logic of giving someone everything for absolutely nothing, but it's the democratic way because these are the same State politicians who think that, when illegal immigrants need lawyers, these lawyers should be paid for by the American people. The puzzling thing is, these people are the inventors of the blame game, we've seen it constantly on the news and in politics today, most of these State politicians, are going on record to claim that we have a white supremacist government, led by President Donald Trump, which is secretly destroying America, from the inside out. There is no actual truth to what these State politicians claim, but these politicians claim it anyways, no matter what city they are representing or whatever news interview they are conducting.

Every time these State politicians are given the chance to blame President Trump, they take it because according to them President Trump, is responsible for all the crime and violence wreaking havoc on their cities. It's not the minorities who are robbing and killing each other in urban communities, it's not the minorities out robbing stores in urban communities, it's not the minorities out selling drugs and killing people in urban communities, it's President Trump and his racist administrations fault. This blame is because these idiots all claim that Trump and his administration are using covid-19 to get rid of minorities and immigrants.

You have to laugh at some of these State politicians though because I don't honestly understand how you can say one thing, but your actions do another, it's like, President Trump does something good, he's still bad, Trump does something that helps Americans, he's still bad. It's crazy because President Trump does something to help out urban communities, something that no President before him has done, still doesn't matter, these State politicians still claim that, Trump hates minorities and does nothing for the minorities.

No matter what you think or may say, democrats, liberals and people that follow them, will always say the same thing, President Trump, is a bad President and doesn't care about the American people. They also say that, Joe Biden is not racist and can somehow fix America. Let's look at Sleepy Joe Biden for a second, he's the 18th longest serving State Senator in U.S. history, but he didn't do anything as VP and he didn't do much of anything as a United States Senator either. All told, he's hasn't done much of anything for the American people, although he's been a government official for over 47 years.

What I also find interesting Is that the people in power like, Joe Biden, Maxine Waters and Nancy Pelosi, have been running our government for decades, these are the same politicians that have been in our government for years, only to be seen pushing the same poisonous agenda. Now since someone fresh has come into the fold, with new ideas and a way to give back to the American people, these people of power hate it, but will do everything they can to get it back to the old way because that's when they were in charge.

These democrats and their people in office, whether it's State Representatives or State Senators, literally can't stand President Donald Trump and since they hate President Trump so much, they are willing to claim that Joe Biden, is the best Presidency nominee candidate they have for America. Democrats and liberals, will continue to try and destroy President Trumps character and smear his name, until the election is all said and done because they know with another four years, they'll lose the power they hold so dear.

This is the only way democrats and liberals can win the election though, they know they have to cheat and steal the election because they can't win straight up, they have to figure out every which way possible, to try and steal the election, the vary election, they claim President Trump is trying to steal. Honestly though, when 46,000 dead people somehow woke up to vote for you or the fact that an entire tractor trailer full of some 200,000 votes, just suddenly disappeared over night, there is honestly no way you can say that there wasn't any cheating during the 2020 election.

We all know the disaster of what the United Postal Service is, combine that with the disaster of mail-in ballots and you have one easy way for democrats to steal an election. The democratic logic is reversed though, these State politicians claim that President Trump is trying to steal the election because President Trump doesn't want mail-in voting, he rather have in-person voting. Since President Trump rather have you go in and personally vote, instead of mailing in a ballot, he's somehow the bad person, but shouldn't that be reversed? Mail in ballots, is an easier way to cheat in an election, the fact that these democrats and liberals fought so hard for it, just shows you that they already had plans to try and steal the election from the beginning.

What's crazy is, people that are not even State politicians, just average everyday Americans, are also claiming the same thing, somehow President Trump is going to steal the Presidency, by not allowing mail-in voting. Seriously, how does that work because I would think it's easier to steal an election with mail-in ballots, rather than someone coming in and personally voting, which President Trump

255

supported and democrats were against? Everyone in the world knows how faulty and easily to manipulate mail-in ballot voting can be, there are even cases going on in North Carolina and Florida today, for mail-in voter fraud, but these democrats push more and more for it. It's puzzling to me how these democrats and liberals, can blame President Trump for trying to steal the election because President Trump is against mail-in voting, yet you would think that whoever is pushing more for mail-in ballots, would be the ones behind the steal.

President Trump doesn't want mail-in votes because mail-in voting has been proven to be fraudulent, but like I said, the real question should be, why are these democrats pushing so hard for mail-in balloting, when they know for fact that, mail-in voting, is an easy way to steal an election? The ideology that these people use just makes no sense at all, but it's very destructive to the American people because all this deception does is divide and separate Americans even more, causing more friction, then there needs to be.

The sad thing is, these people are proud of this, these people will lie straight to your face and be okay with it and you don't have to take my word for it, we've seen it coming out of the mouths of democrats and liberals daily. Even people that have no influence try to open their mouths about how the American people should be okay with the lying, cheating and deceiving, that comes from the democratic party, most of these people are seen on televisions telling President Trump supporters to just suck it up.

Honestly though, how could American be okay with cheaters, I mean there was proven fraud in the election, it was proven that there was clearly fraudulent behavior during the election. So seriously, how can you just tell Americans to suck it up, when you clearly know something is not right? Look I am not saying that these politicians did cheat, all I am saying is that, with all the evidence being brought forth today, with the hundreds of affidavits, to the mysterious boxes coming out from underneath a table, something does seem right here. It doesn't stop there though because there was a mysterious tractor-trailer that just disappeared with over 200,000 ballots in it, but also dead people that supposedly voted.

Therefore, it's kind of hard to see all of this evidence laid out in front of you and claim that there was no cheating during the election. That's what the democrats want though, they want the power and to be in control, this is why they have deceived minorities, especially minority teens, into thinking that white Americans are racist, for simply wearing t-shirts and hats that support Trump. That's right though, even your clothes you wear can determine whether you are hated by these people or not, wearing a t-shirt or even just a hat that supports the U.S. President makes you a racist and an instant enemy to these politicians and their followers.

The harassment and hatred will never stop for President Trump until he is out of office because these American democrats and liberals don't want it to. They will continue to smear his name, but also continue to go after President Trump because Trump took away their power. President Trump also took away their money and gave it back to the people they stole it from, which was the American people. These people don't like that, they don't like the fact that he put the American people first, they should, they should be happy that President Trump put the American people first because that's supposed to be their job too, but unlike President Trump, they've failed at their jobs.

Seriously, democrats spent three and a half years and over 30 million dollars of American tax money to impeach President Trump on false allegations, they blamed President Trump for Russian collusion. While the whole time it was proven that Trump was innocent and the real culprit was Hillary Clinton. Hillary Clinton was charged and convicted for colluding with the Russians, but also spying on Trump's campaign, but it's "disappearing" Hillary Clinton. I call her disappearing Hillary because all the crimes she commits, somehow just suddenly disappears.

She was convicted of corrupt emails that were used to spy on Donald Trump's Presidential Campaign, they all just disappeared, she works with the Russians colluding on the Presidential election, the evidence just suddenly disappears, this is why she is disappearing Hillary Clinton. Seriously, the main focus is on the impeachment because democrats spent over 30 million dollars of American taxpayer's money for investigators and lawyers, to impeach President Trump on false allegations, 30 Million dollars.

Knowing all along that President Trump was innocent and the FBI proved President Trump didn't collude with the Russians, but Hillary Clinton did. I hate to see what these democrats secretly spent on the whole trial because it was declared in the very beginning that, President

Trump was guilty of nothing, no campaign interference, no Russian Collusion, yet, Pelosi and democrats, still tried to impeach him anyway. You can say it's kind of funny because these State politicians know for fact that, Hillary Clinton's campaign was found guilty of spying on President Donald Trump's campaign, but also colluding with the Russians, yet they don't bother to punish or go after her.

Instead they chose to start and investigation into the U.S. President based on false allegations because they don't believe he should be President and they want him out of office as soon as possible. We've also seen this because the entire time President Trump was in office, the false impeachment was still in play, the false impeachment trial lasted for 3 and half years, although it was known from the very beginning to be false accusations. Democrats only did this because they wanted Trump out from the very beginning, these crooked people wanted Hillary to become president, but since the American people spoke up and chose President Trump, they made it their mission to get rid of Trump, by any means necessary.

When you think about it, it's all a bit puzzling because never before in American history would State Officials or politicians, be allowed to impeach a current U.S. President on false allegations. The trial would have easily ended and been dismissed the first week it started, when it was first discovered that the allegations and accusations were false. I guess President Trump is the exception though because they proved Trump was innocent during the first week of the impeachment. Yet, Nancy Pelosi and democrats spent the next three and half years trying to impeach President Trump.

Democrats, led by Nancy Pelosi, were more concerned with getting President Trump out of the oval office, rather than taking care of American citizens. They proved it by allowing this impeachment to go on for two and half years, costing the American people, hundreds of millions of dollars. Then just when we thought it was finally over and these people would stop trying to get rid of our U.S. President, they prove us wrong by blaming President Trump for his response to this horrible covid-19 pandemic.

It's sad because no matter what Donald Trump tries to do as the President of The United States, every move he makes is scrutinized because these people hate him and want him gone. He's the only U.S. President in a decade to give a damn about the American people,

Donald Trump also built his own American empire, Trump didn't leave America for China, like most other U.S. companies did. President Trump stayed in America, kept is company in America and in the process funded thousands of American jobs. You can even say these jobs helped keep America going because hundreds of U.S. companies kept leaving America for China, all thanks to the high taxes and tariffs that, Barack Obama and Joe Biden pushed for.

Thanks to President Trump, American companies brought their businesses back to the United States, President Donald Trump was the ones who lifted most of these crazy taxes and tariffs that Barack Obama put in place. With manufacturing jobs coming back to America, there have been close to 7 million new American jobs created for the American people, jobs that were gone during the Obama administration. It honestly makes no sense to me because before covid-19 hit the United States, President Trump had America seeing the lowest unemployment rates it has ever seen, this includes minorities, veterans and even high-school dropouts.

I honestly don't understand where the hate comes for President Trump, whether it's an actor, musician, sports player, news anchor, journalist or politician, I don't understand the hate. I just don't understand how you can talk bad about a person, who was worshipped by every single American before he became U.S. President. Songs were created by numerous musicians about being Donald Trump, hell, Barack Obama quoted that the American dream, "was to be Donald Trump," so how can these people all of a sudden hate him so much, where they attack him every chance they get?

The more you think about it, the more you realize these people could care less about what President Trump does and more about trying to bash him and claim that he has done nothing for them or Americans. Take for instance huge influential musicians like, Taylor Swift and Billie Eilish, two musicians, who are constantly berating and belittling President Trump because they claim President Trump doesn't do anything for them. It's crazy because if I am not mistaken, President Trump just signed in the Music Modernization Act.

Which makes sure, singers, musicians and songwriters, keep their rights to the royalties of their own songs, but the act makes it a requirement for producers to give these musicians the money they are due. Taylor Swift should be happy and excited about this. I mean she is the one that got screwed by Big Machine, when others bought out the record label and kept all the copyrights to every musicians songs, including all of Taylor Swifts, previously written and produced songs. The Music Modernization Act, that President Trump passed for musicians, gets rid of problems like these, it gives the music creator and song writer, a more reliable way to collect what they are do, but now they also get to keep the copyrights to the new songs that they have created and will create.

I would think this helps out Taylor Swift and hundreds of other musicians, but still her and people like her, continue to berate and belittle President Trump about not doing anything for them, just so they can claim he's a bad person. President Trump passed an actual legislature bill that helps Taylor Swift, Billie Eilish and other musicians like them, from having their music stolen by huge record labels, like Big Machine and other grimy music production companies.

What it all comes down to is the fact that, everyone who isn't a Trump supporter, claims that President Trump does nothing for them, does nothing for minorities, nothing for these rich cry-babies, so this somehow makes him a white racist, who only represents white people and white supremacy. Yea President Trump might say some weird things, yea President Trump might say things he probably shouldn't have, but that doesn't make him a racist or even close to it simply because your opinion is that President Trump, is racist.

This has been proven time and time again, these politicians, especially Nancy Pelosi, calls President Trump a racist and claims that President Trump, is the most racist U.S. President ever, but President Trump hasn't once said anything racist to the American people, Sleepy Joe Biden has though. Then again, every U.S. President before him, said what they wanted to say and spoke how they wanted to speak, should we guilt President Trump for doing what we all do though, should we guilt President Trump, although we know it's not Trumps fault, it's democrats that are pushing this crap?

It really makes no sense to me when you have a person like, Bill Clinton, speaking at the DNC rally, claiming that, "You know what Donald Trump will do with four more years: blame, bully and belittle," which is the exact same thing that Bill Clinton and his democrats have been doing. Democratic cities are filled with gun violence and crime, rioters and protesters have taken over their city streets and destroyed

260

them, but instead of taking the blame, they blame it all on President Trump. They do this while they bully and belittle Americans who support Trump and try to force these Americans into thinking that they somehow made a wrong decision by voting for President Trump.

Seriously though, how can a former impeached U.S. President, who was caught having oral sex and other sexual escapades in the Oval Office, have the audacity to claim that, "Donald Trump's behavior in the Oval Office is unacceptable"? This to me is hilarious because this statement is coming from someone who did unthinkable things in the Oval Office, but also lied to the American people about doing these unthinkable things in the Oval Office and now Bill Clinton, has the audacity to tell another U.S. President that their acts are unacceptable, I mean, talk about being a hypocrite.

Basically it's like Bill Clinton is telling Americans that, forget that I got impeached for having sexual escapades and getting blown in the Oval Office, but the fact that I also lied to you about it. You should still listen to me and believe me when I say, President Trump is bad and what President Trump is doing in the Oval Office, is totally unacceptable. Do I need to be remind you that, Jeffrey Epstein, the rich dude who was secretly killed to keep major secrets quite, had numerous pictures of Bill Clinton, where Clinton was photographed with dozens of under aged teen girls.

Epstein also had a weird painting of Bill Clinton hanging up in his house, where Bill Clinton was sitting in a chair, wearing a blue dress. Not to mention the fact that, Bill Clinton was listed on the flight manifesto of Epstein's private plane, more than 22 times, so Bill Clinton flew to Epstein's Pedo Island more than 22 times, so this is the man you guys want to follow, this is the man you people want to believe? Once again, the logic coming from these liberals and democrats, just makes you continuously just shake your head.

You can see this by looking at what Barack Obama said and claimed, "For close to four years, Trump's shown no interest in putting in the work, no interest in finding common ground, no interest in using the awesome power of his office to help anyone but himself and his friends: no interest in treating the Presidency as anything but one more reality show, that he can use to get the attention he craves." Funny thing about that though, Barack Obama, is the one that craves the spotlight, Obama even wrote a book so he can stay in the limelight, but

261

Obama is the one that helped no one out but himself. All these democrats are nothing but walking, talking contradictions, they talk bad about other people, but forget just how bad they themselves really are. Unfortunately, Barack Obama will never just fade away because he constantly craves the attention that he claims President Trump craves.

Think about it, he's been out of office for four years, but also holds no political position in our government, just like his wife, but we constantly see the Obama's on Television, complaining about just how bad a President, President Trump is. Barack Obama and Joe Biden had 8 years to change this so-called systemically racist government, but he didn't do anything because honestly there was nothing to do, a systemically racist government never existed when he was the United States President.

This was never a problem that was brought to Obama's attention, this was never a problem he actually dealt with because Americans weren't protesting about racial equality or a systemically racist government, we were being convinced and told to accept everyone, even the people that want us dead. This wasn't just during Obama's first term, this occurred until Obama handed the Presidency over to Donald Trump, so how is it that, now that Donald Trump is President of the United States, millions of people are protesting that the government is systemically racist and has been for decades, yet, President Trump, has only been in Office for four years?

It honestly makes no sense to me because these people are following the word of Barack Obama, who ran the United States for 8 years, so if anyone is to blame for a systemically racist government, he would be the one responsible. However, like I said before, Barack Obama didn't bother with dealing with this so-called problem of a systemically racist government because there was no problem of a racist government, until the 2020 election year came. One thing that annoys me the most about the Obama's, besides Barack being Indonesian and not American, is the fact that they think they can speak for every American, they think they can speak for the American people, which they can't.

I mean, do I need to remind you that, Michelle Obama, was heated with women in America after President Trump was elected President in 2016 and even belittled women because she felt she had the right to bash American women for voting for Trump. Michelle Obama, went on record to berate women in America by stating that, "Any women who voted against Hillary Clinton voted against their own voice". Therefore, Michelle Obama basically thinks that she can somehow read the minds of millions of American women because according to Michelle Obama, she is the voice for all women. Michelle belittles million of women, who voted against Hillary Clinton because Michelle Obama claims that these women went against their own voice.

Couldn't be the fact that these women just didn't want to vote for Hillary because they didn't believe the BS she was pushing, nope, that couldn't be the reason at all, it had to be that these women were forced to vote for Trump, yup, that seems to be the reason why they didn't vote for Hillary. I think we have figured out by now that, all democrats, don't think Americans can think for themselves, they don't think American men and women, can actually express their own feelings and use their own voice, especially women.

It's crazy because Michelle Obama went on record to ask American women, "What does it mean for us women that we look at these two candidates, as women and many of us said, that guy, he's better for me, his voice is more true to me. Well, to me that just say's you don't like your voice, you like the things your told you like". It's amazing how Michelle Obama, can ask this of women, but she's not really asking these women this question, it's more like Michelle Obama, is telling other women that they don't like their own voice because they didn't vote for the woman candidate.

It wasn't a women thing, Hillary Clinton was just as corrupt as Barack Obama and people seen right through Hillary Clinton's lies and deceit, American women did use their voice and they voiced that, Donald Trump was a way better candidate then, lying Hillary Clinton. It's funny how Michelle Obama is even talking, like we are supposed to care or give a damn about what she says or even thinks, she's a former first lady, who holds no political office, but is also hated by most American's, but since the Obama's crave attention, we will never be able to get rid of these two foreigners.

In addition, Barack Obama literally handed Congress a fake birth certificate, so seriously, do you honestly think that the Obama's have a problem with lying to the American people? Also, Michelle Obama, claims that American women, are doing what they are told to do, not what they want to do, according to Michelle, American women, can't make up their own mind and they can't express their own voice. What honestly gives you the right to tell women this though, what honestly makes you think that you have the right to speak for other women? Don't forget, during Hillary Clintons campaign, her and her team were actually convicted of spying on Donald Trump's campaign.

Yet, Hillary went on to state that, "When I think of Trump supporters, I think of them, as a basket of deplorable," her exact words, not mine. The hatred for America coming from these people is obvious, but Candace Owens, said this better than anyone, "These people hate America so much, yet these people refuse to leave the United States of America". That is the question on many Americans minds though, Americans like, BT, ABL, Jericho Green, Candace Owens and myself because seriously, if you don't like our country and you hate our country so much, why have you not left it yet?

You are free to leave anytime you would want to, but I guarantee you won't, you won't leave America because you know that the United States of America is the greatest country in the world, if you leave, the results are not the same. America has freedoms like no other country in the world, so if you leave, you won't have the money or power, but you also won't have the freedoms you take advantage of, so this is why many people claim they will leave, yet they never do. Think of the dozens of actors and celebrities, that have made this statement, if so and so gets elected, I am moving out of America, if so and so gets elected, I am moving to another country, but they never actually do move.

These influential people only make this statement because they want their voice to be heard, they never actually would go through with it, just like Barack Obama and Joe Biden, often talked about police reform, but never pulled the trigger. The entire time President Trump has been in office, it's been the blame game, it's honestly crazy, how people can go on television and blatantly blame our current U.S. President for just about anything simply because they do not like President Trump.

It's crazy to me because this is the person who is the President of the United States, forget that you hate him, forget that you can't stand the person, he is the U.S. President and in charge of our nation, it's the House of Representatives job to give him all the help he needs to do his job. The House of Representatives, was designed and created, to represent the American people and the United States of America, no one or nothing else, but President Trump seems to be doing this on his own because the House hasn't helped him once, instead, they've fought him every way possible. In fact, these State Senators are even making Americans lives harder, they are also destroying small American businesses because they've chose to close our country for a virus that is 99.7% curable, a virus they claim is the deadliest virus ever and every American needs to stay inside.

The thing about this so-called deadly virus is that the people that are dying with covid-19, already had underlying problems or conditions, but since they died when they got covid-19, somehow covid-19 because the reason they passed, when several other factors led to their death. This is why we've supposedly had more than 300,000 people die from covid-19, but in reality, people who already had underlying problems, like people with heart problems and the elderly, died because their immune systems were already at risk and when they got covid-19, their immune systems could no longer fight it off with their underlying conditions.

It's been proven to be curable, the President got the virus, he was healed three days later, same thing for the First Lady and his son, they were all fine, they never once worried about a life or death situation, so seriously, how is this the deadliest virus in America, when it's 99.7% curable? This is the democratic logic though, this is the ideology that they use to try and lie and deceive the American people with. These are the same State politicians that think that people should not go out and vote at voting centers, but should go out and stand side by side each other people, so they can protest about how racist President Trump is.

Think about it this way, democrats and liberals, forced every American into a lockdown, which prevented people from talking to one another and sharing their opinions and ideas. These politicians didn't stop there because now communication between others, is only through online social media platforms, yet these vary platforms are increasingly banning certain opinions. Like I said before, these democrats and liberals, deceive us into believing what they want us to believe and they lie to us as much as possible, just so they can stay in power.

Honestly, these democrats are to funny because every single one of them are going on national television, telling the American People and even other State politicians, that we have to accept the election because

265

it was a free and fair election. Uh seriously, have you not been watching the same news everyone else is because these democrats clearly committed voter fraud, they clearly cheated during the election. So seriously, how could you honestly expect State politicians and the American people to accept the fact that you actually cheated to try and win the 2020 election?

I honestly believe this is why democrats and liberals are pushing these statements and pushing the people to accept the results because they don't want the truth or real facts to come out. We know democrats are trying to lie about these incidents because if you take a look at the case where numerous suitcases, were pulled from underneath a table, that was filled with hundreds of ballots for Joe Biden, this was actual evidence, actual video evidence of voter fraud. Still, a democratic assembly member tried to claim that this was already debunked, that they had no evidence, yet this was the first time the video was being shown and the evidence was right there in front of her on video.

Honestly, I am not joking, this female democrat watched the entire video, that showed evidence that there was numerous suitcases taken from underneath a table and counted, after everyone else left, but still, this democrat had the audacity to claim there was no evidence and actually told this lady she has no evidence. You honestly can't say this didn't happen or say that this democrat didn't do something as stupid as making this statement because it was made on national television, the whole world seen her make this statement.

The sad thing was, this democratic made it seem like it was more of an attack on the lady, who was simply showing the evidence that she needed to show, so they could prove their case of fraud, which the video proved their was. That is also why all these cases being dismissed for voter fraud makes no sense at all because there was actual voter fraud, I seen it, you seen it, millions of American seen it, yet democrats and liberals act like they, didn't see it. One person I bow to is, Tomi Lahren, an American commentator, who is not afraid to be truthful.

This beautiful blonde, hit it right on the nail when she posted a tweet that read, "If you can vote for a democrat in November, after what they've done to this country, you really need to have someone take a good hard look at your heart and brain." The chaos, the destruction, the deception, the canceling of cultures, the delusion, it's all coming from democrats in power, but they want you to think and believe that it's all President Trumps fault, so they can steal your vote. Now democrats blame President Trump, for this current COVID-19 pandemic because of his supposed late response to the virus, not only that they call President Trump racist, for claiming that the virus came from China, so it's, "the China Virus," which in all honesty is true because it did.

To label the U.S. President anything other than the U.S. President, would usually get you in trouble, but it's also a position that is the hardest job in America. These people could care less, they berate and belittle President Trump daily and all these democrats should be fired and jailed for ripping off the American people and be traitors towards our U.S. President. If the actions coming from these democratic State Senators weren't already embarrassing enough, it got worse when they started to blame President Trump for the deaths of hundreds of minorities and immigrants because the covid-19 virus, was hitting bigger urban communities harder, then it was smaller communities.

To me, this honestly makes no sense at all because according to these State Representatives and civil leaders, these big cities are all urban cities, that have no white people in them, but to say that the current U.S. President is using the virus to kill off people, should automatically put you in jail for being an idiot and disgracing the U.S. President. The funny thing about what these people claim is that, the so-called bigger urban cities and communities that they are referring to, which are only filled with minorities and immigrants includes cities like; New York City and San Diego. Once again it's their democratic logic that makes them look like complete idiots, not the American people because these people don't care about the truth.

They don't care about helping the American people, they care about helping themselves. These people want to stay in power and they have no problem cheating to do it, especially if it helps them advance their agenda. It's like seriously, this virus started in a Chinese lab and was spread to the United States, President Trump passed a travel ban in January, to at least slow the infection down, but President Trump also did everything in his power that he could to contain this virus, while democrats fought him and blamed him, every inch of the way.

We've seen this occurring daily on national television and even online, by none other than our very own Speaker of the House, Nancy Pelosi, who constantly berates and belittles the President, calling him just about every name in the book she can think of, while letting her own State run into the ground. If you honestly think Nancy Pelosi gives a damn about the American people, you are sadly mistaken, she could care less about the American people and she proves this daily, just by her actions and what she says.

The thing Americans should be worried about is the fact that, our very own House Speaker and most House democrats, have recently passed investigation after investigation, so they could constantly investigate President Donald Trump and his team, at least until something sticks. Not only is Nancy Pelosi, choosing not to bother to help the President fight this uncontrollable China lab created virus, but she chooses to head the investigation into the President Trump and his team's response to the virus.

Don't forget that this is the very same woman that has denied the American people their stimulus package time after time because President Trump and Congress won't give her the money she wants, yea she cares about the American people alright. Honestly though, she is the Speaker of the House, she is the Representative in charge, if anything happens to the President or Vice President, but she chooses to ignore helping the President find solutions to the virus that is still supposedly killing thousands of people because she rather investigate the current U.S. President. I think it's crazy because every single thing that she has brought in front of Congress to try and impeach President Trump with, has been proven to be false, every single accusation is proven false, yet she continues to do it.

I think American politicians have their priorities a little mixed up because this is something the Speaker of the House, liberals and democrats do on a daily basis. When you think about it, when have these politicians ever done something for the American people, they've been in government positions for over five decades, 50 years, yet they've done nothing but lie and deceive Americans. In addition, when did major American cities like, New York City and San Diego, somehow become urban cities and seem to only have minorities living in them?

We know for sure cities like, Chicago, Atlanta and Baltimore are urban cities, but how can cities like New York City and Sand Diego be called urban communities, when their residents are mostly white? It's just another lie they have to push because the truth doesn't fit their

268

agenda, the truth that these cities are filled with mostly white Americans, doesn't help when they are trying to claim that President Trump is trying to killing of minorities and immigrants in urban cities. I mean, I am not making this stuff up and it would honestly be too hard to try to, but actual State Representatives and Senators, are claiming that President Trump is using the virus to eliminate minorities.

These State Politicians and civil leaders go on television and actually make the claim that our government, led by President Trump, is somehow using COVID-19, to get rid of minorities and immigrants, in these so-called bigger urban cities. Since the virus is supposedly hitting these big cities the hardest and they supposedly only have minorities and immigrants in them, President Trump and the government, has somehow contained the virus and used the China lab virus, to target and kill minorities.

It couldn't simply be the fact that, these bigger cities are being hit the hardest because they have millions of people living side by side, all living together in small confined spaces, people of all races and color, so diseases spread easier. It's weird because democrats are known to have hidden agendas, but after time they've all been exposed and charged for their convictions, but somehow that concept has went out the window. Now, politicians, including our very own House Speaker Nancy Pelosi, the Obama's and so-called special DNC speaker, Hillary "Criminal" Clinton, do as they please, with no consequences.

I think what gets me the most though, besides what we've talked about already in this book, is the fact that, these State politicians and civil leaders, lie to the American people like it's nothing. They tell Americans what we are to believe in and if you don't take their side, if you don't believe their lie, you are labeled the American traitor. It's been proven time after time, how much these politicians hate America, especially under President Trumps rule, the numerous cover-ups alone, may have you puzzled. Definitely when you take a look at the Hillary Clinton's government email scandal, where Hillary had a personal server at home and somehow made hundreds of official government emails, somehow just disappeared.

I'm starting to believe this is the democratic way though, they put their faith in criminals, they use criminals as their saviors, hell, Nancy Pelosi gave George Floyds family a folded American flag ceremony, a ceremony that's reserved for our fallen military heroes. Granted, there

269

were a lot of circumstances that led to George Floyd's death and the cop having him pinned down, didn't help, but Floyd was in no way, shape or form, a hero to anyone. Honestly, look at his long criminal record and past, he never did one thing for anyone but himself, he's a hero, he's a guy you start a movement for, he's the guy you want your kids to follow, seriously, I mean, seriously?

Then again, like I stated before, this so-called hero of yours, put a gun to a pregnant woman's stomach, while he robbed her, then pistol whipped her after he was done robbing her, so if this guy is a hero to you people, like you people claim he is, millions of you, got some serious issues. I am dead serious when it comes to this because you guys are claiming that numerous criminals and long-time felons, are your heroes, not only George Floyd, but numerous criminals, people that have committed crimes their entire lives, but also have done nothing to contribute to your own community, are the people you guys are starting movements and protesting for.

I honestly fail to see the upside of destroying your community and killing your own people, for criminals and felons, who did nothing but robbed and stole from your people in that same community. We already know just how full of crap these blm founders are and honestly, if you don't think there is something wrong with praising criminals and attacking police officers, you need help. Honoring people, who rob, steal and kill and attacking the people that keep this from happening to you, shows you certainly lack common sense.

What also gets me is the fact that, these State Senators, politicians and even everyday Americans, go on television and proudly boast their bad opinions and false allegations about President Trump, no matter how wrong or deceitful it tends to be. It really just keeps me puzzled because Nancy Pelosi and other American House Representatives, just approved another investigation, so they can now investigate President Trump for his covid-19 response. I fail to understand how President Trump even has the ability to do his job, when he has Nancy Pelosi and every single democrat, verbally attacking him, coming after President Trump with false accusation after false accusation.

The President, is literally dealing with a crazy foreign virus, that is literally killing American's as I write this book, but Nancy Pelosi and democrats, want to focus on how they can investigate the President, so they can try to impeach him again. The to me is the crazy thing because instead of finding a vaccine or helping out the American people with a stimulus package, these democrats focus on trying to impeach the President, so they can get him out of the Oval Office.

Isn't something wrong here, is it just me that thinks there is something wrong here, we already know that Nancy Pelosi blocked the first stimulus package three times, before her and her democratic cronies approved it, so am I missing something here? These democrats came up with investigating the U.S. President and his team's response to covid-19, which is still killing thousands of people all around the world, instead of investigating to find a cure to stop covid-19. I mean, please tell me if I am missing something here, investigating the President's response to the Chinese virus or investigating to find a cure for this Chinese virus, you tell me, which one is more important?

I know what it is, it must have been a spelling error or spelling mistake because I choose to believe or maybe just hope to believe, that these American State Representatives, can't be so hell bent on getting rid of a U.S. President, where they would choose to ignore the virus, the deadly virus that's killing people as we speak. What scares me and probably most other American's is, these are the people in power, these are the State politicians, who control our American rights, freedoms and liberties, but instead of fighting for Americans, they are fighting more for power, illegal immigrants, foreigners and getting rid of President Trump.

You can see that, I even left minorities out of the list because look at the facts, although millions of minorities hate President Trump and blame all white people, there are a vast majority that don't think like this and think the same way I do because we are all American, doesn't matter what color your skin is. Also, like I said, urban communities do have a big problem with crime and violence, urban communities do have a problem with kids not wanting to be educated, urban communities do have a problem with gangs and drugs, but if we don't start at the root cause of the problem, the problem will never be fixed.

I am all for police reform, I am all for prison reform, but also bringing help to urban communities to stop the alarming rate of death, but abolishing police and blaming other people for the problem that your own people are causing, does not classify as solutions for these problems. Democrats and blm Marxists leaders, know these are not solutions, but they push these solutions anyways because they want minorities to think President Trump is behind all the crime and violence and the only way this violence will stop, is if you give these people what they want. It honestly makes no sense because on one side you have these blm Marxists leaders, trying to take over the world because they want world domination and on the other side you have democrats trying to take over the Presidency because they want to rule America.

I believe all of us Americans are screwed anyways because the people that want to rule America, are led by the State politicians that want to destroy the old ways of America and create there new America. This is why State Senators fight so hard for illegal immigrants and foreigners, they know if they give these immigrants what they want, if they help these illegal immigrants and foreigners out, they'll have millions of more voters. No offense but, if you are trying to help out illegal immigrants, in a time when American citizens are struggling and suffering, you shouldn't have your State job in the first place.

Your job is to focus on Americans, especially in hard times of need, but instead of helping out and focusing on Americans, you are focusing on helping out people over in America illegally. What most Americans have, we have worked hard for, we don't work hard so other people can benefit off of the results of our hard work. If these American State Representatives, have their way, the whole immigration reform will be changed and illegal's will be given free reign of America, without worrying about whether they will be deported or not.

Seriously, as an American State Rep., you can't just give illegal immigrants access to American rights and free money because it's not free money, its hard worked for American money. Money that comes from the backs of Americans, not politicians or congress. I couldn't believe what I heard one day coming from State Rep AOC because ,, besides the many racist claims she just blurts out, she once blurted out that, illegal immigrants deserve free healthcare, free money and free government assistance because they feel left out.

If you look at all the official constitutional laws about immigration, you'll see that illegal is illegal, no matter which way you try to flip it and these people deserve nothing, but a plane trip back to wherever they came from. Therefore, like many others like them, State Senators need to realize that, what's ours is ours, you don't get it and you can't just give it away to other people, just because you want these people to be on your democratic side.

-- Chapter 5 --
More likely to happen or likelier to happen, that's your argument?

One of the biggest ways to look at race and self-entitlement is to take a look at the numerous cases of minorities, who try to sue other people on the basis of race, they use their race as an excuse for the case or even as a merit to the case. We can see this by looking at the case between minority media mogul Byron Allen and the television network, Comcast. Byron Allen is a minority media mogul, that owns several minority television channels and Byron Allen tried to sue Comcast because Comcast wouldn't play his television channels on their network.

Comcast didn't add his channels to their lineup because these channels basically didn't fit their programming, but of course, according to Byron, the real reason was because Byron was minority and these were minority television channels. Because of Comcast didn't want to play Byron Allen's television channel's on their network, Byron felt that he was entitled to sue Comcast for 20 Billion dollar's and use race discrimination, as the basis for his case. Get that, 20 billion dollars, forget that Byron Allen, is probably already a billionaire, but Byron chose to sue Comcast all on the false pretence of race because they didn't include his channels in their network.

Now you would think, if he were suing them for 20 billion dollars, there would be a better reason for him then race right, I mean you are suing them for 20 billion dollars because you are minority. Just didn't make sense that Byron's submittal and deposition for the case, was that Allen was suing Comcast because Allen claimed they were discriminating against him, simply because he was minority and that's why Comcast, chose not to play his television channels on their network. Comcast even told Byron Allen, that they cannot play his channels because of the bandwidth of his channels, but also because his channels didn't fit with their network, but that wasn't good enough for Byron Allen.

Byron felt rejected and felt that since Comcast denied to play his channels, Allen would sue them and claim race as the reason because he feels he's entitled to sue Comcast because it's discrimination. Doesn't matter that it's Comcast's network and this means they can do whatever they want, they choose to showcase whatever channels they

273

want to, you don't get to make that chose and you can't sue them if they don't give in to your demands. It's like, seriously, you are an idiot and you and many like you, are what's wrong with America because how do you justify suing someone for billions of dollars simply because you feel your race entitles you the ability to do so.

Seriously though, how does that make sense, you are trying to sue a company, for a ridiculous amount of money, basically billions of dollars, not millions, billions of dollars. This is all because you feel they discriminated against you and your channel, simply because you are minority. This reasoning has no base to it, this reasoning has no backbone to it and like many others, you can't just use you race as an excuse. This ridiculous case and many like it, are often rejected from our civil courts, only to be pushed to the Senate or Congress, but still they tend to get rejected and dismissed because they usually have no base to them.

Most of these cases based on race discrimination, usually tend to get rejected by Congress and the Senate, but people continuously send these rejected cases back, only to get rejected over and over again. The fact that Byron Allen, even thought it was okay to sue Comcast, for this ridiculous amount of money just on the merit of race discrimination, shows you how minorities, use race as an excuse for everything and how most minorities and immigrants, think they are entitled to whatever you have, whether they worked for it or not.

Comcast eventually won the case because Byron Allen really had no merit or basis to his case and he couldn't prove Comcast did anything wrong. Unfortunately, there are plenty of examples like this and most of the time it's minorities, making statements about racism or discrimination, but most of the time these peoples accusations are usually made up. This was recently played out by a minority television actor, Jussie Smollett, a former actor for the show, Empire, who recently was exposed for lying and making up an entire hate crime assault story for publicity.

This minority actor, went to Chicago Police, with a noose around his neck, claiming that two white men, wearing MAGA hats, assaulted him and while they were assaulting him, they yelled racial and homophobic slurs, poured bleach on him and tied a noose around his neck. When the truth came out, Jussie was exposed for making the entire thing up and it was found out that Jussie, paid two Nigerian-American brothers, who he formally worked with, $3500 to buy a noose and the same clothes and hats, that were used in the robbery.

Faulty and unjust reasoning, are just a few things minorities tend to use when they are making their arguments and you can see this by looking at the case of, a minority man who shot himself, while police arrived on the scene. Since this was supposedly just another minority man, social media went crazy and soon you started seeing riots and protests, all for this minority man, before they even knew anything about the case. Again people assumed they knew better and they started again causing destruction to Minneapolis, but they assumed this was just another unarmed minority man killed by police, they assumed he was just another unarmed minority man.

The truth is, this innocent minority man shot himself, before police could even get near him. That's right, this minority man pulled out a gun and shot his own self in the head and not one police officer fired a shot at him, but still, minorities rioted and protested for this criminal, claiming police shot him in the head. I am not making this up, you can easily read about it in an article that was posted by ABC News. This unknown armed minority man, committed suicide and shot his own self in the head and the police tried to help him, they didn't shoot him in the head, he shot himself and the police didn't even fire one shot, but still, police were blamed for the death of this minority man.

That's the thing that makes all these situations crazy, these people don't wait for the truth, they don't wait to see what the facts are, they automatically assume they know what's going on and to them, knowing this somehow allows them to riot and protest. It's also crazy because the violence that occurred from these riots and protests, for this minority man, who killed himself and wasn't killed by the police officers at the scene, like people claimed, warranted the State Governor, to call in the National Guard.

These people assumed this guy was innocent and just another minority guy shot and killed but the police, but this guy shot himself, he killed pulled a gun out and shot himself, but that didn't matter, these people rioted and protested anyway. These people don't care about the truth and these people don't care about facts, they are always quick to judge everything and make assumptions that are always based on

275

unsound reasoning. Seriously, this armed minority man shot and killed himself, but since this story, doesn't help the narrative, social media quickly flips it to their liking and pushes it as, just another innocent minority man killed by police.

The media continues to blast the story they push, who are now labeling the story as, police shoot innocent minority man in the head, which is nowhere near the truth. We know that there is prejudgment because that is how we find out that this minority man shot and killed himself. The police had to release the video camera feed of the incident because the police were being accused of killing the minority man, even though he killed himself and this incident was seen by several people who witnessed it happening.

To stop the accusations and to stop the violence from these protests, the police released the crime scene video footage, which clearly showed that, the minority man took his own life and police only tried to help him. What's forgotten about most of these incidents is that these people are only encountering police because police are being called on them and the same thing goes for this minority man because the minority man in question was also considered a murder suspect. Many of the cases we encounter today, tend to be the exact same as this one and it always seems to be the police officers fault, but if these people weren't committing crimes, the police wouldn't have been called.

People need to stop believing the fallacies that minorities are the victim because that is nowhere near the truth and people need to stop listening to Lebron James. No matter what, `King Of Beijing` says, police are not waking up and taking their frustrations out on minorities and police are not waking up, deciding okay, how many minorities can I shoot today, stop listening to the fallacies, that these idiots continue to push. Anyone of you that honestly think that Lebron James has suffered from any form of racism, I want you to remember one thing, Lebron James became a millionaire at the age of 18 and a billionaire, by the time he was 30.

Lebron James knows nothing about racism and in high school he was worshipped and from there, the only thing Lebron James, has ever had to deal with is criticism. Lebron, is just like many other millionaire sports players, who are making millions of dollars to play a sport, but they are complaining about systemic racism, when most of these sports

276

players make in one month, what most Americans make in an entire year. The millionaires don't know what it is like to live in poverty, they don't know what it's like to live in violent neighborhoods, they don't know what it's like to watch your sibling fade slowly from drug addiction, but like we discussed before, these people always think they know what's it's like to be you, you don't, they do.

It just gets worse because these millionaire crybabies post their hash tags and they post their hateful idiotic and racist comments. These people also tend to throw in some President bashing posts, but you'll never see these millionaire sports players, bothering to do anything for the people or the urban communities that are dealing with crime and violence because forget taking action, these crybabies think, #hash tagging it, is better. I believe the excuse of race and the blame game, is a huge reason, why these people think they are entitled to freely pass along as much false information as possible, where their argument has sound reasoning or not.

When you are creating cases, racial cases, that are clearly false or when you are justifying arguments, that are based on faulty and unsound reasoning, you are just showing how uneducated you are. Besides their faulty, unsound reasoning, which seems to take the blame for just about everything that goes wrong, this theory really comes into play when it's discussions about minority employment. Also minorities applying for jobs that they don't get or are denied and they blame it on the faulty reasoning, that they didn't get the job, all because they were not white.

It's not that these people don't have the right training or experience for the job at hand, or it couldn't be that they have no experience in that position, but also may have even lied to get the interview, but since a white person got the job and they didn't, the company is racist and they are guilty of committing discrimination against minorities. It's not the fact that minorities, especially minority youths, have no work experience because they choose not to work or the fact that most of these young adults, never finished school or quit school to sell drugs.

So now, because of these choices, they have no education, no work experience and are not able to get many jobs. To these people, it's a push of fallacy because these uneducated minority youth believe that, white people are to blame for all their faults and it's white people, who are the ones solely responsible, for their wrong life choices. Americans, are subject to these unjust and unreasonable examples daily because these people are constantly seen on television, constantly seen on television award shows and are constantly seen on just about every form of media there is, especially online, pushing their false narratives.

It's seriously puzzling, we've seen this occurring more and more and now there are numerous news article stories appearing about, "how white people need to stop committing white racism" because these people claim that, "white racism is the root cause and reason behind the racism occurring in the world" and white people, are the only ones that can stop American racism. It's all puzzling to me because these people tend to react before they think about things and we've seen proof of this.

We watched as these people, rioted and destroyed everything in sight, but also committed violent acts towards others, all because they assumed the police just killed another minority man. The false allegation was spread by someone online and thanks to this false allegation, rioters and looters started to destroy the city. Now since social media activists want justice, these people go out and violently protest, all in the name of this supposed innocent minority man. They violently started riots and protests and these people started this violence, all before they even knew that, this minority man killed himself, the police didn't kill him, he pulled out a gun and shot himself in the head.

Since these people assumed, like they do so many times, they came to the instant conclusion that, this was just another case of a minority man being killed by police and they refused to believe that anything else, could have possibly happened. These social media activists, didn't bother to stop to look into exactly what happened, they didn't bother to stop and look at the facts of the case, they assume they knew, but if they would've took the moment to view the facts, they would have seen that this minority guy actually shot himself in the head, not the police.

Therefore, when I was reading these statements, I had to stop for a second, so I could wrap my head around the statement of, "white people need to stop white racism". This one statement has me really puzzled and if I am reading this right, according to these uneducated entitled lunatics, it's white people, not minorities, that are seen on

278

television committing racism and discrimination against others. I honestly think if you asked these people who they think created blm, they would probably say, it was white people who formed blm because these are the same people that are writing articles claiming that, it's white people, who are rioting, protesting and looting stores.

To these idiots, it's white people who are on television saying the n-word to everyone and it's white people that are in these crime infested urban communities, who are selling drugs, joining gangs, robbing people and committing drive-bys, not minorities. Remember the word I keep using is, fallacy because fallacy, is making an argument for something that is based on totally faulty reasoning, which tends to be the basis for most of the arguments these people are making. Fallacy plays an important role here because there is no real reasoning behind all the fabricated and distorted information they pass.

There is no sound or just reasoning to their arguments and there is no evidence, to what they are claiming, but they still have an agenda to pass and a narrative to follow. When it comes to faulty reasoning or fabricated information, it's not too hard for people to steer the evidence their way and the specialty of the news and media, is deception and misdirection. David Copperfield, was the king of deception and misdirection, but the media puts him to shame and while everyone is watching the right and trying to wrap their head around what's going on, no one is paying attention to the left and the destruction these people are secretly causing.

Unfortunately, the misdirection the media uses, is aimed at white people and now innocent white people are faced with false accusations but tend to be blamed for every ones faults, instead of focusing on the real culprits. The shock that comes with this is, if it's reversed because then it's always a different story and if white people discriminate against minorities or call them anything racist, or say anything remotely offensive, minorities instantly start looting, while screaming racism. The logic behind this reasoning to me is unjust because the thinking is,

It's okay that you just called me the n-word and it's okay that you followed it up with, cracker, I'm white, so I guess you are entitled to discriminate against me and others like me. Seriously, aren't you the ones complaining about racism and discrimination, aren't you the ones who are claiming that you deal with systemic racism because honestly calling white people, cracker, is just as bad as calling you a n****r. That's what's so interesting about all of these movements, you want equality so you riot for equality, you protest for equality, you commit violence acts for equality and you destroy communities for equality, but you don't offer white people equality.

Now you may be calling me a white racist, but let's get that straight, I hate everyone, of every race, who act's ignorant and oblivious to the truth and I don't believe in the concept of friendship because people you think of as a friend, will destroy your life to better theirs, without any hesitation. I also accept everyone, even the Muslims, who think I am an American infidel, to the gay people, who call me homophobic because I don't want to date guys and never had a thought to and I even accept the atheists, who hate my God.

What I seriously can't stand though, is people that use their race as an excuse and people who blame their problems on everyone else, instead of looking in the mirror and I hate to say it, but this tends to usually be coming from our young uneducated, self-entitled minority youth. One of the big concerns that these minority youth tend to ignore is, minority on minority crime because that is one major thing, plaguing urban communities, but minority youth, seem oblivious to it.

We see this daily because somehow it's always more important, when it's a white person or white police officer, killing a minority person because that's news, that's media attention and not the minorities killing, who are robbing and killing everyone. The news stories that are written, are sometimes too crazy to even read, the statistics and the data shown, just makes you shake your head and it's nothing but a repeat of, black on black violence, with numerous cases of, robberies gone horribly wrong. You can see this when you look at the case of 20 year old, Ajani Livous, who was just outright disrespectful to the police officers that pulled her over because her plates didn't match the vehicle she was driving.

Now we all know, this is already a crime because you can't put a registered license plate onto another car, that it is not registered to, everyone knows this, you can't do it, but Ajani and social media ignored this and blamed the pullover all on race because she was minority. If you look at the video, you would probably say, okay just take her away because every other word she said was a curse word and she literally berated this officer, the whole time. Besides the fact that, if you watch this video, you see that Ajani Livous, was so disrespectful to this police officer, that she deserved to be out in jail.

This is the false narrative they push though, this is exactly how young minorities act towards police officers when they are pulled over and they don't care about what they actually been pulled over for because to them, they assumes it's because their minority. These minorities ignore the fact that, they are criminals, who are committing criminal activity because Ajani was driving with no insurance and license plates that belonged to another vehicle, not the one she was driving. Both of these are currently crimes and most people, who are stopped for these crimes, are usually arrested and have their vehicles towed, but since she was minority.

Therefore, Ajani thought she was entitled to do whatever she wanted to and you see this on the video because she literally berated the police officer detaining her the entire time. Without having all the facts, people on social media blasted these Aurora police officers because they believed the false accusations coming from Ajani and her people and they think it's just another bad encounter with police. The false accusations and false narratives, of course, fall into the theory of fallacy because what, Ajani Livous and millions of social media trolls claimed, was nowhere near the truth and the actual police video proved it.

It wasn't the police officers, who were disrespectful, it was Ajani that was the disrespectful one, it was Ajani that was breaking the law and it was Ajani Livous, who was not following police orders. What also falls into this faulty reasoning, they use to make their unsound arguments, these people go online and push their fallacies, before they even know what actually happened, every single time these people act, before they think. It's crazy because these social media trolls didn't know the facts of Ajani Livous's case, once they heard about it, all these social media trolls, instantly rushed online and posted hateful and disrespectful comments about the Aurora Police Department because Ajani and these people pushed their false narrative.

The other interesting part about this case and they false narrative they tried to push was, people were claiming that Ajani Livous never got out of the car and couldn't get out of the car because she wasn't able to walk and required the use of a wheelchair or walker. Fact's and the truth, doesn't really matter to these people anymore, they will flip any encounter with police officers, to better fit their narrative because this wasn't the only time some minority person, lied about a police encounter, to get sympathy from online trolls.

It's sad because no matter how ridiculous their reasoning is, these people are making up encounters, or saying their encounters with the police, were worse than they actually were. This happened to Ajani Livous because when the video of the incident actual came out, it was proven and shown that, Ajani acted like a straight uneducated idiot, constantly cursing at the police officer, while the police officer was completely nice about the whole situation. These people are ruining police officers lives and these police officers, are not doing anything wrong during these encounters, but since it was an encounter with a minority person, they were somehow racist and just harassing minorities again.

Forget that police usually only stop you if you are committing a crime or suspected of doing so, which Ajani and most others like her, were. It's also come down to the fact that, these people don't want equality, they don't want justice, they just want a reason to loot and steal, so they can blame it on racial equality. You've seen this now more than a few times because minorities are starting riots, burning down communities and looting stores, all on the basis of police brutality and the arguments they are basing this violence on, all have faulty and unjust reasoning, behind them.

We can see this confusion and fallacy that they push, if we take a look at the case of, Kyle Rittenhouse, a 17 year old, who was rushed by protestors and shot them, while they were attacking him and pushing him to the ground. Video evidence shows that protesters were rushing and beating on Kyle, who was holding a rifle and when he was able, in self-defense he raised his gun and shot these people who were protecting him. Since Kyle Rittenhouse was a white 17 year old, Kyle is now being branded a murderer because Kyle shot and killed two protesters and wounded a third, after they attacked him.

That's the real fact and truth that, these people are ignoring and not telling you, which to me is funny because these people forget about an amazing thing called, caught on camera. On the video, you can clearly see, Kyle Rittenhouse on the ground, being attacked by several

282

protesters and it was these protesters that rushed him and it was these protesters that threw Kyle to the ground. In addition, if you are rushing and attacking someone, who is clearly holding a rifle, if you don't think they will protect themselves by shooting you, you are an idiot.

Kyle Rittenhouse, was being attacked by several protesters who were hitting and pushing him to the ground and the only way he could defend himself, was to use his rifle and it's these dumbass protesters own fault, that they were shot and killed, they attacked a kid with a gun, who was simply protecting himself. It always reversed though and the false narrative is always pushed first because according to minorities, Kyle was, "A white guy with a long gun, gets to shoot people and then go home and sleep and then get arrested the next day."

Forget the fact that, Kyle is only 17, or forget the fact that Kyle was simple protecting himself, after several protesters jumped him and hit him over the head with a skateboard, but also pulled their own guns on him. Those facts don't matter, all that matters is that, he was a white guy, who got to go home and sleep, after he supposedly killed two men. The story is always half assed though, when it comes to these people because they open their mouths, but usually whatever comes out tends to follow faulty reasoning after faulty reasoning, but still they make these statements because that's what the false narrative is today.

What's also just puzzling about what these people say, even Reverends because one Reverend, who isn't worth a mention, stated that, "If he were minority or brown, they would've opened fire with all they had," he was referring to Kyle, which just shows you that most of these minorities, have no clue what they are actually talking about. If he were minority or brown, they would've opened fire with all they had, who would have? Seriously, who would have opened fire with all they had, Kyle Rittenhouse just shot and killed these people in self-defense because he was being attacked by several other people, who had other weapons of their own.

The crazy thing is, Kyle Rittenhouse was hit in the head with a skateboard, attacked while he was on the ground and while another protester held up a handgun at him, other protesters were attacking him on the ground. So seriously, Kyle Rittenhouse was only trying to protect himself because several protesters were beating him with skateboards and attacking him, while he was on the ground, so

283

seriously, who would have opened fire with all they had, Reverend? Minorities, like this Reverend, will always use race as an excuse, whether minorities are involved in the situation or not and whether it deals with them or not.

The same can be said for the case of Jacob Blake because this fool had guns drawn on him and chose to ignore the police officers yelling at him, while he tried to get to his knife in his car. For the people who think he's innocent, you seriously need to look deep inside your head because you seriously got problems going on up there. Jacob Blake, had the police called on him because he took someone's keys and refused to give them back. While the call to police was coming through, it was stated over the radio that someone at this address had a warrant out for his arrest, non other then Jacob Blake.

Think he's not a criminal, Jacob Blake had a warrant out for his arrest because he was faces charges based on sexual assault, trespassing, hmm, seems familiar and disorderly conduct in connection with domestic abuse. You hear that, Jacob, had a warrant out for his arrest for sexual assault and domestic abuse and you want to claim that this guy was a hero and this guy was a role model for your kids. Also, before we continue about this criminals case, realize that, Jacob Blake, was not shot seven times, Jacob was shot at, seven times and hit four times, so please stop saying that he was shot seven times, when in reality he was only shot four times.

Jacob is a criminal and will always be a criminal, no matter how much his dad protests that he was a good guy because look at the facts, Jacob ignored the commands coming from all the police officers at the scene. After Jacob decided to not listen to the officer's orders, the officers on the scene, tried to subdue him and instead of going quietly, Jacob chose to fight with the police officers. While in a scuffle, the police even pulled out their taser's and tased Jacob because he continued to struggle and fight with the officers. When he finally broke free, Jacob ran towards the front door of his SUV, with the cops still on him and by this time, the police had their guns drawn.

Now, I am no dummy, but when several police officers have their guns pointed at you and are they are screaming at you to stop, you don't continue to your car, unless you are trying to get a weapon or just feel like being shot because you are not that bright. Whether Jacob

Blake was trying to run, or getting a weapon, it was his fault that he chose to ignore the commands coming from the police officers. It's his own fault that he was shot four times, in front of his own kids because he's the one that chose to fight with the police and resist arrest and now he has to suffer the consequences of his own actions.

That's another interesting part that, puzzles this whole dilemma because now, people are claiming, "cops need more training", but do they really, is it really the cops that need more training and not these entitled minority youth, who think they can say and do whatever they want, with no repercussions? Think about it this way though, these parents had 18 years to teach their kids that it's wrong to loot stores and it's wrong to steal and it's wrong to block traffic on the highway and it's wrong to overturn cars, including police cars and it's wrong to destroy buildings and communities and it's wrong to attack citizens. So who really needs the training, the police or these useless hate teaching parents, who have failed to educate these teens?

This is the same excuse they use, when it comes to police encounters in their own communities because these are the same people that are claiming that, police officers harass minorities more and that's why they are seen more in urban neighborhoods. Once again the logic will astonish you because it's not the fact that, minorities are getting harassed more, it's the fact that minorities commit more crime, so there presence is needed pore in urban communities.

It just makes you think though, why would you ever go into these urban neighborhoods, when there is nothing but drugs and gangs, where innocent people are getting shot and killed, for simply wearing the wrong color, it's like nah, I'm good. The violence is displayed daily on your local news stations because think of it this way, what is the one thing that constantly occurs on the news, what is the one thing that constantly occurs daily? There is often many answers that can go here, but the real answer is, murder, everyday on the news, there is a person killed in America, every single day, all around American cities, sometimes numerous killings in one day.

These people are not killed by police, nope, all these are homicides are committed by other Americans. We don't have a police brutality pandemic, we have an American brutality pandemic because innocent Americans are being killed daily, for no apparent or valid reason.

285

What's worse is, white Americans are now being told that since our neighborhoods are usually crime free, it's because of our white privilege and it's because we live in, Sundown Towns.

If you haven't heard what a, Sundown Town is, don't feel bad because I even had to look it up, when I was reading the article on, none other than, Yahoo. These explanations went on to claim that, Sundown Towns, were towns that were solely dedicated to white people and these neighborhoods were mainly white neighborhoods because only white people lives in these towns. The safety and security in these, Sundown Towns, is because white Americans have their white privilege, which allows them the safety blanket of a crime free neighborhood, like having a crime and drug free neighborhood, is some type of privilege.

White people don't live in comfortable communities and neighborhoods because we've had it handed to us and the reality is, every neighborhood in America starts out the same, it's the adaption of the environment that changes the community. Minorities don't like to be stereotyped, but they have no problem stereotyping other people and no matter how you look at it, white suburbia was always considered a better place to raise your kids, then ghetto drug infested communities and neighborhoods. In addition, what I fail to understand is, how can minorities even claim that white people stole their homes?

This to me makes no sense at all because white people didn't steal your home and you have the ability to buy a home just as much as they do, it's called having a mortgage. Then again, they don't like to pay for anything and want everything handed to them for free and now minorities are going into white neighborhoods, screaming at white people, about how you stole our houses and communities. First off, you don't pay their mortgage and you don't pay their monthly house bills and you don't pay their yearly property taxes, hell you usually have never paid for a mortgage in your life, so how can you honestly claim that white people stole your home from you?

That's what is so interesting about these people, they are literally going after white people, claiming white people, need to give up their homes, their jobs, their safety and security and basically everything else, to minorities, for free nonetheless. Minorities are literally demanding that white people move out of communities and give up

286

their own homes to minorities because the white people stole them from them. These ill minded and uneducated people, are making an argument that is completely based on faulty reasoning and it just makes you question everything they do because how do you even back this argument, when there's no factual reasoning behind it?

Your argument is based on assumptions because you are assuming white people have a better life, all because of the color of their skin, but what you fail to realize is, if you worked just as hard as white people have to, you would have the same life. Instead, minorities choose to constantly claim, white people have white privilege and this white privilege gives white people the ability to have a nice home that's in a nice neighborhood, which is in a nice drug free community, but is also protected, by our nice white cops.

Normal people would say no, there is no white privilege, it's just another false narrative that these democrats are trying to push because white people don't just have nice things because of this belief of white privilege, white people have safety and security because unlike you, they work for it and don't just think they are entitled to it. You know the scary part about all of this though and what's more frightening about what's occurring in America, if you have been paying attention to what we have been discussing all throughout this book, you will see that, the people in charge, from minority Pastors, to liberals and democrats, don't put much faith in minorities as a whole.

It's honestly surprising to see that many minorities in charge, are blaming their entire minority faults on white people, but they are also saying if minorities have any traits, they got them from white people. Forget the free individual thinker theory, or being able to have a mind of your own because from what these people say and have said, they don't honestly give minorities a lot of credit and it's somehow always, white people that have to change for minorities. Even the African American National Museum, stated that minorities, have learned everything from white people, we discussed this earlier.

When we talked about the so-called, "attributes of whiteness", that white and minorities seem to have. This is crazy because these powerful and influential minorities, are basically saying that minorities, all around America, have done nothing on their own and have achieved nothing on their own, which we all know is not true and there have been several successful minorities. That's the false narrative that these influential people push and I honestly feel bad for the hundreds of minorities, who have found success in America.

Now even these people are being called, white uncle toms and you can just ask football great and Hall of Famer, Hershel Walker and of course, former officer and the host of, the Tatum Show, Brandon Tatum, who have both been called, white uncle tom's, by other minorities, for simply speaking the truth. It's all a personal agenda push, while they deliberately focus on pushing their false narrative because at the same time they are falsely accusing and blaming white people for everything, these people in power, are deceiving you, feeding you false information, so they can make a power move.

These are also the same people in power, who are calling armed citizens, who are simply guarding or protecting their property, "vigilantes", while they refer to these rioters, looters, attackers and anarchists as, "peaceful protesters". I wish these people would listen more to Martin Luther King Jr., instead of following the fake lead of Fake Al Sharpton because Martin Luther King Jr., did things the right way and went on record to state that violence, was in no way, a good way to fight for justice.

Remember, it was Martin Luther King Jr. that stated, "Violence as a way of achieving racial justice is both impractical and immoral. It is impractical because it is a descending spiral ending in destruction for all. It is immoral because it seeks to humiliate the opponent rather than win his understanding; it seeks to annihilate rather than to convert. Violence is immoral because it thrives on hatred rather than love." Think about these words coming from MLK, for a second because if you read these words carefully, you can see that Martin Luther King Jr., is speaking to us through the grave because violence has taken over American cities and it's a descending spiral of destruction.

As if that wasn't spot on enough, MLK really hits the nail when you see that he states, "it seeks to humiliate the opponent rather than win his understanding" because right now white Americans are being humiliated all across America. They are being berated and belittled by minorities, while minorities turn around and expect all white Americans, to be okay with this humiliation. Most of these peoples reasoning comes from pure hate and these people thrive on hate and

288

they don't care if you know it or not, they hate the white race, therefore, they will always blame the white race for their own faults. You can also look at it this way, if we take another quick look at the killing of Ahmaud Aubrey and we look at his case, you will see that the McMichael's, didn't know this guy, they've never seen this guy before in their neighborhood and all they wanted to do was to stop him and question him.

It wasn't because he was minority, it wasn't because they didn't like Ahmaud Aburey, it was because Aubrey, was a suspicious character, never seen before in the community. Ahmaud Aubrey wasn't just another innocent minority man, just going for a jog, he was an unknown suspicious character, acting like he was jogging, in a community where he's never been seen before, which was also, in a neighborhood that previously had numerous houses, broken into.

This white father and son, the father being a former Sheriff, were going to stop any suspicious person that was in their community, no matter who it was, or what the color of their skin was and they had every right to, seeing that the father was a former Sheriff. The McMichael's, noticed Aubrey, who seemed to be jogging in their neighborhood and they knew he was a suspicious character, who both men, had never seen before in the community. The McMichael's chose to stop Aubrey to question him and during the questioning, Aubrey got into a skirmish with the younger son and during the confrontation, Aubrey was shot and killed.

Since the McMichael's were white and Aubrey was minority, both the father and the son, were instantly blasted by minorities and others, on social media, demanding for the McMichael's heads and before anyone knew the facts, the McMichael's, were branded as murderer's. This is happening all across America right now, if any white person perpetrates a crime against a minority person, it's branded as a hate crime and their heads are called for. Minorities do this because this follows their fallacy of their false narratives, based on unsound arguments and faulty reasoning.

No matter the reason, if it's a minority victim, no matter what the color of the perpetrator or perpetrators are, the perpetrators are instantly blasted online as murderer's by millions of people. These people don't bother to read about or know the facts, but people still think they are

289

entitled to call these white people murderer's, simply because they were white and that makes them automatically guilty. When the truth finally did come out, it was declared that the McMichael's, only tried to stop Ahmaud Aubrey, so they could talk to him and it was Aubrey, who chose to become combative and argumentative.

Once Aubrey got the chance, Aubrey started arguing and fighting with the son and during the fight, the son feared for his life, so he pulled his gun and shot and killed Aubrey. Now someone dying is never a good thing, but it seems that people are always jumping the gun and assuming things, before they actually look at the facts. This case, is prime example of that because the McMichael's, were instantly blasted as murderer's, before they could even give their side of the story, all because the victim killed, Ahmaud Aubrey, was minority and the perpetrators, the McMichael's, were white. Unfortunately, the same thing happens to just about every white person or white individuals, who are seen pulling the trigger, killing minorities.

The false narrative they follow is that, white people are the number one reason why minorities are dying and not just every so often, to them, white people are killing minorities at an alarming rate. The agendas fallacy, is even worse though because not only are minorities claiming that white people, kill them more, now they are under the mistaken assumption and belief, that white people are to blame for their bad environment. They use the false theory of white privilege to help make their arguments and the argument usually, tends to be, minorities live in bad homes, while white people live in nice homes, because of their so-called white privilege.

Minorities live in drug infested communities, while white people, live in drug free communities, it's because of white privilege, basically anything white people have, according to these people, is because of their white privilege. What's shocking and surprising is, forget the old theory of hard work pays off because according to these uneducated and entitled pricks, it's white privilege and not the hard work, millions of white Americans put in, that enables them to live in a nice house and live in a nice safe and secure community.

The fault reasoning that they use is crazy because white Americans try to defend themselves, only to be told they don't know how it is and they are too privileged and that's why they don't see the discrimination.

290

This was evident numerous times when people tried to post the comparisons between, minority pride and white pride because people claimed that, minority pride is stating, "I'm not ashamed of being minority, even though minorities have been treated as slaves for over four hundred years, but I am still proud of who I am".

Which is true, you should be proud to be who you are and yes, you have dealt with slavery, but so has every other single race. Black people were not the only ones enslaved in America, every race was enslaved in America. What these people, State Senators , civil leaders and blm forget to tell you is that, in America, white people were actually the first slaves, not minorities. Like we discussed before, Anthony Johnson, the first recorded slave owner in America, was a prominent black figure, who had four white slaves and one black slave.

Blm hates this fact though, so they try to change it, claiming they are the ones that dealt with slavery, not white people. The difference comes when these people talk about the people who have white pride, because you will see that the theory for black pride, doesn't apply the same here. This is clearly evident because these people claim, those who say white pride, are saying, "I'm proud to be white, the white race, is the best race and always has been". These are also the same people that go on to claim, "White pride, is a message of white supremacy and that's why it's racist".

It gets worse when they claim that, "all lives matters," is a message used to minimize the pain minorities endured for hundreds of years and we don't know what it's like to be minority, so this is why, if you support white pride and are claiming, "all lives matter", you are racist. We can simply look at the logic of the first part of this because how is claiming white pride, any different then claiming minority pride, when you are doing the same thing, you are showing pride for your heritage? The people that believe in this logic, are mainly the problem we are having in America because these are all the self-entitled idiots that push their false narratives, so they can have their 15 minutes of fame.

That's their specific agenda though because this is the false narrative they follow, even though it's a mistaken belief, they push it onto everyone else, while they continue to deceive people, so people forget the fact that, the arguments they are making, are based on unjust and unsound reasoning. The thought alone that, if you are supporting

291

white pride, you are racist and not sympathetic to minorities, just blows my mind because there are minorities, who could care less about anyone, let alone white Americans, but if white American's only show white pride and support their heritage, they are the racist ones, who are discriminating against people, seriously?

The logic that is used honestly makes no sense at all, but these people continue to push their faulty reasoning and if you show that you are proud to be white, this white pride makes you a racist white supremacist, who hates all minorities and supports nothing but white people and white supremacy. It's a mistaken belief, that has been exaggerated into the truth and now innocent white people all around America, are being blamed for the actions of many, simply because the color of their skin.

Whether it's entitlement or just from being uneducated, whatever it is, somehow these influential people in power, have convinced millions of people that white people are the bad guys and it's white people, who are responsible for their own bad life choices. We see this display currently taking place in America where we have minority blm protesters going into white suburban neighborhoods, telling white people that they need to leave their homes and lands because their all living on minorities land and white people stole it from them. That is also the interesting thing about what is occurring in America right now because minorities are demanding just about everything from white people, whether they deserve it or not.

Minorities are now going into white communities because they claim white communities are too safe and this is only because of these peoples white privilege. Since these people all have white privilege, minorities think they are entitled to go into numerous white suburban neighborhoods, trying to cause as much chaos as possible, all because these idiots claim, white people have too much safety. It just does not make sense anymore, we have innocent people killing people in urban communities, but minorities feel white people have too much privilege, so they go into white suburban communities to protest and riot.

The interesting thing about their theory is, if minorities, blm and their followers actually took the time to invest as much in urban communities, as they did in rioting, looting, and burning down businesses, they would probably have nicer, safer communities. These people don't though, they spend more time in blaming white people for their problems, then actually looking at the real problem and this will always leave urban communities, filled with nothing but death and poverty. What minorities and others fail to realize is, there is a real problem for minorities in urban communities, there is a real situation of death, occurring at an alarming rate for minorities and there is dozens of drug and gang infested minority urban communities, but blaming white people is not a solution.

Blaming white people, for something that you guys have to change yourselves, doesn't help you one bit, blaming police for killing you, when it's actually reversed, doesn't help you one bit and blaming President Trump, on the violence and crime in your city, doesn't help one little bit. Let's all take a stand, I'll even stand with you, but the stand will be for the innocent minority children being killed daily in urban communities, the stand will be for the innocent white men, women and children being killed, simply for being white.

The stand will be for the hundreds upon hundreds of minorities that are killed in urban communities daily not weekly, daily. This is where all the change start's, this is where the world starts to make a difference, instead of focusing on fake problems, we need to fix the real problems we all deal with, hash tagging something and protesting online with hateful and delusional comments, does not qualify as taking a stand against racial injustice. Protesting that the American Flag and our American National Anthem doesn't represent American freedoms, is not taking a stand against racial injustice.

Wearing t-shirts that say, black lives matter and painting black lives matters everywhere in the world and even on basketball courts, does not take a stand against racial injustice or equality. It's all a smear campaign, followed by one false narrative, which is pushed by blm and these people in charge because they want to create their new America. They don't give a damn about minority lives, they care about what's good for themselves, they care about staying in power and gaining more, they could care less about Americans and they prove that daily, in their hate speeches and interviews.

What is possibly chilling about the false narrative that these people push is, this fallacy can be the reason for certain killings and we can possibly look at the cases of, Conner Hinnant and Rosalie Cook as

293

examples. Both were white Americans, one a 5 year old child, the other an, 80 year old woman, who were both brutality murdered by minorities simply because they were white, but according to the media, this was not news, so their deaths were not talked about on the news.

Due to this push of false narrative of white blame, Rosalie Cook, was the victim of circumstance because she was an innocent white 80 year old woman, who was brutality stabbed, when she was simply walking out of a store, by a minority criminal, who was just released out on bond. Her murder was just another case, passed over by our major news media outlets because white officers shooting and killing minorities, is more the news story that's fits their agenda. If the case has anything to deal with white people who are the victims, yea they will cover it, but it's slowly pushed off to the side, as protesters being shot and cities being destroyed is the news they chose to cover.

You have to remember, like we discussed before, liberals and democrats own, run and control, most of our news media outlets and these people push the news, they want to push and you can see this evidence, by simply looking it up because if you do, you'll see exactly who controls the airwaves of America. These are not people the people we would originally tend to follow or even like, but they have full control and they will do anything they want to, while you are censored by these people, for anything offensive or anything they deem to be spreading false information, which usually to these people, tends to be anything good about President Trump.

These are the same people that want to educate our children on civil rights movements, starting from Elementary school on up and want our people to learn the democratic way. Forget freedom of speech, forget the freedom to have your own mind, or to be an individual thinker, these people want to teach you to follow their directive and if you don't follow their orders, you are consider an instant enemy. What interest me the most is that, these people choose to focus on police killing minorities, who are well known criminals, but yet they pay no attention to the known minority criminals, killing other minority criminals and basically everyone else.

If you really look at the murder rate and death rate, white Americans are shot and killed more each year, then minorities, but this death rate, should also be alarming because the reality that everyone

294

chooses to ignore is the fact that, minorities do kill more of their own kind, but the same thing can be said for, white Americans. According to FBI data reviews, for 2019, there were 3,315 white Americans killed in homicides and out of these, 3,315 homicides, 2,677 were committed by other white Americans.

The same year, which was basically last year, the results of homicides, were almost the same for minorities because there were, 2,925 minorities killed in homicides and out of those 2,925 homicides, 2,600 of them, were committed by minorities. Therefore, statistics and data reviews, often prove what I have been trying to say all along, white Americans are not your enemy and more white Americans are killed, yearly than any other race, doesn't matter how much you try to flip the truth. What we all should be focusing on as American's, is bringing each other together and stopping the useless acts of violence that has currently been plaguing the United States of America.

How many times have you watched, world star hip-hop, only to see innocent minorities and innocent children, shot and killed by gang members, all because they were wearing the wrong color or because they were on the wrong side of the neighborhood? How many times have you seen videos of minority teens, who are just sitting in their cars, only to be shot and killed in cold blood? How many times have you watched videos of bar fights because in the description, the bar fight turns into an all out gunfight?

The answers to these questions are usually a reflection on the way these people think, but it continues question after question, with no answer or understanding of how to stop the violence or even slow down the rate of homicides, occurring in urban communities. Still you wonder, how many times are we going to have to witness innocent young children being gunned down because some gang members saw their enemy and decided it was a good idea to open fire in broad daylight? We can go on with these types of questions, but I am sure you get the point and you don't have to really go far to see that, black on black crime is worse, then white on black crime.

The truth is, neither one of the races, white or minority, are more responsible for the other ones deaths. White people kill more white people and minorities kill more minorities, that's just the facts of life and we've seen the evidence, where it has been declared by the FBI that, 3,315 white Americans were killed in 2019, compared to 2,925 minorities. All the evidence adds up to be very interesting because 2,677 white Americans, were killed by their own race, while 2,600 minorities, were killed by their own race.

So again, to say that white people are responsible for all of you problems and that white people have a privileged life because of this so-called white privilege, is just plain non sense. We need to educate our children, not teach them hate, but teach them the values of life and everything that comes with it and we need to teach them to respect others, until others disrespect you. Unfortunately the people that are rooted in hatred, will never change and they will always preach hate, whether to their kids, or in our schools. This will always keep society at odds with each other and the only way peace will ever reign, is if we all unite, remember, "We The People," instead of tearing at each other's throats, wondering who gets the last piece of pie.

Instead of peace, we are left with chaos and destruction and the American people are left with people like, Joe Biden and Nancy Pelosi, to speak for them because ,, unfortunately, old Cat Lady Pelosi, is the current, Speaker of the House. To even put your mind around the fact that this lady is our Speaker of The house, just lets you know that there is something seriously wrong with these politicians and they seriously need their heads checked. Nancy "Cat Lady" Pelosi and her cronies, are people that simply boggle your mind and you try to give the benefit of doubt, but all they do is let you down.

Nancy Pelosi, is definitely one of these useless ignorant people because she is supposed to be the voice of the American people, she is supposed to represent Americans first and look out for the best interests of Americans, but all she does is go after Trump and get exposed for her hidden agenda. It's funny how she is always blaming President Trump and Republicans on holding bills or legislature up because ; they want more money, only to find out, her and her democrats are the ones who got denied because they were always requesting more money.

Cat Lady Pelosi and her cronies, do not like the fact that President Trump, represents the American people and now our own, Speaker of the House, is stating that, "I don't think there should be any debates. I wouldn't legitimize a conversation with him." Now I understand if she was speaking about some other State Representative or Senator because

296

sometimes those people are hard to have a conversation with, when they are being told the truth, but nope, Pelosi, was saying this about the current, U.S. President. As a representative of the American people, how can you tell Americans that you wouldn't have a conversation with the U.S. President because you wouldn't call it a legitimate conversation, yet you spout of non-sense all day long?

Nancy Pelosi, like Hillary Clinton and others, should be in jail for all the corruption and deception they push onto the American people, they are guilty of so much slander and defamation of our current U.S. President, they should be jailed. Pelosi, like Barack Obama, does nothing but cause disruption in our country's government and it's funny because these two and many of their followers, are always claiming that there doing it for the American people. Foreigner Barack Obama doesn't represent me, Cat Lady Nancy Pelosi, doesn't represent me, so how can you guys honestly claim you are doing it for the American people, when you are basically doing it for yourselves?

You don't represent the values of the American people because remember, the American people, chose Donald Trump, to be the next U.S. President, the American people chose Donald Trump to represent Americans and you and your cronies, have constantly attacked him, every year since he was elected. You have not helped President Trump in any way possible to better the lives of Americans, you have literally fought President Trump on everything he has done and tried to do for the American people.

It is crazy because Nancy Pelosi and her people claim to represent the American people, yet, they are never seen doing anything for the American people and if they are doing something, it is usually blasting President Trump. In addition to blaming Trump, they blame all recent failed bills on Republicans or are always asking for billions of more money, while they push more chaos, violence and destruction, all over America, stating time after time, it's all President Trumps fault.

The real reality is, these people do not represent the American people, these people do not even represent the voice of the American people because if they did, Nancy Pelosi and her cronies would be listening to the American people and not people that want to destroy our country. The American people are fine with President Trump being in the Oval office, hell, President Trump, was voted into the Oval

297

Office, by the American people, so if you are constantly berating and going after him, how is this looking out for the best interests of the American people. Seriously, how are you helping out Americans, by taking away their chosen voice?

The evidence has already been seen, but also proven, that Nancy Pelosi, always has a hidden agenda, which is exposed by President Trump and herself, over and over again and she doesn't represent the American people because she chooses to constantly attack the President. It's crazy because the American people want peace, the American people want the ability to have the freedom to live their lives freely and not have to worry about being killed for walking down the street and every President Trump focuses on this basic human right, while democrats, choose to step all over it.

I think I still can't get over the fact that she has went on record, stating, "We do the Lords work," when she's approving late-term abortions, basically killing unborn babies, approving higher taxes and also approving free healthcare for illegal immigrants and not the American people. It doesn't stop there, she's approving new prison reforms, that let's convicted illegal immigrants, back out on the streets, yea, Nancy Pelosi, really cares about the American people. Her voice is annoying and reminds me of the old cat ladies and I wouldn't be so mad at her, if she would only show more care about the American people, then she does for illegal immigrants and aliens, but also needs to stop giving away our money, to people that don't deserve it.

One thing to take a look at is this crazy COVID-19 and how Nancy Pelosi and the democrats, stopped the government from helping out the American Citizen's because they were trying to pass a stimulus package, which was totally bogus. Not only was China's COVID-19, solely blamed on President Trump, even though, it was President Trump that put in a national travel ban, while Nancy Pelosi, Joe Biden and the democrats, called President Trump a xenophobia and said they wouldn't have put in a national travel ban.

Therefore, these useless democrats would have killed thousands of more people and still till this day, they blame China Lab's COVID-19, on President Trump and his supposed failed response to this curable, yet damaging virus. Now, they are using the violence form the chaos and destruction they started, with their so-called peaceful protests and

Joe Biden, went on record to clarify this by saying, "Trump is hoping for violence at these demonstrations because it detracts from his failed response to the corona virus". The fact that these democrats, including Joe Biden, keep blaming COVID-19 on President Trump, when they themselves has said that they would have done things different and they would have done better.

Seriously though, how, how would democrats have done better, you basically piggy back of everything President Trump says and it's more the monkey see, monkey do scenario because ,, President Trump, says they do more testing than anyone else, Joe Biden says, we'd do more testing than anyone else. The main thing to realize is, it was President Trump who put in a travel ban to slow the spread, it was also President Trump and Republicans, that passed an American stimulus package, while Joe Biden held firm that, he wouldn't have approved a travel ban and democrats refused to pass the American stimulus package, until it benefited themselves.

Nancy Pelosi and her cronies, are continuously choosing to ignore the violence, ignore the chaos, ignore the rioting, ignore the looting and ignore the COVID-19, while they blame it on President Trump because you know, President Trump, is bad and democrats are honorable, which is something we have yet to see. President Trump and the government wanted to pass an American stimulus package, to help out the struggling American people, through these hard times, due to COVID-19, but Nancy Pelosi and her democrats blocked it because it didn't benefit their agenda.

The American people needed the stimulus for help and were going to be in trouble without it, but Nancy Pelosi, Joe Biden and democrats, didn't care and they proved this, by blocking the American stimulus package, not once, not twice, but three times, so seriously, who's really looking out for the American people? As of August of 2020, it's occurring again because President Trump and Republicans, want to pass another American stimulus package to help out the America people, since most Americans are still left without work.

Nancy Pelosi and her democrats have once again denied the stimulus package, all because they say they want more money as Nancy Pelosi went on record to say, "They come down to, 2.2 trillion, then we can talk." Which to me is kind of funny because if you read most online news articles about the new American stimulus package being passed and who's denying it and who's accepting it, these idiot news writers are claiming that democrats, are not the ones denying the American stimulus package, by requesting more money, but the evidence and statements, prove otherwise.

These are the same statements made, one after another, that are used to attack our current President and no matter how false the accusations are, they will push them because that's their goal, that's their agenda. So once again, who is helping out the American people and who is holding the American people back because it doesn't seem to be our current U.S. President, that's denying the American people? This question I will leave for you to ponder because it really is puzzling to see, Nancy Pelosi, Joe Biden and other democrats, berate and belittle President Trump, but everything President Trump does that is good, they piggy back off of.

It's funny how these people recognize other people and they congratulate other Republicans, while they refuse to show recognition to the man who is responsible for it all, Trump. I honestly am not too sure that I have seen President Trump, doing something bad, honestly, these people are blaming the man he was before, not taking into consideration, the President he's become. Listen, I know he may have said some crazy things and quoted some crazy things, but who hasn't, but also everyone is allowed to have their own opinion, it's called a free country and you can't base these words on his actions as, President of the United States.

As President, this man has done more for the American people, then anyone before him and you don't just have to take my word for it, out away your hatred for the man and look up the facts. From minorities to Native Americans, President Trump is the only U.S. President to donate his entire salary to fundraisers and not taking one dime from the American people, but he is also passing legislature that other Presidents were afraid to pass because they would face certain repercussions. President Trump, is the only U.S. President that hasn't given in to these people that show hatred and dismay for America.

Trump's the only U.S. President that has reformed the old ways of our government and changed the failed traditions that have been controlling power in our government for decades. That's what the real

300

situation could be considered here, these people in power have been running our government for decades, screwing over the American people for decades and as soon as a guy becomes U.S. President, an American, that actually cares about the American people, they go bats**t crazy.

What gets me the most though, all these democrats and liberals, are claiming that they are doing it for the American people, they are going after President Trump for the American people, they are trying to get rid of President Trump, for the American people, why, seriously, why? The American people don't want him gone, you do and democrats, led by Pelosi, have done everything in your power to try to get rid of him, even using false accusations and lying to everyone, which should be a crime and if I am not mistaken, it was the American people that, elected President Trump into the Oval Office.

It was also the American people that backed President Trump, not the democrats, during his fake impeachment trial. It was also American taxed money that you chose to freely use to pay millions of dollars, to DA'S lawyers and investigators, to investigate the President, all on false accusations, false beliefs and false pretenses. What's interesting about all of this is, if these democrats weren't constantly coming after President Trump, Trump would not have to constantly defend himself and President Trump, would instead be able to focus more on the American People.

These people don't care though, especially Nancy Pelosi because according to her recent statements, cat lady Pelosi claims, "Trump and Republicans, are Enemies of the State". Really, "Enemies of the State," let us see if it's President Trump who is the Enemy of the State because President Trump is not the one stirring up all the violence. President Trump, isn't the one holding up legislature that will help the American people and President Trump, isn't the one who is denying federal help, but you know who is, cat lady Nancy Pelosi, Maxine Waters, Kamala Harris and the rest of their democratic cronies, that's who.

We really seen this display of ignorance plays out in Joe Biden's speech because he kept portraying Donald Trump as a bad U.S. President, that wants to hold on to power so much, that Trump is resorting to fear and hatred for his campaign strategy. Of course, after Biden is done with his smear campaign, he launches directly into just how much American supposedly knows him and his family. You can see this because after berating the President, he followed with, "The road back begins now, in this campaign. You know me. You know my heart and you know my story, my family's story. Ask yourself: Do I look like a radical socialist with a soft spot for rioters? It's like, seriously, did you just say that?

Because the answer would be yea, seeing that you have been on record saying that you support the protests and you obviously ignore the violence because you spend more time ripping President Trump and telling Americans, how it's President Trump, who is, "fanning the flames," of violence in America, enticing fear into the American people. Yes, Sleepy Joe, you do look like a radical socialist, with a soft spot for rioters because you and other democrats have, enticed the riots, enticed the looting, enticed the burning of American cities.

Also, with over 100 days of rioting, looting and American businesses being destroyed, you chose to blame it all on the President, while you continuously push to, defund the police, allow illegal immigration, weaken our military, take away Americans guns and approve higher taxes. What was also interesting in Joe Biden's speech, he started with, "the road back begins now", but what does that mean exactly, the road back to when China was making billions, off the American people, or the road back to when Russia was concluding with people like the Clintons and Obama's.

I know, maybe back to the time, when you stated, that you don't want your kids mixed with minority kids because I would seriously like to know where this road begins back to. It's very puzzling because they say one thing, but their actions prove another and they are okay with this, they don't fray from this position and they will push as many mistaken beliefs as they can. It's funny to see all this violence going on, all these so-called peaceful riots, people looting store after store and watch people like Biden and his democrats, that go on to speak and says nothing about the violence, instead, they blame all the violence on President Trump, as if Trump is pushing for the violence.

You can see this in just about every interview that Joe Biden does, he is always blaming the President and most of the time, it's a contradiction to his current actions, "he can't stop the violence because for years, he fomented it". For those Americans, that are not too sure

302

what fomented is, it is the name for someone who instigates or stirs up controversy. This is what democrats are doing right now, they are stirring up controversy and letting the chaos they started reign supreme.

One way to see this is to see what Biden said about President Trump, in a recent interview where he stated, "his failure to call on his own supporters to stop acting as an armed militia in this country shows how weak he is". However, wait, so you want Trump to stop his supporters, but you are not going to say anything to your protestors, Antifa & Blm, who are the ones burning everything to the ground. These statements just shows how weak Joe Biden really is because most of his campaign, has been a smear campaign against President Trump and everything Biden says and claims, just makes you shake your head.

These liberals and democrats watch all this chaos and destruction occurring and they do nothing about it; instead they push their false narrative of a better America. According to Joe Biden, that is only if it is not under President Trump, "I want a safe America, safe from COVID, safe from crime and looting, safe from racially motivated violence, safe from bad cops. In addition, let's be crystal clear: Safe from four more years of Donald Trump," he just could not miss one last opportunity.

The God's honest truth is, if you look up who controls most of these American cities, which are currently being destroyed by rioters, looters and protesters, they are all ran by either liberals or democratic mayors or governors. These are American cities that have been under democratic and liberal control for years, not just while President Trump has been in office. Democrats have run some of these American cities for decades, yet they all blame the violence, chaos and destruction occurring on the President. In addition, the thing to realize is, the President cannot just send Federal troops into an American city, the Governors and Mayors, of that city have to ask for the help.

So right there, the blame falls on them, it's the Mayors and Governors that are the ones letting this chaos reign supreme in their cities, not President Trump, yet these Mayors, including Chicago's, Portland's and Atlanta's, are all blaming the crime and violence on President Trump, all because they claim he is pushing the violence. I mean the sad thing is, these people have taken over the American

303

streets and you say anything wrong, they will show up on your doorstep, rioting and protesting for your head. These people in power, especially Nancy Pelosi and her fellow democrats, say nothing, when they are asked about these riots and the violence occurring, but they have plenty to say when it comes to President Trump.

So criminals, especially convicted felons, are able to do whatever they want to do because they know that these democrats and their follower's, will create legislature for them, so they can be set free for breaking the law. They are enabling violent criminals to be set free, so they can run the streets once again and they enable these rioters and looters, to rip up the streets and burn down business, with little to no consequence. President Trump has already said and stated that he would send the help, but these Mayors and Governors, actually have to request it.

President Trump, just can't send in federal troops, for those of you people saying President Trump, is sending in his own personal war troops, he isn't, not because he is flaming the violence, but because it's the law, he simply is not allowed to do it. What is Interesting about President Trump, as much as he wants to automatically go into these American cities and stop the violence, but he cannot, President Trump obeys the U.S. Constitution, unlike Barack Obama, who used Executive Orders, on numerous occasions.

The American people wanted President Trump in the Oval Office, so they elected him in and since President Trump was elected, he has done many great things for the American people. President Trump is a new fresh face in our government, something new from the normal defiant government that could usually care less about the people who employ them, which is the American people. These are also the politicians, who destroy and defame the American culture, lead personal attacks on our American history and try to cancel our entire American heritage, while they choose to berate our country, but always refuses to leave our country.

That's kind of one of the interesting thing about all these race issues and the excuses that go with them because once one narrative is pushed and believed, the narrative is then pushed by hundreds and believed by millions. You have seen the false race narrative with the current push of minority enslavement because democrats and blm groups, have

304

deceived millions of people into thinking that they are somehow still being enslaved by white people and the government. The deception no longer needs to be pushed because the world is already under the assumption that minorities deal with systemic racism and this to them, is just another form of slavery.

This fallacies of the narrative, is what get's confusing because what actually happened and what these people say happened, tend to be far from in-between because they always exaggerate incidents and use key phrases, to make sure they deliver their point. "A 17 year old Trump supporter is accused of shooting dead to BLM demonstrators in Kenosha," "one man shot dead following clashes between rival demonstrators, according to initial reports, the man killed was wearing a hat emblazoned with insignia of the far-right Patriot Prayer group," these two are just a few lines of despair that these people spit out.

There is always an ulterior motive to what they are saying, they want to make sure they get their point across, their point of course is, the people trying to protect their property and their American right are, 'Vigilantes". While these so-called innocent people, who are rioting, looting and burning businesses and buildings down, are all, "peaceful protestors". They say it because they feel they are entitled to, they feel they are entitled to say things like, "A possible vigilante recruit and Donald Trump supporter, a 17 year old Kyle Rittenhouse has been charged with homicide in the hosting deaths of two demonstrators and the wounding of a volunteer medic Tuesday night. He traveled from his home in Illinois armed with a semiautomatic rifle."

What they fail to mention in their direct attacks of this 17 year old, is that these so-called demonstrators and this volunteer medic, attacked Kyle with skateboards and hand guns, while Kyle Rittenhouse was on the ground, trying to protect himself. Kyle didn't go to their to stir up trouble, Kyle didn't go there to get into fights with protesters, Kyle went there to defend property and the American citizens being attacked and for this, these peaceful protesters attacked him with skateboards and even had hand guns, held close to him.

Then there is those that will say, well he should of not of brought a rifle to the protest and he was against the blm movement anyway, but really though, was Kyle really against the blm movement? I ask this because if I am not mistaken, wearing American flag colors and

305

protecting your second amendment right, is not a crime and does not make you a "Vigilante". It was interesting because Kyle Rittenhouse was interviewed earlier and when asked why he was there at the protests, Kyle simply stated, that he was there because he wanted to protect property.

Kyle did not say anything racist about blm, he did not make any racist comments, he did not condemn blm, or bother to mention any political motivations for his actions and simply stated that, he was there to protect property. This was even recorded on video, where Kyle was interviewed earlier in the day, so it is kind of hard to deny the facts, when they are right there in front of you. That same interviewer, even stated that, they had Kyle Rittenhouse on video, offering medical help to blm rioters, so seriously, how does this make him a vigilante out to kill protesters?

There is no sound argument for this, there is no justification for calling this kid a vigilante, Kyle Rittenhouse, was hit over the head with a skateboard, several times and attacked with guns, which all these people fail to mention, but can be seen in the video, while Kyle was on the ground. These protesters knew Kyle had a gun, they knew Kyle was armed, but they didn't care, they are on video continuously attacking Kyle, while he's on the ground and Kyle trying to fight back, eventually shoots his gun off and kills two protesters and wounds a third.

This is clearly self defense, Kyle Rittenhouse is no vigilante out to kill people, just because he supports the police and America, he was a 17 year old, trying to defend himself, after being knocked to the ground, after being hit over the head with a skateboard. The reasoning and logic, of course that comes from these people, is always non sense and tends not to provide any sound reasoning because to them it's like, your wrong and of course, Kyle Rittenhouse seems like your typical vigilante. Kyle supports Trump and wants to just go out and kill people at these protests, but the video evidence proves otherwise.

What is mind boggling about what these people are saying and writing as news is that, they push their false information, time and time again. This can even be seen here, when people are writing, "Witness reports hold that Rittenhouse was seen near the protests, but not amid them, carrying an assault rifle, before abruptly running unprovoked toward demonstrators, just prior to the murders". No, you are wrong, Kyle wasn't seen abruptly running towards protestors, it's revered, he was running away from protesters, who were attacking him, while one guy tried to hit him over the head from behind, followed by another protester.

When Kyle was hit the head by the second protester, Kyle Rittenhouse, fell to the ground while he tried to run away from these protesters, who followed him, continuously attacking him, especially after he fell to the ground. So now, I am wondering if these people actually watched the video and read the facts, before they made their idiotic assumption. These are the same people that are still claiming that, Jacob Blake was an innocent minority man, who was shot 7 times, when the proof shows he was clearly a criminal and was shot at 7 times, but only hit 4 times.

The facts and the truth do not stop them from passing their false information and statements off as news. You will often see most statements about these criminals are often exaggerated, "Demonstrations erupted in Kenosha last Sunday night after Blake, who was unarmed and not suspected of a crime, was shot seven times in the back by police in front of his children". Some have even gone as far to include, 17 year old, Kyle Rittenhouse and Jacob Blake in the same statement, since they have an agenda, they make sure they push as much fallacy as they can, "The protesters were killed as they demonstrated for the Kenosha police shooting, of Jacob Blake, a 29 year old minority father, on Sunday.

Blake was shot seven times in the back as he walked to his car, where his three young children were waiting for him." Like the first one, they do not tell you the whole story, they tell you what they want you to hear because ; Jacob Blake was the perpetrator that the cops were called for. Jacob Blake already had a warrant out for his arrest for sexual assault and domestic assault, so seriously, how was he not suspected of a crime?

We will get back to that because we know that statement is completely false, but now we get on to the other statement, where these people claimed that, Blake was simply walking back to his car, where his children were. Yea, he was walking back to his car, but what they fail to mention is that, Jacob Blake just fought with the police and was

307

resisting arrest; he also was just tased and had guns being held to his back. Blake was not just walking back to his car, where his three children were, he was running from the police. All this while police had their guns drawn on him, constantly telling him to stop, yet, he chose not to listen and continued towards his car, to either run or get the knife that was in his front seat. Jacob Blake was in no way an innocent man, he was suspected of a crime and police were called on him.

Does not matter though, you can have video evidence, you can have actual proof, but these people will still twist and flip any false information they can, whatever gives them the ability to push their false narrative and agenda. The truth is, African-American's weren't slaughtered by the millions, there private lands were never stolen and they were never put on reservations with low food, while their women were sold off to new husbands of the new America.

Also let us clarify once again, slavery did not build America, yes, it had a hand in building the products and industry of America, but America was already a growing new influence, thanks to their hard working American citizens. These new people were responsible for building the foundation; they built this foundation for America, before slavery was even introduced to them. Remember, the slave trade was already thriving in the, old world, which was mainly comprised of Africa, Asia and Europe and these nations were already profiting off of the slave trade, not Americans, Africans and Europeans.

The Americas, were a new nation to these people, that were not explored and they knew nothing about these new lands, until an Italian explorer set off and discovered South America. While America was in the discovery phase, other American's ancestors were subject to a lot worse punishment and living condition, than your ancestors ever has, but minorities, act like they are the only ones that have suffered from famine and slavery. Also, if you really want to state facts, slavery does go back to over 500 years ago, but during the 19th century and 20th century, before the United States became, a full blown American dominance, most recorded slaves in America, were Irish migrants, bought and brought over from Ireland.

Look it up, history proves it, so technically, for the last 200 years, you have not experienced slavery, as others have. What is crazy is, we should not even be mentioning anything about slavery, we should not give it the reference it does not deserve because there might have been enslaved people in the past, but women and children all around the world, are still being enslaved today. Plus today's America, is not the Americas of the 16th, 17th and 18th centuries, so how can you compare this great nation to the slavery days of the past, it's clear that millions of Americans, have made it past the savagery of slavery, but hundreds of people, who need the constant help and free handouts, continuously bring slavery up.

No offense but, no one can help you achieve your goals and if you have no goals to achieve and you think drug dealing, to get rich is a good goal, then you might want to stay in school. In addition, I hope we already got through that, there is no white privilege, there is only the rich and privileged, there is no white privilege. I am white and I am not awarded with any more privilege, then you are and like myself and millions of other white Americans, we have had to work for everything we have and you will find out that there are millions of white Americans, who work to live.

There is no white privilege and working a 9 to 5 job, 8 hours a day, 5 days a week, turning in 40 hours a week, is not a privilege. Working a job to make sure your family has plenty of food to eat and a home to live in is not a privilege, it is called, hard work and dedication. The truth is, minorities do have the opportunity to do the same thing and some have even taken that opportunity and ran with it, but there are a lot of minorities that continuously blame white people for their bad living conditions and they are never going to change, unless white people changes them.

What I am sitting here wondering is, how, how are white people the ones that can end you pain and suffering, that is caused by other minorities because I would seriously like to know? That's the thing to, please explain to me, the logic behind this because I am so seriously lost in the mass amounts of false information, false deceptions and false accusations, that are clouding the judgment of millions of Americans, all to better one single race.

That's what is going on right now in America, everything is becoming about supporting and making minorities superior to everyone else, but who are these people really helping, is doing this, really helping the minority community? It's a good question to ponder and

309

let's examine each side of the table here, on one side you have, white people and police, okay, not bad. So let's take a look at the other side, let's see what we have, robbers, convicted felons, wanted criminals, thief's, carjackers, drive-by shooters, mass abortionists, numerous drug dealers, numerous gangs, numerous outbreaks of std's and aids, but yea, it's definitely the fault of white people and the police, definitely.

This is the same logic that goes along with the theory that, white people are killing off minorities and since they have white privilege, they are getting away with murder. The McMichael's suffered the consequences from this ill minded logic, all because they were two white men, who killed a minority man and before they could even give their story, they were castrated by millions, simply because they were white and the victim was minority.

This crazy and insane ill logic, somehow entitled, the McMichael's to be labeled murderers, before they could even go to trial, but millions of people didn't bother to wait for the facts, they assumed the McMichael's were murderers and they both needed to fry. For you to even think that way, just shows you how racist you really are because you say nothing about the thousands of minority on minority homicides, occurring daily. Instead you burn America cities to the ground, when minorities get shot and killed by white Americans or police officers, but only if the police officers are white.

It's like you can't be serious, have you completely lost your mind, or did you just not wake up completely today because I can't believe what you just said and this is why minorities will never stop dying because their focus is always aimed towards the people, that are not the real problem. That's what also gets me about this so-called white privilege because minorities use it as an excuse, for everything under the sun, but we've seen the facts and we know it's been proven that, minorities receive more in assistance from the government, than any other race. It's all false because why should white people be shamed for not wanting to live in a drug and gang infested neighborhood and why should white people be shamed for not wanting to live in a crime ridden community, we value our families safety?

Why is this even considered a white privilege thing anyway, don't you want the best for your family, don't you want the best for your kids, I know numerous minority American families that do and I would

310

think providing a nice life, is no privilege, but the right you have because you worked for it. With all the delusion of their new America, I honestly believe these people are trying to erase the tradition of the modern family, the expression of working hard, to provide for your family, has clearly gone out the window.

Now people are crushing the suggestion of a traditional family because it doesn't fit them, since they no longer have families, they think everyone should suffer the same fate. So while they deceive you into feeling sympathetic to their situation, while their accomplices are secretly taking away your home, your religion, your rights, your freedoms, your life and everything else they want to. It starts with this democratic deception that is playing out in our schools and once the world restarts, it will go back to the same thing.

Teachers and professors are trying to erase history because they deem it racist and choosing what to teach these kids and what not to. This is also where the made up wealth gap comes into play because people claim minorities, don't have the same education as white Americans, so they don't get the same job opportunities as white Americans and are left with second rated jobs. This is Michelle Obama's fame to claim, where she constantly talks about how, white people have so much wealth compared to minorities and somehow because of this, white people don't understand her and her people and she blames it all on the so-called wealth gap.

Like we discussed before, Michelle Obama, even went on record to state that, COVID-19, was a blessing for minorities and democrats, to help them change the wealth gap. This to me is interesting because if I am not mistaken, democrats and civil rights leaders, are claiming that, President Trump, is actually using COVID-19, to kill off minorities or all minorities and immigrants, as they put it, so you can see that, none of these people actually know what the hell they are even talking about. Also it's right there in clear view, a democrat is telling you that, she is happy they had a major deadly virus and who cares if it's killing thousands of Americans because COVID-19, will help change the wealth gap of America.

Like I said before, you just can't make this stuff up if you even tried because these people are on television, making these bold statements that are just false and unjust, in every way. Think of the reason behind

311

this supposed wealth gap, think of who's to actually blame for the wealth gap, is it really white people, who are to blame because during the past thirties years, since the early 90's, all Americans have had the same job opportunity. Every American citizen was provided with schooling, whether the schooling was coming from private schools or public schools, you were still provided an education.

Not only have we seen the different schools, played out in numerous movies, these schools in urban communities, often were filled with crime and violence and students who were just unruly and chose not to get an education. Those same people have now grown up and what they chose to do with their life, was their choice, no one told them to ignore getting an education, no one told them not to work, they chose to. Still today, what Michelle Obama states, is not entirely true because minorities, especially minority youths, have higher rates of dropping out of school, or some even tend to skip the whole education system.

Therefore are left with low paying jobs because these people have no formal education, they have no high school diploma and they don't even bother to get a G.E.D. and the only reliable education these people rely on, or that they have, is street smarts and we all know how far that gets you. What I try to express to everyone, from writing this book is, white people, don't control the lives of millions of minorities, every single minority American living today, has had the same opportunity to grow up and better their lives.

It's not white people, who made your life choices and it wasn't white people that, told you to take the path you did. All minorities, just like all white Americans, have the freedom to make their own life choices. They have the right to choice their own path in life, just like these messed up men, now have the right to supposedly identify as, a woman or even a 12-year-old girl. It's not white peoples fault, that half of the minority population has no formal education and it's not white people's fault, that these people live in poor, drug and gang infested communities, it's theirs and theirs alone.

Minority communities, are partly the reason minorities, are being held back and can't advance much in life because these urban communities, are filled with so much death and destruction and this is daily, daily people are being shot and killed, with no future of it ending

312

in sight. Most people tend to forget that the people leading this blm movement, the actual three-blm founders, are actually self-proclaimed and trained Marxists, who proudly states that everyone should only promote minority advancement.

They also think that everyone should move towards dissolving the traditional "nuclear" family, but everyone should also focus more on woman supremacy, by ending male-dominated environments. These are the people that are teaching our children, but also the people that all these youths are following and it's not getting any better. Joe Biden has given in to these people and if elected, he has already stated that he would give these people more power, which will simply give them the ability to finish their destruction of America.

These people have clearly stated that they are against Capitalism; they are against, the constitution, they are against supporting the police, they are against free speech and they are especially against Patriotism. This is also an interesting statement simply because Capitalism gives everyone the ability to prosper in America and make a fortune off your ideas and hard work. That's not only a white thing, that is an American thing and it's not a white privilege, it's a privilege that is given to all Americans because all Americans have the ability to prosper in America.

Instead of focusing on worldwide destruction and destruction of the so-called "nuclear" family, we need to focus more on the education of our children. This is in white and urban communities because that's really the only way Americans will be able to move forward from all this deep rooted hatred. There is no future, there is no wealth advancement and this is not because minorities can't do it, it's because if they do become successful, if minorities are given good jobs or if minorities move into white neighborhoods, it's not the white people living in these neighborhoods, that calls these people uncle toms, it's other minorities.

Other minorities, calls these minorities sell outs, simply because they wanted a better life, then they would get if they were living in an urban community, so they moved into nice suburban communities, so they could have a better life for themselves and their families. The ones that are causing all the trouble, are the minorities that are teaching pure hatred and teaching their children to hate anyone who isn't like them,

313

no matter how nice the other people may be. These are the minorities that, are deeply rooted in pure white hate and this means, their heart is filled with hate, their mind is filled with hate and you will never change the ideology of any of these minorities.

Now, don't get me wrong, there are plenty of white people, that are deeply rooted in hatred too, but it's a not white suburban community, which is suffering from an alarming rate of homicides and it's not white suburban communities that have an alarming rate of robberies gone wrong. So seriously, who could blame other minorities for moving on to better pastures, so their family can have a better life and a better chance to making a more comfortable living? These minorities to me are genius and are smart because they chose to take advantage of their freedom to live in these so-called white privileged neighborhoods.

Contrary to what other minorities claim, many minorities live in white suburbia because it's safe and a better environment for their children, although minorities will argue that fact. Think about that logic for a second though, minorities move into white suburbia, they are called uncle toms and told, it's not a better environment for your children to grow up in, but today minorities are going into white suburban communities, claiming that white people have too much safety and security, while minorities are left with none.

It's crazy because minorities are yelling at other minorities all because these minorities living in white suburban communities, that have nice jobs, are also somehow keeping these other minorities down. This is what I also fail to understand, how are other people holding you back and how are other people keeping you from making the right choices in life. Seriously, you are the person that chooses your own faith, it's no one's fault but your own and if you don't see that, you can thank your parents for raising a retard. What also is interesting about all of this is, how is this even considered a bad thing to do and how is anyone trying to better their lives for themselves, a bad thing, or even a white thing?

This is seen by watching these minority youth on television beating and berating white kids, simply because they are white, they have no real reasoning behind hating these other kids, but since they were taught to hate, these children are just doing what they were taught to do. We have seen several cases of these hate crimes take place, but we

314

have to be careful because in today's America, a hate crime is simply pouring paint on a minority lives matter sign, which someone else painted on the ground. We've recently seen real authentic hate crimes like this documented news report, with video evidence, coming out of Florida, where a group of five young minority teens, beat the crap out of one young white kid, on a school bus, for simply being white and wearing a red Donald Trump MAGA hat.

These young straight hate filled minority teens, attacked one innocent white kid and not just one of them, all five of the minority youth's, all of these entitled hate filled youth's, took it upon themselves to literally beat the crap out of this one white kid, all because he was white and supported Donald Trump. Honestly though, if you don't think this is a problem and if situations like these, don't scream help to you, just realize that, these incidents are happening all over America right now.

If we continue to let it get out of control and choose not to stop to the deep-rooted hatred, our children are going to be suffering the consequences, when they really should not have anything to do with it, their children. The lost ones, fall under the category of uneducated, self-entitled minority youth, that riot and protest about unequal education, but they chose to sit out of class and protest during school because they feel the education they are receiving is unfair. What's funny to me, this falls into the excuses phase again because it was a trend we've seen, that has lately gone away, where there were minority students, having class sit-outs because they wanted minority teachers and counselors, instead of white teacher's and counselor's.

Sound familiar because this was the trend of movements, during the last few years, but now it's full-fledged minority power, and all white people are said they need to learn their real history, like the history we've been taught our whole lives has been false. It is also hilarious when you see a football coach think he is the voice of Americans and tells all white Americans they need to relearn their history because they do not know what it is like to be minority and they do not know the real history of America.

Obviously, someone should have stopped him before he even made the speech because talked about someone who needs to relearn history, he might want to take his own advice and look into when slavery really

315

started. The real history is slavery did not build America, nor was it found up on America and this coach is an idiot, for basically everything he said and he should go look in the mirror, before accusing other white people of something we have no responsibly for.

In addition, white people do not need to go relearn history, we know what the real history of America was and is. You can change it, you can edit it, you can do basically anything you want, but that won't change the fact that there have been dozens of history books, dozens of history movies and dozens of history documentaries, that prove the same thing over and over, no matter how much you try erase our history. What's funny about this is, if white people are doing this to minorities, it's discrimination, but if minorities do it to white people, it's not discrimination, I am not too sure how exactly that works because race discrimination, doesn't have a color.

This protest or sit-out, should be considered race discrimination against these white teachers and counselors because you are claiming that, you don't want to be taught by white people and you feel these white teacher's should be fired because of it. I am sorry, but that is the clear definition of race discrimination because you are discriminating against these white teachers and counselors, claiming they should be fired because they are white and since they are white, they cannot relate to you, so they are not allowed to teach you. You know I would even take their side in some of these movements, but it is just the way they do things, that really has you questioning their integrity.

They are basically walking contradictions; these people claim they want racial equality, so they protest to get rid of white people. What gets me, these white people that are doing nothing wrong, are being cursed at, spit on, berated, belittled, by the same people that is asking for equality. I mean it's just mind boggling, you can literally see these dozens of minorities, saying every racist name in the book, and this isn't just once, this is, cracker this and cracker that and you all need to go home you filthy crackers.

I use the word cracker also because I am white and to me because this is the lighter word, that is said by these people, but it is just amazing, how minorities can ask for equality, when they are constantly seen screaming numerous racist words at white people. This is the same logic that these blm protesters use in their protests, making statements

316

like, "Pigs in a blanket, fry em' like bacon", 'Put them in their graves" and "its open season on cops" and expect the police to still protect you, when you could clearly care less about their lives. That's another thing that's interesting to me, minorities claim everyone other then themselves needs to die, from police to white people and just about everyone else and they claim this is for racial justice, but if you are blaming everyone and attacking everyone else for your problems, why would anyone fight to give you equality?

You are now going to be seen as the enemy because you are telling people that you are going to kill them, so now they will make sure, that every time they deal with you, they make sure they watch their backs and have back up. It doesn't make much sense though because you are screaming, p**s in a blanket, fry em' like bacon and declaring that, It's open season on police, but you still expect police officers to protect you, seriously?

These blm members, liberals, democrats and others, make no sense at all, you are basically telling all police officers, we don't care about your life and we will take it if we can, but it doesn't matter that I don't care about your life, you still will protect mine. Everything minorities do, can be considered borderline racial discrimination and their logic behind it all, is just a fallacy of false lie after false lie and minorities, believe they are free to discriminate against anyone they want, while no one is allowed to do it to them.

You can take the case of these students protesting for minority teachers because they don't want white teachers because seriously, how can you honestly push for these white teachers to be fired, simply because you want them to be. The one thing that I have seemed to find out is, minorities don't care if it affects the lives of other races, they don't care if they make a white family go hungry, or brand a police officer a murderer, to them this is totally acceptable, as long as it benefits minorities. This what makes everything we are talking about a mystery because if minorities, are the only ones to say to be bettering their own race, why do they still feel like they are being held back.

If I am not mistaken, minority only schools and colleges have been opened and around for decades, not just years, but decades providing educations to only black students. The thing that these people failed to realize, if you quit school, sit out of class, or simply don't even bother

317

to show up for class, you are not sticking around long enough to even receive an education. I hate to burst your self-entitled bubble, but you actually have to go to class and learn something, you cannot just swallow a pill to make you smart, like Bradley Cooper. If history has taught us anything, it is that if you want something, you go out and work for it because the only way you are going to get it, is if you get off your butt and earn it, you are really not entitled to anything and this includes a job or an education.

The interesting thing about the education factor is, you had minority students, who were having major protests and classroom sit-out's, at majority white schools and colleges talking about unfair educations, but nothing at all about the educations coming out of, minority only schools and colleges. Most of the protests seem to be this way, coincidence, I think so because like we've been discussing this whole time, they have a narrative to follow and they will follow it no matter how wrong the narrative is or how bad the mistaken belief tends to be.

This makes these education protests and class sit-outs suspect and makes these students, sitting out and protesting, seem insufficient because they are choosing not to go participate in class. If you don't bother to show up for class, you're not going to receive any form of an education and it doesn't matter whether the teacher is, white or minority. You also can't blame white people much on the problem of your education, especially when you have all minority schools that only minorities have the privilege of going to.

Some schools are normally integrated like public schools, which are attended by a variety of races, but there are numerous minority schools and colleges, which only allow minorities to attend them, so complaining about having the wrong education because you go to a white school, with majority white teachers and counselors, is a little contradicting and borderline racist. I wish people would stop playing the blame game though and would like for people to start taking responsibility for their own choices.

I mean, these people are the ones making these choices anyway and you can't blame other people for you not receiving an education, when you put forth no effort into receiving one. This is also the reason for the wealth gap, that Michelle Obama and all these democrats, continuously talk about, but they are wrong because it's not white people, who are

318

the ones keeping minorities from getting good paying jobs, it's the education these minorities have, that is keeping them from decent paying jobs. You can blame white people and say it's because of white corporate America, but if that's your excuse, what's the excuse for Ophra, Byron Allen and minority Sports Club Owners, BET, these are all major minority media companies and minority company owners?

Why are these people not employing mostly minorities, you say it's a race thing, but these people are all minorities, rich Minorities, who own rich American companies. Shouldn't they be the first people offering minorities jobs, shouldn't they be the first people to support their own people, why aren't they doing so? Minorities want to hate and discriminate against white people for not employing them, but they tend to forget that, there are plenty of successful minority American's that own companies and these companies employ thousands of American people.

There is no backlash for these minority owned companies and there is no discrimination or protesting against these minority owned companies because it seems to be only white American companies, led by these so called, white supremacist Uncle Toms that face the backlash from millions of people. We all know these class sit-out's and protest's, are not really about education, I'm afraid not, they are really about minority American students, wanting to learn from, only black teacher's and black counselor's and not wanting to learn from, white teacher's and counselor's.

This race factor, among others, plays an important part of the race problem we have in America because everyone is pushing for division, especially democrats and minorities and they all believe, this is what's best for all, but we've all seen just how great segregation was. These people are following the false fallacies, of the people who only want to destroy America and if this does not change, Americans will never be fully united because to these powerful and influential people, it's better to keep us divided because when we are divided, it's easier for them to deceive all of us.

Americans are all different and that's what makes Americans so unique, we bring the people of the world together, but what we don't do is burn down cities and cancel entire cultures, all on the false pretences and fallacies of everything white, is racist and therefore wrong. This is

319

just another statement added on to the pile of bull, that makes no sense at all, but they make it anyway, just like the one where they claim, all white people need to apologize for being white, not because they did something wrong, but simply because they are white.

History proves that during the 19th century, most imported people for slavery, were Irish migrants, who were brought over by the hundreds to work sugar plantations as slaves and they were white, but still, minorities claim white people, need to apologize for being white. You don't choose what color your skin is, just like you don't choose what family you are born into, you deal with it and you make the most out of life, while putting your faith in the Lord above. Still it's insane because minorities continuously claim that, white people owe them something, but this really just makes these people, walking, talking contradictions.

Minorities claim white people need to apologize for their skin color, but also give everything up to minorities because of their skin color, all thanks to the excuse that their ancestors, were the only people to suffer from slavery. It's like a sleep walker, swearing up and down that they don't sleep walk because they of course can't see themselves sleepwalk, but once they are recorded sleep walking, it's then, these people realize and start to believe what everyone was telling them the whole time.

I thought this analogy was perfect because these people will argue with you till death, until you prove to them that they are wrong and you were right the whole time. honestly, no one owes you anything and just like every other American that came before you, you want something, you go out and earn it, you don't riot, protest and burn businesses down because you feel this is a better way, then actually working for it. Historically, many minority American's, have actually fought for a good cause, MLK, being one of them and they didn't blame it on the color of people's skin. The interesting part is, minorities have always had riots, protests and have burnt buildings down, but has this really changed anything, has it really done anything to better the lives of minorities, especially when it seems they are really only destroying minority owned businesses and urban communities?

Self-entitlement didn't really apply to anything in the past, unless you went out and earned it because back then, the only way you were

320

provided with a good life, was if you went out and worked for it. If they did feel any sort of self-entitlement, they were ignored and this only forced Americans to work harder, putting more focus on what they were trying to achieve, which was equality for all. Unfortunately minority American's tend to riot, loot and protest about inequality today because like we've discussed, to them, it's everyone else fault, that these people are in the situations they are in, not their own.

According to our U.S. Constitution though, all races have the same equal opportunity as everyone else and if you are American, you are entitled to your American rights, but you are not entitled to blame other people, on the bad life choices you've made. That is where the actual separation comes in and this is where the actual wealth gap comes in, it's not a white or minority thing, it's rather, what you chose to do with the opportunities you were provided with, that separates and divide people from each other.

No matter what blm or these democrats want to push, you can't blame someone else, on you not making money, when you choose not to work, or you flip burgers and expect to get paid the same as a professional electrician. Unlike minority only schools and colleges, Trade Schools are available to everyone, every American can easily learn a specific trade, but you have to take the time to go to class and learn about the trade, you can't just complain about an education, without putting in the effort to receive one.

Right now, foreigners and illegal immigrants, have it way better than most American's do, this is all because State Reps. and these illegal immigrants, feel they have some sort of entitlement to American rights. They need to realize that, you are not entitled to anything, if you didn't work for it, especially if you are lazy or an illegal immigrant. People tend to cry and protest about entitlement and they cry and protest about what they supposedly deserve, but you are only entitled to what you've earned and seriously, if you didn't work for it, what makes you think you actually deserve it?

Minority racism, white Racism, Hispanic racism, Latino racism, Asian racism, they are all trends that need to be stopped, but without focusing on the main root and cause, it's useless, whether minorities would like to admit it or not. No one benefits from minorities, saying black lives matters and before you try to write me off, think of it this

321

way, yea of course, all black lives matters, but now you are taking away from everyone else lives because minorities are telling white people and police officers that, their lives don't matter. Even reporters and news writers, are trying to tell white Americans, to commit themselves more to the idea that minority lives matter, like all white Americans somehow hate all minorities and want them all to die, when in reality, this is the media's false narrative.

Due to this insult, which is basically offensive to everyone because you are telling them their lives don't matter and if it was up to you, you would kill all of them off and this is clear because they ignore the violence in their communities, but riot and loot, when criminals get killed by police. Now the world is at each other's throat because you got one-half saying black lives matters and you got the other half, screaming, all lives matter and we are left with no peace in between.

One idiot that clearly has lost his way, is the coach of the Indianapolis Colts because I am pretty sure this guy lives in a mostly, rich white secluded and gated off community, but he thinks it was a good idea to compare the issue of racism to cancer. These coaches should not be really speaking, but saying something like, "Of course all lives matter, but the phrase "minority lives matters," is about unequal treatment faced by minorities, It does not say or imply that only minority lives matter. E.g., when we say "BEAT BREAST CANCER" it doesn't mean we don't care about beating leukemia."

Within that same statement, this coach was basically stating that, saying, "all lives matters," misses the point right now and that's why we shouldn't say it. Not too sure if this coach is even watching the same news as everyone else is because I am not too sure how you can miss the hundreds of people screaming, "p**gs in a blanket, fry em' like bacon" or "Send them all to their graves" because I don't think this counts as, one caring for another's life. Also, if you are saying that, the phrase, minority lives matters, doesn't say or imply only minority lives matters, how come white people get killed, people don't even blink an eye, minority criminal gets killed, world goes nuts?

Nevertheless, according to this idiot, who has the chance to reach out to millions of people, we should still support the mass murders of everyone who isn't minority and should stop saying, all lives matters because it misses the point. We can probably safely say that from video

322

evidence and minorities themselves, I don't want to speak for them, but I am pretty sure you are wrong and to them, minority lives matters, does mean only their minority life matters because seriously, have you even seen the shootings counts lately, I mean these numbers have skyrocketed?

Plus, if you are claiming that making the statement that, `all lives matter`, misses the point, you obviously, don't even know what the point is. Because duh, that is the point of all of this, all lives do matter, including yours. Everyone living today matters and minorities want their people to stop dying and who could blame them, but they are all blaming the wrong people. I am serious, if it wasn't all about minorities and if it's not so racist, why couldn't it be something like, "Our Lives matter too" or "Peace equals equality" or "Color is just a word" or "We all Matter," or you can always go with old faithful, "Thou shalt not kill". Nope, it has to be, "Black Lives Matters" and any other sign is racist and discriminating against minorities.

What I find interesting about the whole thing, like I've stated before, numerous people are going around stating, "well saying, minority lives matters, doesn't, just mean it's only minority lives that matters and people are missing the objective of what we are saying, when they say all lives matter." To me this is very interesting because when people are asked about a white person being killed by cops, they ignore it and say that's not the same thing, even if it's a minority police officer shooting and killing a white person, which we all know, happens way more in America and it's been proven, by me and the FBI.

So seriously, how is this not the same thing, how can you say minority lives matters, but any other life doesn't? We can see this also my taking a look at the case of Justine Damond because Justine Damond, was a 40-year-old white Australian-American, who was fatally shot and killed in 2017, by a minority police officer, working for the Minneapolis Police Department, the very same police department, who helped in the death of George Floyd.

The police officer, shot Justine in the abdomen, as she walked towards his car and Justine was unarmed and barefoot, but no protests for her, no riots for her, no chaos for her. The sad part, just like everything else ewe have talked about today, there were protests for this police officer, a Somali-American Minneapolis Police Officer, who fatally shot an unarmed white woman. Justine was just being a nice neighbor, calling the police because she thought she heard a female either being raped, or having intercourse in her back alley, after the police cleared the scene as okay, Justine, unarmed and barefoot walked up to the police car and knocked on the window.

Startled, the police officer, who already had his gun drawn, shot Justine, hitting Justine once in the abdomen, before she even had a chance to say anything to him. This poor innocent woman was just another fatal statistic to liberals and democrats and even police departments and to minorities, Justine was white, so her life didn't matter. You don't have to take my word for it, you can watch a video on this, where the journalist goes around in Australia, asking people who are protesting for, George Floyd, if they even know about one of their own, Justine Damond. Most of these people didn't even know who Justine Damond was, but knew who George Floyd was, a criminal killed by police.

If you watch the video, you will honestly lose your respect for humanity because these people have no problem telling you that Justine's life didn't matter and not for any other reason, then she was white. One lady interviewed even blamed all of crime and violence all around the world, on white supremacy, even when asked about Justine Damond, who was a white Australian-American killed by the same police department. It gets worse though because numerous people, even shocked the journalist with their answers because when people were asked, if all lives matters, most of them said, "at this current moment, NO".

This should be concerning to Americans and we should be worried about statements like these because these people, are expressing and cultivating their white hatred, among other countries and nations and therefore these people are making it to where, everything white is racist and wrong. We've seen instances like this play out numerous times, before in America, but no world-wide chaos, no world-wide destruction, only if it's a minority person being killed by a white person because then it's, let's burn this s**t to the ground.

Therefore, we all know it's not about all lives, it's about minority lives and they only want to better minority lives, while everyone else has to somehow just automatically get out of their way, while they hand

324

everything over to them for free. I would believe people that, saying minority lives matters, means all lives matter, but the evidence and the actions of all these minorities prove otherwise and some of these minorities, have even went on record to make sure everyone knows that, the only lives that matter, is theirs.

Kamala Harris, Joe Biden's VP nominee, has even proved this to Americans because not only is her identify up for negotiation, Kamala Harris, was recently asked about how the federal government should respond to COVID-19 and where they should send the resources and basically to Kamala, it's all about race. Kamala Harris, simply stated, that the government should make the decisions on where these resources should go, based on race and on the basis of skin color, so only people of certain skin color, minorities, get the resources.

What's crazy is this is supposed to be a woman, who was elected to represent the American people and not just one race of people. Just don't tell her that, also don't mention anything about identifying as an Indian-American because now Kamala Harris, is somehow a representative of colored people claiming to be African, yet Kamala Harris, has no African blood running through her vein's. For those of you who think I am lying, like we have discussed before, Kamala Harris is half-Indian, Half Jamaican and you can ask any Jamaican if they are African and they would probably punch you in the face.

In addition, I am no genius, but I am pretty sure to be identified as an African-American, you have to be from Africa, or have some sort of African blood running through your veins, Kamala Harris has neither. It all keeps you guessing because they say one thing, only to write another and whatever they say, they flip and twist so it sounds just right and once it sounds right, they pass it on to the people. I would take their side, if saying minority lives matters, really did mean that all lives matters to these people, but it doesn't, to these people, minority lives are more important than everyone else and they will fight tooth and nail, to tell you that.

We've seen the numerous amounts of evidence that has been provided to us on a daily basis and it doesn't stop there, if any issue, has anything to do with the color white, these people constantly aim to destroy it. The entire white culture is being assassinated and it's undeniable, that minorities go online and post negative comments and

325

racist remarks, about white supremacy and how black lives matters more than everyone else and when white people try to defend themselves, they are the racist ones. We've talked about the separate groups before, but there are now minorities that have taken a step further and they are creating initiatives, to provide minority only communities to minorities.

It is also clear and evident, when you look at these certain initiatives for minorities, which are being created by minorities, only for minorities and we can take a look at the Initiative coming from these two female minorities, who are creating and starting the, Freedom Georgia Initiative. This is just one initiative that is going to be used to only better the lives of minorities because it's basically a group of 19 minority families, who have purchased 96 acres of land, in Georgia and will be turning the entire 96 acres of land, into a self-contained, self-sustaining minority community.

This to me says the opposite of what these major influential white and minorities are saying because it's obviously, minorities want to only better the lives of minorities and everyone else, is just in their way. Therefore, these people saying the phrase, black lives matters, doesn't mean, all lives matter, contrary to what this Colt's coach and people like him have stated. It's obvious to minorities, any white person or police officer, can basically go jump off a cliff, these people wouldn't care and these people wouldn't bat an eye, matter of fact, they'd probably even give us all a little push.

The shock now is, these insane belittling statements are not just coming from minorities, nope, they are now being made by everyone from rich white individuals to rich white millionaires. All people who live in secluded white communities and go home to their comfy million dollar houses. Nevertheless, they make statements about white guilt and how white people just don't understand the meaning behind, minority lives matters. Honestly, we were behind it at first, we were behind the fact that minorities are dying at an alarming rate, where you went wrong is when you started going after white people, for no reason at all, other than the color of their skin.

We started not caring when you started killing other minorities during these riots and protests, we stopped caring, when an innocent 5 year old, was shot in the head and executed because he was white and

326

we stopped caring, when people started burning down communities for criminals. Still, rich people feel they are the voice of Americans, so they go on television interviews and speak their minds, but these people have no right to speak for anyone but themselves, but they think they are entitled to tell Americans what to do and tell Americans what to say, all because they think they have some invisible influential power.

It's also puzzling because it's not white people, who are often seen on television calling minorities the n-word or berating everyone on television and you don't see white people, making racist remarks and threats towards minorities and contrary to what everyone believes, police officers, are not the ones on news every day, robbing, stabbing and killing people. Not only is it puzzling to see these statements, I find it interesting because minorities claim this is all due to systemic racism, which is confusing to me because minorities, are the ones, who love to keep themselves separated.

This is clear and evident because minorities are the ones who have created separate groups, not for just a few things, but for just about everything. Americans are already subject to their daily dose of white hate, it's become okay for everyone, not only minorities, but everyone to berate and even attack white Americans, all on the basis of their skin color. We've all seen the numerous television shows, created by minorities only for minorities that showcase minority history, minority heritage and ancestry, while promoting hate and discrimination, with no repercussions.

I think the kicker is, how can these people honestly say that they're subject to systemic racism, when minorities themselves, have the opportunity to go to only minority schools and colleges, that, have all minority teachers and counselors, teaching and counseling, at these all minority schools and colleges; talk about being subject to institutionalized racism? This is the kicker because minorities complain about institutionalized (systemic) racism, yet they are the ones that have separated themselves from everyone else, but also separate groups, that are aimed to only better minority lives.

You are clearly showing support for black supremacy because you raise your fist in support of the Black Panthers and you protest that only black lives matter, how is this not considered supporting and trying to dominate with black supremacy? Then again, none of this matters because it's more likely that these people will never change their opinion of white people, until they become the dominate race and it's highly unlikely that they'll ever stop rioting, looting, robbing, shooting and killing other's to better their lives.

-- Chapter 6 --
Chaos and Confusion, will always cause,
Disruption and Delusion!

As America descends further into chaos, democrats and House members, are continually choosing to ignore the destruction in their cities, ignore the chaos occurring within America. Instead, these politicians focus on President Trump because to them, they think the chaos they started, is a good way to get Americans to hate Trump and turn to the democratic side. These democrat's and blm Marxists want the chaos, they want their cities being torn apart because it causes confusion with the American people and this confusion helps them push their narrative with more ease.

You have everyday Americans who are questioning, just what the hell is going on, but then on the other side, you have other Americans, who believe the false propaganda these democrats are pushing, this is also where the disruption plays a role in everyday lives because it's all one big delusional lie. The hate from these people is cast every day and we have all been subject to the damaging rants that are now coming from these leftists, blm Marxists and democrats. These politicians and influencers, go on huge rants about how white people, living in America, are racist towards minorities, therefore they all demand that white people give up their entire lives because these people claim they only got it because of their white privilege.

Most of these useless rants usually turn into long lists of demands for white people and show how white people are supposed to give up everything simply because they are white. The message coming from these people is just insane, forget about minority justice for the innocent minorities being killed, also you can forget about minority justice for the innocent minority children being killed from stray bullets because these people only go after white people. Like I've stated before, it's somehow all white peoples fault, somehow we are the ones to blame for minorities having so much crime and violence occurring in their communities.

We discussed this before, now, white people living in America, are being told that they are to give up their safe and comfortable paid for homes, their safe crime free communities and their safe comfortable lives because having all these things, also just a nice life in general, is a white privileged life. It's an insane way of thinking because according to these simple-minded people, working hard to provide a safe and secure life for you and your family, is somehow a white privilege, doesn't matter that you have had to work for it your entire lives. The funny thing is that, these liberal and democratic mayors and governors are blaming the crime rates in their cities on Trump.

Besides other mayors who open their mouth about things they shouldn't, the Atlanta Mayor went on an interview and simply stated that crime in her city was up, simply because of President Donald Trump. The crime rate has spiked in Atlanta because of police reform, but this mayor, who called for and passed the police reform, thinks' that the rise of crime is not because there are less police thanks to her and her cronies, no, according to this Atlanta Mayor, it's all President Trumps fault. Unfortunately, this simple-minded democratic logic doesn't stop with her though, there are several other State mayors of American cities that are doing the exact same thing.

These democratic mayors passed police reform, they also defunded the police, which in turn caused crime to skyrocket in their city, but it's not the police reform, it's President Trump. Think of it this way, in Chicago alone, democrat Lightfoot's city, hundreds of people are being shot and killed weekly, there was even a recent funeral service that was being held, where 15 people were shot during the funeral. A funeral, for a dead gang banger, was taking place and their rival gang banging buddies, took it upon themselves to commit a drive by on the funeral, shooting and injuring at least 15 people.

The sad reality is, this is only one democratic ran city, where violence and chaos tends to run rampant and these State mayors solutions, blame it all on President Trump and see how far that gets them. Think about it, in Chicago, Baltimore and Atlanta, all people of leadership roles, from the city mayor to the Police Commissioner, are minorities, yet every single one of these three cities, has the highest crime rates recorded in America. The people in charge of Chicago, including mayor Lightfoot, are all minorities or minorities that hold major positions, Yet, these people ignore the crime and push the chaos, while their community's burn to the ground, all thanks to their hatred of Donald Trump.

What I don't see is, any fair equality for Americans though, you will often notice most of these blm leaders and democrats are demanding equality, but demanding this equality be given to them by white people, who they assume need to give up everything, only to receive nothing in return. That hard worked for home, given up for free, that paid for car, given up for free, the inheritance from your family, given up for free, the land you just bought, given up for free, sounds to me like, these people don't want racial equality, they want domination.

That's what is so mind-boggling about how these people are protesting for equality. All these demands for white people to hand over their homes and security to minorities, are supposed to be done for free. You inherit a house, hand it over for free, you get inherited money, you are to donate all of it to minorities, you live in a nice house that you still work to pay for, you are to give it to them for free. This isn't coming from just me either, look up recent and past news interviews, these statements are coming directly from the mouths of these blm leaders and democrats.

They spout off list of demands for white people because according to these people, all white people owe minorities something. Unfortunately after listening to these demands for about five minutes, you'll get the feeling that these people could care less about equality and more about free hand outs, while they try to become superior to white people. You can see this by examining the motives of the blm movement and how it changed so quickly, if you look at it, the motive went from protesting about police brutality, to protesting about how all white people are white supremacist, who owe minorities everything under the sun.

One of the greatest basketball players of all time, well now he will always be questionable, but Lebron James, a voice for minorities, opened his mouth and stated that, "Every time a minority man walks out his front door, he is hunted down like a dog". Lebron James, made this statement to the news, but also posted this statement online, after an unarmed minority, was shot and killed by two white Americans. This so-called minority was stopped and questioned as to why he was in an unknown neighborhood, the minority then got into a fight with one of the white men and ended up being shot and killed.

The minority was a known criminal and was confronted by these two white men, a former sheriff and his son, but after a short argument, the minority turned violent and started fighting with the son, after a brief fight broke out, the minority, was shot and killed. Lebron's thought, this minority man was innocent no matter what he was convicted for and all minority men, are hunted down like dogs and shot dead in the streets by police officers. Of course the truth is far different from what Lebron James and others like him believe and they tend to ignore the fact that, this supposed innocent minority man, was actually robbing houses in the area.

Aubrey was simply stopped and questioned, but when found to be lying, chose to fight with the son, who then feared for his life and shot him in the scuffle. Still, according to Lebron James, minorities, blm leaders, their followers and democrats, these two white men shot and killed this unarmed minority simply because he was black and they'll get away with it because they have white privilege. Since he was black, these white men, will get away with killing him because they were white and they have white privilege, doesn't matter that he was a criminal or felon..

This is their platform narrative, this is the fallacious argument these people make, democrats think death, chaos and inner city destruction, is a great way to get white people to hand everything over, although they only seem to be dividing Americans. These liberals and democrats, are allowing their own police stations and federal buildings to be set on fire, they are allowing their own state parks and national monuments to be destroyed and anyone who says anything to stop them, is deemed un-American and traitors to the American people.

Now, these millions of people, are destroying our American history and destroying our American city streets, all in the name of minority justice and minority equality, justice they don't really believe in because we all know it's more about democratic and racial superiority, than it is about minority equality and justice. We are a country of rhetoric because we are now seeing ex-President Obama, who failed as a President, but who was also in office for two terms and did nothing for minorities, back for his fifteen minutes of fame. Democrats and liberals are now claiming that if President Obama were still in office, he would have fixed all the problems, better than President Trump has.

We all know the truth though, Obama had eight years to do more for his country, but he did absolutely nothing to better the lives of Americans, but President Trump, did everything he said he would do, but also everything he promised he would. Just to be clear, Barack Obama wasn't a millionaire until he became U.S. President, being U.S. President made Obama rich and now, the Obama's are multi-millionaires, not to mention we still pay him for being a former President. Barack Obama had 8 years in the Oval Office and the democrats never bothered to go after him, never bothered to investigate him, but they also never bothered to second-guess anything Barack Obama pushed for.

In addition, Obama's administration, was even stated to actually be guilty of working with the Russians, yet they tried to impeach President Trump, for asking Ukraine officials about his competitor, which was proven to be false. For the first three years of President Trump's office, he's had to face an impeachment brought on by false accusations, he's had to face a global virus and pandemic killing hundreds, but he's also had to deal with democrats investigating him on how him and his team responded to this global deadly virus, which is still killing people.

Think of it this way, President Trump, has backed several statements over his four-year term, but something as simple as stating, "Make America Great Again", has somehow made President Donald Trump a racist white supremacist. Something as simple as saying, "Make America Great Again", is being described as racist and white Americans are getting beat up or picked on for saying it, but also for simply wearing a hat that has, "MAGA" on it. A hat that represents America and states that we want to make America great again, is considered racist and whoever wears the hat or says this statement out loud, you are a supporter of white supremacy.

It's crazy because President Trump wants the American people to be number 1, like we were before, so he claims, "Make America Great Again", but since President Trump is making this statement, it automatically makes him a racist and a supporter of white supremacy. It's just insane because these liberals and democrats, hate America and these are American State politicians, who are supposed to be representing the American people. Americans voted these people into office, including our great President Donald Trump, who wanted to make sure America was taken care of first. Barack Obama's eight-year mission was different, he wanted to bring Americans and Muslims together and wanted acceptance.

It was all about acceptance, acceptance for everyone, Obama wanted us to accept all people for who they are and look where that got us. We've accepted people for who they were and that was not enough, they wanted more, we gave these people an inch, instead they took a mile and now these are the same people destroying our country from the inside out, while they all blame it on President Trump. Let me give you a few statistics from Barack Obama's 8 years in the Oval Office, to start off, we all know about the Snowden trial and how Barack Obama and his administration, spied on millions of Americans, but Obama also gave billions to Iran and armed the terrorist group ISIS.

The kicker of his entire 8-year run was the fact that, Obama apologized to foreign countries that clearly hates Americans, Obama apologized to these countries for our so-called failed American Foreign Policies. Don't forget, Barack Obama's administration, led by Hillary Clinton, covered up the incident that happened over in Benghazi, where Americans and foreigners were killed due to their negligence. Barack Obama also sold 20% of our Uranium to Russia, a country that was the basis for President Trump's impeachment and the country that Sleepy Joe Biden is currently claiming that is going to be messing with the 2020 election.

Barack Obama, did nothing for Americans but divide us, he did nothing for the minority community and now Barack Obama is back, coming to divide Americans once again. Somehow, we still have to suffer the consequences of Obama's failed Presidency. This is not just talk either, you can look at Obama's Presidency and you can see for yourselves that Obama did nothing for the American people or even minorities, he focused more on immigrants and foreign countries, just like Joe Biden did. Barack Obama and Joe Biden, promised to do a lot of things for the American people, but also the minority community yet, they never did.

One simple example, they said that they would fix healthcare and they would make drug prescriptions cheaper and more available to the American people, they didn't, President Trump did. Barack Obama and Biden both claimed they would fix this problem, they knew that Americans were driving across the border to Canada to buy their prescription drugs because it was cheaper to drive to Canada and get their prescriptions, then to buy their prescriptions in America.

Think about that though, Americans need these prescriptions to live, we need these pills to keep us alive, yet these drug companies could care less because all they see is the money they are going to make off each pill. Obama and Joe Biden, never did what they said they were going to do, but President Trump did, Trump took on this problem and

President Trump put an end to these crazy drug prescription prices. Now that we have chaos and confusion, Barack Obama, has decided to pop up and support Joe Biden, a guy who has gone on recorded claiming that he doesn't even want his own children in schools with minority kids because "they are jungles".

Unfortunately, urban communities have become the new hotspot for these blm movements and these communities are being destroyed one by one, minority owned businesses that took years to make successful, are being burnt to the ground in mere seconds. Not one of these democrats or blm leaders, have asked their people to stop the destruction or chaos, in fact, we've seen most of these people, including State politicians, pushing the chaos and destruction, pushing the crime and violence. It's still unclear how destroying your own community and burning down other minority owned businesses that are in your own neighborhood, results in you receiving racial equality, but this is what these politicians and blm leaders claim will do the trick.

The scary thing to look at is the fact that, since most of these democratic ran cities have defunded the police, shootings and killings, have skyrocketed and communities led by these liberal mayors are becoming instant killing fields. These blm leaders, led by democratic and liberal State politicians, called for the police to be abolished and defunded, but now, crime has drastically risen. Still the continuous rise of crime and violence, is not their fault, no, it's not because they chose to defund the police, the fault all lies on President Trump and his administration.

Take a look at July 4th weekend alone, there were hundreds of shootings recorded in numerous democratic ran cities, where minorities were the main perpetrators. Look at some of these statistics for the 4th of July, in Chicago, there were 89 Americans shot, 17 killed, in Philadelphia, there were 31 Americans shot, 7 killed, in New York City, there were 64 Americans shot, 10 killed and in Atlanta, 31 Americans were shot and 5 killed. Hundreds of shootings, hundreds of minorities being shot and killed, hundreds of minorities being shot, yet no one seems to want to stop this from happening.

This doesn't account for the rest of these democratic ran cities in the Unites States, this only accounts for four cities, all over one weekend, a weekend that was supposed to be of celebration, but turned deadly for hundreds of people. The sad thing is, most of these shootings, robberies and killings, if not all of them, were perpetrated and committed by minorities, not white people, not police officers, minorities. This is what is occurring right now in America, minorities are being allowed to tear apart our country all for racial equality and minority justice.

Their able to destroy an entire culture all for racial equality and if anyone says anything to the contrary, you are branded racist and supporters of white supremacy. These democratic mayors, are allowing hundreds of people to destroy federal buildings, destroy major businesses, commit violence against police and citizens, but also burn everything to the ground, all in the name of equality. The funny thing is that, these democratic State politicians, claim these people, were allowed to protest peacefully, which is true, but at the same time, none of these protests have been peaceful. Seriously, how is destroying and burning down a building at a protest, peaceful?

How is shooting and killing innocent minorities at these protests, peaceful? Seriously, how is assaulting police officers, throwing bricks and Molotov's at police officers and attacking police officers, who are merely doing their jobs, peaceful? The real reality is that, none of these riots and protests were peaceful, all these protests were violent protests, where people destroyed property, attacked cops and even shot and killed innocent people. These are not the results of peaceful protests, so seriously, how can you go on record to claim that you are okay with these riots and protests because these people are allowed to peacefully protest, when they are not very peaceful?

One liberal reporter, even had the balls to ask, even after all this chaos occurred, "Well aren't people allowed to peacefully protest, thanks to the 1st amendment?" Yes, these people are allowed to peacefully protest, but peacefully doesn't mean you destroy everything in sight, peacefully, doesn't mean you throw bricks and bottles at police officers, peacefully doesn't mean you destroy federal buildings and peacefully, doesn't mean you burn down and loot businesses in your own community.

All of this circles back to our previous talk about how it all starts from home because most of the destructive youth, who are behind these riots and protests, tend to come from broken homes, where there is no guidance or discipline. These are often the misinformed youth, who have no father figures, they have no control and they tend to have no sympathy towards other people, they do what they want, no matter who tells them otherwise, especially the police. These misfit youths often blame other people for their faults because like we've discussed many times before, they believe it's everyone else fault, so these youths often become violent and destructive, but also tend to get easily offended by everything.

People from all races live in low-income housing areas and all these communities are hotbeds for crime and violence, most of the youth that live in these communities, are usually the ones responsible for the rise of crime and violence. Since these are typically housing projects or trailer parks, these communities don't have much money flow through the community, unless it's from government assistance, so these young teens tend to quit school and turn to selling drugs and joining gangs. For these teens, selling drugs, is a better way to make money because they see no future in going to school and getting an education, they see no future in working a 9 to 5 job or getting a career, that's too much work for them.

They see no benefit in working for $9.00 an hour, when they can make over $500 dollars a day, selling drugs in the hood, all these youths see is money and as they grow up, all they know is selling drugs and shooting people. Forget about an education, forget about working a job, forget about having a career, most of these kids from these bad neighborhoods, whether it's the projects or trailer parks, see no benefit in any of these things. Since they see no benefit in any of these things, they drop out of school to join gangs and sell drugs because they claim school and an education, is too much work for them to manage and just isn't for them.

Since these democrats have brainwashed these youths into thinking that the government is oppressing them, but also holding them back, so these youths turn to destroying their own communities, destroying national monuments and statues and destroying minority owned businesses. Besides the fact that, these democrats preach help, but offer no help, some of these people, white and minority, choose to live in these bad communities and they do this because they know the government will give them assistance, whether they work for it or not.

This fact, is a proven statistical fact, food stamps, government assistance and welfare, are the three prime examples because people in these bad neighborhoods, tend to abuse these programs, so they can do as they please, without having to work for it. Another reason for all the disruption and chaos going on in America right now, civil leaders and democrats, are telling these minorities that they are not receiving the government assistance they need, when in fact, it's proven that minorities, immigrants and even foreigners, receive more in government assistance, then white Americans do.

The damage also comes from this un-American State Rep, AOC, who thinks illegal aliens and foreigners, should have more rights than Americans, but not only that, she's fighting for illegal aliens to get reparations and free money. This State Rep., along with others, are the politicians who constantly blame President Trump for everything, yet they do nothing for Americans and continue to let their States be torn apart by racist movements and groups. Many Americans in these bad communities constantly receive government aid and assistance, they are constantly given the help they are needed through several different programs.

Still according to these blm leaders and democrats, it's not enough as they continue to demand more. What's funny about this demand is that, it only goes one way, these civil leaders and democrats, want minorities to feel that white people, are trying to be superior to them, so they cause chaos and confusion, which then leads to disruption and delusion. Once the chaos was started, it was just a matter of time before the confusion of what was really happening started to sink in, everyone thought the movements were about police brutality, only to find out, it was about white Americans and their so-called white privilege.

After the confusion sat in, then the disruption started to play out because major cities all around America, were being torn apart, while federal buildings, were being lit up in flames night after night, disrupting the daily lives of the American people. Then the last step, which was the delusion these people pushed of a false reality because with the chaos already occurring and the disruption of our daily lives now constant, their delusion of a false reality was forced on to the American people. It's delusional because civil leaders and State politicians, want Americans to believe the chaos and disruption is being caused by President Trump and his followers.

Yet, these politicians, are the ones pushing for and causing all this turmoil. These State politicians, are the ones who are in control of their American cities, but they all chose to let them be burnt to the ground by violent rioters. Unfortunately, these politicians could care less about the American people and they will continue to follow their delusional theory until they are blue in the face, all the while telling Americans that President Trump is wrong and these people are our only saviors.

This is the thought process of these blm Marxists and their followers, they think that it's everyone else fault, they are in the situation they are in, especially white people, not their own. White people, are the reason that their own race is dying or being killed at an alarming rate, white people, are the reason they have no education, white people, especially President Trump, is the reason why they have so much black on black crime in their communities, at least that's what they claim.

I mean, it simply couldn't be the fact that these people choose not to work hard for anything or the fact that they choose to drop out of school to sell drugs or the fact that they, have the highest abortion rate amongst Americans, nope, couldn't be. The harsh reality of today is that, minorities are getting away with racism and discrimination against white Americans, while white Americans, are punished for saying anything offensive or racist back. If white people do say anything back, we are the racist ones that are discriminating against minorities and should be punished. How does that honestly work?

How does that show equality for everyone? How does that ask for racial equality and minority justice? Seriously, it makes no sense because these people are blaming an entire race on the actions of a few. Instead of being reasonable and debating this opinion because when you really think about it, it's ones opinion, but because of this hateful opinion, minorities are beating and even killing innocent white Americans simply because they are white. Honestly, how does this make any sense at all? In addition, when you think about it, what kind of message does this send to our youth? In fact, what it does represent and inspire, is people like this useless piece of crap minority, who thought it would be a good idea to kneel on a white 2 year olds neck and take a picture, while claiming black lives matters.

How is this honestly seen as something that would be okay to do, this was a two year old child, how would you honestly think this was a good idea? Seriously, how do you justify kneeling on an innocent two year olds neck, while your friends hold his hands behind his back, throwing deuces and claiming blm, just because the child is white?

What's just sad and upsetting about this is that, minorities in the comment section of this photo were mad that this minority man and his girlfriend were arrested for what they did. Dozens of minorities, were cursing out white Americans and the police who arrested him just because this guy was arrested for what he did to this poor 2 year old.

The mother should also be in jail because when asked about it, she simply stated that, "oh he wasn't hurting the baby", although you can clearly tell the baby is crying in the photo. That's the delusion of today's chaotic democratic society, minorities, are upset that this man was arrested for assaulting an innocent child and it simply proves that, no matter how offensive the crime, minorities will ignore the truth and protect their kind. For those who think I'm kidding or don't believe me, take a look at the gruesome murders of a white couple, by a group of five minorities, four males and one female, who car-jacked the white couple, then kidnapped the white couple and took them to a remote location.

The reason I bring this case up is because this white couples gruesome death occurred back in 2007 and these useless minorities would eventually be convicted for the gruesome crime in 2009. Unfortunately during the trial, you had minorities claiming that these five useless individuals should not be killed and not be sentenced to death for what they did. People actually protested for them not to receive the death penalty, but if it were white Americans who did the killing, it would have been prosecuted as a hate crime and they would all be sentenced to death.

These useless minorities, car-jacked this innocent white couple simply because they were white, then kidnapped this white couple and took them to a secluded rental house, where they raped the white male numerous times, then cut off his penis and as if that wasn't enough, they shot and killed him, while his girlfriend was forced to watch the whole thing go down. The innocent girlfriend suffered far worse though, these useless minorities, showed no mercy as they raped her numerous times, urinating on her in the process and when they were finished with her, they cut off her breast, then shot and killed her.

So seriously, who's getting beaten and murdered for the color of their skin, again? Are minorities really being tortured and killed every time they walk out their front door like this idiot Lebron claims or is the reality far worse then what we think it is? We constantly continue to see innocent white Americans, even white kids, beaten or even killed simply because they were white. White people in America, are simply being targeted and tortured because the color of their skin and this is only getting worse because to minorities and these blm leaders, shooting and killing white people, is totally justified. Now, even our kids are not safe anymore because minorities have no limits to the horrible things they'll do to white people.

The sad thing is that, we really are seeing a dramatic change in our society and it soon won't seem safe to even walk on city streets, especially if you are a white American male or female, who supports the American Flag. The white racism abuse is everywhere and has taken over America, innocent white Americans no longer have a say and if we do speak up, we are told we are the racist ones. That's one of the viewpoints of blm leaders, liberals and democrats, that I fail to understand, it's one that has mind-boggled many Americans because white Americans are experiencing racism every day, just like everyone else.

Not all white Americans are rich and privileged, not all white people have money just handed to them, many white Americans have to work hard for what we have and experience just as much discrimination and racism as anyone else. It's insane how these people claim white Americans aren't subject to racism or discrimination, but you watch as all of them go on national television and call white people every racist name in the book. White people, are constantly subject to racism and discrimination, it's just a matter of how much we have to deal with, but it's crazy to claim that only minorities experience racism.

Along with all the other mind-boggling claims that come from these blm leaders, liberals, leftists and democrats, this one usually takes the cake, but also is what helps these blm leaders push their one race narrative. As I stated before, these low-income urban neighborhoods and communities tend to be major hotspots for all this mass chaos and confusion because these are the people that use the government to get ahead in life, so they rely on what the government tells them, whether they are lying to them or not.

Let's take a look into the abuse of certain programs and how it's not really white Americans, who are the ones holding minorities back. In addition, white people are definitely not the cause or the problem for all the problems occurring in these urban communities. As we discussed before, food stamps and welfare, were created to help out families in need, definitely young single mothers, working two to three jobs to provide a better life for their kids, they were also created to help out families, who were on hard times and in desperate need of serious help. Now, three decades later, you have people, whole generations of families, that have lived off welfare and food stamps for not only years, but decades, never lifting a finger to work for it.

The difference is clear when it comes to these food stamps and welfare recipients compared to hard working taxpayers because hard working taxpayers, can ask for government assistance, but be denied, often being told you make too much or you simply do not qualify for help. Instead, these people want you to still work hard at your job, still work to live paycheck to paycheck, so they can deny you help, but give the help to people that want to sit on their butts and not work because they believe work is too much or too hard.

As a non-working, non tax-paying American, you can easily walk into any State or local social services office and get help and assistance instantly, there's multiple programs available for those that make the bare minimum or nothing at all because they choose not to work. You will also notice these free loading food stamp and welfare recipients at grocery stores across America, standing in line with a cart or two, full of all kinds of junk food and things they clearly could never afford on their own.

These freeloaders usually stand in line with both carts filled to the brim, while the hard working American taxpayer is standing behind them, holding a basket of food that they hope will last them to their next payday. This is something I have never really fully understood, tax-paying Americans usually have to work to live, sometimes 2 or 3 jobs and a lot of Americans usually live paycheck to paycheck. Also often have to watch every dime they spend, while you have people on welfare and food stamps that are able to live comfortably on the American tax dollar, without a care in the world.

These food stamp and welfare families, do nothing to contribute to society, they don't bother to work or even bother to get a job, yet democrats and liberals, easily fund these people's lives because if they do, they know these people will always vote their democratic way. This theory also comes into play when you look at illegal immigrants and foreigners because these State Senators, especially State Rep. AOC,

342

think and often claim that, these illegal aliens should have rights, sometimes more rights than American citizens. Not only do these State Senators claim that these illegal immigrants should have rights, their schooling and their education, should also be free. It doesn't stop there though because these illegal immigrants should also all be given free money, free homes and even free healthcare, although they are over in America, illegally.

What worries me is, these are our so-called American State Representatives making these claims, the politicians, who were voted in to represent the American people by the American people. Instead, these State officials are constantly seen on television protesting that illegal immigrants, although they are over here illegally, should still receive American benefits. Not only should these illegal's receive American benefits, but these illegal's should also be entitled to Americans rights.

Forget about asking for help if you are a hard-working tax-paying American, don't expect help because hard-working taxpaying Americans, white and minority, all supposedly make too much or don't seem to qualify. Of course liberals and democrats, have no problem with giving away our hard-earned taxed money to foreigners and illegal immigrants. This falls in line with the democratic narrative though, they want the chaos, confusion and the disruption to occur because the more people are confused about what's going on, the less they start to question.

Forget about Americans and bettering our way of life, these State politicians, rather put Americans on the back burner, whether we agree with it or not. We see this occurring daily in America, riots and chaos have taken over democratic ran cities, protesters are out destroying federal buildings, destroying police stations and even lighting court houses on fire. While all of this chaos is going on, these democratic State mayors and governors, stand idly by and watch it all go down, some have even pushed and inflamed these riots.

In addition, what's crazy is, these democratic mayors and governors, stood by and watched their cities be destroyed by constant riots, they watched as the public's safety was jeopardized, but also watched as their police officers were abused and pelted by rioters and protestors. Still, according to the head democratic leader, Nancy "fake" Pelosi, all this chaos and violence was President Trumps fault.

Seriously, according to her and every single democrat, President Trump was somehow the one to blame for all the crime and violence occurring in these democratic ran cities. Not these liberal and democratic State mayors, who stood by, while these rioters and protesters ravaged their cities and communities. Remember, thanks to this simple-minded logic, if you are a patriotic American, who supports the American national anthem and American flag, you are a racist white supremacist, who hates all minorities.

The logic usually coming from these politicians tends to makes no sense at all, still, according to these State politicians, if you support the American flag, you are un-American, if you support the American national anthem, you are un-American and racist. It was this ideology that brainwashed most minorities into thinking, we are somehow back in the days of slavery, where all minorities are slaves, but also oppressed by the white man. I still think it's crazy how these blm Marxists leaders, liberals and democrats, have convinced hundreds, if not millions of minorities that, minorities still face slavery today.

The thinking makes no sense, the opinion makes no sense because the claim is that our four fathers, even though without them, we wouldn't be where we are today, were all white supremacist slave owners, who did nothing for the minority people. This is now the false reality that these far left blm leaders, liberals and democrats have pushed, the false narrative of an, all white society that somehow controls the lives of minorities, but also keeps all minorities oppressed.

According to these people, there is no more progression, there is no more progress to be made, so they urge rioters and looters to burn down everything in sight. These people push these rioters to fight the police as much as possible, destroy and burn down any federal buildings they can, all for equality. Forget the fact that, great influential minorities, have protested and died fighting for racial equality, forget the fact that, minorities have come a very long way, thanks to the ending of things like segregation, nothing matters to these people.

The fact that there are minority millionaires and billionaires complaining about being oppressed, like Ophra and Lebron, who alone could probably buy this whole country, should be the warning sign. It's insane when you think about it because according to these crazy minded leftists, liberals and democrats, minorities still need to be secluded to a group and given reparations because they can't seem to get it on their own. Forget how far minorities have come because these blm Marxists, leftists and liberals, have tricked minorities into thinking they are still oppressed slaves living in the past. For minorities, these politicians have managed to destroy any equality they have fought for over the years and now, what started out as peaceful movements, have slowly turned into hostile takeovers by the Democratic Party and these blm Marxists leaders.

This nonsense is being seen daily, whether it's coming from people being interviewed on the news or people writing online fake news articles about nothing of importance, where they usually blow things way out of proportion. One fake news writer on yahoo, one of just the many they tend to have, was writing about African Americans and guns because you know, the only black people in America are African-Americans, even though most of them are not even from Africa, nor have they or their family members, ever set foot in Africa.

After getting through a few, you are an idiot for writing this paragraph thoughts, you tend to see that this article and the writing of this useless article, is what's wrong with America. The writer of this article, obviously has drank the Kool-Aid, like all these other simple minded people because according to her, this is the first time minorities have owned guns and because of this, there are certain stereotypes of minorities, who own guns. Forget the fact that, during the 80's and 90's and even the 20th century, minorities, white and Hispanic gang members, were shooting and killing each other every day with illegal guns.

Gun violence, was at an all time high in certain cities and because of this, these cities created crime units, specifically to focus on gun violence that was coming from these gangs, but this writer obviously never seen the movie, Colors. I mean, the article just gets worse and worse as you continue to read it, but the kicker is, like every other leftist, liberal and democrat, she also blames all the gun violence and city destruction on President Trump and his administration, but also his millions of followers. When a Senator spoke about the rise of these armed minority men and the possible outcomes of what could happen, this news article writer called this State Senator rhetoric.

He also went on to explain that his thinking, "echoes that of President Trump and other Republicans, who have taken an increasingly antagonistic tone towards protestors and members of the blm movement." She also went on to state that, "Trump has referred to the movement as a, "hate group" and repeated talking points in favor of tough policing. The President and his supporters, meanwhile, defended a white St. Louis couple, captured on video pointing guns at black protestors simply walking by. According to fox news, the couple told the police they retrieved their firearms after spotting armed protestors."

She also goes on to claim that, other members of President Trumps circle, have taken to calling blm protestors, "Marxists", who has been, "planning to destroy the police for years". So where do I start because there is so much wrong in just these few statements alone, it's mind-boggling how she was even allowed to pass this article on as news or that she actually thought it was a good article to write. First off, like we discussed before, the white St. Louis couple she is referring too, had guns because they were trying to protect themselves after armed rioters and protestors, broke down their personal locked iron gate.

This white couple, didn't just grab their guns because they saw armed protestors simply walking by, like she claims, no, this couple grabbed their guns because armed protestors broke down the locked iron-gate to their private property. This couple was on their own private property, trying to protect themselves from these looters and protestors, who took it upon themselves to break down this white couples iron gate and trespass on to their property, screaming about how they were going to kill them. These rioters and protestors, weren't simply marching by this house peacefully, these useless protestors broke down this couples private locked iron-gate and continued to argue and threaten to kill this innocent white couple, who were simply trying to protect themselves.

What's really worrisome is the fact that, there is no truth anymore, every single one of these yahoo articles, written by her and writers like her, only preach hate. All of these writers say nothing to condemn the chaos, violence or destruction occurring in these American cities, it's just the opposite where everything white, is the problem. If you are white in America, like this St. Louis couple, anything you do is a crime, you try to protect yourself or your home from these rioters and looters, it's a crime.

You try to stop protestors from burning down you business, it's a crime, it's come to where, if you don't give in to minorities, you are to suffer simply because you're white. That's also a scary thing to think about these days, these minorities are listening too and following these destructive leftists and blm Marxists leaders, who are telling minorities that, all white people should die, all white people should be killed off and all white people are racist bigots. The truth is easily ignored by these people, as they continue to push their fake news and propaganda out to millions because they want the country at war. These people want the country in turmoil, if it is in chaos, it's easier for them to keep Americans divided and separated, with their lies and deceptions.

You can see this from news writers like this writer, simply because of what she claimed, this is something we've talked about before, blm leaders, have gone on record, claiming to be `Marxist's` groups and claiming they will burn everything to the ground, if they are not given what they want. Numerous black lives matters protestors were on record saying the exact same thing, one after another, "we are trained Marxists, we are trained Marxists", and that's why these people are tearing down and destroying their communities.

Not according to this writer though, also most democrats, it's President Trump and his supporters, they are the ones labeling these so-called innocent peaceful blm protestors as Marxists. Therefore, you can see what I mean about narrative and even motive, these blm leaders, their followers and most democratic State politicians, make bold statements and bold claims, but then turn around and blame other people for these statements or claims. Blm claimed they were trained Marxists, no one else did, blm did and the evidence has clearly been seen of this.

This is why I am left puzzled when these people turn around and make claims that, it's not them making these outrageous and ridiculous statements, it's President Trump and his followers. They are the ones guilty of making these statements and causing all this chaos and destruction that's occurring in these Americans cities. Certain Americans, including myself, just want the world to get back to normal because I am sorry but everything white, is not racist and blaming white people for your own problems, is not going to solve the problems minorities have, nor will it even touch the base of the root of the problem that minorities have.

Think about this for a second, people have burnt down their own communities, people have burnt down minority owned businesses, people have burnt down police stations, people have burnt down courthouses and people have burnt down public national monuments and statues, all in the name of racial equality. Urban communities and neighborhoods, now lie in ruins, all simply destroyed because these people thought it would be a good idea to burn it all down to the ground, all in the name of racial justice and equality.

After everything we discussed though, does this honestly make any sense at all, does destroying everything in sight, but also destroying dozens of urban communities, really advocate for minority justice or equality? I don't honestly think it does, I mean, you are burning communities to the ground, your own community, not someone else community, your own community. I think minorities already have a hard time as it is when it comes to cleaning up urban communities, but when people are coming through and destroying their communities, they are left trying to replace, what these people chose to destroy.

The sad thing is that these are not white people coming in and destroying these urban communities, this is blm leaders and their followers, which makes no sense because if you were advocating for equality or justice, why would you loot grocery stores and destroy your own communities? Then you have these liberal and democratic American State mayors and governors, who were elected and tasked to provide public safety for their citizens, just idly sitting by, while crime increases and violence takes over their streets. They all have the same narrative, this narrative is to blame President Trump and his supporters for being white supremacist, oppressing these people living in urban communities.

What's mind-boggling to me is that, these rioters and looters, the ones being called peaceful protesters by these blm leaders, leftists, liberals and democrats, have chosen to destroy dozens of businesses, even with the storeowners standing in front of their stores, storeowners, who plead to these people to not destroy their businesses. These rioters and looters didn't care about the owners pleas, they went on to destroy their property's anyway, which is crazy because these rioters even beat up most of the store owners, some almost to death, people, who were simply trying to protect their businesses from being looted and destroyed.

I say it's mind-boggling because these blm leaders, liberals and democratic State politicians, have chosen to turn a blind eye to all of the chaos and violence occurring to American citizens, but they also ignore all the assaults and murders occurring to business and storeowners. Time after time, these State politicians, from city council members to State Senators, are seen on television dodging major questions about the rise of crime, while most of them come back around to the fact that, somehow it's all President Trumps fault. President Trump is somehow responsible for the rise of crime and violence, Not only that, President Trump's the one that's to blame for all the chaos and destruction occurring in these democratic ran cities.

The whole blm movement shouldn't be supported because not only have minorities already had to fight tooth and nail to have successful businesses, thanks to a failed economy and communities with no gentrification. Now, hundreds of blm protestors just cost minorities their entire lives in mere seconds because they burnt down their businesses, all in the name of minority equality. However, these storeowners were minorities and these businesses were minority owned businesses, in mostly minority communities, so seriously, how is this movement all about minority equality?

The logic coming from these people makes no sense at all and forget arguing with these people because if you have a different opinion, you are always wrong and they are always right. These are also the politicians who try to be altruistic towards Americans living in these low-income urban neighborhoods because they want you to feel they are helping you, they want you to feel you need them, but in reality, they are using you to stay in office for another 30 years. These liberals and democrats also love to help out people who are over here illegally and people who choose not to work because these are the very same people, who tend to easily follow their lies and narrative of help.

It all sounds lopsided to me because the working class American, is the one that pays taxes on everything from money earned to store groceries, year after year, only to hope that they have enough money to retire, when they reach the age of 65. Unfortunately, this isn't who appeals to these liberals and democrats, they want people they can easily deceive into doing as they wish, people who tend to have no say or opinion, in the matter at hand.

Nancy Pelosi, is key to all of this because she is the ringleader of all this chaos and destruction, but of course just like everyone else, according to her and her followers, it's all President Trumps fault. Nancy Pelosi even went as far to call our American federal troops, President Trump's storm troopers, after Trump sent them in to clean up the American streets. Think about that for a second, the United States President sends in federal troops to stop the chaos occurring to American cities and the Speaker of the House, berates him for it. All these liberals, leftists and democrats, have only one narrative they want Americans to follow and if we don't get in line, they try to destroy your character, so anything you say, will be considered just another conservative lie.

The narrative itself is scary enough, millions of minorities have latched on to the slave theory and now we have nothing but chaos in our cities. These liberals and democrats, led by Nancy Pelosi, have tricked millions of minorities into thinking, President Trump, is the one who is treating all of them like slaves, keeping all minorities oppressed. What's worse is, these liberal mayors and governors, are all on television blaming the gun violence and crime in their cities, on President Trump, which to me is kind of weird because these city mayors, were the ones elected to provide public safety to their citizens, President Trump can only step in, if they ask him to.

These politicians were elected into office by the American people and they are representatives of the American people, who have been tasked to provide public safety and security to its American citizens, I am not too sure where the confusion comes in. These are the American cities that are controlled and ran by liberals and democrats, who defunded the police and called for police reform, but now deal with crime and violence running rampant in their cities and communities. In these liberal and democratic ran cities, crime has skyrocketed to the extreme, we witness the dangerous reality of what is happening daily, although these liberal and democratic mayors, claim were wrong.

For example, we can take a look at Seattle, Washington, where Seattle's mayor claimed, "in police-free zones, we could have a summer of love", but in reality, Seattle, seen crime increase to over 525%, compared to the same month back in 2019, 525% increase. Portland, Oregon, where all the chaos was getting out of hand, but the Portland City Council went on record to claim, "Defunding the police was a victory. We're not done", but Portland, has seen crime increase to over 240%, compared to the same month in 2019, 240%.

It's worse when you take a look at some of the shootings and the death rates coming from these other major American cities. That's why it's finny to see these liberal and democratic mayors, continue to claim these are all just peaceful protests. We can look at New York City, where there has been an 130% increase in shootings, compared to last year, but the NYC mayor, went on record claiming that, "we think defunding police is the right thing to do". We honestly don't need to mention Chicago and the great democratic mayor Lori Lightfoot, who tends to put reality and truth in the closet, while she lets craziness and insanity, run rampant in her city.

Mayor Lightfoot's Chicago, from May to July, had an unprecedented 1,130 shootings, which 212 of these shootings were fatal, yet mayor Lightfoot claimed that, "it's time for our city to seriously look at cutting the police budget". Which this to me is mind-boggling itself because Chicago is one of the most murderous cities in America, they alone have more homicides than any other city, yet there own city mayor, wants to defund the police because she claims the police officers trying to keep her city safe, are the problem, not the minorities killing each other.

All of these cities have experienced a major increase in crime and violence, thanks to police being defunded, but it doesn't matter to these State mayors and governors, they all could care less because to them, the more destruction these people cause, the better. The liberal and democratic ways of thinking is part of this whole chaotic problem we have, these are the politicians, who thought that defunding the police would somehow stop crime from occurring in their city. It honestly makes no sense because you would need serious data to back this statement up, but when there is no truth to what you are claiming, how can you defund the police and think that crime would stop?

I mean, seriously, these State politicians, are the ones that went on television to tell their own citizens that, since we defunded police, social workers, are going to respond to your home break-in or domestic disputes. I guess they never watched the television show cops or seen the outcomes of some of these dangerous domestic disputes, which quickly turn violent, where police offers have lost their lives. Now, according to these genius State politicians, social workers will be responding to these domestic calls, but social workers will also be the ones dealing with police issues.

Now, these social workers will have to worry about their lives as they answer and respond to these violent domestic calls, where shots have often been fired. When we talk about these simple-minded people, we can also include illegal immigrants and illegal foreigners because there has been a rise of stabbings and killings, perpetrated by illegal immigrants and illegal foreigners, who are over here illegally. Although we have State Reps., protesting for these people to have rights, murders perpetrated by these illegal outsiders, are increasingly on the rise and some of these murders, are just gruesome, from stabbings and shootings, to people being beheaded for no apparent reason at all.

One immigrant, who was just released from prison, where he was serving time for murder, was being dropped off at his car by his friend, then after a short argument, this immigrant turned on his friend, instantly shooting him, then calmly pulled off as his buddy laid there bleeding to death. This was an illegal alien, who was just released from prison for murder, only to be sent back to prison for the exact same crime, after he killed his friend, who was just giving him a ride. Seriously, how would social workers be able to respond to situations like these, how would a social worker be able to stop a husband, whose hell bent on shooting his wife or ex wife and kids?

We've already seen this occur in Seattle, seriously, already there was a social worker, was killed responding to a domestic dispute. Yet, the case was ignored by the media because they don't want Americans to know the truth, which is, their democratic logic never works. It's crazy when you think about it because these people don't care about American laws, these people don't care about what's right and what's wrong, they do as they please and these State politicians are there to let these rioters and looters get away with it.

Remember, democrats are the ones who created bills that allowed protesters and rioters to walk, after they were arrested for causing chaos and destruction, not Trump. It's all about rights and laws really, these State politicians want more money to pass their laws, they want more rights to increase their power and they will help anyone that will take their side and vote their democratic way. This is why we supposedly have close to over 11 million illegal immigrants and foreigners, living in the United States of America that Joe Biden claims he would be giving citizenship to, if he's elected President.

If these people are all over here in America illegally, why is a former State Senator, even talking about giving these people citizenship, they are illegal immigrants, not legal Americans? The weird thing is, Sleepy Joe Biden is making this statement, like he somehow knows exactly where these people are and if that is the case, why are these people not being deported back to whatever country they came from, they are illegal immigrants? If not, how would you know that there are over 11 million illegal immigrants living in the United States, but also, how is this even allowed, how are there over 11 million people living in our country illegally?

When you think about it, this is a spit in the face to the legal immigrants and foreigners, that came over to our country the legal way because these people had to go through the process of becoming legal, while these others will merely be handed citizenship for being here illegally. It seems as if these State politicians, will bend over backwards for illegal immigrants and others, but when it comes to the American people, they don't bother to put forth much effort. They will gladly give away our hard-earned money, also our hard fought for American rights, to people over in America, illegally.

I'm puzzled to as why this is even happening in America, also why are we even talking about something like this because this should not be occurring, the American people should not be pushed to the side for illegal immigrants and foreigners, but the fact that they are, means that these American State politicians, have failed Americans. This is also why these people living in America, illegally, could care less about becoming legal, they have everything handed to them, but also have State politicians fighting to give them more, so why would they.

Don't get me wrong, this doesn't apply to all immigrants and foreigners, like I said before, there are legal immigrants and foreigners over in America that came over to America the right way. What I am mostly referring to are these illegal immigrants, who take advantage of the system, who are often led by State Rep. AOC and her squad because these State politicians claim illegal immigrants and foreigners, should have American rights. This is what gives these illegal immigrants the thought that, since these State politicians claim they deserve American rights, maybe they should be out protesting for them, although these people are over here illegally and should be given nothing but a deportation flight back home.

It's crazy because State Rep. AOC and her so-called squad, also can't stand President Donald Trump, but also America, so they'll do anything they can for illegal immigrants and foreigners, this includes destroying America and the lives of Americans, if they have to. Prime example of how much they hate Americans, is to take a look at this new bill that is currently being proposed in the House because if you haven't heard of the, New Way Froward Act, you might want to hold on to your seats for this one. We all may remember how bad the proposed, New Green Deal was, a whacked out of the mind deal, that these politicians fully supported, but this new bill being pushed by State Rep. AOC., and 43 other democratic constituents, takes the cake.

This new bill or legislature that these State politicians are pushing, is said to be exactly almost as long as the U.S. Constitution and ultimately would create a whole new country for immigrants. Other politicians in the Senate that disagree with the bill, have claimed that, "The bill would entirely remake our immigration system, with the explicit purpose of ensuring that criminals are able to move here and settle here permanently, with impunity". However, it gets worse, other House members went on record to claim that, "the New Way Forward Act, is the most radical single piece of legislation we've seen in this country. It makes the Green New Deal look like the status quo".

These statements are all coming from State Senators and House members, who are blown away by what State Rep. AOC, the squad and these other 43 democrats have proposed with this new bill. The real reality is that these democrats, including State Rep. AOC, could care less about Americans and more about their political agendas and we see it daily because democrats and liberals, will go on television and constantly make these fallacious statements and claims.

Lie after lie, deception after deception, false truth after false truth, fallacious argument after fallacious argument, these State Senators push their narrative, until their so blue in the face, they forget what they were even claiming in the first place. I honestly think it's insane how these State Senators make these outrageous statements, that no one in their right mind would ever make because there is no truth to them, but these State Senators make them anyway. State Rep. AOC and other democrats, are prime examples of this because her and other democrats, went around promoting this, New Way Forward Act.

Simply claiming that, "convictions, should not lead to deportation," basically claiming that, even though these illegal immigrants may have committed a major crime, they should not be deported for committing this major crime. Although they are over in America illegally, they should still be allowed back onto the streets after committing major

354

crimes. Again, illegal means illegal and the democratic logic that comes from State Rep. AOC and other democrats, is just mind-boggling to say the least. These are not simple minor convictions that these State Senators are referring to, no, these are felony convictions such as, armed robbery and murder, convictions that usually land people in prison for years.

Still, according to State Rep. AOC and other democrat's, these illegal immigrants who commit these major felonies, should not be deported after they commit these major felonies. Instead, they claim that these illegal immigrants should be jailed in prison, on the American taxpayer's dime, and when they are released from prison, these illegal immigrants are to be released, they should not be deported.

It's just insane when you think about it, but you can also forget about immigration programs because these State politicians, led by State Rep. AOC, wants all of our immigration programs to be canceled, not some, she wants all to be cancelled. State Rep AOC, also wants all illegal immigrants currently living in America, to instantly be granted American citizenship, instantly be given free healthcare, but also free living expenses. This might sound a little familiar to what we were already talking about, maybe it's a coincidence that, State Rep. AOC backs Sleepy Joe Biden because Sleepy Joe Biden just made the bold statement that once elected President, Sleepy Joe, would grant over 11 million illegal immigrants, American citizenship.

Therefore, not only do State Rep. AOC, Sleepy Joe Biden and other democrats, believe that illegal immigrants, over here in America illegally deserve rights. These State Senators, also think they should be given free homes and even free healthcare, all on the American peoples dime, of course. The sad thing about all of this is not the fact that, these are American State politicians fighting for illegal immigrants, but it's the fact that, these are American State politicians, who focus more on illegal's, then Americans. Honestly, name one bill of legislature that was put forth by State Reps., Alexandria Ocasio-Cortez of New York, Ilhan Omar of Minnesota, Avanna Pressley of Massachusetts and Rashida Tlaib of Michigan, that didn't have an agenda of helping out foreigners and illegal immigrants, rather than Americans.

These State Senators, are so un-American it's pathetic and the scary thing is, they are not afraid to show it. They have no fear of berating America or berating President Trump because they do this daily in front of the American people, without a care in the world. As American State representatives, these women have done nothing for the American people, seriously, these women are always seen on television, telling Americans, how President Trump is a neo-Nazi racist and bad for the American people, I think it's reversed.

It doesn't stop there though because according to these politicians, President Trump, is responsible for the crime and violence. In reality, they all can't stand the fact that, President Trump puts the American people first, instead of illegal's and terrorists, like these State Senators tend to do. These four women were elected into the United States Congress, don't tell them that though because if you do, you're racist and objectifying these women. The truth is, they should be representing the American people and no one else, they were elected to represent the American people, not the people who came over here illegally to enjoy our freedoms.

What's interesting is, it's a proven fact that, most minorities choose to live in drug and gang infested neighborhoods, all due to the enticement of the money. If you look at national statistics for the past few decades, you will often see that the government has always provided more assistance to minorities and immigrants living in these communities, more than any other race. So, what these State Senators seem to claim is redundant because it's always the same demand, somehow illegal's and even foreigners, deserve more rights than Americans, although they already receive more assistance then most white Americans.

It's crazy because illegal immigrants and foreigners, have easily slipped into these crime and drug infested communities all over America simply because the police were too busy dealing with people being shot and killed, rather than being able to focus on people, who are over here illegally. All you really have to do is, look at the statistics and data reviews compiled over the years, you'll see for yourself. Especially if you take a look at the polls recently completed over the past few years that show you the difference between, who the government assist's and who they don't.

If you look at most of these recent statistics taken, especially FBI Data reviews, you will often notice that white American's, were often given less assistance from our government then minorities, immigrants and even illegal immigrants. Still, doesn't matter though because State

Reps., blm leaders and civil leaders, claim these people do not receive the assistance and feel they are entitled to so much more, whether they deserve it or not. Last time I checked though, being over here in America illegally, doesn't entitle you to anything, except a trip back to whatever country you came from, you don't get free money, you especially don't get free healthcare, which is something most Americans themselves don't even have or receive.

What some of these State Senators do just seems to keep you puzzled, but one thing is for sure, they don't care about the American people, they care about their agenda, which is to better the lives of their immigrants and foreigners. This is why they often gear their hatred and blame towards President Trump, since President Trump cares more about the American people, rather than illegal's and foreigners, this somehow makes him a racist, no good President. It's crazy because this is how it should be, every State Senator sitting in office, should be putting the American people first, but it doesn't happen and we can see this by looking at this new stimulus package, where they are given billions to foreign countries and foreign aid, but only $600 dollars to each American citizen.

It's part of the 900 million dollar American covid-19 relief stimulus package, yet, the American people that seriously need the help, are only going to be receiving $600, while Egypt and Asia, get's over a combined 2.7 billion dollars. Think about that though, State Senators are okay with giving each American citizen $600 dollars, to help somehow stop the bills from piling up, while they give billions away to other countries, in a bill that's supposed to be for the American people.

It honestly makes no sense because here's what some of these foreign countries would be receiving when the bill is passed because remember the House and Senate, has already passed this bill onto the President. Sudan get's $700,000,000, Ukraine get's $453,000,000, Israel get's $500,000,000, Asia R.I.A. get's $1,400,000,000, Egypt get's $1,300,000,000, Cambodia get's $85,000,00, while the American people get's an extra $600. Honestly, if you think these American State politicians, really care about the American people, I have a beach for sale in Upstate, New York, you interested?

This to me is crazy because think about it this way, the government, mostly democrats, passed a bill on to the U.S. President to sign, that would give over $4,500,000,000 billion dollars to foreign countries, while democrats complaining that Americans getting a little over $200,000,000, is too much. If every American living today gets about $600 dollars, that would only equal to over $200,000,000 dollars, if at most close to $250,000,000. Therefore, that's still leaves over $650,000,000 being held from the American people, while our government hands billions over to foreign countries.

If you honestly don't think something is wrong here, you are part of the problem because we should not be sending money to foreign countries in the first place, not when millions of Americans, are suffering and losing their entire life savings because they now have no way of making an income. It makes no sense because these liberals and democrats, claim that President Trump, is the one that hates the American people, President Trump's the one that's not doing anything for the American people, but the evidence proves otherwise.

This is what makes all of this so puzzling, these State politicians blame President Trump, claiming he's a bad American President, but people never realize that House democrats and House Republicans, are the ones, who are supposed to be the first line of defense for Americans. President Trump, is there to back up their decisions, once they approve a bill, it's sent to his desk for approval, so I fail to understand how all these democrats can blame everything on President Trump. The sad thing is, these liberals and democrats have no limits to what they will do or what they will say, they will use any chance they can to change the course of history, but also to get rid of Trump.

It's really interesting because even Barack Obama got in on this when he used a democrats funeral service, democrat John Lewis's funeral, to berate President Trump and talk about how bad of a President, Trump is. It's funny coming from a former President, who did nothing for minorities during his Presidency, but claims that the current President, who actually has, hasn't helped out the minority community at all. Barack Obama, constantly made promise after promise, but never fulfilled those promises. Obama also said he was going to somehow fix everything, but, him and sleepy Joe, did nothing that they said they would and now they berate a U.S. President, who has done everything they didn't.

Like I stated before, look at the facts and statistics for his Presidency, President Trump, has literally done more for minorities, then Barack Obama and Joe Biden combined. One simple example, is the fact that, President Trump, not Barack Obama, signed a bill of legislature to invest over $100 billion dollars to urban communities for development. Over $100 billion dollars, to help minorities in urban communities better their lives and their surroundings.

Did Barack Obama ever do that, I think not? Did Joe Biden or Barack Obama, ever do anything for urban communities or ever pass bills to give money to minorities to help them develop their communities, I think not. President Trump did, not only did President Trump pass a bill of legislature to give billions to minority communities, he also invested in the future of minorities, by helping out minority schools and colleges. This is what's crazy about Barack Obama speaking up about President Trump, the whole basis for Obama being re-elected was because Barack Obama, was going to help minorities and better the lives of minorities, yet, he never backed or passed one bill to do so.

Now, Barack Obama, wants to berate and belittle a President, that has done everything he didn't and more because Barack Obama, feels this President, is a bad man and should not be President. What always gets me about Barack Obama though, is the fact that, Barack Obama, focused more on letting men into women's bathrooms and Americans accepting Muslims, Islam and the hateful ideology of Jihad. All this, although Islamic Jihadist and most Muslims, including State Rep Illan Omar of Minnesota, hate Americans and are taught to hate Americans from a very young age.

Think I am joking, I'm not, State Rep. Illan Omar of Minnesota, has backed State Rep. AOC, with everything she does, but now State Rep. Omar, is also claiming we shouldn't help out Israel because she simply hates them, just as much as she hates the people she was hired to represent. State Rep. Omar, is not an American and it's a shock that, her and State Rep. AOC are even U.S. congresswomen, because of the hatred and distain, they show for America and the American people, especially the American President. This is also the very same State Rep. that went on record in 2013, to prove her faith to Allah and devotion to al-Qaida, during an interview on Belhadan, a Minnesota Middle Eastern community channel, talking about Muslim issues.

In this 2013 interview, she praised Allah, talked crap about our American values and praised al-Qaida, she even went on record to say, "when Americans say American, you don't distain the name, so when we say al-Qaida, why do we do it." It's like seriously, these people hate Americans and have been taught since birth that Americans were infidels and the enemy, you are an American State Congress woman, praising these people, how do you even have a job?

Although the evidence is clear that she hates America and the American people, she went even further with her hatred, when she went on record to claim that she, "hopes Americans can find the grace of Allah". This is an American U.S. Congress member, who is clearly stating that she hates our God and hopes for Americans to instead, worship her false God, Allah, but not only that, she's on record stating that, al-Qaida makes her proud. An American U.S. congress member, stating that she praises Allah, a prophet that hates Westerners and praises al-Qaida.

The group responsible for Osama Bin Ladin and possibly part of 9/11, but also one of the most dangerous domestic terrorist groups there is, State Rep. Omar praises them and tears apart the American people, for hating them. The bad part about this is, we are letting State Rep. Omar do it, the American people elected her into United States Congress and now she is a domestic terrorist, slowly trying to tear apart our country from the inside out. Wasn't this what Iran, China, N. Korea and Russia, were always trying to do in the first place, incorporate spies into the United States of America, seems to me like they succeeded.

Are these people not the ones always getting exposed for trying to get people into high ranking positions in America, so they can secretly destroy our American values, from the inside out, I think this may be the same problem we have here. Think about it this way, not only has State Rep. Omar, constantly shown her distain and hatred for America, she was also the State Rep. that referred to the tragedies of 9/11 as, "just something that happened." It's crazy because according to this American State Representative, 9/11, as bad as a travesty as it was, to her, was just something that happened to Americans. Unfortunately though, with the constant attacking of President Trump, State Rep. Ilhan Omar now, claim's she never said any of these things, although the interview was recorded and published on national Muslim television for the entire world to see.

For State Rep. Omar, to sit there and deny these statements, knowing that she made these statements, just shows you how much these new politicians will, lie, deceive and manipulate people into

360

getting what they want as they secretly destroy our American values, one by one. This really just goes with the leftists, liberals and democratic lies occurring these days because State Rep. Omar said it, the statements were watched by hundreds, if not millions. Still, according to fact checker's and democrats, she did not say it, President Trump is lying.

That's another thing that is funny about these liberals and democrats because they blatantly make these ridiculous statements, then retract these statements and claim that they didn't say them, President Trump said them, it's really just mind-boggling. Back to Barack Obama and it's interesting that, after a proven failed Presidency, Barack Obama now thinks he has the right to tear down our current President, who has done more in three and half years, than Barack Obama did in 8 years or during his entire political career.

Look at the statistical polls for unemployment for minorities and immigrants, you will see under President Trumps U.S. Presidency, unemployment itself, is the lowest it's ever been recorded and jobs have grown ten-fold, since Trump became President. Barack Obama had 8 years to help the American people, instead Obama chose to focus on foreign policies, but also foreigners and immigrants, instead of Americans. We also can't forget that during Obama's Presidency, about the 13 million Americans were on unemployment, which was the highest it's ever been recorded.

We have already discussed Obama's money, which is, Americans made the Obama's rich, Barack Obama didn't become a millionaire until he became the U.S. President. With his salary as U.S. President, something President Trump donates, Obama became a millionaire, then after his failed Presidency, he became a multi-millionaire, thanks to American taxpayers and book deals. President Donald Trump, built a billion dollar empire and has more knowledge of the American working class, than any other elected official, so why wouldn't Trump be great for Americans, we have already seen what he could do in 3 1/2 years?

Barack Obama, wasn't a millionaire until he became U.S. President, Obama never even ran a business or company, he also never had to worry about thousands of employees, Barack Obama stole the Presidency and made himself and his family rich, all thanks to the American people. I say stole the Presidency because if you really look at the facts, good ol' Barry, which is his real name, if ya'll didn't know, was supposedly born as a foreigner in Hawaii to an Indonesian mother and Kenyan father. We all know about the controversy surrounding Barack Obama's birth certificate, I mean, this guy gave U.S. Congress a fake birth certificate. Barack Obama claimed it was a real one, but Obama also had dual citizenship in Kenya and Indonesia, which is a no no and excludes you from becoming U.S. President.

Want proof, according to article 11, section 1, in the United States Constitution; it states that, if you carry multiple citizenships, you are not eligible to run for President of the United States, there you have it, plain and simple. We know Obama is not American and it was proven before Obama even took office, but the fact that he supplied a forged birth certificate to Congress, should have been a warning to everyone. Now, if you look at his name, Barry Soetoro, you will find nothing but articles on Obama and Obama's citizenship conspiracy theories.

Barack Obama's citizenship was called into play time after time, yet he never once provided an actual authentic birth certificate, only the forged one he provided to Congress, during the trial. This to me is shocking because anyone can purchase a copy of their birth certificate through the right channels, all American birth certificates, are available through each State and can be supplied to you, once the documents needed are approved and verified. Why is it that a person, who claims to be American, but who is also trying to become the President of the United States, couldn't seem to provide a real birth certificate to Congress? Seriously, why is that though, when everyone in America can use Vital Records and receive a copy of their birth certificate?

Still till this day, Barack Obama's birth certificate remains a mystery and has yet to be brought forth, but instead of Obama's birth certificate, the media switches the focus towards President Trump and his taxes. At the same time, you are ineligible to become U.S. President if you have dual citizenships in other countries, yet, Barack Obama, was still somehow able to become President, without providing a verified birth certificate to the United States Congress. That's right though, Barack Obama, was born of foreign decent, had siblings and parents of foreign decent, also never maintained his American citizenship, had dual citizenship in other countries.

Yet, like some strange unsolved mystery, Barack Obama, was still able to become President of The United States. Here's the kicker though, Barry or Barack, whatever you want to call him, attended

American high schools as a foreign exchange student and even attended college as a foreign exchange student, who would become a foreign policy major and the President of Harvard Law Review. Which to me is kind of interesting, he was the President of Harvard law, yet, he knew being a foreigner wouldn't allow him to become the U.S. President, so instead, he forges a birth certificate that claims he's now American, whose name is Barry Seotoro.

What's even more interesting is that, the last name Seotoro, was the surname that was often used by his mother, Ann Dunham, who changed her last name, just as much as Barack Obama changed his mind. What I fail to understand is, how can an immigrant, who was often declared a foreigner all throughout his young adult life, but who was also noted to having dual citizenship in other countries, be elected as President? I mean, Barack Obama himself, knowingly handed in a forged birth certificate to congress, which Obama swore up and down was real, so seriously, how was Obama even eligible to become A United States President?

Also, the fact that his mother's maiden name, was changed several times and these names weren't always all the same, this makes you question why that would be occurring and why his mother, would change her name at least 4 times, only to settle on Ann Dunham. Obama, screwed over Americans for 8 years and now he is trying to screw over Americans again by taking the side of Sleepy Joe Biden, a man who's a well known racist and has literally been recorded making some of the most outrageous racist statements ever.

That's also interesting to me because we've seen what President Trump has done in just his first 4 years and we finally have a U.S. President, who has helped out more Americans, than any other President in U.S. history, including Barack Obama. Still, according to Barack Obama and other democrats, President Trump, is a bad President for the American people, who does nothing but hurt the American tradition and culture. Due to this opinion that they have, President Trump should somehow be stopped because he's racist and un-American, but also isn't doing anything for the American people, but democrats supposedly will.

Like we discussed before though, President Trump, has done more for the urban community and minorities, then Barack Obama and Joe Biden, has ever done. You don't even have to take my word for it, you can easily look up statistics and yearly data reviews, to see what Barack Obama has done, compared to what President Trump has done, in half the time. President Trump, has also gotten Americans out of the worst deals in American history, the deals Barack Obama apologized for to foreign countries like, Iran and China, who were literally screwing us over with bad deals and tax tariffs.

President Trump stopped all these wrong dealings, not Joe Biden, not democrats and especially not Barack Obama. With President Trump in the Oval Office, American manufacturing companies and businesses, are also being brought back to America. The very same companies that left after Barack Obama pushed high corporate taxes, which then forced these companies to leave. Barack Obama's high taxes, made it cheaper for companies to move overseas to countries like China, rather than keeping their businesses in America. President Trump provided the tax cuts and tax breaks, to these American companies, which brought these manufacturing companies back to America.

He was also responsible for stopping State Rep. AOC and other democrats, who wanted to give illegal immigrants free rights, free American money and free healthcare. President Trump, put a stop to all of the crap coming from these State politicians, not Barack Obama, not liberals, not democrats. The crazy thing is, President Donald Trump, has been in our government for only four years, while all these other State Senators and politicians, whether republican, democrat or liberal, have been in our government for decades, not just years, but decades.

You can also see what I mean by taking a look at how long some of these top State political officials have been in our government, they've been in their position for decades. Yet, each one of them they haven't done much of anything for America or the American people, but cause chaos and division. Nancy Pelosi, Speaker Of The house, has been in our government for 33 years, Joe Biden, former Vice President, has been in our government for 51 years, Maxine Waters, has been in our government for 47 years, Chuck Schumer, has been in our government for 45 years and Obama has been in our government for 20 years.

Still, all of these liberals and democrats, blame the problems they haven't solved in decades, on a U.S. President that has only been in the government for only 4 years. For those of you reading this, who believe in what Barack Obama and these democrats love to claim, which is, President Trump is a racist, who is bad for the American people, but also bad for the American economy, let me share something with you. Besides what we've already discussed, I'm not too sure why Barack Obama, is even hating on President Trump, when back in high school, Obama himself, went on to claim that, his American dream was to be Donald Trump, Obama even stated, "The American dream is to be Donald Trump," not to be like Donald Trump, but to be Donald Trump.

So why is Barack Obama hating on Donald Trump now? The fact that is already well known is, President Donald Trump, is far from racist, yea he might say some off things, but what government official doesn't, but the real racist Presidential Candidates are Joe Biden and his democratic party. Unlike Joe Biden, President Trump, is an equal opportunity employer and has been known to hire hundreds of minorities, while Sleepy Joe Biden, doesn't even want his kids in the same schools as minority children because according to Joe Biden, these public schools are jungles.

In the short span of just four years, President Trump, has unequivocally done more for America and the American people, including minorities, Asians and Hispanic Americans, more than any other President besides, maybe George Washington and Abraham Lincoln. To simply sum this up, take a look at something as simple as unemployment, where you can look at recent statistics and you will notice during President Trumps four-year term, America has seen the lowest unemployment rate that has ever been recorded. This applies to all races, which even includes our uneducated youth, who dropped out of school and our veterans.

This is led by the lowest minority unemployment rate, which is at the lowest rate, it's ever been recorded, even lower then when we had a minority U.S. President in the Oval Office. A president who served for eight years, but let the unemployment and jobless rate skyrocket to over 13 million unemployed Americans. Not only is minority unemployment the lowest, but the same goes for Hispanic Americans, Asian Americans and even high school dropouts, who have no high-school diploma, no GED, but they also now have the lowest unemployment rate that's ever been recorded.

What seems to be missed by people, is the fact that, this is just what President Trump has done for unemployment and the American people, this doesn't scratch the surface of what he's been able to accomplish. Not to mention what President Trump has done for the American people by adding over 7 million new American jobs, since he was elected into the Oval Office. Seriously, how is President Trump a bad President for the American people again, how is President Trump bad for America, when he's done more in four years, then others have done in decades?

President Trump, is a true American and supports America completely and he's stated this time and time again, but Barack Obama and his democratic cronies, hate his love for America and they want President Trump to fail. Since President Trump is simply too smart for them and won't fail, these liberals and democrats try to make up as many lies as they possibly can, hoping that one of their little white lies, eventually sticks. You have to keep in mind, these are the same democrats and liberals that knew for fact there was no actual Russian collusion between President Trump and Ukraine.

This was proven to them by the FBI in the very first week of the investigation, still, knowing their allegations were false, democrats chose to impeach Trump for Russian Collusion. The interesting thing about democrats and their Russian Collusion theory, is the fact that, democrat Hillary Clinton, was actually convicted of Russian Collusion, yet democrats went after President Trump for conspiracy to commit Russian Collusion. These State Senators and State politicians, also tried to impeach President Trump for trying to expose a crime, while they are now trying to replace President Trump, with the very person, who committed the crime.

Democrats and liberals, spent millions of American tax payers' dollars, on lawyers and investigators for a trial that lasted almost three and half years, knowing from the very beginning that there was no Russian collusion and President Trump, was guilty of absolutely nothing. These liberal and democrats lies have no bounds either, as we've all seen lately, these liberals and democrats, blame President Trump, for just about everything. From the gun violence happening in their own democratic ran cities, to the federal buildings being burnt to the ground, somehow it's all President Trumps fault.

I'm sure I've said this a few too many times, but it's just so mind-boggling and puzzling as to why these State politicians, whatever the party, would allow chaos, violence and destruction, to run rampant in their American cities just so they can blame it all on President Trump. It seriously makes no sense at all, as to why these State politicians, not matter how much they hate President Trump, would be okay with our country being sent into turmoil. Major American cities like, New York, Portland, Seattle, Chicago, Atlanta, Philly and Baltimore, are experiencing chaos, night after night, while these State governors and mayors, chose to do nothing about public safety for their citizens.

What's insane, is the fact that, these State politicians are also the democratic politicians, who are telling people it's not okay to open businesses, but also not okay to even open churches. It's definitely not okay to open bars and restaurants and it's especially not okay to go to President Trumps Presidential campaign rallies because you might easily contract COVID-19 or spread the disease. It is however okay if you want to riot, loot and protest in crowds of hundreds, side by side against President Trump, that's perfectly okay.

It seriously makes no sense at all, but the fact that these are American State politicians pushing this, should scare all of us because if these State politicians, tried this crap anywhere else, they'd be fired and exiled from the government. If any State official spoke bad or wrong of their World Leader, these State politicians or officials, would be jailed or exiled from their government position, yet, American State Officials do it on a daily basis. Remember those old school movies about how Russia, China and Japan leaders, were always trying to secretly get people into the American government, it's like now they seemed to have succeeded.

Take a look at the so-called Squad of State Rep. AOC and her cronies, you will see exactly what I am referring too. Candace Owens, an intelligent minority voice for Americans and someone who we should all listen to, but, she said it perfectly when she stated. This is your daily reminder that we shut down America, impoverished millions, forced businesses to fail and homeowners to foreclose, over a virus that has a 99.96% survival rate. And the democrats are demanding we continue the lockdowns for everyone but their protestors". I hope she's not mad that I used her name or her statement, but what Candace said was spot on and thanks to a curable supposedly deadly virus, democrats shut down America and kept millions of Americans from working or even living.

This is because these State politicians claim it's too dangerous to even go outside, without a mask on, or two masks, unless of course, you want to protest against the President, then being outside in groups of hundreds in close proximity, is totally okay. That's the crazy thing about these statements coming from democrats and liberals, they are okay with hundreds of people being in close proximity to riot, protest and loot, but not okay with people going to hospitals, churches, bars, stores, restaurants or socializing in confined spaces, without being six feet apart.

According to these State politicians, all these places, including small businesses and churches, should still continue to remain closed. Blame after blame, comes from democrats and liberals and like I said before, Barack Obama even stooped as low as to use a fallen State Representatives funeral, State Rep. John Lewis, to tell Americans, how bad of a President, Trump is. That is how much these democrats and liberal hate President Trump, any chance they are given to bash President Trump, they will take it and this includes attacking him at other State Representatives funerals.

How much of a spit in the face is that though, here lies a fallen hero and State Representative of the American people and instead of giving a eulogy about how great of a man he was, you choose to bash our current U.S. President and tell Americans how bad of a President, you think he is. You should honestly be ashamed of yourself, for even doing this, but it's Barack Obama, the guy who has no shame. It's the thought's coming from these simple-minded State politicians though, what they think and what they say, is often a far stretch from the truth. The funny thing about this one though is that, this funeral bashing was all coming from Barack Obama.

The U.S. President before President Trump, who had 8 years to do what he said he would do, yet, did nothing he claimed he would. Is Obama really even American, I'm still waiting to see that birth certificate. I also find it funny when you look up Barack Obama's family and sibling's, Wikipedia, takes you straight to Barack Obama and his wife and kids, no information about his siblings at all, even though Barack Obama, is said to have a sister of Indonesian and Kenyan decent, not American decent. The funeral, wasn't the only place Obama used as a platform, now, Barack Obama, can be seen on just about every network he can be, conducting some kind of interview.

This is where Obama tries to poke his nose where it doesn't belong, whether it's warranted or not, which we know most of the time, it's not. Barack Obama is no longer President, he is no longer in control of any political position, he no longer really even should have a say, yet, Obama still thinks he can say whatever he wants, no matter how much of a lie it is. It's crazy because Barack Obama has a long history of insulting President Trump and now Barack Obama somehow thinks Joe Biden, a known racist, who even went as far as passing legislature jailing hundreds, if not thousands of minorities, can fix the broken problems of America.

The proof and truth is in Barack Obama's Presidency, democrats, can gather all the data they want and manipulate all the data they want, it doesn't stop the fact that President Trump has already did everything Obama said he would do and then some. Now Barack Obama, wants to poke his two cents in and by some miracle, 4 years later, Barack Obama, has all the answers and believes Sleepy Joe Biden, can fix everything. Although they both had eight years to do the things they promised to do, they often talked about the problems, but never really did anything to fix the problems.

Sleepy Joe Biden, has been in our government for over 5 decades and has done nothing for the American people, just incorporate lies and now can't even put a sentence together. I got a feeling, Biden should coin the phrase, "come on, man" because that quote is going to make him some money. This happens a lot though in America, tax-paying Americans, have made hundreds of politician's rich, American taxpayers pay their six figure salaries. Yes, I said that right because most politicians, including State mayors and governors, all make close to or over six figures, while all these six figured salaries, are paid for by the American people.

It was also funny when Michelle Obama, another person becoming rich off Americans, claimed that President Trump puts her into a deep depression, like she somehow encounters or deals with him on a daily basis. Michelle, who holds no political position, but who is also just as far left as her husband, recently slipped up on her new web show, when she was caught stating that, "Covid-19, is an opportunity for us to change how wealth is distributed". It makes no sense because this is the lady that is constantly on air telling Americans our President, is racist, yet, she only pushes things that benefits her family.

These political influencers, like Michelle and her husband, could care less about Americans and our way of values or way of living, all they care about is money and power, but also how they can get their hands on more of both, Michelle Obama, proved this by stating that Covid-19, is an opportunity for them to change wealth distribution. Also after a long line of crap, after being asked about our essential American workers, Michelle Obama stated that, "Often doing invisible, but yes, essential work and I struggle with it because I'm not sure that we treat them like they're essential".

So, let me get this straight, first you insult them by saying they are doing invisible work, which is already a slap in their face, than you go on to say that you think we don't treat them like they are essential, yet, you just claimed these people are doing invisible work, with you somehow struggling with it. You are on television talking about we need to fix this so-called wealth gap, instead of pushing to help take care of our essential workers or stopping the destruction of urban communities. Does this make any sense at all though, I honestly don't think it does, but she is an Obama, so can we really expect much?

What's insane is, she holds no political office, she's only a former first lady, even her husband, no longer holds any political office, still, she somehow struggles with the way essential workers are treated, but all you see coming from her is complaints about a wealth gap. So seriously, why is she even speaking, why is she even calling essential work invisible, but yes essential? She is a nobody in particular, she is not anyone famous, she is not anyone political, she holds no political office, she's just another minority female, that thinks she has more say, then she actually does.

Even if you listen to her talk, you can tell that she thinks and probably feels that, all the first ladies that came before her were useless and she even verbally assaults the current First Lady because she's said that the current First Lady, was just as racist as her husband was. It's funny how people can sit there and talk crap about other people, yet, they fail to look in the mirror and see what the real problem is, the Obama's themselves are far from respectable people. The way the Obama's think, personally is a joke, they'll do anything they can to remain in the spotlight, from radio shows to book deals.

The fact that they are foreigners, posing as Americans, simply takes the cake, but then again, if you want to prove me wrong, I would gladly like to see a valid birth certificate, one that's not forged. I mean, look at what President Trump did for minorities, compared to what Barack Obama did for minorities. This is what all the drama is about, minorities feeling they deserve more because they've been oppressed by a systemically racist government, led by President Trump. Barack Obama, constantly talked about prison and drug reform for minorities, he also talked about how he was fighting Congress to get money for urban communities for redevelopment, so they could invest more in urban development, yet, Barack Obama, never did one thing for minorities.

Unless you count making himself and his wife rich, then he did everything for minorities. In three and half years of being in the Oval Office, President Trump, has not only invested in numerous bills of Legislature for minorities, but like we discussed before, President Trump, also passed a bill to invest over $100 billion dollars into urban communities for job and community redevelopment. That's only what's he done so far for minorities, President Trump has also signed three bills of Legislature to help out Native Americans, one bill even gives them compensation, for the land they lost in the mid 1900's.

President Trump's EPA, (Environmental Protection Agency), has given over a $100 million dollars to Flint, Michigan, to help solve the water infrastructure problem they've had since the early 90's, so their citizens can finally have access to clean drinking water. President Trump, has even went as far as to sign the, Save our Seas Act, which funds $10 million dollars a year to clean the garbage constantly littering our oceans, lakes and our seas. This is only a third of what President Trump has done for America and the fact that people, including the Obama's, are saying that he's not good for Americans, just speaks volume to their character.

The fact that these politicians can't deny is, President Donald Trump, is a great U.S. President and Americans are proud to have him as our U.S. President. Americans should not have to be subject to these temper tantrums coming from liberals and democrats because they hate the fact that Trump is our U.S. President. What's crazy is, the American people voted him in, this is why we have elections, yet, these liberals and democrats, can't accept this fact and they will do whatever they can to get rid of President Trump, this includes cheating during the 2020 Presidential election.

You would think a President that has done great things for United States and the American people, whose said it time and time again that, he puts Americans first, would be a good thing, but nope, according to the Obama's, liberals and democrats, President Trump's a bad U.S. President. These idiots now refer to President Trump as, "Mr. Make Matters Worse", although the evidence proves otherwise. Liberals and Democrats, have really never focused on giving any money to any minority communities, nor do they tend to pass bills for urban development, unless of course, there are illegal immigrants living in those communities.

Because then they'll do everything they can for that community. Sleepy Joe Biden, is the same way and sleepy Joe, was the one who went on record to claim that, he doesn't want his kids in the same schools as minority kids. It's insane how these democrats claim President Trump, is the racist one, yet, it's Joe Biden's whose been quoted for making the most racist statements towards minorities, you can possibly think of. Now, after years of racist remarks, Sleepy Joe Biden, wants to appeal to minorities.

During an interview with Charlemagne the dummy, Sleepy Joe Biden made the racist statement that, "if you don't know whether you want to vote for me, or Donald Trump, you ain't black" and yes, sleepy Joe, actually said this on national television. This dude actually went on national television and claimed that, if minorities vote for President Donald Trump, in the upcoming election and not him, they were not black. Crazy and insane things, have been said by Joe Biden, time after time, now Joe Biden, just did something even more puzzling, he selected an even more racist VP candidate, Kamala Harris as his running mate.

Forget the fact that her own heritage seems to be called into question because she was born to Indian and Jamaican parents, who emigrated to the United States, yet she claims she's African-American, although she is half-Indian and half Jamaican. What's really puzzling about it all is, the fact that she is trying to hide, what people have already been told, which is, her family has strong ties to a Jamaican Sugar Plantation slave owner named, Hamilton Brown. Mr. Brown, was a former Irish slave owner, who owned Sugar Plantations in Jamaica, the origins of Kamala Harris's heritage and lineage.

It was stated that, Hamilton Brown, recruited hundreds of Irish migrants to work as slaves on his Sugar Plantations, even after the British Empire abolished slavery. Now, you may think to yourself, well if she is related to him, why is it a problem, and it wouldn't normally be, but when Kamala Harris is denying this heritage, but her father is saying it's true, you start to question who to believe. Kalama Harris, is the same person that claimed her and her family celebrated Kwanzaa, an African-American, minority-American tradition, that was created by a black American, but her family supposedly celebrated it, although she was raised in a French Indian-American household.

When her very own father, Donald Harris, confirmed that his paternal grandmother, was Christiana Brown, a direct descendant of Brown. Kamala Harris, claimed this was completely false, then gave in and said it was true, but only after she was chosen to become a V.P. nominee, so with this info, you tend to question her character. But if it's true, if Kamala Harris, is tied to a former slave owner, it's puzzling because isn't this what all these millions of people claim to be destroying our American national monuments and statues for, are they not causing all this chaos because white peoples ties to slavery?

Are these people not claiming that these public statues supposedly represents former slave owners and confederates, who wanted to continue the enslavement of minorities? Hamilton Brown, was a prominent Sugar Plantation owner in Jamaica and was even credited for creating an entire town called, Brown Town. During the first half of the 19th century, Mr. Brown was on record as a prominent Irish and Jamaican slave owner. Mr. Brown, even went as far to advocate against the abolition of slavery and he was known to constantly downplay the slave trade in Jamaica, so Hamilton could keep profiting from using Irish and Jamaican slaves on his Jamaican Sugar Plantations.

It isn't too hard to go to ancestry.com, to see if all this is true, but two things are known for certain and that is. One, Hamilton Brown, was a well-known and documented Irish and Jamaican slave owner and two, her father, Donald Harris, of Jamaican lineage, wrote an article that was published in the Jamaican global back in 2018. This article referred to his Brown family heritage and the fact that it's proven, Donald and his daughters, are descendants of Brown. Kamala Harris's father, Donald Harris, who is of Jamaican decent, wrote an article, about him and his daughter's family lineage back in 2018, two years ago.

This was where Mr. Harris described his ancestors, as well-known and prominent slave owners in Jamaica, who owned Jamaican Sugar Plantations. Like I said, if it's true , it's true, but the puzzling part was when Kamala Harris denied this claim by her own father, denied her Jamaican lineage and denied her heritage because she claimed to be African-American. We as Americans, know this is not true, Kamala Harris's mother and father, were both foreigners, who emigrated to the U.S. and Kamala Harris identifies as, half Indian and half Jamaican, not even American Native Indian because she's native to India.

So seriously, how does that make Kamala Harris the first African-American VP nominee, how is she labeled the first African-American VP candidate and first woman of color, when Kamala Harris, is not even African-American or of African descent? Kamala Harris, has no ties to African heritage at all, her mother's not of African descent, her father's not of African descent and she's barely even classified as a full-fledged American. It honestly makes no sense because why would you lie in the first place, this is your heritage, this is your father speaking of your heritage, why would you deny this is your heritage?

This tends to happen a lot with State politicians though, they say one thing and stick to that one thing, no matter if it's truthful or not, unless it's something that contradicts what they've previously said, then they just switch their story all together. Most of what's being said by these democratic politicians, even American civil leaders and activists, doesn't make much sense because they'll say one thing, only to claim and literally do the opposite, always contradicting what they've previously said. Americans often see this play out on television, mostly during political interviews, we've all seen these news interviews where these State politicians, civil activists and even news anchors, make certain statements.

The kicker is if their past statements contradict anything these people are claiming now, because then, these past statements and past interviews, are erased or buried and claimed to have never been said. Especially self-entitled know-it-all, Barack Obama because even Mr. Obama, has been caught behind the scenes, making some very interesting statements to other democrats about Joe Biden, one of these statements made from Barack Obama was, "Don't underestimate Joe's ability to f**k things up".

Another statement that kind of sticks in my mind is when, Barack Obama, was also caught behind the scenes saying, "And you know who really doesn't have it? Joe Biden". This opinion of his, won't be shared in front of the cameras, Barack Obama is Sleepy Joe Biden's best friend, which contradicts, what Obama has said in both of his statements. The Democratic Party, wants you to think that Barack Obama and Joe Biden, are close friends and you got it all wrong, they don't hate each other and you're crazy Barack Obama, never made these statements about Joe Biden, yet, Barack Obama, was secretly recorded making these exact statements.

It doesn't stop with democrats and liberals though, look at news writer and activist Shaun King for example. Shaun King, is a well-known un-American writer, civil rights activist, human rights activist, racial injustice activist, blm supporter and co-founder of Real Justice PAC, and he hates Trump. You will see exactly what I am referring to because Shaun King, is known for being a huge supporter for the black lives matter movement, but who is also trying to supposedly fight for all the racial injustices occurring to minorities.

This is a quarter of what is listed as his work credentials, but back in 2018 Shaun King, went on record to bash Joe Biden and Kamala Harris, who Shaun King claimed that, "both Biden and Harris, helped build and advance mass incarceration in America". In the 2018 post, Shaun king stated that, "I'll be frank and tell you two democrats that I am 99% sure I won't be supporting, primarily because of their dismal history on criminal justice reform over the course of their entire years, which is Joe Biden & Kamala Harris. They both helped build and advance mass incarceration."

Now, that seems like a fine statement to make and yea it might be true, they have both built their political careers on mass incarceration, but also mass illegal immigrants, mass racism, mass segregation, but that's not why I'm bringing his statement up. I am bringing Shaun King's statement up because now, two years later in 2020, Shaun King, recanted his statement about Kamala Harris and re-tweeted that, "That's it for me. I am incredibly proud to see a brilliant black woman and HBCU grad, chosen as a Vice Presidential nominee. I've done political work my whole life. It's rarely things dreams are made of. Kamala Harris is the most progressive VP nominee in American history."

The story with these people tends to never be the same, it always changes and Shaun King, is just one example and now you have everyone from fake news journalist to State politicians, saying one thing, only to change it around completely and say something else. You would think this wouldn't be allowed to happen or these people would be called out for making these contradicting statements, but then again, you would also think that these people of influence, would have more character than that. I honestly don't understand why people would do this, they said it, they know they said, it's been recorded on television of them saying it, but they still claim they didn't say it.

This is why racism has taken the dangerous turn it has in America, people are expressing their opinions and pushing them onto others, forcing these people to follow their opinions, even if these people do not want to. These hateful opinions being pushed, are turning dangerous and even sometimes violent and we've seen this by examining what we've discussed a lot, which is white people, being assaulted for simply being white, this includes white children. A very sad example to look at as a result of these violent opinions, is the one we talked about before, which is the case of innocent Cannon Hinnant.

Innocent white 5 year old, Cannon Hinnant, was outside in his front yard with his siblings, when his minority neighbor, walked out of his house with a gun, walked up to 5 year old Cannon Hinnant and literally shot him in the head, leaving him there to die, as the neighbor calmly walked back into his house. Cannon Hinnant, received no media frenzy, no one protesting about his death and it's all because this savage killing doesn't fit the democratic Medias narrative. This brutal killing doesn't fit the case of it being white on black crime. Innocent white 5 year old, Cannon Hinnant, was riding his bike, in his own front yard with his siblings, when their neighbor walked out, put a gun to his head and pulled the trigger.

This gets no news coverage, this gets no media attention because 5-year-old Cannon Hinnant, was white, not black. It's sad because these people push their hateful opinions and other people act on these hateful opinions, and commit horrible racist acts towards others and this is just one case in a sea of many. However, it's these hateful opinions that are enacted out by millions and people that should be held responsible, like the piece of crap minority, who shot innocent Cannon Hinnant, get away with murder because it's other people's opinions that, what this useless pos did, was okay.

If you think I am joking and you think people didn't support this minority thug, but also that these opinions can't turn violent and are not vicious, you can easily view the actions of a private leftist group, who started a fundraising page for this thug, with the headline reading, "Justice for Daruis Sessoms". These people actually claimed that, pos Darius Sessoms, the one who shot innocent Cannon Hinnant, for no other reason, then he was white, the guy who everyone saw pull the trigger and shoot innocent Conner, deserves justice and not to be put in prison.

This piece of crap organization with over 16k members, actually started a fundraising page to claim that, Darius Sessoms, needs justice, not innocent 5 year old, Cannon Hinnant, who pos Darius just killed for being white, Darius needs justice. This should be worrisome to Americans, people like this don't care about what happens to the other race, they will always support minorities. We can see this because this was the statement on the page of this racist organization, about pos Darius. "Darius Sessoms has been accused of a heinous act that he didn't commit." This is all propaganda from the far right Trump propaganda machine to make minorities look bad.

We cannot sit idly by while our President plays fast and loose with the laws. That's why we need to back Darius against these outrageous allegations. #blacklivesmatter". You get that though, these people ignore the fact that, pos Darius Sessoms, was just seen by everyone committing the murder, multiple people seen this him walk up to Cannon and pull the trigger, then cowardly run back into his house. Yet, these people claim Darius did absolutely nothing wrong and they are lying about the whole thing, making it about black people.

Cannon's father ran outside after he heard the shot, but was left begging for help, while he held his dying son in his hands, trying to stop the bleeding coming from Cannon's gunshot. It honestly makes you worry as a country because I kind of wish I was making this stuff up, but this is what's actually occurring in America right now. People are backing criminals and thugs, who are killing innocent people, even children because they believe the opinions of the people in charge, which is, it's white versus black.

These people say they need to back Darius Sessoms, from these outrageous allegations, but these are not outrageous allegations, Darius Sessoms, did walk up to this poor innocent kid and shoot him in the head, then run back to his house. So seriously, how are you defending a man that is clearly guilty of murdering an innocent 5-year-old kid? What's worse is, this pos is a child murderer and committed this act out of spite simply because Cannon Hinnant was white. This dude should receive no justice and deserves to be shot by a firing squad, just to make sure he suffers. It's crazy to me because like we discussed many times before, these people don't care about the murderers or killers themselves. Just like this group, they blame it all on President Trump's white supremacist administration, while they claim that they cannot sit idly by, while President Trump, plays with the laws.

The thing that I can't get over is the fact that, this organization group called these, outrageous allegations, but they also claimed that, Darius Sessoms, didn't commit this heinous act, although they know damn well, Darius, literally walked up to innocent Cannon Hinnant and blatantly shot him in the head, without any warning. This is the left and democrats specialty though, they ignore the truth and blame it all on President Trump, but in reality, this was a heinous crime and Darius Sessoms, did do it.

Darius, was the one seen committing this heinous crime, so it honestly makes no sense why these people would deny this and blame it on President Trump because he's supposedly making minorities look bad. It makes no sense because President Trump, didn't walk out and shoot this innocent white kid, President Trump, didn't hold the gun to Cannon Hinnants head and instantly pull the trigger, it was a minority thug. So seriously, who's giving who, a bad name here? This falls in line with what we've talked about before, people don't care about the truth, they don't care about facts, they will use fallacious arguments to push their opinions onto others, opinions that are speared by hatred and violence.

These people will easily switch the truth to better fit their narrative and they don't care if people know it, they don't care if people already know the facts, they will still push their version of the truth. The sad reality of what these people do and what these people claim, can sometimes be a mind trip, but still millions of people follow these hateful opinions. Now, the world has become filled with sick degenerates, which is sad because these aren't normal people, nope, these are our State politicians, civil leaders, parading behind the scenes as normal people.

I say this because if you look at some of the comments that were posted about the innocent killing of Cannon Hinnant, you will see just how ruthless and vicious people or politicians can be. Take for instance, Terrell Kent, a hard working American from North Carolina, whose name was used to post some pretty disturbing things about Cannon Hinnant. The sad thing is, Terrell Kent himself, didn't post this comment, he was just one of many Americans that have their names and images used.

Now, these people, who have been used by others, receive tons, maybe even hundreds of messages, from people asking why they would post something as disturbing as they did, yet, these people have no clue what post or comment, they are even talking about. Terrell Kent, was one of these people because someone used his account to post a hateful comment about Cannon Hinnant. A viscous comment that was posted from his account page read, "Ion give a s**t he is white it's time for revenge we tired shit over with now we shooting ya'll go cry to your momma."

At first it seems like grammar would be the key, but when you take a look into where this post came from, you realize that this was not posted by Terrell Kent, just some imposter pretending to be him. It's Terrell's name and photo that's being used as props, along with many others and the leftist, liberals and democrats, have no problem using Americans as guinea pigs. Blm Marxists, civil activists, leftists, liberals and democrats, will flip any statement they can, as long as it benefits their narrative and it doesn't matter just how bad these statements tend to be. Another user named, Dante Salvador, had his account and name used to post an even more disturbing comment that read, "Blew his little white privileged brains clean out of his head! #blacklivesmatter."

Now, this comment was supposedly said about an innocent 5 year old, who was killed for simply riding his bike while white. I honestly think this is the same case as Terrell Kent because I honestly hope these are not real postings or comments, if they are, this just makes you scared for the future of America. I honestly fail to believe that people are this ruthless and this heartless, to where they are berating and belittling a 5-year-old kid, who was shot in the head simply because he was white.

It does make sense when you think about what's going on in America right now because each of these posts or comments had the #hash tag of black lives matters at the end, so they all fit the narrative of blm and these far leftists because their narrative is to destroy everything white. Seriously though, there has to be something else behind it because to make post or comments about the death of an innocent 5 year old and claiming that your happy that someone blew his head off, because he was white, is coming from someone who is, deeply, deeply disturbed. I mean seriously, from the lies these people spread to the deception they cause, to the chaos and destruction they intensify, to the violence taking over American streets, honestly, when will it stop, when will these people say, okay, enough is enough?

Many Americans, including myself have had enough of the BS these people are causing, we don't ask for much as Americans, we just want to be able to live a comfortable life, why is that such a crime? Why are white people subject to all this chaos and violence simply because it's peoples opinion that, were all racist bad people. In reality, we just chose to live in safe and secure neighborhoods, so we can make sure our kids have a better life, why is that a crime again? Honestly, what gives minorities the right to demand white people give up there, bought and paid for homes because minorities think they are somehow entitled to it, they didn't work for it, so how are they entitled to it?

White Americans, have the right to live free just like everyone else and city Mayors and Governors, are the ones responsible for providing public safety, but they also play the blame game and place all the crime and violence on President Trump. White people, have no white privilege, we don't have a card we can simply swipe that gives us everything, most white people, are hard working tax-paying Americans, just like everyone else. We have no affirmative action, we have nothing simply being handed to us, most hard working white Americans, work for a living and tend to live paycheck to paycheck.

It's crazy because we were raised with the philosophy of, if you want something, if you want success, if you want to make something of yourself, you go out and work hard for it because no one is going to just hand it to you, you actually have to work for it. You don't get things handed to you simply because you choose to riot and protest or burn everything down because you think you are entitled to it, especially when you haven't lifted one finger to work for it, honestly though, how do you think you deserve it?

That's also the situation here, the 80's and 90's, even the early 2000's generations, were taught about respect, hard work, success and discipline, these newer generations, aren't taught about anything and are often left to fend for themselves, which then leaves most of them making bad decisions. This turns them into little spoiled brats, who thinks everything, from money, to jobs, to houses, you name it, their supposedly entitled to it and you can forget about these people working for it, that's just too much for them to do. In addition, people, mostly minorities, need to stop claiming that minorities built this country because we all know, that is nowhere near the truth and the fact that people are claiming this, just shows how ignorant they are.

Listen, our founding fathers, weren't minority, our generals in the Revolutionary War and Civil War, weren't minority, our first U.S. President wasn't minority and according to history, the first recorded slave owner in America, had four white slaves, one minority slave, so please stop saying minorities built this country. Saying minorities built this country, is like saying minorities created the Deceleration of Independence, which helped create a new nation, you can honestly get out of here with that BS because while American colonists were building their nation, minorities were too busy being traded off by their very own people.

This way of thinking goes along with the democratic narrative and liberal agenda being pushed by these leftists, liberals and democrats because the more minorities feel entitled and enslaved, the more they will vote the democratic way. It's often because minorities, are tricked into thinking, white people and even President Trump, are at fault here, not the liberals and democrats, who were proud to send this country into chaos. Prime example, is to look at democrat John Thompson, of Minnesota because Thompson is prime example of just how crooked and messed up these democrats tend to be.

This democrat, who should have never been elected in the first place, brought a group of blm protestors, over to the house of the Minneapolis Police Federation President, where democrat Thompson, went on an epic rant, which was geared towards this Federation President, but was really just all about racism. Forget the fact that this dumbass, was just elected into the House of Representatives, to represent the American people, not just minorities. Don't tell democrat John Thompson that because according to democrat Thompson, "blues lives don't matter and white lives, sure the hell don't matter".

Besides the fact that, this statement is coming from an American State Representative, who was chosen to represent the American people, this douche-bag went on a rant, making some of the most offensive and racist statements possible, statements that should never be said by a State Representative of the American people. It was bad enough that democrat Thompson, was already calling to burn down the entire Town of Hugo, Minnesota, which is crazy because this is an American State politician, protesting to burn down an entire American town, not for any other reason than the fact that the Minneapolis Federation President, lives there.

As democrat Thompson and his crowd of ignorant blm protesters surrounded the MF Presidents house, they basically demanded him to resign. They accused the Minneapolis Federation President of, "fostering a toxic culture within the Minneapolis Police Department". Simple fact though, like we discussed before, in 2019, 1 minority American, was shot and killed by the Minneapolis Police department. In 2020, 1 minority American, was killed by the Minneapolis police department, who just so happened to be George Floyd, a criminal who was caught passing counterfeit money, resisted arrest, while he was high on fentanyl and Meth.

So seriously, there is no toxic police culture, unless you account for the black on black crime that has taken over communities because that is toxic, minorities dying every day by the hands of other minorities, is very tragic and is very toxic to the minority culture. This isn't the worst of it though and the reason I call democrat John Thompson a pos because just like every other liberal and democrat, they get away with saying some of the most outlandish and racist statements ever, while other Republicans and even President Trump, are usually scolded for non-racist statements.

A neighbor of the Minneapolis Police Federation President, was even holding up a, blue lives matter sign and John Thomson told this neighbor to, "Stick that sign up your ass". Yes, I said that right, a sign that represents the lives of Police Officers, the people, who put their lives on the line for the American people every single day, democrat John Thompson, an American Representative, told this American citizen, to stick the "blue lives matter" sign up their a**.

It got worse because democrat John Thompson, even claimed that the Minneapolis Police Federation President, was a member of the Ku Klux Klan and even went as far to say that, the MPFP, was supposedly the grand wizard of the Ku Klux Klan. Now, I know you are thinking, well John Thompson, said he was a member of the KKK, that's not really bad and yea, that's not. However, when democrat Thompson went on to state that, "why the f*** we so peaceful in this (homophobic slur) neighborhood, F*** your mother***ing peace, white racist mother***ers," kind of changes the whole dynamic of his so-called peaceful protest, don't you think? It's just mind-boggling when you think about it because not only was this the exact statement coming from a newly elected House member.

The way John Thompson spoke about white people, was just embarrassing in itself because Thompson, acted like he had no formal education, but was only hired to represent minorities. I honestly couldn't believe my ears when democrat Thompson, went on record to claim they should burn down the entire town or State when he said, "This whole goddamn state burned down for $20 goddamn dollars, you think we give a f*** about burning Hugo down? Blue lives don't mean s**t to minorities, F*** Hugo Minnesota!".

First off, like I said, democrat Thompson, might not be educated enough to tell the difference between, a Town or a State because democrat Thompson, tells the crowd to burn down the entire town of Hugo, which Thompson refers to as a State. I am sure by now, you've seen that most of these leftists, liberals and democrats, have no clue how to fix the mess they created and started, but they will still do or say anything, to try and act like their the victims. The fact that people, led by these State politicians, are going to peoples private homes, trespassing on their private lawns, to protest about something they don't experience at all, makes no sense at all.

It makes no sense because these blm protesters, led by democratic Thompson, traveled to someone else home, trespassed on their property to berate and belittle them, but also threatened to even kill them, if they didn't agree to give in to what they were requesting. I don't know what honestly gives people the right to go to someone else home, trespass on their private property and berate them, even threaten to beat or kill them because they won't give in to their ridiculous demands.

Seriously though, how is this right, how are you liberals and democrats okay with this, how are you okay with putting American lives in jeopardy, how are you okay with people going into other people's homes and physically assaulting them? I mean, the mind-boggling part is that most of these State Representatives could care less about the American people, but why would they when they got millionaires like Ophra, Taylor Swift and Lebron James, telling Americans how we supposedly didn't want Donald Trump, as our President, yet, it was the American people, who elected him. Besides the fact that I lost so much respect for Taylor Swift, who I felt sorry for when she got screwed by Big Machine, but now, she has gone far left and claims that, President Trump, is bad for Americans.

She even went on record to state that, "Americans didn't want Donald Trump as President". It's funny how President Trump, became the U.S. President because he was elected into the Oval office by the American people. Still, according to Lebron, Swift, liberals, democrats and many others like them, the American people, didn't want Donald Trump as President, even though Americans, voted him in. That's why it's funny to see democrats fighting so bad for mail-in voting because we all know that it's a rigged system and you can simply look at States like, California and Florida, to see this.

These States still currently have mail-in voter fraud lawsuits, but of course according to democrats, you can't steal an election with mail-in voting. What makes everything more interesting is the fact that, President Trump knows mail-in voting is a rigged system, President Trump, knows mail-in voting is not a good thing, but because President Trump thinks this, President Trump, is somehow going to steal the election, if mail-in voting isn't allowed. Wait what, so let me see if I got this right, going to the polls and voting, is going to steal the election, not mail-in voting, ballots that can be sent in by anyone, anywhere, whether their authenticated or not, cannot help steal an election.

Once again, here is the famous logic of leftists, liberals and democrats at its finest and now Miss Swift, is even opening her mouth and claiming that President Trump is somehow going to steal the election because he's not allowing mail-in voting. It's sad because I used to like Taylor Swift, I mean, she alone, is sexy and her attitude is awesome, but just why, why did she have to go to the dark side? President Trump, has proven to be a better U.S. President and I've proven it, but you can simply look up for yourself and see the great things he's done.

I wish people would stop believing the hype that these leftists, liberals and democrats, are pushing and start looking at the real culprits behind all the madness and chaos. In the end, after all is said and done, people are going to realize that these far left liberals and democrats, have been lying and deceiving you the whole time. For instance, if the heritage and lineage statement or lie, wasn't bad enough, State Senator Kamala Harris, is the former California State Senator, who claimed illegal's, should not be arrested or even deported. Instead, these people should be released onto American streets, but also given free-living arrangements, free tax money, free healthcare, even free medical marijuana healthcare, all on the American peoples dime.

Keep in mind, this is the same California State Senator that ran in the 2016, who only got like 6% of the democratic vote, which was barely enough to become a democratic nominee. Kamala Harris, was one of the State Senators in the 2016 democratic debate, who went on a rant aimed towards Joe Biden, where she berate and degraded Joe Biden for his racist remarks and his trend of passing bad legislature. Seriously, four years ago, Kamala Harris in a debate with Joe Biden, berated him for his bad legislature during his entire tenure as a government official.

It was funny because Kamala used the analogy of her having to take a bus to school, after she emigrated into public school systems, like somehow Kamala Harris, was the only one that rode on a bus to school when she was younger. Her statement also proves that she was a foreign student after she emigrated to the United States of America as a child. It's interesting because she was born to an Indian American immigrant and a Jamaican born father, yet, Kamala claims to be African-American and the first woman of color to hold the office of vice President.

Now, to see these two as President and Vice President Nominees, makes you just shake your head because Kamala Harris, despised Joe Biden, now, four years later, which was once a hatred for each other, has turned into love for each other. Seems to be a familiar trend with these democrats, I hate you, I now like you, I hate you, I now like you, I hate you, I now like you, it seems to be a continuous thread of contradictions. It's crazy when you think about it because Kamala Harris, went on record, numerous times to degrade Joe Biden and his failed policies, but now, they are somehow best friends.

California State Senator Kamala Harris, went from hating and despising Joe Biden because she deemed him an ignorant racist, who was known for passing bad legislature, to now, thinking the world of

Sleepy Joe Biden. State Senator Kamala Harris even went on record to claim that, Joe Biden can fix America, although President Donald Trump already did, after Barack Obama and Joe Biden, broke it. You have to suspect something is going on when their motto is, "build back better", but I am sitting here thinking, wait, once Donald Trump, was elected, the country was on the path to remarkable things.

President Trump, added more jobs than any other U.S. President, President Trump decreased our unemployment rates, manufacturing jobs have been better than ever before, so seriously, what are we, building back better? People think Kamala Harris, is a great choice for VP nominee and would be great as a VP, but why, who claims this, when her actions have proven otherwise? Kamala Harris, is the same Sate Senator that wanted to put you in jail if your kids skipped school, she was also the same State Senator that didn't believe in releasing wrongly convicted offenders, she's also the State Senator that funds private prisons. American writer Shaun King knew this and that's why he stated that, he wouldn't be supporting Kamala Harris back in 2018.

Nevertheless, like all other fakes, King soon recanted his statement and claimed that Kamala Harris, is the most progressive VP nominee ever. Keep in mind that, before Kamala Harris, was chosen to be Joe Biden's VP nominee, she didn't identify herself as a minority woman, but after being chosen to become a VP nominee, Kamala Harris, identifies and is declared as, the first African American female VP nominee. A self-described Indian-American woman, who is of Indian and Jamaican decent, now identifies herself as An African-American, claiming to represent the African-American community.

Seriously, you couldn't make this stuff up even if you tired to, it's just so unbelievable sometimes, you just shake your head and keep telling yourself, it will all work out in the end, although it only seems to being getting worse and worse. If anyone with a brain says anything, if they have any inclination of asking these people what they are doing, these people try to write you off and destroy your character, so people won't listen to anything you say or claim to be true.

This is the specialty of the liberal and democratic parties, they don't like American history, they don't like American heritage, to these people, our history represents white supremacy because they claims it's all built by racist white men. Our country was built by white men, but what tends to be lost in translation, is these men founded a nation to protect the freedoms of all men, woman and children, some of these men, even fought and died to protect that right. You can't get mad at them for what your ancestors did because people tend to forget that, African migrants, along with Irish Migrants, were sold to white colonists, they were not stolen, no one went over to Africa or Ireland and stole people. Your own so-called African ancestors, sold you to the white man, your ancestors cared for you so much that they sold you to the highest bidder.

North African Moors, were the founders of slavery, these people saw you as a trade commodity, they saw you as nothing more than an item to trade, which they traded at will and even protested against the stopping of slavery, after the British Empire abolished slavery. So seriously, how can you say the white man enslaved you and owes you something, when slavery ended hundreds of years ago and was technically started by your very own ancestors? This form of slavery is long gone, everyone, including yourself, has the opportunity to make a living in the United States.

You are not entitled to anything, simply because your ancestors were slaves, which in reality, only applies to like a third of the minorities living today, maybe even less. What everyone fails to realize is, people that actually come over here from Africa, real African-Americans or the people that are actually of African descent, are doing better right now in America, then most minorities. It's often because Africans or African-Americans, don't sit around and wait on the government to take care of them, they actually get out and work for what they got, just like many white Americans.

Kamala Harris is a liar and Joe Biden is just as bad, both of these people push hate and racism, they both claim they are not racist, yet they've both been on record, making racists statements or racist remarks towards others. The sad thing is, you can easily look up Joe Biden's speeches and see the crazy statements or remarks that Joe Biden has said or made, but still, some people think, Joe Biden, would be a good candidate to run our country. God help us because Joe Biden can't even put together a sentence, let alone run a government.

This is also why Nancy Pelosi is trying to pass an amendment that would unseat a President, if he is to unfit to be President, people think she's doing this for Donald Trump, but Pelosi's really doing it just in case Joe Biden wins, so Kalama Harris can replace him. What Biden and these democrats, are promising to provide Americans, is a scary thing to look at because if you have been paying attention, you will see that, it is more about taking American rights and money and in turn, using them to provide free homes, free lives and free healthcare, to illegal's and foreigners.

That's always been the liberal and democratic pitch, we'll provide you with an entire life, but you have to vote for us, but also do as we say and think how we think, no matter how wrong you may feel about what we tell you. The truth is very different then the reality these politicians push, but that's okay for them, this is what these leftists and democrats want, they want people to think the way they do, that way it's easier for people to be deceived into falling in line. These people in charge behind the scenes, control the chaos, they control the deception and they all use President Trump, as the escape goat, it's their narrative, no matter how bad it is, they're still going to push it.

Everything has now become divided and because of this division, everything is now, white versus black or black versus white, white income verse minority income, white safety and security versus minority safety and security. The great Dr. Ben Carson, said it perfectly when he stated that, "We, the American people are not each other's enemies. The enemies are those people behind the curtain jerking everybody's chains and trying to divide us up by age, by race and by income."

This is what these State politicians love to do, this is what they tend to focus on, they could care less about the American people because all they want is to make sure they stay in power and to do this, they will lie and deceive as much as possible. We've already seen this coming from Michelle Obama, when Michelle claimed that the Covid-19 virus, was a way for America to redistribute the wealth flowing in America. Michelle holds no political office, so just imagine what actual State politicians are able to do. There is nothing about uniting Americans because this is not what these people in charge want, they want Americans divided, they want Americans confused and separated, not knowing exactly what's going on.

When people are confused, but also kept separated, it's easier for these State politicians to push their false narrative, which is, white people are racist and a systemically racist government. Think I am crazy, think I am making stuff up, okay, take a look at what blm

Marxists leaders, posted the second day after they found out that Kamala Harris, whose ancestors were slaves owners, was chosen by Joe Biden to be his VP candidate. If you do, you will see that these blm Marxists leaders, supports Joe Biden and Kamala Harris, two politicians, who have put more minorities in jail, then any other State Senators.

Blm despises President Trump and Vice President Pence, although President Trump and VP Pence, has done more for the minority community, then Joe Biden and Kamala Harris combined. The logic behind this is very puzzling to me because on one hand, you have Joe Biden, a proven racist against minorities, who has even stated he doesn't even want his own kids mixed with minorities, joined by Kamala Harris. Who is a proven descendant of slave owners, but who also lied about celebrating something as simple as Kwanzaa.

On the other hand, you have an American President and Vice President, who has not said anything racist towards minorities, but has done nothing but help minorities and put the American people first. It's puzzling how these blm Marxists leaders and their followers, claim President Trump and VP Pence, are the leaders of a systemically racist government, who hates minorities and wants all minorities to suffer because these very same people claim, Joe Biden and Kamala Harris, are not racist against minorities, like I said, puzzling.

Let's talk about that for a second, systemic racism because when you look up to see what the definition of systemic racism is, you will see that it's actually referred to as, institutionalized racism and not systemic racism. Nevertheless, when you take a look at the definition of institutionalized racism, you will see that it is described as, a form of racism that is embedded as normal practice within a society or an organization. Okay so wait, I have a question, wouldn't having minority only schools and colleges, minority only award shows, minority only television shows, minority only television channels, minority only support groups, minority only fundraisers, be considered normal practice for minorities today in America, wouldn't this be kind of be considered institutionalized racism?

White Americans, can't even have their own white television show or channel, they also can't even have their own support groups without being labeled racist or being called racist for supposedly forming a white supremacist group. Old classic movies like, Gone with the Wind and Casablanca, but also television shows like, Dukes of Hazard, have been stricken from television play because minorities claim these movies and television shows, are racist and offensive to them. Try that in reverse, let white people protest that minority shows and movies are offensive to them, have white people protest about taking something off the air, they would still be labeled racist and would get in trouble for discrimination against minorities.

It's a one way street these days and everything is being turned into, minority this and minority that, but the real problem isn't being tackled, the real root of the problem isn't being solved and will never be solved because these people think erasing everything white, is somehow going to solve all their problems. Seriously, white people can't do or say anything without offending someone, while numerous minorities have shouted out racist words and made racist statements towards white people, raising their fist for black power, yet, it's offensive and discrimination, when white people do it.

White Americans, were charged with a hate crime and discrimination for simply painting over a blm sign, a painted sign, seriously though, how is that a hate crime? These white people painted over a blm sign, a sign that was painted on the ground and their tried for a hate crime, minority woman does the same thing, she's not charged for a hate crime, basically nothing happens to her. You can often see these differences by watching your local news or reading news articles, about how white people are being arrested for simply saying "white power", while they raise their closed fist to minorities.

These simple gestures coming from white people, have now become a hate crime and discrimination. Minorities raise their fist to support, the Black Panthers, a known racist hate group, also go on television calling white people every racist name in the book, that's not a hate crime, nor is it discrimination, like I said many times before, it's all one sided. Let's go back to that definition of system racism because like I've stated before, minorities, have their own categories in television and film, which you will often see titled as, Black Cinema films, Black Lead Films and Black lead television shows.

Yet, if white people try to do the same, if white people try to have their own channels or shows, they are labeled racist and in trouble for discriminating against minorities. Minorities, are the only race in the entire world that can keep everything separated, keep their own people divided from other races, then turn around and complain about the separation and divide. This goes for televisions shows, movies, schools, colleges, support groups, even the NRA because they have an all minority NRA, but still minorities riot, loot and protest, burning down everything they can because they say they are being separated and divided by white people.

It makes no sense to me because minorities are the ones that focus on keeping their race separated from everyone else, it's not white people keeping them separated. Seriously, might not even be a strong enough of a word here because minorities keep themselves separated, but they also tend to keep things this way on purpose. Minorities only do things if it benefits the black race and we've seen this time and time again, so seriously, how are white people the racist ones again pushing for separation and divide? If white people only show support for their race, their the racist ones, if they do things to only benefit their race, there the racist ones, yet, minorities do this constantly and get away with it.

Minorities, claim systemic racism, but the truth of the matter is, minorities, are the ones that keep their race separated from the rest of us Americans. Let me rephrase that a little, most minorities and democrats, are the ones that want to keep us separated and divided. There are many minorities, who I respect dearly, that have finally stepped up and tried to get these other minorities back to thinking normal, but it's easier said than done.

Let's clear this up too, there is a huge difference when it comes to minorities and blm as a group, they are not the same, blm, is a ruthless Marxist group, who sees all white people as wasted space and will never respect the white race. Regular minorities, who don't fall for the BS, are hard working tax-paying Americans, who want a future for themselves and their families, just like everyone else. The blm movement, is no longer about minority justice or racial equality, if it was, they wouldn't be destroying their own communities. These people wouldn't be burning down minority owned businesses and they especially wouldn't be killing their own people.

This is the thing that gets me because it's all about minorities, these people are on television, commercials, interviews, talking about change and how white people need to change to end racism. Yet, every single one of these blm protesters, ignores the constant death occurring in urban communities, being committed by minorities, not white people. This is what pisses me off, everything has somehow become about minorities, everything from television commercials to television shows, has to now incorporate some minority or minorities in it, if it doesn't, it's automatically labeled racist.

It makes no sense because that's their culture, that's not the white culture, so why do white people have to bend to the minority culture, if all minorities want to do is, erase ours? We don't live like minorities, we don't talk like minorities, plus, minorities are literally the ones causing all the death, so seriously, why should we bend to your ridiculous culture? The even more interesting part about all of this blm bull is, if you donated money to the blm movement, it didn't actually go directly to minorities, it went directly to Actblue. A non-profit organization, which is ran mostly by democrats, who passes out the money raised for blm, to whom they see fit.

Seriously, look at where these so-called blm fund came from and see where they go, you will notice that most of the billions of dollars goes to Joe Biden and his administration, along with Bernie Sanders and other democrats. So again, the ones holding minorities back and taking all their money is liberals and democrats, yet, these liberals and democrats, have convinced millions of minorities that, its white people. It's ridiculous because blm protestors, can discriminate against white people, they can claim all white people, are racist, yet, white people, can't even defend themselves, we're supposed to just sit there and take the racism and discrimination.

If we say anything about it, we're the ones labeled racist, not minorities, who are causing the racism and discrimination on a daily basis. What I don't understand, but is also something I've asked many times is, how you can you destroy your own community for criminals, but ignore the innocent minority men, women and even children, that are constantly being killed in your own communities? White people, are not killing people in these urban communities, white people, are not committing drive-bys in these urban communities, white people, are not the ones killing innocent minorities in these urban neighborhoods, so seriously, how are white people to blame again?

Seriously, minorities, literally commit more violence towards each other, than any other race in the United States and it's been proven that almost 90% of crimes committed against minorities, were perpetrated by minorities, 90%. It's a known fact that more minorities have been killed in America, by the hands of other minorities, then by any other race in America, this includes white people and police officers.

We already discussed that in 2019, criminals or felons, who were shot and killed by police officers, estimated at about 14 minorities, while over 7,400 minorities, died by the hands of other minorities. This is the truth, these are known facts, but the problem is that these deaths are not being addressed, this death rate is not being addressed because blm and minorities have convinced themselves that these facts are wrong and it's white people and police officers, who are killing minorities more.

Like I've stated many times before, civil leaders, blm leaders and their followers, could care less about the truth because according to blm leaders and their followers, they want white people and police officers to, "just stop killing us". Fourteen minorities, who were shot and killed by police officers, doesn't really seem to compare to the over 7,400 minorities, that were murdered on urban city streets, by their own race, doesn't even come close. So holding up a sign that claims white people and police officers need to, "just stop killing us", honestly makes no sense, when it's coming from people that rob, steal and kill each other, every single day.

What people fail to realize is, before George Floyd, was accidently killed by the Minneapolis Police Officers, the Minneapolis Police Department had 1, minority killed by police in 2019, just 1. So, seriously, how are police officers killing off minorities in Minneapolis, when they barely made the mark with one? Look at Chicago, so far in Chicago, just one city in America, just one, there were 753 recorded minority homicides, homicides perpetrated by other minorities, 753 minorities in one year, compared to the 14 minorities that were shot and killed by police officers. It's insane when you think about it because these hundreds of minority injustices, are occurring in urban communities every single day, to black people by black people.

Still, blm and their followers, blame it on other people, mainly white people, not themselves, this is why they often destroy everything around them. Democratic and leftists State mayors and governors, stand idly by and do nothing at all, while the crime and gun violence increases in these urban communities. The murder rate skyrockets, still, all the death and violence, is not on their shoulders, it all somehow falls on the shoulders of white Americans and police officers. These State politicians and city council members, sit back and watch their cities and communities be burnt to the ground and there city businesses being destroyed.

This is what these politicians want, the more chaos and destruction they cause, the more they can blame it on President Trump and his racist white supremacist government. What these State mayors, governors and democrats, fail to tell you is, more police officers have been shot and killed during these riots and protests in the past six months, then minorities that were killed by police, in the last three years. You don't even have to take my word for it, you can easily look up these statistics by looking at FBI Data statistics and reviews, where you'll see what I am referring to.

The reality is, these are no longer peaceful blm protests or movements, they were never even peaceful to begin with, as soon as these protests started, minorities and even white people were rioting, looting and burning things down. Since it was a movement that liberals and democrats thought would be able to help push their narrative, they latched on like leaches. It's almost like Bill Murray, in the movie, "Groundhog Day", these liberals, leftists, blm Marxists leaders, civil leaders, activists, democrats and their millions of looters, followers and rioters, wake up every day, not knowing exactly how to stop the chaos and destruction they started and created.

Since they don't know how to stop the chaos, they spend the rest of the day being confused as to what just happened. These people do this because they play the blame game and use the race card, so they can turn a blind eye to all the chaos and destruction going on, since they don't actually know how to stop the mess they caused, started and inflamed. The logic these people use, is insane to say the least because when did it become okay to discriminate against someone all because of their race. Isn't that what we have amendments for, isn't that what you are protesting and rioting for, equality for all people or is it just equality for minorities?

Seriously, white Americans, are being attacked and discriminated against, all for simply being white and the sad thing is, this is now affecting poor innocent defenseless kids and defenseless old white people. We have all seen the news stories of these pos minorities, who are seen sucker punching old white people, who are simply walking down the street, minding their own business. What's wrong with our country, is the fact that there were people, especially minorities, in the comment sections of these videos, praising these minorities for what they were doing, even though the old white people did nothing wrong, it's okay because they were white.

To think it's okay to beat on anyone, let alone an old person, white or minority, who can't really defend for themselves, makes you a pos, you and your parents should be ashamed of yourselves, obviously you were raised like an animal. Minorities, often see discrimination against white people as okay and they encourage other minorities, including their own kids, to constantly berate and attack white people, all for something they have no personal experience with, slavery.

As one of the most admired influencers, Denzel Washington, once stated and what I dedicated a whole chapter to, which is, it all starts from home. This plays an important role here, discipline starts at home and knowing what's right and wrong is learned from your parents, you learn respect from your parents. One thing we all learn is, you respect the elderly because they've probably had a harder life, then you ever will. Discipline and respect, are two things that are long gone, the father figure, is now being trashed and now minority kids, are being taught to hate white American kids, because of what our ancestors did hundreds of years ago.

Young minorities, are taught and raised to ignore the fact that American history, clearly shows North Africans and Arabian Moors, started the slave trade and these African Moors, the originators of the slave trade, were highly responsible for selling their own people for animals and comfort commodities. Why do you think it was called, the slave trade, it was given that name because it was a world trade and something that was seen as normal at the time, that means all races, from all over the world, headed by African and Arab Moors, sold people and profited from slavery. White colonists, only participated in the global slave trade because it was known as a profitable platform and the truth is, white Americans, stopped the global trade of slavery, not the African and Muslim people who started it.

Africans, Arabs and Muslims, wanted slavery to continue because people were their most profitable trade commodity and they despised, the Thirteen Colonies and the British Empire, after the Thirteen Colonies and the British Empire abolished slavery. For white colonists, people weren't the greatest trade commodity, our crops, our fruits and our labor, were our greatest trade commodities. We valued people and instead of focusing on slavery, white Americans, led by President Abraham Lincoln, abolished slavery and instead created the American workforce, where all people were created equal and had the right to be free. That's what these public American national monuments and statues represent; they represent the Americans that have sacrificed life and limb, so Americans and their families have a better life.

These people didn't just do this for white Americans, remember, most Americans in the North, didn't even participate in slavery or profit from slavery. The one thing it comes down to as we discussed many times in this book, is the fact that, every ones ancestors were slaves at one point in time, minorities were not the only ones that had slaves as ancestors. The faulty and unjust reasoning, behind all of these convictions and arguments, makes no sense at all and this is often because these fallacious argument's, have no truth or base to them and it's all really about racial domination and blm looking out for themselves.

Don't believe me after all we have discussed, let me leave you with a little bit of information about these blm leaders that you may not know. Without saying her name, if you look up the facts, you will find out that, one of the founders of blm, has multiple million dollar homes, not just one or two, but multiple million dollar homes. She also lives in an all white million-dollar community, but yet, she is protesting that minorities don't get the treatment or privilege that white people get, although she has more privilege then most Americans.

What it all comes down to is the fact that, these blm founders, State Senators and their followers could care less about wanting racial equality or even racial justice, they want to run the country and they will destroy anyone who disagrees with them or gets in their way. This is the unsound democratic logic and false ideologies that these blm founders, State politicians, civil leaders push, they twist, bend and feed these false ideologies to the American people, so the vast opinion is that everyone of color is the victim of enslavement and oppression.

This even includes minority millionaires, while everyone else in America is stuck working hard, trying to make a living, but always left asking, "seriously America, seriously?"

Acknowledgments:

First and foremost I would just like to acknowledge and give thanks to my parents for everything they've done for me and for making me the man I am today. I know my Angel momma, is looking over me and always will be and I thank my father for everything he's taught me and everything he continues to teach me. My mother will always be watching over me and I will always think of her lovely smile. I appreciate them because my mother and father, are two people that has had more faith in me, then I sometimes had in myself. My parents will always be my guidance and inspiration and I will always thank them for making me the man I am today.

I wrote this book to be different, I wrote this book my way and the way I wanted it to come across, as if I were asking and answering these questions all myself. I also didn't write this book to stand out or be different, but I did want the book to be different in a way that I talk about the real facts, the real troubles that we seem to be experiencing in America. Since no one else wants to, especially State politicians. Everything that is going on, makes no sense at all, but I hope I put some thought into your minds and people will start waking up.

I want to also acknowledge all the secret influencers that inspired me to write this book. From family members to conservative influences all around America, that actually care about what is happening to America, thank you from the bottom of my heart. I want to thank people like Candace Owens, Brandon Tatum, Jericho Green, Adam Calhoun and other's for their inspiration and for their daily voice because they speak the truth and tell you how it really is.

I want to thank all Americans, all true red, white and blue, stand for the American Flag and National Anthem Americans, we are strong and we will not let these weak people take over. I believe in the American people, I believe in my people and we will not stand for these non-Americans coming into our country to try and change our American Values and Beliefs and everyone who stands up for these American values, I salute you!

References & Research:

Schumaker, Erin, (June 5, 2020), *What the latest research tells us about racial bias in policing*, Retrieved from abcnews.go.com/us/

Garcia, Carlos, (June 22, 2020), Black Lives Matter activist Shaun King says statues of Jesus Christ should be torn down, but just the white ones, Retrieved from theblaze.com/blazemedia/

Macdonald, Heather, (July 3, 2020), There is no epidemic of fatal police shootings against unarmed black Americans, Retrieved from yahoo.com/news/

Ankel, Sophia, (July 18,2020), National Museum of African American History apologizes for chart listing attributes of "whiteness", Retrieved from yahoo.com/news/

Feller, Madison, (July 23,2020),`I knew we were going to be History-Makers`: How this city approved reparations for black residents, Retrieved from yahoo.com/lifestyle/

Jarvie, Jenni, (July 15,2020), `You're not welcome here.` The painful reckoning playing out in a Wendy's parking lot, Retrieved from yahoo.com/news/

Morrow, Brendan, (July 24, 2020), Lebron James group donates $100,000 toward paying Florida ex felons' fines so they can vote, Retrieved from yahoo.com/news/

Harsanyi, David, (July 27, 2020), *The Chicago Gun Myth*, Retrieved from yahoo.com/news/Chicago-gun-myth

Lee, Kurtis, (July 30, 2020), Column One: He prays for Chicago as violence takes children's lives and Trump threatens with federal forces, Retrieved from yahoo.com/news/prays-Chicago

Whitehouse, *Trump Administration Accomplishments*, Retrieved from whitehouse.gov/trump-administration-accomplishments

Mock, Brenton, (August 6, 2019), *What New Research Says About Race & Police Shootings*, Retrieved from Bloomberg.com

Hughes, Trevor, (August 15, 2020), Record wave of deadly shootings hits US cities. More police aren't the answer, activists say, Retrieved from yahoo.com/news/

Allen, Nick, (August 15, 2020), Barack Obama reportedly said: `Don't underestimate Joe's ability to F.. things up`, Retrieved from yahoo.com/news/

Sattler, Jason, (August 16, 2020), Trump has a plan to steal the election and it's not clear democrats have a plan to stop him, Retrieved from yahoo.com/news/

Linker, Damon, (August 23, 2020), *The only way Trump can win*, Retrieved from news.yahoo.com/only-way-trump-win

Cwik, Chris, (August 24, 2020), `This is why we don't feel safe`: NBA, NFL speak out about Jacob Blake shooting, Retrieved from sports.yahoo.com/

Lyman, Bryan, (August 24, 2020), Republican National Committee resolution condemns Southern Poverty Law Center, claiming `obvious bias`, Retrieved from yahoo.com/news/

Chung, Andrew, (August 25, 2020) *Special Report, Shot by police, thwarted by judges and geography*, Retrieved from yahoo.com/news/

Golden, Hallie, (August 23, 2020), Defund the police: can other cities learn from Seattle's stumbling blocks?, Retrieved from yahoo.com/news/

Khan, Amina, (August 16, 2019), Getting killed by police is a leading cause of death for young black men in America, Retrieved from latimes.com/science/story/

Seyton, Joe, (May 7, 2020), Lebron James says Black people are `literally hunted every day,` Numbers tell a different story, Retrieved from westernjournal.com/

Ruiz-Grossman, Sarah, (August 27, 2020), *These are the victims of the Kenosha Protest Shooting*, Retrieved from yahoo.com/huffpost/

O'Kane, Caitlin, (August 28, 2020), US Marshalls say they found 39 missing children in a 2-week operation, Retrieved from yahoo.com/news/

Myers, Kristin, (August 28, 2020), *Survey: Over 1/3 women say financial situation has worsened under Trump*, Retrieved from finance.yahoo.com/news/survey/

The Grio, (August 29, 2020), Byron Allen's $10 billion racial discrimination lawsuit against Charter Communications allowed to proceed, Retrieved from yahoo.com/news/

Baer, Jack, (August 29, 2020), Pete Carroll urges white people to learn America's 'real' history: 'Black people can't scream anymore', Retrieved from sports.yahoo.com/

Relman, Eliza, (August 29, 2020), Trump & The GOP want voters to fear 'chaos and anarchy' under Biden, but not the corona virus that's killing 1,100 Americans a day, Retrieved from yahoo.com/news/

Ballesteros, Carlos, (August 20, 2020), *Chicago looting proves Black America deserves reparations – hears why*, retrieved from yahoo.com/news/

Cwik, Chris, (August 31, 2020), Colts owner Jim Irsay explains why saying 'all lives matters' misses the point right now, Retrieved from sports.yahoo.com/

Abcarian, Robin, (September 2, 2020), White people will contort themselves to justify the killing of black people, Retrieved from yahoo.com/news

Ho, Jennifer, (September 1, 2020), With Kamala Harris, Americans yet again have trouble understanding what multiracial means, Retrieved from yahoo.com/news

Kessler, Jim, (September 3, 2020), *If Black lives truly matter, stand your ground laws must go,* Retrieved from yahoo.com/news/

Robillard, Kevin, (September 1, 2020), *Joe Biden turns speech condemning riots into Television Ad*, Retrieved from yahoo.com/huffpost/

Jansen, Bart, (August 31, 2020), Biden hits back on Trump attack's: 'Do I look like a radical socialist with a spot for rioters?', Retrieved from yahoo.com/news/

Kim, Whizy, (September 9, 2020), *Trump banned white privilege training – Now Scholars are on strike*, Retrieved from yahoo.com/lifestyle/

Obiedallah, Dean, (September 11, 2020), *White Privilege is real. I lost mine after 9/11*, Retrieved from yahoo.com/news/

Bernstein, Brittany, (September 21, 2020), Black Lives Matter removes language about disrupting the Nuclear Family from website, Retrieved from yahoo.com/news/

Pitts Jr., Leonard, (September 15, 2020), If you're focused on black deaths in Chicago, you're willfully ignoring what police do to us | Opinion, Retrieved from news.yahoo.com/

Noah, Trevor, (September 9, 2020), Trevor Noah nails what's being forgotten amid Black Lives matters restaurant clashes, Retrieved from yahoo.com/huffpost/

Carlson, Tucker, (February 6, 2020), Criminals would be protected from deportation under bill AOC and other House Democrats back, Retrieved from foxnews.com/opinion/

Orecchio-Egresitz, Haven, (August 24, 2020), Chaos will continue in Kenosha until the cop who shot Jacob Blake is fired or arrested, local BLM activists worry, Retrieved from yahoo.com/news/

Evans, Zachary, (September 1, 2020), *FBI reports Chicago gangs have formed pact to shoot cops `on sight`*, Retrieved from yahoo.com/news/fbi-report

Kay, Natalia, (September 1, 2020), MSNBC's Joy Ried Says `BLM doesn't riot` blames Trump for encouraging violence by `White Nationalist Mobs`, Retrieved from breakingreports.org/

Rufful, David, (August 17, 2020), `We coming from everything you motherf****rs took from us`: Democrat John Thompson holds rally Running for State House, Retrieved from breakingreports.org/

Papenfuss, Mary, (August 28,2020), White Supremacists were `on a hunting spree` in Kenosha, says Wisconsin lawmaker, Retrieved from yahoo.com/huffpost/

Owens, Jake, (August 27, 2020), Ravens demand arrest of officers involved in shootings, police reform bill from Mitch McConnell, Retrieved from sports.yahoo.com/

Brodigan, (August 31, 2020), Two Black Lives Matters speakers declare `open season` on cops, time to `Put them in their graves`, Retrieved from louderwithcrowder.com/

Young, Shalize Manza, (September 13, 2020), Frank reich and Colts execs just sent a powerful message about white privilege, Retrieved from sports.yahoo.com/

David, Javie E., (September 10, 2020), NYC business leaders urge `immediate action` from de Blasio to fix Big Apple's rot, Retrieved from finance.yahoo.com/

Wolford, Brooke, (September 23, 2020), Ban on natural hair discrimination passes in House. `Everybody should feel empowered`, Retrieved from yahoo.com/news/

Jibilian, Isabella, (September 23, 2020), Elizabeth Warren, AOC blast Wells Fargo CEO for blaming `very limited pool of black talent` for the banks trouble hitting its diversity-hiring goals, Retrieved from yahoo.com/news/

Roscher, Liz, (September 23, 2020), Disappointment, frustration, failure: The sports world reacts to Breonna Taylor decision, Retrieved from sports.yahoo.com/

Justich, Kerry, (September 23, 2020), Uncle Ben's changes name to Ben's Original amid criticism over racist imagery: `We listened. And we learned`, Retrieved from yahoo.com/lifestyle/

The Week Staff, (September 27, 2020), *The Black Wealth Gap*, Retrieved from yahoo.com/news/black-wealth-gap

Tyko, Kelly, (September 27, 2020), Cream of Wheat to remove black chef from the box as it updates imagery in wake of calls for racial equality, Retrieved from yahoo.com/news/

Neumann, Sean, (October 6, 2020), *Michelle Obama delivers `Closing Argument` for Joe Biden over Donald Trump*, Retrieved from yahoo.com/entertainment/

Manns, Keydra, (October 9, 2020), NYC cancels $900 million payment to teachers due to financial crisis, Retrieved from yahoo.com/news/

Marina, Fang, (October 9, 2020), Pelosi unveils 25th Amendment Bill to clarify how to remove Presidents from office, retrieved from yahoo.com/huffpost/

Evans, Zachary, (October 10, 2020), Minneapolis business at site of George Floyd killing threatens to Sue City over `Autonomous Zone`, Retrieved from yahoo.com/news/

Bendery, Jennifer, (October 11, 2020), *Trump signs 2 Laws addressing Missing and Murdered Indigenous Women*, Retrieved from yahoo.com/huffpost/

Bush, Gerard, (October 11, 2020), *Pride in America can not only be certain brand of white man's pride*, Retrieved from yahoo.com/news/

Sacca, Paul, (November 20, 2020), BLM founder calls for Biden to sign radical legislation to `abandon police, prisons and punishment paradigms`, Retrieved from theblaze.com/

Heltzel, Jon, (November 26, 2020), Obama says Republicans have created "this sense that white males are victims" which doesn't gibe with both history and data and economics, Retrieved from theconservativeopinion.com/

Austin, Michael, (November 28,2020), `Anti-Hate` group leader at race conference says it's time to `kill the white man`, Retrieved from westernjournal.com/commentary/

Troiano, Joshua, (December 10, 2020), AOC furious that Republican Congressman are fighting for Trump instead of `starving and small businesses`, Retrieved from mediarightnews.com/

Huston, Warren Todd, (December 28, 2020), Pelicans coach Stan Gundy calls himself `Poster Boy for white privilege`, Retrieved from briebart.com/

Newkirk, Donovan, (December 29,2020), Harvard Panel: Not all who give birth are women, adopts term `birthing people`, Retrieved from rfangle.com/

Zanotti, Emily, (February 2, 2021), Chicago Mayor Lori Lightfoot: Donald Trump to blame for Chicago public school issues, Retrieved from dailywire.com/news/

Cox, Isa, (February 17, 2021), NYC Schools asks parents to reflect on their `whiteness`, become `white traitors`, Retrieved from westernjournal.com/news/

Statistics, data reviews, facts and information about Slavery or American History, were Retrieved from these sources:

https://en.wikipedia.org/wiki/Slavery,

https://en.wikipedia.org/wiki/Atlantic_slave_trade,

https://www.history.com/topics/black-history/segregation-united-states

https://www.gettysburgflag.com/history-of-american-wars

https://www.mphonline.org/worst-pandemics-in-history/

https://www.statista.com/studies-and-reports/digital-and-trends

https://www.ushistory.org/us/index.asp

https://www.usa.gov/history

https://www.cdc.gov/nchs/fastats/deaths.htm

https://www.worldometers.info/

https://usafacts.org/

https://www.who.int/news-room/fact-sheets/detail/the-top-10-causes-of-death

https://www.statistics.com/

https://nces.ed.gov/